4/94

4/94

Obsession

Also by Steven Gaines

Simply Halston: The Untold Story
Heroes and Villains: The True Story of the Beach Boys
The Love You Make: An Insider's Story of the Beatles
(with Peter Brown)
Me, Alice: The Biography of Alice Cooper
Marjoe: The Biography of Evangelist Marjoe Gortner
Also the novels *The Club* and *Another Runner in the Night*

Also by Sharon Churcher

New York Confidential: The Lowdown on the Big Town

OBSESSION

The Lives and Times of Calvin Klein

Steven Gaines
and Sharon Churcher

A BIRCH LANE PRESS BOOK
Published by Carol Publishing Group

A Birch Lane Press Book
Published by Carol Publishing Group
Birch Lane Press is a registered trademark of Carol Communications, Inc.
Editorial Offices: 600 Madison Avenue, New York, N.Y. 10022
Sales and Distribution Offices: 120 Enterprise Avenue, Secaucus, N.J. 07094
In Canada: Canadian Manda Group, P.O. Box 920, Station U, Toronto, Ontario M8Z 5P9
Queries regarding rights and permissions should be addressed to Carol
Publishing Group, 600 Madison Avenue, New York, N.Y. 10022

Carol Publishing Group books are available at special discounts for bulk purchases, for
sales promotions, fund-raising, or educational purposes. Special editions can be created to
specifications. For details, contact Special Sales Department, Carol Publishing Group,
120 Enterprise Avenue, Secaucus, N.J. 07094

Manufactured in the United States of America
10 9 8 7 6 5 4 3 2 1

The Cataloging-in-Publication Data for this title may be obtained from the Library of
Congress.

ISBN 1-55972-235-5   LC 94–070741

For James A. Urban Jr. and John Hawkins,
and for Michael Taylor and Margot Churcher

Never forget that all these people are primarily visual people. They are designers, window dressers, models, photographers, graphic artists. . . . They value the eye, and their sins, as Saint Augustine said, are the sins of the eye.

—Andrew Holleran, *Dancer from the Dance*

ACKNOWLEDGMENTS

Despite Calvin Klein's roadblocks and personal pleas to associates and relatives, as well as a barrage of letters imploring, "I . . . have not authorized this book and I am asking my friends not to speak to . . . anyone . . . involved . . . ," over one thousand individual interviews were conducted and nearly ten thousand pages of documents were obtained and reviewed for this book.

The authors would like to offer their gratitude and appreciation to the many people involved; however, this is not possible, since hundreds of favors were granted and interviews conducted with the assurance of anonymity. We salute all those kind people for their confidence and generosity. Happily, we are able to publicly express our gratitude to the following people who contributed by word or deed to the contents of this book, including Zack Carr, Sam Shahid, Sydney Salenger, Reginald Peters, Susan Romeo, Lizzette Kattan, Peter Rogers, Bill Rancitelli, Alan Rish, Paul Rackley, Glen Plaskin, Elinora Parkinson, Gail Osman, Laura Odell, Paul Jabara, Diane Molinaro, Nick Mottola, Abe Morenstein, C. David Heymann, Gene Momberger, Kathy Di Montezemolo, Ethel Mirkin, Madge Miller, Robert Ianucci, Murray List, Ph.D., Larry Mark, Karen Mann, Ulf Lundqvist, Alexander Lieberman, Kenneth J. Lane, Martin Price, Charna Phillips, Rabbi Herschel Schacter, Joel Permison, Lisa Phillips, Olga Petroff, Mr. and Mrs. Irving Pais, Marjory Okin, Don Newman, Linda Most, Jon Miller, Ralph Garner, Richard Mineards, Lefty Farrell, Diane Feldman, Steven Karten, Ed Gittelman, Molly Ann Acker, Sophie Acker, Daisy Aldan, George Ahern, Neil Bieff, Michael Blum, Irv Brooks, Wilma Brooks, Jean Lesser, Derek Callender, Alan Cohen, Florence Chernoff, Jane Sternberg Cohen, Tillie Greenberg, Ron Ciner,

Elaine Ciner, Carol Chesney, Al, Paul and Lillian Edelson, Leslie Fanning, Shirley Rosen, Barbara Fuchs, Marty Friedman, Yvonne Fitzner, Norma Hauptman, Jerry and Rochelle Goldberg, Michael Sigmund, George Simonton, Alice Smith, Mitchell Speilberg, Ida Speilberg, Frances Speilberg, Barbara Stevens, Walter Teitelbaum, Janet Vella, Faye Wagner, Barry Wasserman, Scotty Watt, Marilyn Randall, Robert Rubin, Ruth Rosenzweig, Ronnie Roberts, Ernest Sapp, Shelby Schmitt, Barry S. Rosen, Milton Shlansky, Ed Schneider, Laura Schwartz, Beverlee Sclar, Harry Shanker, Sharon Berkowitz Spiegel, Alan Spritzer, Mike Steinberg, Lou Goldman, Audrey Goodman, Arlene Hecker, Irene Katcher, Susan Kaplan, Rina and Myron Katz, Shirley Kerner, Fredda Kleiner, Fred Kleiner, Peggy Kestenbaum, Kaaren Lee, Cynthia Mailman, David Millstein, Ed Millstein, Irma and Murray Kopstein, Wendy Lipkind, Charna Phillips, Tim Bascom, Thomas Bolan, Esq., Abel Rapp, Dr. Diane Beckworth, Dan Armante, Conrad Bell, Richard Bernstein, Bill Blass, Steven Biedermann, Jack Bianchi, Julie Britt, Michael Borden, Lawson Bowman, Richard Johnson, Fran Boyar, George Rush, David Burns, Michael Casey, David Chapman, Val Cook, Mildred Custin, Susan Cowell, Joe Dakota, Sal DeFalco, Gina Epworth, Michael Fesco, John Flanagan, Michael Foley, Nat Forman, Marilyn Funderbunk, Jenny Garrigues, Bob Garey, Matilda Gemellaro, Milly Graves, Betty Ann Grund, Judith and Don Guerra, Nikki Haskell, Dennis Hand, R. Couri Hay, Natalie Herman, Edward Jones III, Baird Jones, Susanne Klevorick, Cindi Klar, Etta Sherman, Babs Simpson, Barbara Slifka, Gwenn Randolph Franklin, Audrey Smaltz, Pat Shelton, Frank DiGiacomo, Billy Smith, Mark Smith, John Stedila, Norma Stevens, Harold Streitman, Richard Golub Esq., Tiffany Telter, Charles Suppon, Nancy White Thompson, Robert Turner, Stephen Wayne, Edward Wilkenson, John Weitz, Willy Woo, Nicholas von Hoffman, Myra MacPherson, Joseph Mancini, Mrs. Arnold Cohen, Sidney Zion, Jan Zimolzak, Jennifer Hyde, Ernie Volkman, Mai Hallingby, Jim Grissom, Robert Frye, Gene Sampieri, John Davis, Ellen Alpert, Dan Arje, Bill Avery, John Blair, Patricia Burke, Edward Caracci, Jack Clark, Robert Cuelar Rogers, Vivian DeMilly, Thomas Demakis, Ed Diamond, Richard and Robert Lasko, Mark Ellingbow, Joe Eula, Catherine Fahringer, Harvey Fishbein, Harvey Feller, Robert

Forrest, Ted Foley, Barbara Gerard, Seth Gordon, Stephanie Mansfield, Brad Gooch, Wendy Leigh, Milton Grossman, Andrea Hyde, Randy Kelly, Larry Kramer, Mary Lewis, Bill McCarthy, Gary Lisz, Theresa Mahar, Penny Irwin, Bruce Mailman, Roger McFarlane, Gerard Malanga, Tom Monaster, Joe Mulligan, Leo Narducci, Gustavo Novao, Charles Peterson, Mark Quigley, Radu, Dominique Ransay, Mike Romano, Bobbie Rothstein, Chris Royer, Lee Schrager, Myra Sheer, Mike Shibel, Martin Siegel, Linda Stein, Patrick Taylor, Billy Tsutsos, Jeffrey Trachtenberg, Robert Treadway, Daniel Tripp, Tom Twomey, Peter Wise, Ben Petrone, Kent Holland, J. Wallace LaPrade, Maurice Brahms, Sam Bolton, Robert Jon Cohen, Michael Pye, Senator Franz Leichter, Susan Crimp, Kimberly Kenney, Lydia Encinas, Paul Hallingby Jr., Dianna de Martino, Mrs. Russell Skillin, Elaine Rosenberg, Jerry Thayer, Ulla Gabay, Michael Pucillo, Larry Rosenzweig, Shep Cogan, Myra Ursal, Harvey Mann, Robin Weir, Audrey Goodman, Karen Mann, Allen Tucker, Linda Stein, Robert Feiden, Clovis Ruffin, Jack Hyde, Harvey Fishbein, Harold Streitman, Susan Kaplan, Warren Hirsh, Eleanor Lambert, Stanley and Ruth Trachtenberg, Beth Luttinger, Stephen Franks, Robert Taylor, Dustin Pittman, Fredrick Behrends, Joe Valaquette, Bill Robinson, Richard Esposito, Russ Radley, Ken Maley, Michel Zelnick, Pamela Plummer, Tom Alston, John Lunning, Lou Jacobs, Tony De Stefano, Harold Randall, Lydia Encinas, Chuck Ortleb, Wilhelmina Sobel, Jack Clark, Gene McDermott, Bart Gorman, Artie Engels, Sam Schwartz, Ivy Schwartz, Kenneth Lindahl, John Coyle, Raymond Jacobs, Gene Sampieri, Keith Sherman, Don Robbie, Alan G. Millstein, Michael Datoli, Gus Ober, Rita Schreger, Rita Schprechman, Ed Schneider, Faye Topal, Barbara Stevens, Paul Cuniliffe, Sam Greenberg, Andrew Wentick, Craig Douglas, Douglas Grover, Andris Kurnis, Glenn von Nostitz, Mike Weber, Wayne Barrett, Rafael Madan, Chris Berry, Berna Cosner, Steve Rickenberg, Linda Drogin, Martin Friedman, Steven Fried, Murray and Irma Kopstein, Martin Siegel, Thomas Naegele, Robert Treadway, Sydney Weinberg, Ted Bocuzzi, Tom Miller, Sean Kellerher, Estelle Berk, Len Bressack, Jim Friday, Dan Klores, Aaron Retica, Al Nahas, Felisa Neuringer, David Barr, Richard Chernela, Gregg Fields, Dan Sheffey, Joe Cydal, Herbie the Butcher, Irma Kopstein, Joe Mullins, Peter Rothchild, Ann Brearley, Maurice Bidermann, Terrance White, and Marylyn Aronstein.

Martha Trachtenberg intrepidly did the research for this book through heatwaves, hail, library closings, and the birth of her son, Michael Griffith. Our thanks also to Martin Garbus and Edward Rosenthal at the firm of Frankfurt, Garbus, Klein and Selz for their counsel and support, and to Melvin Wulf at Beldock Levine & Hoffman.

Steven Gaines would also like to thank his father, Isidore Gaines, Janet M. Chandler, who transcribed thousands of hours of interviews, David Groff at G. P. Putnam's, Donnie Evans, Paul Solomon, Jeffrey Ulman, Esq., Jean Claude Baker, Bernard Berkowitz, James Mackin, Steven and Susan Feldman, Sydney Butchkes, Joseph Olshan, Gladys Guadalupe, Moses Cardona, Sharon Friedman, and Warren Frazier at John Hawkins & Associates. Also, a tip of my hat to Frank Nowicki and Jonathan Canno for their stalwart friendship.

Sharon Churcher joins Steven Gaines in thanking our agent, John Hawkins, who believed in this book. She also expresses her gratitude to Laura Handman and Kate Rowe at the firm of Lakenau Kovner & Kurz, and to the many journalists and publishing executives who have provided her with a support network, including Peter Bloch, Joe Conason, John Cooney, Don Forst, Rod Gilchrist, James Greenfield, William Grimes, Bob and Kathy Guccione, Charlotte Hays, Jonathan Holborow, Diana McLellan, Sue Reid, Randy Rothenberg, Susan Roy and Paul Palmer.

This book has traveled a long, winding, and uphill road to publication. Michaela Hamilton, Elaine Koster, and Alan Kaufman at Penguin/NAL are owed a great debt of gratitude for the first incarnation of this book. Later, G. P. Putnam's Sons president and publisher, Phyllis Grann, became this book's advocate, and her contribution is deeply appreciated. However, it is due to the determination and vision of the book's primary editor at Putnam's, George Coleman, that this biography exists. George Coleman struggled for ten years to see this book written, and his blood, sweat, and tears are on every page. A huge debt of gratitude also goes to Bruce Shostak, who graciously gave the book its final home, and to everyone at the Carol Publishing Group, where the publisher, Steven Schragis, had the tenacity to put *Obsession* in the stores.

Steven Gaines
Sharon Churcher
February 1994

Obsession

CHAPTER ONE

Unable . . . to reach sex through love, I started
upon a long quest in pursuit of love through sex.
                                        —J.R. Ackerly

"**I** am holding your daughter," said a man's voice on the telephone.

Calvin Klein tried to clear his head. He had been fast asleep when the phone rang, and for a moment he thought he was still dreaming. It was just after eight o'clock in the morning, an unusual hour for Calvin to still be in bed. On most days he would have already been at work at the office. He was, by nature, a driven man, a workaholic, obsessive in all aspects of his life. For him, he said, more than four hours of sleep was a "waste of time," and anyway, when he slept too long, he woke "with more lines and wrinkles." Since image and youth were perhaps the thirty-four-year-old designer's greatest commodities, he didn't want any more of *those*. Yet, uncharacteristically, on this cold and overcast Friday morning, February 3, 1978, Calvin Klein had stayed in bed.

As he tried to shake himself into consciousness, the strange, high-pitched voice on the phone continued. "I want a hundred thousand dollars in twenties by two-thirty this afternoon," the man said in a curious, lilting accent, not quite Spanish, not quite French. "If you call the cops, don't drop the money, because the deal is off and I will know because you're being watched. You will get to see your daughter when I get the money and I'm safe with the money."

A chill ran up Calvin's spine. "This has got to be a joke," he said, and then he repeated it again, his voice rising in anger, *"This has got to be a joke!"*

"This is no joke," the man insisted. "I'll put your daughter on the phone." Calvin could hear the man's voice drop as he turned his face away from the receiver and said, "Marci, pick up the phone."

There was a short pause and the sound of an extension phone being lifted, and then the petrified voice of his eleven-year-old daughter came on the line, shrieking, *"I love you, Daddy! I love you, Daddy!"*

Calvin could tell she was in a wild panic. In his mind he could see all four and a half feet and eighty pounds of her, shaking, tears spilling down her round cheeks. She was a sweet, trusting little girl whose kisses were wet and whose smile was shy and lopsided. His heart could have burst from the anguish he felt as she kept shouting hysterically, *"I love you, Daddy! I love you, Daddy!"*

"Are you all right?" Calvin cried.

"I'm all right!" she managed to shout before the receiver was snatched away from her and the man got back on the phone.

For the first time it really sank in. Marci had been *kidnapped*.

Without a second's hesitation, Calvin asked, "Where do I drop the money?" A hundred thousand dollars was a small, small price to pay for Marci's safety. Of course, you couldn't put a price on his baby's life, but Calvin, who was worth hundreds of millions, would gladly have paid fifty times that to get his daughter back unharmed.

"Two-thirty at your office. I'll call you," the man said, and abruptly hung up the phone.

Calvin listened to the empty static on the other end for a moment before dropping the receiver back into its cradle. "Nothing could be more painful," he said of that moment. "Death couldn't be as bad as not knowing what's happened to your child." If only he had asked her to stay in his apartment last night. And Jayne—his ex-wife—was away on vacation in Fort Lauderdale and had left Marci in the care of baby-sitters. He would *never* forgive Jayne—or himself—if anything happened to his baby. Marci was all the world to Calvin. He *adored* this child, this most lovely of all his creations, who lavished on him pure, unquestioning love in an otherwise tension-filled existence. She was his "only reality," he said, and he would murder any bastard who touched a hair on her head. "Inside, I am like nails," he said. "I will kill."

In another moment Calvin was dialing the number of his business partner, Barry Schwartz, at his home in the New York suburb of New Rochelle. Barry, a mainstay of Calvin's life, would know what to do. More than friends, closer than brothers, he and Calvin were partners in a grand plan that had amassed for them a garment-center empire and transformed Calvin's name into one of the most recognized trademarks in the English language. Although their lifestyles were worlds apart—Barry was a suburban family man who shunned Calvin's fast-lane, glittering life—there was a bond between them so tight that it melded at the seams. When Calvin told him about the ransom demand, Barry was speechless at first. Then he said that he would set right out for Calvin's apartment and that in the interim Calvin should enlist the advice of their attorney, Charles Ballon. Nicknamed "the Ambassador" by those who had seen him negotiate, Ballon was one of the shrewdest corporate lawyers in America and a partner of the legendary attorney Louis Nizer. Roused by Calvin at his Sutton Place home, Ballon said that he would report the phone call immediately to the police and the FBI no matter what the kidnapper had threatened. He told Calvin to get a grip on himself and sit tight until the cops arrived.

Calvin threw on a pair of chino pants, a white sweatshirt inscribed "Property of Amherst College," and brown hunting boots, a souvenir from Paris. He looked for all the world like a college junior on his way to class; boyish, sexy, clean. It was an image that tantalized millions of women. It wasn't simply that he was handsome—indeed, he was hardly conventionally attractive—but there was something compelling about him. The way he moved and stood and spoke drew women to him, half to mother him, half to take him to bed. He was a big man, six feet two inches tall, yet only 160 pounds, lanky and V-shaped, like Gary Cooper gone fey. His eyes were a soft hazel, alternately penetrating and seductive. His strong chin was set off with a deep cleft, his sandy-brown hair luxuriantly thick and studiously mussed.

Although the mass adulation pleased Calvin, he was self-conscious and insecure about his looks just the same. He fretted his whole life that he was too thin for his height and had recently begun exercising three times a week at the European Health Spa to add some meat to his bones, a losing proposition. He had for years suffered from a nervous stomach, and food was never much joy to him. In fact, he was so tightly coiled that he could easily drop four pounds in a day by forgetting to stop for meals. "I sometimes wonder," he once mused aloud, "why I don't just disappear." Perhaps more than his skinny body, he was embarrassed by his red blotchy complexion. Even at age thirty-four he was still plagued by adolescent acne, and his cheeks were lightly mottled by small scars and pits, the remnants of which had been filled in with silicone injections by a Fifth Avenue dermatologist.

As Calvin waited for his lawyer and the police to arrive, he smoked his first Marlboro cigarette of the day and gulped black coffee. Oblivious to the breathtaking view from his apartment windows, he paced back and forth, distractedly picking at the skin on his palm. He lived in a forty-sixth floor penthouse aerie at the Sovereign, a glass-and-cement monolith at 425 East Fifty-eighth Street that loomed a block behind the elegant mansions of Sutton Place. Floor-to-ceiling windows overlooked the East River to the borough of Queens and, on a clear day, three states beyond. To the west and south the sparkling Manhattan skyline provided an even more startling vista, while forty stories below, the tramway floated on slender steel bands to and from Roosevelt Island.

The apartment was like a movie set, the *echt* millionaire's high-tech bachelor pad of the seventies. The lacquered walls in the living room had been designed to rotate at the touch of a fingertip, changing the size and shape of the space at whim. The seating was sparse save for built-in platforms with slabs of suede upholstery and soft throw pillows. The living room's centerpiece was a large, oval, one-thousand-year-old fertility stone from India. The occasional tables—polished rubber constructions set on subway pipes—were accented by sweeping yellow orchid sprays and cacti in straw baskets. At one end of the living room, strung from wall to wall under a six-foot ficus tree, was the most peculiar decorative touch of all: a black-leather hammock.

The bedroom was dominated by a double bed, a platform in an upholstered frame that hovered mid-room, like an altar. On one side of the bed sat a porcelain bowl holding the finest rock cocaine money could buy; on the other, a bowl filled with a small mountain of chalky white Quaaludes purchased on the black market at five dollars a pop. At the foot of the bed stood a large-screen Advent projection television and videocassette player equipped with an extensive selection of straight and gay porn films. Behind the bed was a bulletin board covered with clippings of his magazine advertisements, a snapshot of Marci smiling and showing her braces, and photographs of a shirtless male model in blue jeans. There were framed photographs everywhere—by Ansel Adams, Avedon, Scavullo, Bruce Weber—leaning in stacks against the walls, along with the lithographs Calvin had collected over the years, including a Miró signed "*à Calvin Klein, amicalement.*" Nowhere to be found were any bright colors; almost the whole apartment was decorated in Calvin's signature neutral tones of tan and beige.

In fact, the only conventionally cheerful room in the place was Marci's bedroom, a room Calvin made a great point of keeping for her. It was filled with toys and furry animals, and one wall was lined with brightly colored metal lockers. Marci was the last vestige of what had once been a normal life. Calvin had divorced her mother, the former Jayne Centre, in 1974, after ten years of marriage. At the start it had seemed like a storybook union—Bronx style; two cute and talented young kids who fell in love, had a baby, and worked hard to get ahead. Jayne was a pretty young girl, warm and innocent, with strawberry-blond hair that fell in a shimmering bob to her shoulders. Their first apartment was a three-and-a-half-room rental in Forest Hills, Queens, that could have been a stage set for a situation comedy, with its wall-to-wall shag carpeting and a Naugahyde dinette set. Marci was born on October 21, 1967, and while Jayne stayed home and cooked and cleaned, Calvin took the E train every day to his job as an assistant designer in the garment center. On weekends they drove his old green Plymouth to the Bronx to see his parents. Everyone said what a lucky baby Marci was to have been born into such a happy family.

But Calvin was far from happy. There was a void in his life, a yawning space, unfulfilled and undefinable; not just his burning ambition to get ahead but some larger, insatiable thirst for a kind of passion he did not know with Jayne. Calvin had repressed his sexual desires for many years, but when the money started pouring in, along with new, fast-track friends, it gave him courage to experiment. He rapidly metamorphosed from the sweet Jewish Bronx boy into an aggressive and status-conscious entrepreneur. It soon became clear that the Bronx marriage and the Bronx wife did not fit. "If you have to go elsewhere for sex, then why be married?" Calvin said. Jayne's response was to quote Calvin's partner, Barry: "Calvin Klein is a very easy man to get along with if he gets exactly what he wants."

Calvin Richard Klein didn't get to where he was in one of the world's nastiest businesses by being soft. In an industry in which fortunes and reputations were made and lost in a season, he had risen on a certain wave, adept, surefooted, predicting trends so skillfully that Madison Avenue marketing experts regarded him as an oracle of public taste. His designs were clean, sensuous, and practical, capturing a market made up of millions of prosperous young mothers and career women, the baby boomers of the "Me Generation." He had already won every accolade the industry had to bestow, including the equivalent of an Oscar, the Coty Award, for three years in a row and was the youngest designer ever elected to the Coty Hall of Fame. His yearly paycheck was $4 million, and that didn't include millions of dollars of profits his company paid down to him at the end of every fiscal year. His women's ready-to-wear was so hot that it had spawned a host of licenses that included shoes, scarves, sheets, sunglasses, pillowcases, and furs. As his company entered 1978, Calvin was embarking on what was thus far his most daring venture. That very week, he was flooding the market with his new designer blue jeans. Calvin intended to take one of the most utilitiarian American commodities, dungarees, recut them high in the crotch and tight in the buttocks, and transform them into one of fashion history's most unlikely status symbols. He expected to sell *1 million* jeans the first year alone, raking in more than $12 million—and that figure probably would be revamped upward twofold. The following month, he planned to launch an even headier, more daring venture—the unveiling of his first fragrance-and-cosmetics line, which, if it caught on, would be another goldmine, projected to gross $10 million its first year. And then, in June, a menswear line would hit the stores, for which he already had taken another $10 million in orders. It was possible that Calvin Klein Inc.'s 1978 grosses might well hit $200 million.

But if his business life was filled with unimpeded success and accolades, his personal life was in lurching disarray. Calvin was, at his core, a hopeless romantic, never seeming to find requited love. He was a man obsessed with physical beauty, a voyeur who inhabited an erotically beautiful world of his own creation. "He would fall in love with beautiful people all the time," said one close friend, "both men and women. He would go gaga over them . . . and he was never sure what he was." Since the breakup of his marriage to Jayne, his seeming inability to connect with man or woman was a great puzzlement and the source of haunting unhappiness. Although he knew how to navigate in business, in affairs of the heart he was lost. "I like people who complicate my life," Calvin admitted, "but I always seem to pick the wrong ones."

The "wrong ones" were straight, and the complication was that none of the strapping, heterosexual lads who so electrified Calvin wanted to settle down. And then again, neither did he, for in his heart Calvin wasn't gay. For certain he enjoyed being sexually intimate with men, but it was only women with whom he fell in love. Tied tightly in this conundrum, doomed to perpetual rejection, he was constantly mending his broken heart by drowning himself in a sea of sex and drugs. As Calvin once bragged, "I've tried everything, knew no limits. . . . I stopped at nothing. . . . I would do *anything*. . . . I'll say that anything I've wanted to do, I've done." His compulsive search for love and sex sent him out on a nightly jet-set merry-go-round on which there was no gold ring. Studio 54, which had opened less than a year before, became his clubhouse, an easy place for him to pick up the kind of muscular, all-American boys who were his *specialité*. He would spend hours cruising the crowd, leaning against the circular center bar, heavy lidded, high and drunk on a dangerous combination of vodka, Quaaludes, and cocaine. To pass the time he flirted with the bare-chested bartenders until out of the crowd appeared a young man who caught his fancy. Although Calvin was shy, seduction was an easy task for him: Most men and women were so impressed that he was Calvin Klein that they tumbled into his arms. If his conquest was special enough, he would take him home to the platform bed at the Sovereign, or if he couldn't be bothered with a houseguest, he would lead his nightly catch down to Studio 54's private basement "Playground."

Alas, Studio 54 was a benign venue compared to some of Calvin's sexual pursuits. He was becoming a familiar face in back-room bars, where, if Studio 54 was having a slow night, he could drop in for anonymous relief in the dark. For more leisurely sexual pleasures, Calvin favored a bathhouse, like the "8709" in Los Angeles, where one night, wearing only a flimsy white towel slung around his hips, he prowled the brightly lighted hallways as other half-naked men gaped at him, slack-jawed in amazement, as he strolled by. And if going out was too much trouble altogether, there were always the courtesans of the night. Studio 54's owner, Steve Rubell, carried a pack of Polaroid pictures in his pocket of available call boys. And if none of them took his fancy, Calvin could simply dial his local gay madam and have a hunk from Chippendales sent over to his apartment, like ordering in Chinese food.

Yet if Calvin was indulging himself in wild permissiveness, he privately took little delight in it. Ultimately, after the late nights and wild times had ended and the drugs were gone and the boys had left and Calvin was alone, he was profoundly depressed by the sordidness of his existence. In some deep, inner core of himself he hated it—hated the emptiness, hated himself. In his heart, he was still just a sweet Jewish boy who spoke wistfully of "spirituality, love, marriage, commitment." Nevertheless, he found himself being sucked farther into this bacchanalian whirlpool, drowning in it. The dichotomy between how he behaved and what he wished for himself was ripping him apart.

At this moment in his life there was only one innocent, unsullied thing left, and that was Marci. Yet even his child had not been left unscathed by Calvin's lifestyle. Marci was a student at Manhattan's exclusive and expensive Dalton School, where she was a daily object of derision by her classmates. "Your father is a faggot" was a constant refrain, making the little girl sick with shame. Jayne was as upset as her daughter. "Just ignore them and don't pay any attention to what they say," Calvin's ex-wife counseled her child. "Don't even bother to answer them. You know who loves you and who your father is." But it was impossible for the eleven year old to ignore the constant taunts. What did it really mean that her father was a "faggot"? Something horrible and shameful at the least. She asked every adult she could confide in when she got them alone. "Is my daddy gay?" she would implore, her greenish-blue eyes filled with tears. And she was invariably told, "Of *course* not."

It tore Calvin apart that Marci was teased because of him, that he had hurt her this way, however unavoidably. He knew that Marci adored him and that to her he was a hero, so handsome and famous.

And now this: kidnapped—because of him and his fame and his money. The netherworld in which he indulged, this dark and shocking demimonde, had exposed him to an entire supporting cast of weirdos, drug dealers, addicts, perverts, and creeps. And as with many who have fame and wealth and power, Calvin was disliked by not a few, hated by many. There were hundreds of people who felt he and Barry Schwartz had screwed them over and were hungry for revenge. The man who had called him on the phone this morning could have been *anyone*.

Or the piper wanting to be paid.

If only he had asked Marci to stay with him the night before, she would have been safe now. He paced and smoked cigarettes and prayed to God and cried as he waited for Barry and Ballon and the FBI to arrive. He kept wondering, What's going on in Marci's mind? Is she safe? Are they hurting her? Certainly she knew that her father would pay anything, do anything, go to the ends of the earth, to get her back. He tried to remember, for a moment, what it was like when he was only eleven years old.

CHAPTER TWO

I was always the favorite.
　　　　　　　—Calvin Klein

When Calvin Richard Klein was eleven years old, he was a shy little boy with sandy hair and freckles, so painfully thin that his belt rested on his bony hips. While other boys his age would rather be at the Polo Grounds or playing basketball in the schoolyard, Calvin's favorite place in the world was a discount women's retail store on the Grand Concourse in the Bronx named Loehmann's. For Calvin there was an excitement to Loehmann's that no game of baseball or ring-a-lievo could match. He would follow closely on his mother's heels as she went up and down the aisles, his eyes wide with curiosity, picking through the racks of clothing with her, carefully examining the Claire McCardell and Norman Norell samples, trying to figure out how they were made. He watched fascinated as portly women pored over the discounted dresses and suits, looking for that perfect size 14, sometimes stripping to their wholeslips in the middle of the store when the communal dressing rooms were full, while their children played in the aisles or ate knishes bought from a street cart on the Concourse by their bored fathers. And while Mickey Mantle and Pee Wee Reese were heroes to his contemporaries, young Calvin Klein was more intrigued by the store's legendary proprietor, Frieda Loehmann, a craggy old lady always dressed in black who used to ride the freight elevators in the New York garment center searching for bargain merchandise from overruns and samples, paying with a roll of bills she kept hidden in her bloomers.

For Calvin's mother, Flore, whom everybody called Flo, Loehmann's was something of a mecca. Flo was a clotheshorse whose love for a new outfit was barely second to that of her love for her family. She was a woman of medium height with teased blond hair and sequined eyeglasses who *loved* to get dressed. She took tremendous pride in putting herself together every morning, *fapootzed* every day of the week, from her vermilion lipstick and blue eye shadow to her I. Miller high-heeled shoes. She was a "shopaholic," as Calvin once referred to her, and it seemed as if she wore a flashy new outfit every week. But Flo didn't bargain-shop. It had to be "good stuff." She would save up her salary and every two months go on a shopping binge, sometimes traveling all the way to Levine and Smith on the Lower East Side of Manhattan, where she could find designer labels at a discount price. "She loved beautiful clothes," said Calvin, "and she had no sense of money. She would spend outrageous amounts on shoes and hats, for a middle-class family. In the forties, she was buying shoes that were one hundred dollars a pair, hats for two hundred dollars. . . . I mean, she was outrageous in her day. She'd have white fleece suits lined with black persian lamb—when you think of the Bronx, you don't think of clothes like that. We weren't really wealthy, but she managed. My father was . . . a great guy who allowed his wife to spend all their money on clothes." Maybe, Calvin said, "she spent too much money."

Flo and Calvin inherited this consuming interest in clothes from Flo's mother, Molly Stern, a former seamstress for the dress designer Hattie Carnegie. Calvin worshiped his *bube* Molly. She was a wizened, white-haired old lady, with gnarled fingers and a thick Yiddish accent, from whose sewing machine sprang a dazzling array of garments. The bube knew how to make everything from slipcovers to the most beautiful evening gowns, which seemed to come tumbling out of her head without the aid of patterns. According to family legend, Molly Stern could have been a successful designer herself had not fate relegated her to life in a tiny notions store on 204th Street in the Mosholu section of the Bronx, a few blocks down the hill from the building where Calvin grew up. It was a shabby cubbyhole of a store where Grandma Stern sold buttons and trimmings and took in seamstress work. Toward the end, when things got really bad, Flore took her in and shared her care with her older sister.

The old woman's life had not always been so dreary. As a pretty

young immigrant from Austria at the turn of the century, Molly
Graff married a man who seemed like a terrific catch for a husband—Max Stern, a young dentist just starting his practice on the
Lower East Side of New York. The naive and innocent bride moved
into an apartment on East Third Street with her new husband and
within the first few years of marriage gave birth to a daughter, Flo,
as well as another girl and a boy. During her last pregnancy it
slowly began to dawn on Molly that her husband had a secret
shonda—he was a gambler of an uncontrollable nature: Dr. Max
could not stop betting on the horses, and he gambled away every
cent of his earnings. At first, Molly prayed that it was only a phase,
that it would pass, but as time went by, she realized he was like an
addict, and as their assets dwindled, Molly went crazy with unhappiness. While other dentists were getting rich and moving to pretty
houses in the suburbs, all of Dr. Max Stern's money went to the
racetrack and bookies. At one point, he was so desperate for gambling money that he took down all the draperies that Molly had
painstakingly sewn by hand for their apartment and sold them in
the street. Eventually, he deserted the family and disappeared,
heavily in debt, in Chicago. Little Flo, distraught at the desertion,
never forgave him. His cruelty broke Molly's heart as well—but not
her determination. Indefatigable, she raised the children all by herself, sheltering and clothing them the best she could, eking out a
living with her sewing machine, to which she ended up tied so
many years later in the Bronx.

To Calvin, his grandmother was far from a tragic figure. She was
a heroine. She had triumphed over life's indignities with her Singer
as a weapon. He worshiped his bube to the day she died—when he
was fifteen years old. He was her *shayna tottala*. He loved to watch
her wizened fingers move the fabric through the silver tongue of
her sewing machine. Indeed, his bube's sewing machine so fascinated Calvin that Flo finally gave him one of his own for his birthday. Every day after school, instead of playing with the other boys,
Calvin went to his room to sew. Flo's cronies remembered that on
mah-jongg nights at her house, Calvin would be sequestered behind a closed door in his room from which the gentle humming of
the machine would emanate. He loved in particular to make
women's clothes, and on one occasion he designed an entire ward-

robe for the dolls of his younger sister's friends. As he became more ambitious, he tried his hand at making dresses for Flo. Although this hobby made him something of an oddball for a little boy, he seemed sure of himself and became determined not to let other children's teasing faze him. In fact, he seemed determined not to let it appear that anything fazed him—on the outside. "I never went through the thing most young people do," said Calvin, "going to school and not truly knowing what they want to do until later in life. I mean, I had a major head start—at age five I had a pretty good idea of what I wanted to do." What Calvin wanted to do was design women's clothing.

This was not an easy ambition in the Mosholu Parkway section of the Bronx, a lower-middle-class haven for struggling second-generation Jews who had survived both the Great Depression and the Holocaust, a neighborhood of gentle conformity in which parents' greatest hope for their children was financial security and youngsters were expected to attend college and pursue conventional professional careers as doctors and lawyers and accountants. Yet Flo found no trouble with her son's aspirations. From the moment he was born on November 19, 1942, whatever her angel-faced, talented *tottie* wanted to do was perfectly fine with her. "He's going to be a great fashion designer," she would tell anyone who would listen. "My son is going to be famous." She was so consumed with her ambitions for him, "you'd dread going to the supermarket where she worked," one neighbor said, "because all you'd hear about was Calvin." Even his Protestant name, Calvin, was in some ways an extension of her master plan for him. "Everyone was shocked when Flo named him that," said a family friend. "It was untypical, strange, and partly her own vanity to want him to be so different."

Calvin's stooped, subdued, Hungarian-born father, Leo Klein, was less comfortable with his son's interest in women's clothing than was his wife, but Leo didn't have much to say about it—or about much else in the household. He was a thoughtful man who took a stand only when thoroughly provoked. To Calvin, Leo was a sad and distant figure whom he greatly loved but with whom he was never able to communicate. There was affection between them, but it was unspoken and never demonstrated. Like many fathers at the time, he seemed worn down to docility by the struggle of making a living. In later years Calvin deeply regretted not having made an effort to be closer to his dad. Still, "Calvin had the greatest respect for his father," said a close friend, "and nothing could be said that would cast a negative picture of his father. Leo was a loved and wonderful man, a fine gentleman who would never do anything dishonest."

A grocer by trade, he had come to this country at age eleven with his older brother Ernest, and together the two had worked six and seven days a week building up a series of superettes. But Leo had little to show for it. Leo had once owned his own store in Harlem, "Barry's," named after Calvin's older brother, but failing physical health had relegated him to a position as a salaried employee at his brother's prosperous store, Ernest Klein and Co., on Sixth Avenue and Fifty-fifth Street in Manhattan. This servitude to his brother had become a matter of abiding bitterness to Flo, who felt that when Ernest opened his prosperous Manhattan store, he should have taken Leo in as a partner and that Leo had been ruthlessly squeezed out of the honeypot. It irked Flo that Ernie and his wife, Ada, lived in a suburban neighborhood in an expensively decorated home, while in her own house she worried constantly about money. Ada was a particular target of Flo's wrath, and Flo even "sat shivah" for her sister-in-law. And she didn't let Leo forget his brother and sister-in-law's transgressions, either. "I told you so," she would say time and again. "I told you your brother would cut you out one day." The lack of money and Ernie and Ada's prosperity were harped on with daily regularity. Calvin remembered that the lack of money was all his mother and father talked about at dinner. Determined to keep up a good front, Flo took a job as a cashier at the checkout counter at the Met Supermarket on 204th Street to supplement Leo's earnings.

Over the years Flo became a strident and opinionated kvetcher whose personality dominated her household. Flo made the beds, did the wash, cooked dinner, and bought everyone's wardrobes. Flo paid the bills, chose the restaurant, picked the TV program that everybody was going to watch, and chauffeured the family car because Leo never got a license. "Leo, sit up straight!" she would yell at her husband; "Leo, hurry up!" she would call as she walked briskly ahead of him down the street. After twenty years and more of this kind of steamrolling, Leo retreated to a position in front of the TV set in the hallway of their apartment. He was so broken and quiet that Flo's mah-jongg partners nicknamed him the "gray mouse." When the players would converge on the Kleins' apartment for a noisy game of tiles, Leo would remain oblivious, glued to the TV set. "He'd be sitting in the foyer," remembered one of the players, Laura Schwartz, "and he'd never acknowledge us."

Calvin's family lived at 3191 Rochambeau Avenue on a tree-lined street in a six-story prewar brick building that had fallen into comfortable shabbiness. The wine-colored velvet banquettes in the lobby were stained from children playing on them, the brass mail-boxes were in need of polishing, and the once-ornate chandeliers were chipped and missing crystals. Nevertheless, it was a warm and happy place to live; all the tenants knew each other by their first names, and mothers would scold one another's children. At dinner-time, a rich potpourri of food smells filled the hallways, and in summer, apartment doors were propped open with chairs to catch a cooling breeze.

The Kleins lived on the top floor in apartment 6A, the largest line in the building. It was a sunny, one-bathroom corner apartment with huge windows, ten-foot-high ceilings, and penny-a-foot mold-ings on the walls. The senior Kleins slept in a room with double glass doors, originally meant to be a dining room, opposite a narrow living room, hardly ever used, with wall-to-wall carpeting, heavy satin drapes, and fussy French provincial–style white sofa and chairs. Flo sheathed everything, from lampshades to footstools, in a protective layer of custom-made plastic slip covers. The occa-sional tables were cluttered with tchotchkes, and against one wall stood a console piano on which Calvin's younger sister, Alexis, would rarely practice. Beyond the room-sized foyer—large enough to set up a bridge table for Flo's mah-jongg games—there were two bedrooms, one for Alexis, and another across the hall that Calvin shared with Barry, his older brother, born April 12, 1938. This cor-ner room was the best of the lot, with windows that overlooked the tree-shaded Mosholu Parkway and the schoolyard of P.S. 80 across the street. The room was decorated with bright blue wall-to-wall carpeting and twin beds. Its shelves housed Barry's extensive collection of 45 r.p.m. records and Calvin's growing menagerie of parakeets, turtles, and lizards as well as a spotlessly clean tropical fish tank.

The Kleins seemed comparatively affluent in their building, populated by garment-center workers or proprietors of small local shops. Flo owned a mink stole, a treasured status symbol of middle-class Jews in the fifties, and every summer, while many other families in the building sweltered in the Bronx, the Kleins rented a shanty of a bungalow in crowded Rockaway Beach, Queens, a block from the ocean. They were also the first family in their neighborhood to get a TV set, and not only did Flo and her three children have extensive wardrobes, but the Kleins owned a washing machine, four window air conditioners, and separate telephones for each child.

In fact, this affluence was something of an illusion, and one that Flo was determined to foster. "Flo was a bragger," said Tillie Greenberg, who has known Flo Klein for thirty years. Added her daughter, Elaine Ciner, "She lived up to the Joneses, and she'd make a daisy seem like a rose." Her outspokenness often irked many of her neighbors. "She never had anything nice to say about other people," said Tillie Greenberg. "She would always find something to argue about." Jon Miller, one of Calvin's friends, agreed. "She wasn't overly bossy, but she let everybody know that she had something to say." Herbie, the kosher butcher on Bainbridge Avenue, remembered: "Flo was a character. She once didn't like the meat I sold her, and she called me up and said, 'Stick to the veal chops!' " Although Flo's home was open to all of her children's friends ("Sit down and eat!" she would implore, referring to her legendary cheese blintzes), the older women complained that she was tightfisted with her money. When members of her mah-jongg group would buy new "tile" cards each year from a local store where an extra twenty cents was tacked on for charity, Flo bought her cards elsewhere to save the additional two dimes. Another lady who lived in the neighborhood remembered that when Flo worked the checkout counter at the Met Supermarket, she would evaluate the food she was ringing up. When Rochelle Goldberg, whose husband owned the local candy store, bought ice cream, Flo asked loudly, "Do you really need that?"

It was not an easy job for Flo's children to have a mother who was so opinionated and demanding, but of the three, Calvin fared the best. "Flo wasn't a mother to any of her children, except Calvin," claimed their neighbor, Tillie Greenberg. Calvin didn't annoint himself his mother's favorite child, "but I think my brother and sister felt that," he admitted. "My brother used to refer to me as 'the King' in the house." Calvin never had to make his bed or pick up after himself. "My mother did it all," he said. However, this did not mean that he was immune to Flo's constant kvetching. The biggest battle was over food. Flo would "constantly be shoving food at me," said Calvin, "and I absolutely refuse to eat even if I'm starving. I'll sit there and not say a word and she'll want me to eat and I'll be hungry and I will refuse to do it." Both Calvin and his older brother, Barry, developed persistent stomach problems as youngsters. Finicky eaters with poor appetites, the boys were both whippet-thin and suffered from chronic acne, caused, Flo believed, by their bad indigestion.

Like many of her generation—the children of European immigrants—Flo held the medical profession in high regard, and her children were no strangers to doctors' offices, in particular, regular visits to a dermatologist for their acne. However, when a doctor couldn't cure an ailment, Flo insisted that an enema could. She was a firm believer in the Old World, eastern European panacea of high colonics for everything from the flu to headaches to pimples. Flo was also of the opinion that enemas were good for the soul and mind as well as the body. In later years Flo's enemas became a grim family joke. When Barry got married at age thirty-two, Flo's sister took his new bride aside and said, "You better learn how to give your husband enemas."

In many ways the boys did not have it as bad as their younger sister, Alexis. Born January 18, 1950, Alexis was the lost child of the family, a cute little girl with a halo of blond hair. Friends remember that Alexis was a "surprise child," unexpected in the family planning. Nevertheless, Alexis was a child who ostensibly wanted for nothing, with a beautiful wardrobe, an expensive doll carriage, and the best collection of "Ginny" dolls in the neighborhood. Yet she grew into a moody youngster, and if Flo was critical of her sons, she relentlessly found fault with her daughter. Sometimes Alexis rebelled. "One day Flo threw a fit because Alexis spilled all her perfume down the toilet deliberately," said Judy Deutsch. "Alexis was always doing obnoxious things. I think Alexis needed attention whether it was negative or positive. I don't think her mother liked having a girl." Although she was later to prove herself academically by earning a master's degree in accounting, Alexis was usually in the slower classes at school, best remembered by her classmates for her painstakingly neat penmanship. Neighbors also remembered her resenting the lack of attention paid to her by her mother, who was often short and cutting with her. Like her older brothers, Alexis was a "latchkey kid" who had her own key to her parents' apartment so Flo could go her own way. "My daughter knows how to make an egg," Flo declared, "and if she doesn't, she can starve till I get home."

While Alexis might have been a disappointment to Flo, it was her eldest son, Barry, who broke her heart. In Flo's worst nightmares she never could have dreamed that Barry would be cursed with the same illness that destroyed her father and his family: compulsive gambling. At least now she had a name for it. Gambling was not an unusual preoccupation for young men on the Parkway, but while Barry's contemporaries went to the track or placed small bets with each other, Barry bet large sums of money daily through bookies. Jerry Goldberg, who owned the candy store Barry frequented, said, "Barry could win a thousand dollars a minute and lose three thousand a second." He was usually in such desperate need of money that on the odd occasion he baby-sat for the Goldbergs for extra cash, sometimes with his kid brother, Calvin, in tow. "When I came home," Jerry Goldberg quipped, "I had to check my kids to see that he didn't hock them." When not at one of the sixteen tables at Sam Pistone's pool hall shooting billiards for a quarter a ball beneath a haze of smoke or haunting the pay phone with calls to the *New York Daily News* for hockey and basketball scores, Barry Klein could be found almost any time of the day loitering on a corner across the street from his grandmother's notions store, slouched against the railing that stood on either side of the subway entrance, placing bets with Louie, the local bookie.

"What are we going to do with you?" Flo would wail to Barry when he came to her asking for a loan to pay the bookie. "This has to stop! You'll be the death of me yet!" Flo never knew what trouble Barry would get into next. One afternoon while Barry was out, a character who used the alias Lefty Farrell arrived at her apartment door with some terrible news. The loan sharks were holding Barry prisoner in return for $1,400 he owed them. Lefty was a pal of Barry's, alternately feared and worshiped by the younger kids as a bully who became their protector when gangs from other neighborhoods descended on the Parkway looking for trouble. Out of the generosity of his heart, Lefty said, his cold blue eyes filling with tears, he had already paid Barry's kidnappers $500, but unless somebody came up with the additional $900 to pay Barry's gambling debts by 3:00 P.M., he would either be "shot or thrown into the river" and Flo would never see her eldest son again.

On the edge of hysteria, Flo gave Lefty $145 that she had hidden in the house and promised him that she had another $500 in her savings account in the bank. That would still leave them $255 short. Lefty said that because he loved Barry so much, he would sell his own car to come up with the remainder if Flo emptied out her bank account. He drove Flo to the bank, and she withdrew $500 in hundred-dollar bills and gave it to him.

Later that night, when Barry came through the door, Flo flew into a hysterical rage, crying, *"Thank God you're safe! Thank God you're safe! What I went through for you today!"*

Barry stared at his mother wide-eyed. "I don't know what you're talking about," he said calmly.

Flo related the whole story to him—how she gave Lefty Farrell every penny she owned to save Barry's life, adding that Lefty had sold his car to make up the difference.

"Bullshit!" Barry cried. What loan sharks? What debt? It was a scam! he vowed. Flo had been had. With Barry sheepishly in tow, Flo headed directly to the local police station and filed a complaint against Lefty Farrell, who was charged with extortion and thrown in jail. He pleaded guilty to a reduced charge of petty larceny and was sentenced to a year at Rikers Island prison. To this day, he swears his version of the story is true and that Barry Klein double-crossed him to save face with his family. Indeed, twenty-five years later, at a reunion of all the people who had grown up around Mosholu Parkway, Barry Klein came up to Lefty with tears in his eyes, hugged him, and said, "Please forgive me. I'm so sorry for what I did to you."

Thus went Flo Klein's life. A husband who had failed her, a son who gambled, and a daughter with whom she was at war. As far as Flo Klein was concerned, the future of the family, all of her aspirations and dreams and hopes, were invested in the life of one person, her perfect son.

Calvin.

2

Those who grew up in Calvin Klein's neighborhood in the fifties and sixties say there was something magic in the air in the Mosholu Parkway section of the Bronx, "like a time warp of innocence," said one resident. Illegitimacy and divorce were unheard of. So were welfare and drug addiction. This was a neighborhood enthralled with life and its possibilities, inhabited by a young generation with an irrepressible vision of the future for their young. They call the Bronx "the borough of parks," but in the early part of the century this hilly ward north of Manhattan was perhaps better known as a haven for immigrant and second-generation Jews seeking better housing than for its bucolic fields. The opening of the first subway line to the Bronx in 1904 brought waves of Jews escaping from the tenements of Manhattan's Lower East Side. So many new apartment buildings had been built in the borough between the two great wars that by the late 1940s nearly half of the population was Jewish, over half a million strong, more Jews even than in the new state of Israel. Mezuzahs guarded the doors of each apartment, and on the high holy days, the schuls were standing room only.

The upscale address for Jews in the Bronx was the Grand Concourse, "the Park Avenue of the Bronx." This four-and-a-half-mile-long boulevard was the site of the finest apartment houses the Bronx had to offer, many of them with the then rare luxury of elevators, the priciest even with doormen. If the Grand Concourse was first-class, then Mosholu Parkway, where Calvin Klein grew up, was a poor second. Although the Parkway, as everyone called it, was also lined with apartment buildings, they were far less elegant and more affordable. The six-mile Parkway itself connected Van Cortlandt Park to the Botanical Gardens and the Bronx Zoo. The Bronx River, which once flowed where the Parkway stands today, still runs underground, and pumps worked twenty-four hours a day under Calvin's school to keep the foundation dry. To the south of the Parkway, on Villa Avenue, there was an enclave of Italians families, mostly the children of bricklayers and mason workers who helped build the apartment buildings, and slightly to the north of the Parkway there was a large settlement of Irish families who were responsible for the construction of the subways.

Most Jews in the Mosholu Parkway section attended the Mosholu Parkway Synagogue, where Calvin was bar mitzvahed and Flore Klein made "modest but consistent" contributions over the years, according to its rabbi, Herschel Schacter. But while the synagogue was the center of religious activities, daily life in this area revolved around the Parkway. It was on this broad, maple-lined street, with wooden benches and a bicycle path, that the local citizens would congregate. In the summer months the adults would linger late into the night, waiting for the muggy air to cool before returning to their small apartments. The narrow iron railing that delineated the Parkway was a magnet for the neighborhood children, who sat or leaned on it for so many thousands of hours that the iron itself began to bend. Said Larry Rosenzweig, who grew up there with Calvin, "We never thought of going to Manhattan. You can't believe the life we grew up in—two hundred kids, their asses over a fence for five, six, seven years, everyone knowing everyone else. But there was something there, a challenge, an intellectual competition. Some of us became doctors, some guys became little businessmen, some relatively famous." Some very famous. Dubbed "a cradle of stars," the Parkway was home to such celebrated alumni as actor Martin Balsam, designer Ralph Lauren, comedian Robert Klein, producer Gary Marshall, his younger sister, actress and director Penny Marshall, musician Joshua Rifkin, disc jockey Dave Herman, movie producer Herb Nanas, and publisher Gloria Leonard, to name just a few. The Parkway seemed so nurturing to its denizens that Ralph Lauren fondly described it as a "college campus."

Almost all of the kids who sat on the rail attended P.S. 80, in-

cluding Calvin Klein and Ralph Lauren, who later designed the
school's logo. P.S. 80 was an imposing, U-shaped brick building
that sat on a rise directly overlooking Mosholu Parkway. Because
P.S. 80 embraced a baby-boomer generation from kindergarten to
grade 9, it was an unusually large school of over eight hundred
students. The school was noted for its high academic standards,
ensured by its staff of mostly old-maid, Irish Catholic schoolteachers, each one more laden than the next with powder and rouge and
flowery-smelling perfumes. Everyone in the school, students and
teachers alike, lived in fear of Pearl Thaler, the principal during
Calvin's time. She was a big-bosomed woman only five feet tall, a
"terror in size-two shoes who could throw fear into the heart of a
grown man," said a former student. A dedicated educator and strict
disciplinarian, Thaler prowled the hallways, classrooms, and
schoolyard, always on the lookout for wrongdoers. On one occasion Thaler caught Calvin running up and down the school stairs
with some friends, and she terrorized the cringing boy for five minutes in a stairwell. In his school records it was duly noted under
"Conduct" that Calvin "needs improvement in self-control."

When Calvin started kindergarten in 1948, Flo made sure he
was immaculately dressed and groomed, the little Beau Brummell
of the school. "Calvin's mother always dressed him up," Wendy
Lipkind, who was in many of his early classes, recalled: "I remember him in these unusual colored shirts, like pale mauve or violet or
pink, magnificently laundered and ironed. He wore them with little
bow ties. The other boys might have worn white shirts and ties on
special days, but Calvin's were very unusual. It was the overall ge-
stalt." As Calvin got older, he showed his own flair for fashion and
became a neighborhood trendsetter—the first to wear white bucks
and pants with pleats down the side, and while most kids wore
low-budget pants and sneakers from Fordham Road, Flo took Calvin to buy his wardrobe in Manhattan.

Over his ten years at P.S. 80, Calvin earned consistently high
grades—in the 90s in English and social studies and in the 80s in
art and music. From the start, however, academics left Calvin cold.
His great love in school was art. In Mrs. Goodblatt's first-grade
class he was able to cut out copies of autumn leaves with consummate skill, and in Mrs. Simonetti's second-grade class Calvin built

a dollhouse complete with matchboxes for bureaus and cut-up toilet paper rolls as chairs. By third grade he demonstrated a precocious facility in drawing, precise and mature, and he began to spend hours every day sketching the comic-strip character Katie Keene, attiring her in a various assortment of gowns and suits. He also liked to make pencil drawings of women in fancy gowns. "It was in his genes," said Linda Most, who would watch him sketch. "It was in his blood." Perhaps Calvin was best remembered at school for his execution of a large mural on the wall of the stairwell just outside Pearl Thaler's offices. The mural was so elaborate and professional that students and teachers have not forgotten it in four decades. By age twelve Calvin was so good that on weekends he went to the Art Students League in Manhattan and took classes in life drawing and sketching.

As he got older, he began to carry a sketch pad with him wherever he went, doodling designs whenever there was a spare moment. Lillian Edelson, a neighbor who also worked at nearby Montefiore Hospital, remembered that one day Flo came in for X rays and brought Calvin with her. Perched nervously in the waiting room, the boy told Edelson that he wanted to become a fashion designer, and to be pleasant, she asked him to suggest something for her to wear. Calvin took out his sketch pad and designed a suit for her on the spot. "That's all right for when I go to work," Edelson said, "but what about when I go out?" Calvin turned the page and deftly drew an elaborate ball gown.

Calvin's penchant for drawing women's clothing did not make him especially popular among his peers, since sports were a preoccupation for most boys. "He was a bit of a fish out of water," Beverlee Sclar conceded. Although on school questionnaires he dutifully listed among his interests "baseball and hockey," at heart Calvin hated sports. He found athletics boring—mostly because he couldn't compete like the other boys and threw a ball with a limp overhand, like a girl. In the schoolyard or during gym periods, Calvin watched from the sidelines and sketched women's clothing while the other boys played catch. "Calvin did not do what we did," said neighborhood boy Larry Rosenzweig, "no basketball, no stickball. He didn't play cards or go to the track or hang out on the rail, asking for cigarettes."

Of all the people in Calvin's young life, it was probably his junior high school art teacher, Nedda Arnova, who made one of the most important contributions. Arnova not only recognized his potential; she praised his abilities instead of mocking them. She was another window into the world outside the Bronx. A tall, unattractive spinster who taught gifted students in the special art classes, Arnova quickly came to be adored by Calvin, especially the way she dressed in exotic outfits of silks and cashmeres, accessorized with long scarves flung over her shoulders. In autumn, when she returned from vacation, she would spin fantastic tales about her overseas voyages. Calvin would listen spellbound. "Arnova was very proud of Calvin," said Judy Deutsch. "It was almost like she was his surrogate parent, because she had no children." She was also very strict, and students were allowed to draw only what she told them to. Calvin defiantly kept a sketch pad hidden under his desk and drew women's clothing instead of working on his class assignments. He even dared to be mischievous with her, periodically knocking her favorite snack—a banana—off her desk onto the floor, stepping on it, and then breaking into hysterical laughter, a prank for which he was detained many times after school.

Prankster or not, as time passed, Calvin felt even more of an odd man out. He even talked differently: His broad Bronx accent softened and turned vaguely effeminate. In his pubescent years he shot up in height, over six feet tall, and he developed a gooney toe-to-heel walk that made him an object of derision. "Everybody got hysterical because he used to bounce," said Molly Ann Acker. "He used to hop when he walked, if you watched him. It was like he was on a trampoline." Self-conscious about the way he looked to begin with, as he entered his teen years, he was besieged daily with a new crop of erupting pimples which no amount of Clearasil could conquer. One winter, in desperation, he purchased a bottle of a new product on the market called Man Tan, a clear liquid that turned skin a tan color. The only problem was that Calvin smeared the liquid on his face unevenly. When it dried, it left the outlines of his fingers on his cheeks in yellow streaks of dye.

Gawky, Man Tanned Calvin was irresistible prey of the neighborhood toughs, and one year an Italian gang called the Golden Guineas ambushed both Klein brothers near the Parkway. Calvin and his older brother started running for home, but with the toughs almost upon them, they ducked for cover into a convenient apartment building and raced up six flight of steps to the roof, where they were trapped. The gang overpowered Calvin and tied his arms tightly with several lengths of electrical wire before he finally got loose, physically unharmed but very shaken. He raced home and sobbed as he told his mother the story. Flo was outraged to hear that those *telenah* would dare touch her flesh and blood and took her sons directly to the local precinct to lodge a complaint. When the police tried to dismiss it as "just kids roughhousing around," Flo blew her top. By the time she was through, the desk sergeant had sent out two cops to talk sternly with the parents of the Italian kids.

The general consensus of opinion about him in the neighborhood was overwhelming. He was different. "There was just something about Calvin that wasn't clearly defined," said one girl from the neighborhood. "It became more obvious in junior high school. He just seemed like one of the girls. In the eighth grade, when boys were going into adolescence, you didn't feel Calvin's maleness, those male hormones. You felt a softer person."

Molly Ann Acker declared, "Calvin liked things women liked. He liked women's clothes. He'd tell girls, 'You look nice in your lipstick.' "

One neighborhood girl, Sheila Messer, wouldn't even go out with him. "There was something feminine about him that turned me off. He was tall and skinny and pimply and gawky. He was very nervous in general and had this habit of wriggling his leg around a lot."

Calvin was only too aware of the world's assessment of him, and it tormented him more than anybody could guess. Calvin knew what a *faygeleh* was. He had heard the word used derisively around his house as long as he could remember, the Yiddish for "little bird" or "fairy." But that word was meant for hairdressers or male nurses, not good little boys from the Bronx. He would not, could not, let it be true. The only solution was to try to act normally. "Normal" in the Bronx meant marriage and kids. "The assumption in the neighborhood was that you would marry," said Ed Schneider, who also went to P.S. 80. "Homosexuality was not even discussed. I remember saying to my rabbi, 'If Adam and Eve only had two sons, where did the rest of us come from?,' and I got smacked in the face. Even straight sex was not discussed. In Calvin's neighborhood, being acceptable and being accepted by your group was the main thing."

Yet amid all this turmoil and doubt, there was one light in his life. It was another boy, and if Calvin had been able to express his feelings more openly at the time, he might have said that he was in love with this boy. He was handsome and strong and tough and masculine—all the things that Calvin could not be—and when they were together, Calvin felt strong and normal as well. In his heart, he wanted in some way to be connected for the rest of his life with this boy—Barry Schwartz.

CHAPTER THREE

Barry was the only person Calvin trusted.

—Jon Miller

On the surface, Barry Schwartz was a most unlikely best friend of Calvin Klein's. "The two didn't share anything in common that I could see," said Alan Cohen, one of Barry's close childhood friends. Joel Permison, another friend, said, "How those two got together I'll never know. I would never associate Barry Schwartz with Calvin Klein." And yet, as another childhood pal put it, "Calvin's last name was Barry, and Barry's last name was Calvin. They were synonymous."

Perhaps that was because as incompatible a pair as they seemed, the two were ineluctably drawn to each other. Apart, they each seemed wanting in some way; together they made a nicely rounded person, a yin and yang of personalities and interests that worked for them like finely meshing gears. While Barry was short and dark-skinned, with coarse features, Calvin was tall and soft. Barry was athletic and confident. Calvin was reserved but had all the style and sophistication that Barry lacked. Barry was tough and self-assured; Calvin, aloof and high-strung. While Calvin was always impeccably groomed, Barry usually wore blue jeans—until Barry's mother began to send Calvin with him to shop. "From age five or six we were inseparable," Barry Schwartz said. "I spent my whole life growing up in Calvin's house. Calvin spent the same amount of time in my house. We'd sleep over, we'd eat together, we'd meet after school." The two even took private Hebrew lessons together to prepare for their bar mitzvahs.

Even as children, the two shared one great bond: They dreamed about getting rich together. They were going to become entrepreneurs together. Calvin was going to be the idea man, and Barry was going to run the business side. Their dreams weren't small-scale, either, and they formulated a whole series of grandiose schemes, including starting a chain of supermarkets or pet stores. "I would buy all the pets," Calvin said, "and Barry would run the business." Their efforts in this direction started when, at age six, they teamed up to hawk iced tea together on the street. "When Calvin and I were eight years old," said Barry, "we used to sell newspapers on the Parkway. We'd get the *Daily News*, the *Daily Mirror,* and we'd get a bundle of fifty papers and put them on our shoulders. I think they were four cents in those days, and we'd sell them for six cents. The weekends the papers were more, so you made more money. And I held the money. That's what we joke about today. Because even then, I held the money. And at the end of the night, I'd divide it up. I'd give him some, and I took some for myself."

The boys had been introduced by their fathers, who owned Harlem grocery stores in the same period and rode to work together on the train. Yet the two boys developed a closeness that was independent of their families. "The whole relationship was Calvin's and mine," said Barry. "It wasn't from our parents, because our parents didn't really socialize at that point." In fact, when the boys were young, Flo, in her characteristically abrasive manner, made some comment that so infuriated Barry's mother, Eva, that the two women stopped talking to each other for over fifteen years. But Calvin was not going to allow this to separate him from Barry or, for that matter, Eva. Calvin adored Eva, and eventually the two sons insisted that their mothers make up, which they reluctantly did, but even then the truce was tenuous.

Barry Kent Schwartz was born on May 25, 1942. He grew up in a second-floor, three-room apartment that overlooked an alleyway at 3120 Bainbridge Avenue and 205th Street, just a few blocks away from where Calvin lived. The building was a plainly built brick mid-rise, blackened by gusts that blew up from the subway that rumbled below. It had none of the gracious stonework that gave Calvin's Rochambeau Avenue apartment house so much charm. Unlike Calvin's spacious apartment, the Schwartz's flat was spartan and claustrophobic. Barry and his older sister by four years, Clara, shared one small rear bedroom, while his parents, Harry and Eva Schwartz, slept on an old pull-out sofa in the living room. Much of the family's time was spent in a narrow kitchen, where a small window looked out over the sunless alley.

Eva, who sometimes worked as a cashier in the family grocery store, was a youthful woman with short black hair. Of all Barry's friends, she was especially fond of Calvin, whom she considered a good influence on Barry compared to the other, rougher kids her son consorted with in the neighborhood. Although Barry loved his father deeply, the two had little rapport during the boy's younger years. Harry Schwartz was a bull-like man with a pasty complexion and untidy gray hair. His manner was gruff and surly—"You took one look at him and you thought he was going to bite," said Beverlee Sclar—but friends and family alike remember him as a man with a soft and generous heart. "My father worked very hard all of his life," Barry said. "I never knew him except as a person who'd come home and look at the newspapers and fall asleep in a chair because he worked fourteen hours and he was exhausted. He worked six days a week and slept half of Sunday. He yelled, hollered, and screamed, and as a boy, I was scared of him."

When Barry was eight years old, in 1950, Harry opened the Sundial Supermarket in Harlem at 170 Lenox Avenue between 117th and 118th streets in an area of run-down tenements and brownstone rooming houses. Only three and a half square miles in area, Harlem was densely populated with a quarter million blacks who struggled under some of the worst living conditions in America. Many of the white, mostly Jewish store owners had begun to flee the neighborhood, but not Harry Schwartz. Harry liked it there and for the most part got along well with the local residents. Said Barry's friend Jon Miller, "I would describe Harry as the mayor of 117th Street. There were bad guys on every block. You had to be tough. Tough or crazy."

Although the Sundial had a rather ambitious logo of an "S" inside an outer ring of miniature sunbursts—and Barry would later describe it as a "chain" of supermarkets—it was a humble-looking place, a hundred feet wide, with six aisles, tin ceilings, and linoleum floors. The clientele, which was made up almost entirely of poor neighborhood blacks, were fond of Harry as well, for it was not unknown for him to allow more needy families to run up a bill when cash was tight.

Yet the Sundial Supermarket was not as simple as it seemed. According to local police as well as many others who knew him, it was from the Sundial that Harry ran his subsidiary business—that of a well-liked and well-connected small-time loan shark and bookie. Horses and numbers were a natural extension of Harry, anyway, who loved to gamble himself and had even once been arrested, in 1955, for "loitering for gambling" in a dice game. The charges were later dismissed, and Harry was often on the phone six hours a day conducting his secondary business. ("He wasn't ordering groceries," said Jon Miller.) Dozens of people who did not come to the Sundial to shop were in and out of the store throughout the day to see him in his office.

One reason why Barry didn't get along with his father was that in so many ways they were exactly alike. Not only did he have the same facial expressions as his father, Barry talked in the same gruff manner, and from the time he was a child, Barry shared his father's passion for sports. One of Barry's best childhood memories was of being taken to the Polo Grounds by his father. Barry was enchanted by the old stadium and rode the train there after school whenever he could, lingering during baseball batting practice to scavenge the balls hit into the the empty stands and later sell the balls for two dollars each during games. Even Calvin caught the bug and landed a weekend job there at the press gate; like a good boy, he turned his entire earnings over to Flo.

Calvin was especially fond of Barry's older sister, Clara, whom everyone called by the Yiddish declension "Kayla." They were something of kindred spirits, both artistic and creative—Kayla made some of her own clothes—and both outsiders. Kayla carried a massive 180 pounds on her five-foot-three-inch frame and was known by all as the jovial neighborhood fat girl. On sunny afternoons when Barry was out playing basketball with the other kids, Calvin would seek out Kayla in the Schwartz's apartment. They'd sit in her room and talk for hours, about their families and themselves and their dreams. Over the years Calvin came to realize that underneath the public persona of a happy fat girl, Kayla was a desperately lonely young woman who could not find a boyfriend. Through most of her life she was on fad diets, but on late afternoons Kayla could be found drowning her misery in an ice cream sundae at the candy store.

2

Although Barry Schwartz lived not far from Calvin, his apartment building was not in the same elementary school district, and for his first six years of schooling Barry attended P.S. 56. He was a fast study and an impatient student, easily bored by school. Yet his grades were far above average, as was his IQ. In 1955, when he was eleven years old, he transferred to P.S. 80, although he was never in any of Calvin's slower classes.

As a teenager, Barry grew into a combative, determined young man. "Barry had a sexual magnetism about him," Jane Sternberg remembered. "But he also had a selfishness that would make a lot of people uncomfortable." As he got older, his love of sports combined with his zest for risk taking, and like so many others in his immediate circle, he became a frequent gambler. "He would bet on two cockroaches," said Ron Ciner. But unlike Calvin's brother, Barry, Barry Schwartz was a smart gambler. "If he had two marbles and it was marble season," Jerry Goldberg recalled, "at the end of the day Barry Schwartz would wind up with fifty marbles." However, horses and cards, not marbles, were Barry's favorite indulgence, and the racetrack and poker soon replaced the ballpark as his primary diversion.

Barry even enlisted Calvin in his gambling adventures. Calvin soon found that the possibility of winning large amounts of money filled him with adrenaline. He was determined to be his friend's equal, and the track and weekly poker games became a diversion for him as well. Barry remembered that "he and I went to Belmont together when we were fifteen years old. We went to the trotters at night."

When Barry wasn't at the track, he was a fixture at Sam Pistone's pool hall. "I really was a good pool shooter," said Barry. "I have one thousand hours into that." Pistone's also happened to be the favorite hangout of Calvin's brother, Barry, and he and Barry Schwartz became friends as well. In many ways Barry Klein was a much more logical friend for Barry Schwartz than was Calvin. "Barry Klein was a hero to Barry Schwartz," Don Guerra recalled, "and Barry Klein was much closer to Barry Schwartz than Calvin when they were teenagers. Barry Klein was the gambler that Barry Schwartz wanted to be."

As for Barry's romantic life, as a teenager he was an unapologetic womanizer. Barry liked to play the field, and it seemed he had a different girlfriend every few weeks. This preoccupation with girls added an extra impetus to Calvin's need to prove himself, and he dutifully started to date. But while most teenaged boys were obsessed with "make-out" dates during which they necked passionately with a girl in an angora sweater, when Calvin invited a girl to his bedroom, it was to spend an evening on the telephone playing practical jokes on strangers. Calvin did pluck up the courage to ask out Lefty Farrell's cousin Fredda Kleiner, but she rebuffed him, saying, "I'm not interested in this little skinny Calvin. I like steak."

Flo worried about her favorite child's shyness with girls. Although Calvin had occasional dates throughout his adolescence, something seemed amiss to her. Finally, Flo called the mother of a young girl with whom Calvin had a platonic relationship to make a "*shiddach*." Calvin was only in his early teens at the time, and the girl's mother was amazed.

Since the idea of a sexual relationship intimidated Calvin, he did the next best thing by finding a "safe" girl to go out with, someone who was virginal and conservative and wouldn't think of having sex any more than he would. Calvin found such a girl in Diane Goldhammer, a neighborhood girl who was a "kindred spirit," according to Goldhammer. At the time they started to date in their early teens, Diane was "short and dumpy," as she described herself, although she had a sweet face and dark, flowing, Pre-Raphaelite hair. She was also an aspiring artist with whom Calvin shared much in common. "He was a joy," she said. "He spent many hours at my house drawing, and we would go to Manhattan all the time to visit museums and see the costume collections." They would go clothes shopping together, and Calvin would blithely spend hours advising her on styles that slimmed her short frame. One evening that Goldhammer remembered fondly, Calvin took her for dessert at Toffinetti's, a restaurant on Broadway in Manhattan's theater district. The two sat in a window seat, and for hours Calvin charmed her by critiquing the clothing of the people passing by in the street, rattling off his philosophy of taste and style.

Barry Schwartz "was never far away," Goldhammer said. "The three of us were together a tremendous amount of the time." As for Calvin and Barry's friendship, "Barry was the other side of Calvin. It was an incredibly wonderful friendship. And yet Barry had his own identity. You know how some people have a deaf ear to music? Well, Barry had a deaf ear to fashion. But he was always accepting of Calvin's artistic ability. He never, like some kids, put it down, like 'Come on, let's go bet on the horses. . . . What are you doing with a sketch pad?' They were just like a hand in a glove together, and I was like the third part of it."

Eventually, however, being the third part of a hand in a glove has its limitations, and Diane introduced Barry to a girlfriend of hers, Sheila, and the four of them began to double-date. "Calvin and I sort of became 'the couple,'" said Diane, "but it wasn't the type of relationship like Sheila and Barry had. It was more of a friendship." Diane and Calvin and Sheila and Barry would often go out to the David Marcus cinema together and afterward to Jahn's ice cream parlor. Goldhammer remembered that at other times they would go somewhere private so that Barry and his date could neck, and she and Calvin just watched and giggled. "It wasn't a romance," she said. "We didn't feel that it was really our fault that it wasn't [sexual]. The nice thing was that it was hardly relevant to our friendship, and I felt that to be very beautiful. I felt that we could be with Barry, who was hot and heavy half the time with whomever he was with, and we were kind of just along and having a wonderful time and it wasn't an issue—at least to myself."

"In the very beginning," said Diane, "there was such an unrest in him, such a searching. I felt that he had a burning drive, that he would be somebody. He just made himself nuts sometimes. Some people are able to find their center and put everything in perspective, but he didn't. He would blow things up so that they were absolutely earth-shattering. He was very hyper. When things would disturb him, his gait and bounce would become more pronounced, and his left leg would start to shake."

Calvin's relationship with Goldhammer continued into high

school. While Barry had chosen the local Bronx high school, De Witt Clinton, a rough-and-tumble all-boys school, Diane and Calvin both wanted to attend one of the Manhattan high schools that specialized in careers in the arts. Calvin's choice was the High School of Industrial Arts, which specialized in advertising and drafting. He was thrilled when his acceptance letter arrived in the mail in the early spring of 1957. It meant a long subway ride to Manhattan every day, but it was also a ride far away from the Bronx. All along he had known he was destined for something greater. Wilma Brooks remembered that when they were about ten years old, she and Calvin swapped autographs in turquoise ink. "We had these conversations about being famous," Brooks said. "We all said we would be famous, but Calvin was the only one who really believed it."

The graduation picture of him that appears in the P.S. 80 yearbook is that of a smiling, clean-cut youngster with a high pompadour and pudgy nose—not a hint of the attractive man who would soon emerge. Beside the picture was an odd inscription: "Industrial Art . . . Fashion designer . . . Shut your mouth! Go away! Girls, look at Calvin K."

Many years later, Calvin's P.S. 80 friend Linda Most read in the newspapers that the now world famous fashion designer was going to make one of his rare personal appearances at Bloomingdale's department store in Manhattan to publicize the launching of a new line. Most was feeling pangs of nostalgia the day that she arrived at Bloomingdale's. She took a seat in the front row of folding chairs and waited expectantly as the room filled quickly with a crowd of adoring fans. Finally, with fanfare generally accorded a movie star, Calvin was ushered into the room surrounded by a phalanx of store executives and publicity people. He bore little resemblance to the nervous, skinny kid Linda Most had known at P.S. 80. He was still gangly, but years of lifting weights had hardened his muscles, and the vestiges of his adolescent acne had been smoothed over with hundreds of tiny silicone injections. Moreover, there was something radiant about him, glamorous and transcendent. The boy who had never belonged had been transformed into one of America's greatest media stars. As he was seated at the table where he was scheduled to sign autographs, he seemed uncomfortable and aloof, as if all the attention embarrassed him. Linda Most sat smiling at him for a few minutes until she finally caught his eye and a flicker of recognition crossed his face. Suddenly, as it dawned on him who she was, his face lit up as if he were a little boy again, a kid from the Parkway. He jumped up from the table and rushed around to where Linda Most was sitting, throwing his arms around her, hugging and kissing her cheeks and asking how she was and what had happened in her life. But after only a few moments, someone from his staff gently tugged him away, and in an almost frightening transformation, he became cold and distant and went back to being Calvin Klein again.

3

Going off to the big city and a new school was a tremendous thrill for the fourteen-year-old boy from the Bronx. Not only was Manhattan where the "real world" started, but at the High School of Industrial Arts, Calvin hoped he would no longer feel like such an oddball. Whereas in the Bronx he had been ridiculed as an effeminate outsider, at Industrial Arts, said Calvin's high school friend Marylyn Aronstein, "there were so many kids who were off-the-wall that we were kind of sedate in comparison." And whereas in the Bronx it was unusual to admit to artistic talent and aspirations, at Industrial Arts everybody could boast of some creative ability, and many were much more gifted than Calvin. Indeed, Calvin's classmates included the budding poet and photographer Gerard Melanga and the aspiring fashion illustrator Antonio. At Industrial Arts, Calvin was no longer a "fish out of water," as Beverlee Sklar remembered him at P.S. 80, but now a small fish in a big pond.

At the time Calvin attended the High School of Industrial Arts it was split into two buildings—an annex on East Fifty-first Street, which Calvin attended for his first year, and a larger, decrepit building on East Seventy-ninth Street that was so ancient it once housed wounded Union soldiers during the Civil War. Founded as a vocational high school in 1936, the school still emphasized trades in the arts, although an academic curriculum had been added. Courses included cartooning, drawing, illustration, package design, creative writing, and physical education (which included learning golf and tennis swings). Although this new, artistic atmosphere seemed the perfect opportunity for Calvin to come out of his shell, for the most part he remained a shy young man who kept a distance from his fellow students. Thirty years later, only a handful of them would remember he was even there.

In high school Calvin shot up to his full six feet two inches in height, and although he was not traditionally handsome—if anything his acne had grown worse—a sexually appealing young man began to emerge. Indeed, when he broke through his shyness, he had a kind of cocksure charm, and his muddy green eyes could turn seductive. Still, with most people Calvin was distant and cool, and other than the nervous shaking of his leg, he managed to maintain what appeared to those around him an arrogantly aloof exterior.

Calvin's major at Industrial Arts was fashion illustration, and he was one of only a handful of boys in that field. While he loved the mechanics of illustration, haunting art supply stores and becoming the first in his class to use press-on type and Rapidograph pens, his dedication to his craft didn't seem overwhelming. In fact, during his last two years at Industrial Arts he would often play hooky for days at a time and go to the racetrack with Barry or bury his nose in the racing results at school. At one point he won $1,500 and bought himself a beat-up used car. Making money sometimes seemed more important to him than becoming a star in the fashion industry. "I'm going to become a manufacturer," he told a school friend, "not a designer. I'm not going to work for somebody else." And if he couldn't make it in the garment center, he was prepared to go another route. Marylyn Aronstein said: "Calvin and Barry were hell-bent on opening a supermarket, and eventually a chain of them. The object of the game was to make money. That was Calvin's main objective. It was a serious commitment to being successful. He wanted all the things that we were raised to want."

There was one thing he didn't want, and that was to be associated with homosexuality. Many of his closest friends in the school were other young men who were also closeted in their sexuality. One closeted young gay student who was friendly with Calvin in high school would also date girls to keep up pretenses, and on occasion he and Calvin double-dated. One night, they even triple-dated with Barry Schwartz and his girl. The three couples wound up "parking" in Barry's car in a secluded, dark spot. As Barry and his girlfriend began to neck, "Calvin and I would try to follow along, like taking a cue," Calvin's friend recalled.

There were other students, however, who were far more liberated in their sexuality than Calvin and his friend and were openly gay or part of a group of young drag queens who also populated the student body. These "queens," in particular, offended Calvin, who was disgusted by the way they flaunted their sexual ambiguity. On weekends the group would hold drag parties, dressing in clothing they designed, then bring photographs of themselves to school later in the week. The photos would be passed around class to much laughter and screaming, and everyone would critique the clothing, everyone except Calvin, who couldn't bring himself to glance at the photos. "Calvin hated that [scene]," remembered Aronstein. "He didn't even want to be *near* [gays] at school."

Most of Calvin's classmates had no idea just how deeply conflicted he was. Some were positive he was straight; others simply assumed he was homosexual. "There were any number of overt homosexuals in that school," said Calvin's classmate Derek Callander, "but not Calvin. In those days homosexuality was a lot less acceptable than it is now, and I don't think he wanted to get tarred with any particular brush, because it might get in his way . . . and [he would] find himself in a position where his career might be hurt by it. I always got the impression that sex, so far as Calvin was concerned, was pretty much like anything else, a tool to be used. Calvin struck me as being a very calculating person, someone who heavily weighed the odds and didn't do anything unless it could do him some good."

One skill that Calvin would hone during his high school years was his capacity to charm and win over those with power and influence. Many of his classmates regarded their drafting instructor, Miss Gerson, as a moody and difficult woman. "If you were a slight hair off in your architectural rendering," one student said, "that would be cause for a D." Gerson also had a peculiar habit of tilting her head to one side and dangling her arm behind her shoulder as she spoke, and she was the object of constant mockery behind her back. One group disliked her so much that they poured brown paint into her coffee cup and guffawed when she took a sip of it and spit the liquid out over the floor. But not Calvin. Calvin cultivated Miss Gerson. Soon after Miss Gerson announced in class that Pablo Picasso was her favorite painter, Calvin's artwork suddenly began to take on a distinctly Picassoesque style. This culminated with Calvin beginning to sign all of his class work "Picasso."

"What are you doing?" asked one of his classmates when she saw the signature.

"If it's good enough for Picasso," said Calvin, "it's good enough for me."

Indeed, the signature certainly met with Miss Gerson's approval. "She fell for it," said Derek Callander. "After that, Calvin could do no wrong. Calvin was a man who knew even then which side of the bread the butter was on." There was a great deal of resentment toward Calvin when, at the end of the year, he was given one of the highest marks in the class. "Brownie points are brownie points," said Callander.

Calvin's popularity with instructors was especially irksome to many students whose consensus of opinion was that Calvin was not particularly talented. "He was definitely *not* the person you'd vote mostly likely to succeed," said his classmate Cynthia Mailman. Yet Calvin was beginning to exhibit a skill that would eventually allow him to outdistance his fellow graduates; he was a brilliant copyist, with an uncanny ability to mimic the lines and styles of the great designers, then subtly alter their work to make it his own. "If you looked carefully," Derek Callander said, "he was entirely derivative. His early fashions, the ones he did in school, it's Dior and Chanel."

Though Calvin never seemed to realize it, the teacher he admired the most at Industrial Arts, Olga Petroff, did not reciprocate in her opinion of him. Petroff was a svelte woman of innate style and taste who started her career in the design room of Henri Bendel's before opting for the security of a teaching career. "I had a great verve for teaching and living, and it wasn't only in fashion," she said. "I would give opinions about seeing things differently not only in fashion but in everything that one could be inspired by, in art, in fabric, and seeing so many different nuances that all came together. I would encourage my students to go to museums and see paintings and the colors different artists used and look at color and color combinations . . . and the light of satin and the dullness of flannel and bring them together. I could close my eyes and see Calvin with his wide eyes watching me and listening so attentively," Petroff said. "I know that he adored me, that I know, very much."

However, as a talent "Calvin was not outstanding," Petroff judged. "There were many talented students among the group, and I wouldn't put him in the top group. He had a simple, clean line and a good eye, but I didn't spot anything in him that I thought would be a great designer. Even today his designs are all just paste rather than really good design. Yet he had the keen sense of judgment to know whether something was good or not. He had style more than great design. His talent was in having an eye and knowing what will go with what, along with the help and guidance of others. As far as real design, I never thought he had that." Tactfully, Petroff hid these misgivings from Calvin, who was entranced by her cosmopolitan lifestyle. One of his favorite memories of his high school career was when she invited a small group of students to her apartment in Manhattan around the Christmas holidays. The students lounged on overstuffed print pillows on the polished wood floors while Petroff served them biscuits and tea from a big silver samovar and they strained to make urbane conversation. "He was quiet and shy," said Petroff. "He had this kind of aloofness. I didn't think he integrated with the other students in the class too well. I don't think he had much confidence in himself, either. It seemed to me as if he didn't have any direction."

After Calvin graduated, he kept in touch with Petroff for a few years, and then they drifted apart. Many years later, however, Petroff was pleased to discover an invitation in the mail to one of his fashion shows. Retired by now, she had put on many pounds and was no longer the slender fashion plate Calvin remembered. "I should have had judgment and not gone to see him after the show," Petroff said, "but I went in to congratulate him and tell him that I was pleased to see him doing so well." As Calvin looked her over, Petroff could see the dismay in his eyes at how she had changed physically and left the showroom feeling rattled. "The next year, I never received an invitation because he evidently had his eye on slim fashion-conscious people and I didn't fit into that scheme anymore. He just didn't want to have a heavy, clumsy woman around there. I felt hurt by this kind of rejection."

Petroff was not the only one from the High School of Industrial

Arts who felt rejected. A great many of the 375 students from his graduating class and its alumni association later came to resent Calvin. Even while he was at the school he began to distance himself from it. There is not a single picture of the lanky eighteen-year-old Calvin in the yearbook, perhaps because he was either self-conscious about his pockmarked complexion or regarded the school as a closed chapter in his life that he did not care to look back at and reminisce about. "He decided not to be in the yearbook," said a school friend. "He hated things like that—pooh-poohed it. It was too sophomoric for him." The only reference in the book to his existence at all in the school is on a brief list of "camera shy" students: "Calvin Klein, 3191 Rochambeau Avenue, Bronx. Fashion Designer." Since the time of his parting, the school's most famous graduate has virtually turned his back on it. Numerous requests for his assistance from the alumni association—some as simple as for a donation of his sketches for display in the hallways—have been consistently ignored. Sometimes his decision not to cooperate has been more pointed. Nearly twenty years after he graduated, a group of young students from Industrial Arts went to visit his showroom through an appointment arranged by one of their mothers, who was a secretary at the headquarters of Calvin Klein Inc. But when the teenagers arrived, "they got the doors slammed in their face," said Shelby Schmitt, the president of the alumni group. "There had been some 'mistake' about Calvin's availability, and he had no time to see anyone. The kids were very disappointed, and I had a lot of crying."

Perhaps the most hurtful slight felt by his fellow students was when Calvin's graduating class of 1960 held a gala reunion party. If he had attended, he would have been their most honored and revered guest. But Calvin never even responded to the invitation. The general feeling among his schoolmates was that they were deliberately being snubbed. "We are all annoyed," said Cynthia Mailman, "People felt that it was nasty, really, to forget your roots completely. So we all made a pact to never, ever, buy Calvin Klein clothes again."

Fresh out of high school, Calvin took a summer job in Freedomland, a vast amusement park in the marshy east Bronx shaped like the United States, where Co-op City now stands. Now eighteen years old, he was no longer the ugly duckling, yet neither was he quite the beautiful swan. Although he was still a skinny fellow with a bouncing gait there was an infectious magnetism about him, some indefinable star quality, sexy and charismatic. His self-assurance, which had once irked his peers, was beginning to be tempered by a dash of humility. His smile could warm the coldest heart, and when he wanted to be solicitous, he could make the most wretched soul feel transformed into the most important, appreciated person in the world. It was a talent that came naturally to him, and over the years his easy conversation became a weapon in his personal arsenal that he could brandish at will to win over the most reluctant of subjects.

He was, in the fall of 1960, a young man brimming with enthusiasm for his future, certain that real life would begin for him at the Fashion Institute of Technology (FIT). Although it was in theory an excellent springboard into the fashion industry, FIT—or the "Fairy" Institute of Technology or "Faggots In Training," as it was jeeringly dubbed by Calvin's acquaintances in the Bronx—didn't seem as if it were preparing him for the real world at all. Industry old-timers, who had clawed their way up the ladder from the shop floor, didn't hold much respect for anyone who would think of going to "college" to get into the garment center. Indeed, classes at FIT were pedantically oriented to learning a trade, and in his first year Calvin felt obliged to take a series of tedious craft courses, like sewing and patternmaking.

Calvin was also irked at some of the direction he was given at FIT. "When I was at design school," he said, "I was taught all of the tricks, how to put seams in every different place and how to stitch the seams and how to put flowers on something or put large buttons on something. You can create all sorts of tricks. Well, to me, the most interesting thing is to create something very beautiful, very attractive, very well cut, very well proportioned, and very simple."

At least one important contribution FIT made to Calvin's growth was that he coped with the boredom by cultivating his editorial skills. Eager to learn, he sopped up everything he saw and heard about fashion and began to develop an implacable opinion of what he deemed good or bad. He acquired a passion for expensive fab-

rics, particularly natural yarns of cotton and silk, and developed a
snobbish contempt for anything synthetic. He also began to affect
an equally emphatic dislike for bright colors, and muted shades of
browns and beiges became his great favorites. He was creatively
sparked, he said, by the work of Jacques Tiffeau, an obscure
French-born designer whose New York–based company, Tiffeau-
Busch, specialized in young sportswear with a modern look. And,
like thousands of other young students, he was fascinated by the
work of American designer Claire McCardell, who virtually invented American sportswear by designing practical yet fashionable
women's clothing for everyday life. Some of the highlights of his
time at FIT were the frequent trips the students made to the Costume Institute at the Metropolitan Museum. At this repository of
clothing and costumes collected from all over the world, Calvin
was allowed into the archives to examine original garments by great
designers like Chanel and Poiret. He loved fabrics and textures,
and he spent hours at the institute, poring over the old fabrics like
an archaeologist examining rare fossils.

4

It was while Calvin was attending FIT that something remarkable
happened: He fell in love with a girl. For those who had dismissed
him as a sissy dress designer, it was nothing more than miraculous
that Calvin had not only fallen in love, but he had won the heart of
the prettiest girl on Mosholu Parkway, Jayne Centre.

Calvin and Jayne had known each other throughout most of their
childhoods, even before she added the "y" to her name to give it
some distinction. Jayne was the girl all the other girls envied and all
the boys wanted to date but never could. She was the girl who
didn't seem to fit, the girl the other kids in the neighborhood
thought of as "goyim Connecticut." Even the way she walked her
pedigreed boxer dog along the Parkway seemed aristocratic, with
her head held erect, looking straight ahead as she went, not a single
one of her strawberry-blond hairs out of place. "Jayne was gorgeous
from head to toe," Sheila Messer remembered. "That's why Calvin
picked her." Barbara Stevens recalled, "She had that aura of being

unique. She stood apart a little bit. She had a sophistication about her, a little bit of class."

Ten months younger than Calvin, Jayne lived directly across the Parkway from him, and if he stuck his head out of his bedroom window, he could see her building, number 116 East Mosholu Parkway. She was an only child, doted on by her parents and spoiled and indulged. Her father, Harry, was a veteran of the garment center and worked as a salesman for various companies, including Puritan Fashions, the largest dress manufacturing company in the world. The lived in one of the better buildings in the area, where the apartments were known for their "sunken" living rooms. Jayne attended P.S. 94 until the seventh grade and then P.S. 80, where she was a class officer in her senior year. The following fall, she caught up with Calvin at the High School of Industrial Arts, where she majored in textile design.

Friends were aware that for a long time Jayne had an adolescent crush on Calvin and gave him shy smiles at they passed in the school hallways. One day, Calvin's friend Molly Ann Acker said to him, "Ask her out, what have you got to lose?" Fred Kleiner said, "When we were thirteen or fourteen, I remember being with Calvin at a dance one evening at the Jewish center social hall, and I looked around at the different girls. I was interested in Jayne Centre, and I was somewhat jealous of Calvin because he left with Jayne and walked her home. She was wearing a black dress, and I thought she was *the* most attractive girl at the dance."

Although Calvin and Jayne dated sporadically throughout school, the relationship took years to catch fire, and Jayne continued to go out with other boys. There was a period when she dated the son of the landlord of her apartment building, Michael Steinberg, whose parents were so rich it was rumored they bought him a new car when his old one got dirty. Another of Jayne's beaus was Barry and Calvin's friend Jon Miller. Miller remembered his astonishment when Jayne finally got serious with Calvin. "She typified the small-town girl who dated a football captain," he said, "and Calvin was anything but a football-captain type." But Calvin had something that the other boys did not: sensitivity. While most young men bored Jayne, since all they knew how to talk about was sports, Calvin seemed positively cosmopolitan and interested in really getting to know her. They would discuss fashion and art and textiles—Jayne's particular field of interest—or the latest fads in music and dancing. Unlike other boys she was seeing, Calvin wasn't constantly trying to persuade her to sleep with him, and as Jayne developed into a bosomy, sensual young woman, she was grateful to be in the company of someone who wasn't always coming on to her sexually. "They were really nice together," said Molly Ann Acker, "because they liked the same things." Said Judy Deutsch, "I remember they used to hold hands and walk with their arms around each other. Yet they were both very strange. Nobody really understood what the attraction was." Yet attraction it clearly was, because the two couldn't bear to be apart or take their hands off each other. They rode the subway together holding hands, necked under the ersatz stars in the Loews Paradise on the Grand Concourse, or made out in the backseat of cars on dates.

It was no real surprise to others that Jayne was attracted to Calvin. In many ways Calvin reminded people of her father, Harry Centre, with whom Calvin shared a certain softness. Harry was a dapper man with thick eyebrows, impeccably mannered and nattily dressed. When he spoke, he enunciated each word very carefully in a high-pitched voice, and he wore so much toilet water that the elevator in his apartment building was redolent for hours after he was in it. Said Molly Ann Acker, "Harry was very effeminate in the way he spoke and walked. Once, when we double-dated with Calvin and Jayne, my date said to me, 'If you laugh when you meet her father, I'll kill you.' " It was also the talk of the neighbors that Harry maintained a separate bedroom from his wife—unheard of at the time in the Bronx. "He had a bed in the corner," said Alice Smith, "with red satin pillows on the floor. Frieda lived her own life. She even went on vacations without him." Nevertheless, the two seemed totally dedicated to each other and satisfied in their relationship.

Although Flo and Leo adored Jayne from the moment Calvin walked her into their apartment—Jayne was so warm and natural she could win over anybody—Frieda Centre heartily disapproved of their daughter's relationship with Calvin. "Her mother didn't want her to get serious with Calvin," Alice Smith recalled. "She said she wanted her daughter to marry a rich man." As the years passed, however, the Centres began to accept the relationship, for it became clear that Jayne was devoted to Calvin, who also seemed besotted. For one thing, Jayne was about as different a woman from his mother as he could find. She was tender and unthreatening, and she let him take the lead. She also seemed as convinced as he was that he was destined to become "somebody." In her company, he felt relaxed, and friends remembered that Calvin started to develop a sense of humor when he was around her.

Nevertheless, the relationship followed an on-again, off-again pattern for years that mirrored Calvin's ambivalence about himself. When Jon Miller would meet him in the street and ask how it was going with Jayne, Calvin would shrug and reply either, "We just broke up," or, "We just got back together again." The main impediment to the relationship seemed to be Jayne's desire to marry and have children. Calvin told himself that he really loved her, and he wanted offspring as well. But his career aspirations came first, and he wasn't so sure that marriage was going to further them. It wasn't until they were both attending the Fashion Institute of Technology that the relationship became more of a reality for both of them.

Calvin shared some of the feelings of his deepening relationship with his friend Wilma Brooks late one balmy summer night on the Parkway. There had been a group of young people from the neighborhood lounging on the rail and gossiping. Finally, long after the moon appeared, only Calvin and Wilma remained. The conversation took an intimate turn, and Calvin lowered his voice and began to talk haltingly about Jayne and how much he loved her. Wilma remembered thinking there was some problem that he could not quite bring himself to admit. "He was scared, really scared," she remembered. "I think he knew he was gay. It was hard in that neighborhood. There was a lot of pressure on you to get married. He had all these plans and really wanted to be a manufacturer with his heart and soul. But Jayne wanted to get married, and he was afraid it was going to 'fuck him up.' He was afraid he was going to have responsibility he didn't want to have. He said he didn't want to live without her. And he was afraid of living with her."

5

After only two semesters at FIT, Calvin became restless, "champing at the bit," said his school chum Marylyn Aronstein. "His attitude was 'Let's get on with it. It's a great big world.'" He was so bored that one day, instead of attending classes, he paid a visit to his high school teacher Olga Petroff. "He seemed very discouraged," Petroff said. "He was going to FIT, and he sort of loped along. He wasn't enthusiastic. He was confused, and I felt sorry for him, but I really couldn't give him the attention at the time."

Eventually, Calvin began to contemplate quitting school and left after his first year. Although he continued to live at home with his parents and the rent was paid, he was in desperate need of pocket money, and on May 8, 1961, he took a job as a copyboy in the art department of *Women's Wear Daily,* an influential daily trade publication dutifully read by the industry. He wanted to be hired as an illustrator but took the copyboy job he was offered instead. Calvin was convinced it would be an excellent place for him to get a foothold in the business. Yet none of the busy journalists or editors were interested in the sketches of an ambitious copyboy. During the time Calvin worked for *Women's Wear Daily,* it was run by James Brady, a cigar-smoking man about town who brooked no nonsense from his employees. Calvin regarded Brady with such awe that he never even spoke a word to him. Years later, when Calvin was a celebrated designer, he confessed to Brady that he had once been employed at *Women's Wear Daily* as a copyboy. "I thought I could break into design that way. But no one at *Women's Wear Daily* thought I had any talent." Brady laughed and said that he didn't remember Calvin at the newspaper.

"Of course not," Calvin said. "I was so terrified of you, I hid in the men's room when I saw you coming."

Although Calvin probably learned more about the machinations of the fashion industry from his six months at *Women's Wear Daily* than he did from a year attending FIT, working as a copyboy turned out to be another dead end for the twenty-year-old. Defeated and glum, at mid-semester he reenrolled at FIT to complete his senior year. A school co-op program, during which he worked gratis at a series of grimy, undistinguished garment-center houses cutting fabric or gathering up dropped thread, did little to sate his hunger for the big time. Finally, in January 1963, after what seemed like an interminable year of treading water, Calvin graduated from FIT with a degree in fine arts. He did not attend graduation, and his diploma was mailed to him.

CHAPTER FOUR

He was like a son to all the women.
                                        —Ethel Mirkin

Calvin's first job out of FIT did not exactly set the world on fire. "I earned fifty-five dollars a week working for a company that made dresses out of a fabric it called 'whipped cream,' " he remembered. "The dresses sold wholesale for $6.95 and in the stores for about fourteen. When I went into the shop to cut the first samples at eight A.M., my boss would be watching *Captain Kangaroo* on television. That was the mentality of some Seventh Avenue people. After three months of *Captain Kangaroo* and 'whipped cream,' I asked my boss for a hundred-dollar raise."

"You're crazy," his boss told him.

"You're probably right," Calvin said. "I quit!"

Next, Calvin decided to look for a job in coats and suits. While many young designers were attracted to the big bang of haute couture, with its lush evening gowns and international following of glamorous women, for Calvin the coat-and-suit business was where money and security lay. A good suit was bread and butter; it was what well-dressed women wore year-in, year-out, whether to work, to lunch, or to church on Sundays. However, the coat-and-suit business was also one of the last fortresses of old-fashioned dreariness left in the garment center, a segment of the market pretty much untouched by the youthful trendiness that swept the rest of the business. The great majority of coat-and-suit houses were family businesses owned by men in their sixties and seventies, and the stodgy products they put on the market reflected their wariness of change.

There were, however, two or three coat-and-suit houses that were prestigious, and one of Calvin's top choices for a job was at Dan Millstein's company. Millstein's several divisions were best known for top-of-the-line, form-fitting coats and suits trimmed with luxurious fur collars and sold only in the better stores, like Peck and Peck and Saks Fifth Avenue. There were also several lesser-priced lines as well as a small made-to-order clientele that consisted of movie stars, divas of the Metropolitan opera, and fashionable society ladies. The Millstein name had become familiar to every American household through his clever promotional gimmick of loaning different outfits each day to *The Big Payoff*, a national daytime TV quiz show on which they were modeled by former Miss America Bess Myerson.

Millstein's reputation was so great that each year scores of students would flood the firm with their portfolios. Calvin set himself apart by writing an intelligent and endearing letter requesting an interview—not with Dan Millstein himself but with one of his best-known stylists, named Faye Wagner. A fortyish former model with flame-red hair, Wagner's designs were so popular with the public that she was one of the few in her field to have clothing sold under her own label: "Dani Juniors by Faye Wagner." (In the confusing nomenclature of the time, the highly paid, mostly European-born patternmakers were called "designers," and the people who drew the original sketches were called "stylists.") Wagner was flattered by Calvin's letter and agreed to meet with him. Just as he had hoped, the middle-aged woman was beguiled by the lanky boy who sauntered into her office for the interview. "Cal was wonderful," Wagner said of that first meeting. "His touch, his sketches, were just the kind of stuff that I liked, the kind of things that I did." What Wagner did not realize was that Calvin had seen her work in the newspapers and knew just the kind of sketches she would like. While Calvin sat in her office, Wagner called Dan Millstein and said, "I have a boy down here who showed me a few of his sketches, and they're beautiful. I'm very interested in him, and I think you should be, too."

To Calvin, Dan Millstein was a living legend, the Louis B. Mayer of the coat-and-suit moguls. He was a debonair man in his early fifties who knew the value of image and glamour. Unlike entering most garment center showrooms, with fluorescent lights and pipe racks and overflowing ashtrays, walking into Millstein's terraced showrooms at 205 West Thirty-ninth Street was like entering a plush Paris salon. The showroom had thick red carpeting and gilded Louis XIV furniture, and the walls were hung with French impressionist art, including a Renoir and a Monet. He and his sable-cloaked wife, Rose, lived in an antique- and art-filled mansion in Lawrence, Long Island, kept a pied-à-terre at the Hampshire House Hotel on Central Park South in Manhattan, and owned a winter retreat at the Savoy Plaza in Palm Beach. His thousand-dollar suits and big black limousine completed the movie-mogul image.

He was also a tyrant and a monster. Millstein had an "ego a mile long," said Audrey Goodman, his daughter. Charming and witty when he wanted to be, he could just as easily be mean-tempered and ruthless, slinging obscenities during fits of hair-trigger temper. Despite the luxurious trappings, his shouting matches with employees were more appropriate for the pushcarts of the Lower East Side. There's not much of a Harvard Business School atmosphere in the garment center to begin with, but Millstein was usually down in the gutter with the best of them. Once, when he didn't like the way a collection was turning out, he screamed at the designers, "This line is made for fucking *lesbians!*" On another day, when a buyer complained that the fox collars on a shipment were too skimpy, Millstein chased her out of the showroom, bellowing, "*I didn't fuck the foxes!*"

When Calvin was ushered into the manufacturer's palatial office for his job interview, the first thing he laid his eyes on was a signed photograph of Marilyn Monroe hugging Dan Millstein, wearing the clinging suit that Millstein had made to order for her wedding to Joe DiMaggio. Millstein perfunctorily leafed through Calvin's portfolio, a cigarette burning between his fingers, and after a minute grunted acquiescence. Calvin was put on staff as a sketcher for $75 a week. When he came home that night to Rochambeau Avenue and told Flo and Leo about Marilyn Monroe and the Renoir, he was a hero.

Unfortunately for Calvin, he was assigned to work not for Faye Wagner on the eleventh floor but for a stylist named Maria Prinzi in the "Missy" division of the company nine floors below. Prinzi was regarded as a good "idea person" in the company, and Calvin's primary responsibility was to translate her ideas onto paper. This was not an easy task for a young man as opinionated as Calvin, and although at first he and Prinzi got along well, there soon developed a grating friction and competition between the two that made Calvin's workdays miserable. Calvin's penchant for designing for tall, slim women did not serve him well in the "Missy" division, which derived its name from a clever ruse designed to flatter women up to size 18. While he slaved in a windowless cubbyhole churning out sketches, Prinzi would criticize and ridicule them, and Millstein would insist his coats looked "schmaltzy." "Dan had taste," said Calvin, "and understood clothes that were well proportioned. But his bread and butter was flash-in-the-pan clothes—such as one hundred percent camel's-hair coats with special seaming and an interesting cut. . . . Dan was a manufacturer, not a designer. . . ."

Calvin was not without his admirers at the company. Even the other young male sketchers began to appreciate "young Cal's" appeal. "I was very impressed with Cal," said George Simonton, a designer who also started at Millstein. "He was very bright, and I knew he was star material. He had something—and I don't know that it had to do with his talent. He was different from the rest of the people there. It was his look. He's good-looking now, but he was absolutely gorgeous then."

Yet the person Calvin most needed to appreciate him was Dan Millstein, who, when he was obliged to acknowledge Calvin at all, would refer to him only as "What's his name" or "the boy." Calvin would show Millstein his sketches, and the man would bellow, "I *hate* them. They're all *terrible*. You don't know what the hell you're doing!" Although Calvin grew to hate Millstein, he also had a lot for which to be grateful to him. Working for him was an unparalleled indoctrination into the nuts and bolts of a gritty industry. "I learned a lot, because he threw me into the snake pit," said Calvin. Millstein taught Calvin to be tough about quality; he watched as his boss would simply run his hand over a fabric and know if it was good or "crap." He taught Calvin to have respect for buyers and build a rapport with them. It was also Millstein who introduced Calvin to the world of haute couture by taking him to Europe for the first time to see the Paris collections. For a kid who had never before been farther than the Catskill Mountains, Paris was a thrilling adventure. Weeks before the trip it was all he talked about to Jayne and his family, and he spent hours planning his wardrobe and practicing his rudimentary French. On the way to Europe in the plane, he sat in the coach section, while Millstein and his wife traveled first-class, but when they arrived in Paris, Calvin was given a room in the same three-star hotel as the couple, the swank George V, just off the Champs Élysées. Although Millstein kept him busy working most of the time, Calvin was able to steal a few spare moments to investigate Paris. The Parisians fascinated Calvin. Even the lowliest *vendeuse* in the smallest boutique on the Faubourg St. Honoré was more stylish than the average American society woman. Calvin haunted the clothing stores looking for new ideas, and although he was not much of a gourmand, every bite of food in the restaurants where the Millsteins took him was sheer heaven.

However, Millstein didn't bring Calvin to Paris as an act of generosity. The manufacturer wanted to take advantage of Calvin's unique talent for copying. At the time, it was common practice for American manufacturers to plagiarize Parisian fashions. "They did what was called 'line-for-line' copies in those days," said Calvin, and the great Paris fashion houses, aware of this wholesale theft, demanded that in order for an American manufacturer to attend the showing of a collection, a fee, or "caution," of several thousand dollars had to be paid along with a guarantee to buy at least two articles of clothing. The garments Millstein bought were usually given to his fashionable wife, but not before they were temporarily dismembered in his New York offices so that exact copies could be manufactured. However, the many garments Millstein did not buy had to be copied from memory, and this was where Calvin came in. Millstein would bring Calvin with him to view the collections at Nina Ricci or Saint Laurent, and when a model came down the runway wearing an outfit that Millstein liked, he would nudge Calvin in the ribs. Calvin would methodically commit to memory every detail, and when the show was over, he would race back to his hotel room and deftly sketch what he had seen. "Copying was a *big* business in those days," said Calvin, "and if you were an important

American designer, you got a front-row seat at Dior or Balenciaga or Givenchy, and there was a lot of prestige attached to that." However, Calvin was less impressed by where he was sitting than by what he was looking at. "I really couldn't understand the clothes for young, modern Americans. My head was in a completely different place, and Millstein didn't really understand what I was talking about. I wasn't impressed by the fact that I got a front-row seat—I didn't even want to be there. I didn't see the significance of it. I found it was more fun to run around Europe and look at how everyone was dressing and be inspired by what was happening on the streets."

As time went by, it became clear to him that Dan Millstein was a man who was next to impossible to please—and he was not alone in this assessment. Ethel Mirkin, who worked in promotion for Millstein for twenty years, remembered Millstein as a "tyrant"—the appellation most frequently given to him by his staff. Millstein's nephew Alan, who toiled at his company for ten years, said, "I don't think that most people 'worked' for him. I think most people were so afraid of him that even if they wanted to quit they didn't have the courage to tell him."

"He was an impossible man with a colossal temper," Calvin remembered.

One of Calvin's petty responsibilities that he loathed the most was keeping track of the suits and coats that Millstein loaned to the TV quiz show. One day, after Calvin misplaced the list, Millstein fired him on the spot, screaming, "Get out! Get the fuck out!" Calvin raced from Millstein's office, his face burning, and enlisted the aid of one of the firm's patternmakers, a Polish refugee named Abe Morenstein. Morenstein helped Calvin search for the list for over an hour; it finally materialized from under a pile of sketches. Calvin sheepishly took it to Millstein's office, who glanced at the list and snarled, *"You just fucking saved your skin!"* Calvin was so relieved to have his job back that he threw himself into Abe Morenstein's arms and broke down in tears. On another occasion, Calvin claimed that Millstein almost killed one of his employees: "Right in front of me I watched Dan literally give one of his patternmakers a heart attack! It was one of the most frightening things I've ever seen. Everyone else who worked for Dan was deathly afraid of him. One day, he started screaming at one of the patternmakers—a sweet man named Jack. Dan was violently abusive, and Jack's face started to turn red, and he suddenly fell to the floor and started gasping for breath." On another occasion, Calvin claimed that Millstein actually lunged at him. "He actually raised his fist," said Calvin, who stared Millstein down. "You're an old man," Calvin told him. "I can't believe you're crazy enough to get into a fight."

"That was the caliber of most of the Seventh Avenue people," said Calvin. "The fashion world can be a jungle filled with manufacturers who come up from the bottom and are so tough, insecure, and greedy that there is a kind of animal killer instinct in them. It's a fiercely competitive business, and Millstein was the epitome of that world."

Still, it disturbed Calvin that a man who was so successful had to be so vile and combative, and one day, in an airplane coming back from a business trip, buoyed by a drink, he summoned up his courage and ventured to ask Millstein, "Why do you talk to people that way?"

Millstein glared at him and said, "I like to make people shit in their pants."

Calvin never bothered to try to fathom Millstein again after that. Instead, he became determined to get away.

2

There was another, more trenchant reason other than Millstein's abuse that made Calvin so unhappy working for him: homophobia. While the public's impression of the fashion industry was that it was unusually hospitable to homosexual men, in practice this was simply not true. Only the most famous haute couturiers could afford to be open about their sexual proclivities. For a junior employee in the New York garment center in the sixties to be known as gay was a kiss of death. This was an industry where it was a mark of honor to be a ladies' man; you were not only expected to be married, but it was winked upon to cheat on your wife. Moreover, Calvin was beginning to get tired of the nagging chant around the office—as well as at home: "When are you going to get married?," or, "Why aren't you married?" Jayne, too, was asking the same questions. With one eye on the clock Jayne was showing no little anxiety over whether they would ever get hitched and start a family. Calvin dutifully paraded her around the Millstein offices as a display of his heterosexuality, but he was still living at home with his mama, and it was unusual for an attractive young man like him to be single.

Back in the Bronx there was constant pressure from Flo. She had given up hope of Calvin's older brother, Barry, ever getting married; Alexis, as it would turn out, never would marry. Flo's dreams of producing a new generation of little Kleins lay with Calvin. "When are you going to get married?" was a topic he dreaded, and yet she brought it up every other day. Perhaps another, even more compelling reason to be married at the time was the draft for the Vietnam War. The draft was in full swing by the mid-sixties, and there were precious few ways for Calvin to get a deferment. The most realistic possibility was to get married. Thus, as the pressure from all sides intensified, Calvin finally decided that taking a wife was more valuable to him than the freedom he so treasured, and in 1964, he broke down and proposed to Jayne. She was thrilled, but no more than Flo Klein, who spread the word through their Mosholu Parkway neighborhood like wildfire: Calvin and Jayne had set the date. The only naysayers were Jayne's parents, who were concerned about whether Calvin would be able to give her the kind of comfortable home they had provided for her.

Indeed, there was still the very real problem of how the young couple were going to survive. The prospect of paying the rent on their own apartment, let alone furnishing it, was daunting. Although as soon as Jayne graduated from FIT she began working as a free-lance textile designer and would be able in some small way help supplement Calvin's paltry salary at Millstein's, it would be next to impossible to make ends meet. "He was a very poor boy," Ethel Mirkin said, "and he didn't have any money. He didn't have any bank account, and he lived from hand to mouth." The only alternative Calvin had was to look for a better-paying job. On the sly, he went to the offices of Walter Teitelbaum, who ran a service that supplied sketches for suits and coats to various manufacturers, including Millstein. Although Teitelbaum's firm was not an employment agency, in hopes that Calvin would become a client and buy his sketches at a new job, Teitelbaum agreed to get him an interview with a manufacturer even more famous than Millstein, Seymour Fox. Fox was in a league of his own in the fashion business, a mogul even wealthier than Millstein. Fox was known not only for his exquisite, high-priced fashions but for his grand lifestyle, replete with stretch limousines and a beautiful mistress, the *Women's Wear Daily* columnist Carol Bjorkman. One day during a lunch break from Millstein's, Calvin was granted an audience with Fox. Calvin tried his best to impress the manufacturer, but after the interview, Fox called up Teitelbaum and handed down his verdict, which devastated Calvin when he heard it: "Charming but not talented."

Calvin hinted to Millstein several times that he would like a raise but was given only icy stares in reply. Now that a wedding date had actually been set, Calvin was not sure what he was going to do. One day at the company offices there was a small birthday party for Dan Millstein, who seemed to be in an unusually expansive mood. Calvin's friend, the patternmaker Abe Morenstein, took pity on him and decided to intervene. Morenstein went up to Millstein and entreated, "Mr. Millstein, Cal is getting married soon, and he doesn't know how he's going to make a living."

Millstein turned beet red and began to harangue Morenstein in a roar that could be heard all over the showroom, "Well? What is it your fucking business?" he barked. "What's it to you?"

Millstein's wife, Rose, heard the commotion and went over to Morenstein and asked him what was wrong. Morenstein responded that Calvin was too poor to get married and that her husband had refused to give him a raise. "Oh, that's a shame," said Rose, who marched over to talk to her husband. A few minutes later, Millstein summoned Abe Morenstein over and said, "Abe, call that fellow, what's his name?"

"What's his name" Klein slunk over to Millstein, who begrudgingly snapped, "Twenty-five dollars more and that's it. If you don't like it, you can take a fucking hike." Calvin left the office that day grinning from ear to ear over his new $100-a-week salary.

In spring of 1964, Calvin and Jayne were married in a civil ceremony at city hall by a justice of the peace. The glowing young cou-

ple returned to the Millstein offices, where a party was thrown for
them in a back room featuring a spread of cold cuts from the
nearby Dubrow's cafeteria. A few weeks later there was a formal,
catered wedding for family and friends at the Hampshire House
Hotel. The Hampshire House was considered an impressive venue
for a wedding for two kids from the Bronx. "It was a very different
wedding than I had ever been to," their friend Jane Sternberg remarked. "It was a different class for the average Bronx person. It
was sort of aristocratic." High-class or not, all the Jewish traditions
were followed. The couple were married by a rabbi under a *chuppa*
in a splendidly ornate room overlooking Central Park. Flo, in a
black sheath dress, wept sentimental tears of relief during the ceremony, and Alexis served as the maid of honor. Calvin and Jayne
made a strikingly handsome young couple standing under the traditional arbor of flowers. Calvin wore a tuxedo; Jayne, a white, short-
sleeved, ankle-length gown trimmed with hand-sewn lace that
flared out from her bodice and a pillbox hat with matching lace-
trimmed veil. Later, after a roasted chicken dinner, there was an
orchestra and dancing, which included the hora and the bunny
hop.

Egged on by Rose, Dan Millstein also helped arrange the honeymoon, for which he loaned Calvin an eye-popping five hundred
dollars. Ethel Mirkin remembered that Millstein arranged a room
for the newlyweds at the Nevele Country Club, a popular honeymoon destination in the Catskill Mountains. Millstein called the
hotel and told them that Calvin was one of his name designers.
"They gave him a free week," said Mirkin. "Maybe they thought
we'd pay for it, but we never did."

The week they returned from their honeymoon, Calvin and Jayne
moved to their first apartment together, a one-bedroom, $110-a-
month rent-controlled flat at 68-38 Yellowstone Boulevard, Forest
Hills, Queens, in a building named the Benjamin Franklin. This
large, white-brick doorman building, with white pillars to imitate
an antebellum mansion, was filled mostly with young couples just
starting out. Calvin and Jayne's apartment was on the first floor,
with windows facing the courtyard, where burbling concrete fountains were flanked by planters stocked with artificial flowers that
the building management changed to mimic the real blooms of

each season. Jayne was fiercely proud of their first home, and she delighted in choosing the decor. She bought the apple-green and hot-pink tweed living-room carpet from the previous tenant, and Calvin bit his tongue as Jayne's choice of furnishings were delivered. The apartment's foyer was turned into a dining room, where an Italian Provincial–style table was covered in a floral-print cloth and surrounded by tall wicker-backed chairs. On the walls were some Picasso lithographs, purchased when "we went to an auction and Calvin lifted his hand up," said Jayne. The sunken living room, two steps down, separated from the foyer by a wrought-iron railing, was furnished with chairs of rose-colored silk, a tuxedo sofa in olive green, some green-painted chests from Jayne's mother, and large KLH stereo speakers, a status symbol of the time. Also prominent in the room was Jayne's baby grand, which she rarely played anymore. Although Calvin privately worried that the apartment looked middle class, their neighbors and acquaintances considered the newlyweds' home terribly chic and cosmopolitan, as they did Calvin and Jayne themselves, right down to the frozen canapés Jayne served or the cocktail Calvin drank before dinner. They even scraped together the money for a weekly cleaning girl. To their friends the young pair exuded an air of sophistication and worldliness. Calvin seemed to know all the trendy movies to see and all the new "in" spots in Manhattan at which to eat. "Calvin was *fun*," said Jane Cohen, "Oh, yes, the two of them together, interesting and fun, and Calvin just loved to laugh."

Yet at home life was not so amusing. Jayne discovered that Calvin was so engrossed in his work that she saw even less of him now that they were married than when they were dating and he had put aside time for her. Soon after the marriage she noticed he seemed distracted and absentminded; he frequently forgot appointments with her and all but ignored special occasions like birthdays. "He kept losing his wallet, and Jayne kept having to cancel all the credit cards," a neighbor recalled. "She was so annoyed at him." Yet Jayne was so much in love with him that she wanted to know where he was every minute and phoned him frequently at the office. Before long, Calvin began to feel overwhelmed and haunted by his young wife. He worked late almost every day, coming home tired and cranky. Even on the weekends he labored for hours on his sketches. A few months after they were married, their old friend from the Bronx, Molly Ann Acker, came to visit them. Jayne seemed tense and unhappy to her. "Jayne said it was really tough," said Acker. "Calvin was busy a lot, and she felt kind of abandoned." Etta Sherman, a neighbor in Forest Hills, remembered Jayne telling her that when she walked down the street, young men turned to look at her. "At least *somebody* is paying attention to me," Jayne quipped.

"Jayne was very supportive of Calvin," said Jane Sternberg, "but it was just a very difficult marriage. I remember Jayne complaining that in the early years Calvin was so involved in his career, it was hard on her. She didn't have the closeness with him that she would have liked. I don't think that Jayne felt loved during her marriage in the way that Jayne needed to feel loved. . . ."

Not long after, Calvin's former High School of Industrial Arts teacher Nedda Arnova gave an exhibition of her artwork at a gallery on Fifty-seventh Street, and she made sure that Calvin and Jayne were invited to the opening. Calvin was thrilled to see Arnova again, and he and Jayne chatted with her for a while before strolling around the gallery to look at her work. The wise old teacher sensed something odd between the couple, and as they got out of earshot, she turned to Judy Guerra, who was standing nearby, and whispered, "Somehow I don't think this is going to be forever."

3

Barry Schwartz's dreams were just as stalled.

His life, if anything, had turned into even more of a bleak trap than Calvin's. "When I was sixteen," Barry said, "and I graduated from high school . . . so I hung around the Parkway and I went to the track everyday. I hustled and played crap and shot pool." Finally, Harry Schwartz laid down the law, and Barry went to work for him at the Sundial Supermarket. It was a brief time of reconciliation between Barry and his father. "I spent six days a week, morning till night, working at the Sundial," Barry said, "and everything I learned, every bit of practical knowledge that I got, I got from my father. He gave me the greatest gift that any father could give any son. He taught me how to run a business and really how to be successful."

But neither Barry nor his father wanted him to be stuck in a Harlem grocery store for the rest of his life. Harry always wanted his son to be an accountant, and Barry enrolled at the New York University School of Business in Washington Square. However, "After three months at NYU," Barry said, "I found myself one hundred hours behind in my accounting homework. I got 'no credit' in every subject. That's when I gave up . . . I went back to work for my father, stacking groceries, ringing a cash register. In the winter I froze my ass off because there was no heat in the store. I used to walk into the store in the morning, and it was so cold that the bottles of cooking oil had cracked—that's how bad it was." As the years passed, Barry began to hate the Sundial. Eventually even the army seemed like a better alternative, and he enlisted in the early summer of 1964. That August he was sent to Fort Dix, New Jersey, for basic training.

In the interim, there was now another, full-time family employee at the store—Kayla Schwartz's new husband, Harvey Spielberg, a slovenly, shifty sort of fellow. Although the Schwartzes couldn't stand the sight of Spielberg, big-hearted Harry Schwartz graciously paid for an expensive wedding and helped find the newlyweds an apartment on the fourth floor of his own building, but it wasn't long before Harvey was in hock to his neck with gambling debts. Shortly, Harry Schwartz was paying his daughter's rent and doling out cash to Spielberg. It was no big surprise either when Harvey was arrested and fined $25 for bookmaking, and then five months later again arrested for grand larceny for diverting funds from a cleaning store where he used to work. He was found guilty of grand larceny and sentenced to a year in New York City's Rikers Island prison. When Spielberg was paroled from jail, Harry Schwartz, out of love for his darling Kayla, gave his son-in-law a job at the Sundial Supermarket.

It wasn't long before that, too, turned into trouble. Spielberg and a twenty-six-year-old grocery packer at the Sundial got the brainstorm that they would take a $5,000 bank loan and use the money to start a numbers racket, but Spielberg wound up squandering most of the money. "After that," Spielberg would later tell police, "we thought we would work on junk [narcotics], but it didn't materialize." Not only didn't it materialize, but one of the first buyers with whom Spielberg tried to consummate a deal turned out to be an undercover agent from the Federal Bureau of Narcotics. One day, a team of federal agents descended on the Sundial and hauled Spielberg off. He was threatened with a long jail sentence—unless he cooperated with the authorities and turned informant. It wasn't much of a choice, and Spielberg remorselessly turned stoolie for the feds, snitching on drug dealers. A stormcloud was gathering over the Sundial.

It was Harvey Spielberg who was supposed to open the store on the morning of October 13, 1964, but Spielberg claimed he had a flat tire that morning. Instead, he phoned his father-in-law and asked him to open. Harry Schwartz dragged himself out of bed, stopped at a local luncheonette for breakfast, and made his way up to Harlem by subway. When he arrived at the Sundial at about 7:45 A.M. he unlocked the door and gates, and disappeared inside. Not more than a few minutes went by before one of Harry's long-time employees, William Miles, arrived at work. Miles was just about to enter the store when the door burst open and a black man ran out clutching a coat under his arm, as if he were trying to hide something. Miles was too shocked to say anything to the man, and hurried into the store to see what was wrong.

The first thing Miles saw was blood—blood everywhere—on the counter, on the shelves of food, in pools on the floor. Then he saw Harry's coat and hat strewn on the floor and the cigar box, in which he kept some of his bookmaking cash, lying empty next to them. There was no sign of Harry. "Harry! Harry!" Miles called out. Only silence.

In a panic, Miles raced out the door into the street and sprinted down the block to a police phone box. "There's blood all over the place!" he shouted into the phone. "My boss is missing, and there's blood everywhere!"

Ten minutes later, the police found Harry Schwartz. He was dressed in his white grocer's jacket, kneeling on the sawdust-covered floor of the walk-in freezer next to a stack of fresh-packed young poultry. His wispy gray hair hung over his forehead forlornly, his cheeks were pale and flaccid. Puddles of blood had soaked into the sawdust on the floor from a wound under his left arm. During a struggle with his assailant he had been stabbed under his left bicep, slitting the cephalic vein and brachial artery. Then, fighting all the way, he had been dragged down the aisle, knocking over cans of groceries as he went, and shoved into the big walk-in freezer. The heavy wooden door had been secured with a knife sharpener, trapping him inside. Harry tried to tie a makeshift tourniquet around his arm to cut off the flow of gushing blood, but had passed out and bled to death while pawing at the door for help.

Barry had only been in the service two months when he was summoned to the sergeant's office at Fort Dix and told that his father had been in a serious accident and he was needed at home. He had no idea just how bad an "accident" his father had been in until he was speeding up the New Jersey Turnpike, listening to the news on the car radio, when it was announced that a Bronx grocery store owner named Harry Schwartz had been murdered. Barry drove directly to the Sundial, where he seemed in a trance as he spent hours with the police trying to figure out what had happened. The next day the *New York Post* ran the headline "Stabbed Harlem Shopkeeper Dies Locked in Refrigerator," and the entire neighborhood turned out in force for the funeral at the Riverside Chapel, including many Harlem residents and customers from the store. As Harry's casket was carried out to the hearse, somebody in the crowd was heard to say, "There goes the last white bookie in Harlem."

The Chain Store Food Employees Association, the Negro Labor Committee, and the Associated Grocers of Harlem pooled a $2,500 reward for the arrest and conviction of Harry Schwartz's murderer, but nobody who knew Harry thought they had to search very far to find the man responsible. In the minds of his family and friends, it was Harvey Spielberg who had caused his death. Police surmised that the robbery was an inside job planned by Spielberg, who arranged for an accomplice to hide in the store overnight and lie in wait for Harry Schwartz. The police eventually found the alleged accomplice, a neighborhood junkie, but there wasn't enough concrete evidence to bring charges against him or Harvey Spielberg, and the file on the murder of Harry Schwartz remains open to this day.

Soon after Harry's death there was an apocalyptic confrontation between Barry Schwartz and Spielberg, and Barry fired him. Kayla left with Spielberg for a new start in New Orleans, Louisiana. The next that was heard of them was that Harvey Speilberg was peddling cemetery plots to poor blacks. Unfortunately for the deceased, the plots were below sea level, and all the corpses eventually washed out into the Gulf of Mexico. Kayla Spielberg died a few years later of complications from a chronic stomach ailment, and Harvey followed her to the grave as a result of a heart attack in 1988.

Barry's worst fears had now been realized. Pleading that he was the sole support of his mother and would have to take over the family business, he was given a hardship discharge from the service—out of the frying pan into the fire. Now, more than ever, he loathed the grocery store with a bitter, abiding hate. Still, Barry decided to make the best of the Sundial and became determined to turn it into a legitimate money-maker. He worked hard—a minimum of 75 hours a week—turning the Sundial around. "Barry was a very shrewd businessman," remembered his pal Mike Sigmund. In fact, under Barry's stewardship, grosses at the Sundial quadrupled. This success renewed Barry's childhood dream of opening a chain of supermarkets, and in an ironic turn, it put Barry in a position to help his old friend; he gave Calvin a job working at the Sundial on Saturdays. The pay: twenty-five dollars a day, plus all the groceries he could eat.

CHAPTER FIVE

If you ever see Calvin Klein, tell him he broke my
husband's heart.

—Edith Morenstein

It was no small humiliation to Calvin that he had to work Saturdays at the Sundial to make ends meet, and after nearly two years
of drudgery at Millstein's, Calvin's unhappiness became palpable.
Being stuck in an airless cubicle, a nameless drone, was like a jail
sentence to him. The tension between Calvin and Maria Prinzi was
now the talk of the office. "Jealousy" was Faye Wagner's opinion.
"The boy was brilliant, and his work was beautiful, but you know
. . . women . . . can cause a lot of havoc, and she did. He wanted to
quit so many times." Perhaps if Millstein had given Calvin a raise
or a promotion, it would have eased his burden, but the manufacturer wouldn't hear of it. "The tyrant wouldn't give him more
money," said Ethel Mirkin.

To intensify his discontent, Calvin grew to loathe the gaudy
clothes he was forced to sketch for Millstein. "Bright yellow, orange, and lilac suits with long-haired fox collars and cuffs that
sometimes ran down the front of the three-quarter-length jacket
and around the entire border of the suit. Real hooker clothes!" Calvin described them. "I needed the job and had to design those suits,
but fortunately, I never saw anyone wear one of them."

Then one day, he did. Calvin was walking down a Manhattan
street when he saw a woman coming in the opposite direction
dressed in a Millstein outfit he had helped design. "She was wearing a yellow suit," Calvin remembered, "with the yellow fox collar

and cuffs, a yellow hat, a yellow handbag, and yellow shoes. . . . I was sick to think that I had been part of making that outfit possible." Calvin decided at that very moment that he had to renew his quest for another job.

Through business contacts, he was recommended for a position at Halldon Ltd., a large coat manufacturer owned by an old-time European refugee named Louis Shlansky, who had started the firm in 1917. Halldon was best known for its fake-fur coats, which were sold in "moderate-priced departments." An interview was arranged for Calvin with Shlansky's son, Milton, who ran the company. Calmer and more gentlemanly than Millstein, Milton Shlansky had several reasons to want Calvin on board. First, for a low-profile company like Halldon, stealing one of Millstein's sketchers would be something of a coup. Second, Calvin would help lend a more youthful image to the aging firm. "It was to our advantage to hire a young man like Calvin," explained Milton Shlansky, who promised Calvin a bright future with the company, pledging to allow him more freedom with his creations than he had known at Millstein's. His starting salary was a whopping $20,000 a year, and his four-year contract provided for further salary increments and paid vacations. Calvin was thrilled with the offer, and that very afternoon he triumphantly marched into Dan Millstein's office and quit. Millstein didn't bother to say goodbye. It wasn't for many years that Calvin Klein would ever cross his mind again.

Life at Halldon was considerably different for Calvin from the shoulder-to-the-grindstone, daily soap-opera drama at Millstein's. From the start he was treated like a promising designer on the way up, an investment the Shlanskys expected to pay off. "He was probably the most intelligent young man I ever had work for me," said Milton Shlansky. "He was the only employee that I had who never counted or begrudged me how much money I was making." Shlansky was also sympathetic with the fact that the kind of coats Calvin was being asked to design for the company were not his forte. "He hated fake furs," said Shlansky, "but we were interested in making money, not so much in style and fashion." Calvin understood making money, but he believed that mixing good style with workmanship would result in good profits.

In fact, Calvin's early work at Halldon was inventive and sleek, considering the parameters of price and style within which he was marooned. He did several lines of coats in tweeds, gabardine, and wool twills, some with tab fronts and high collars or flap pockets with accent buttons, priced at $35.75–$45.75 wholesale, which budget department stores snatched up. "I think Calvin's main talent," said Milton Shlansky, "was his selection of what the woman wants, that excellent feel of timing of the country and what will be accepted. He didn't have to initiate the styles. He's able to select the best and change and modify, to take a collar from one coat and a sleeve from another or a yoke from one and a back from another . . . his coats did exceptionally well."

Shlansky deliberately was setting Calvin up as an upcoming star. "I put his design room right off the showroom," said Shlansky. "Then, as the big buyers came in, I would bring Cal out and introduce him to the merchandise people." Meeting these key industry middlemen was perhaps the greatest bonus at Halldon for Calvin. He began to develop a personal charisma, a mixture of shyness and confidence, unique and powerful for someone so young. Many of the buyers and writers he met were older women with a soft spot for a kid so cute, and Calvin took advantage of every provocative smile and wink. "He knew communication," said Shlansky. "He knew how to handle people, and he could read people. He was brilliant in that department, no question about it."

It wasn't long before Calvin's name began to appear in industry publications, including the influential *Tobe Report,* an industry newsletter subscribed to by stores and manufacturers that depended heavily on it for sources and trends. Calvin's first mention in the *Tobe Report* was in late April of 1967, when the newsletter reported that "Cal" Klein had designed "diagonally cut chinchilla and puffy ottoman" fake-fur coats that were "both shapely and . . . pretty." In August his name again appeared in the *Tobe Report,* this time with the unusual notation that Calvin was "one of the more aggressive and imaginative young coat and suit designers." Marjorie Dean, who wrote reviews for the newsletter and saw much of Calvin's early work, said "He had a lot of moxie."

On his first Christmas at Halldon, Calvin insisted that the Shlanskys buy expensive pieces of luggage as promotional gifts for a long list of industry buyers and writers and editors. Gifts for that many people came to a phenomenal amount of money, and Louis Shlansky, who saw this as little short of payola, was shocked. "You're kidding," he said. "They're never going to take it."

Calvin urged him, "Just listen to me."

Shlansky shrugged and said, "Okay, Cal. But how are we going to get the luggage to everyone?"

That was no problem, said Calvin. He would personally hand-deliver the gifts; that way the buyers and press would know exactly from whom they were coming.

2

In Calvin's deepest core, no matter how much the twenty-five-year-old resented his marriage to Jayne, he wanted to make it work. The convention of joining with one person for eternity had been ingrained in him since childhood. What's more, he loved Jayne in his way. But at the same time, he found her affection smothering, and the sheer effort of being married drained his creative spirit. Then, in January 1966, something happened that momentarily gave him respite: Jayne became pregnant. He had always wanted to be a father—it was one of the reasons he had talked himself into the marriage in the first place—and perhaps a baby would be the magic elixir that would sweeten their life together.

For a while it seemed to do just that. Jayne's pregnancy was a romantic time for them, a period so loving and caring that one of their neighbors in Forest Hills said she herself became pregnant because she so envied their happiness. Calvin remembered Jayne's pregnancy as "the happiest time of our lives." They took a romantic trip together to Europe, and Calvin behaved like the consummate tour guide. In the face of the additional expenses having a baby would incur, they overspent wildly, dining in the best restaurants and treating themselves to wardrobes of new clothes. Neighbors remembered that Jayne came home with the chicest maternity wear ever seen in Forest Hills.

On October 21, 1966, a fat, adorable little girl they named Marcia Robin Klein arrived, and Calvin went mad over her. He felt weightless whenever he looked at her. She was the most perfect, beautiful baby in the world, and best of all, everybody said she looked just like him. Hardly anyone was more excited than Flo Klein, who was so proud to learn she was a grandmother that when she heard the news on the phone she came rushing out of her Rochambeau Avenue building shrieking to all the neighbors, "It's a girl! It's a girl!" That same day, Calvin raced through the offices at Halldon, telling anyone who would listen that he was a new father.

Then, in a few brief months, all the joy was gone. The baby slept in their bedroom, she cried when she needed to be fed, and Calvin couldn't get any sleep at night, leaving him tired and irritable all day at work. When the euphoria of fatherhood dissipated, he was faced with the reality of diapers and pediatricians and bills, bills, bills. Although he could hardly afford the rent, they moved to a larger apartment, where Marci slept in an alcove off the kitchen. As time went by, Calvin went back to burying himself in his work. "He was in his own world," said Etta Sherman, "his own, artistic little world. Jayne was really unhappy being alone and lonely."

The harder Calvin worked, the more Jayne's feelings of estrangement grew. She had given up her job and now felt increasingly isolated. "In the evenings," Etta Sherman remembered, "Calvin would get home really late, so Jayne would usually come upstairs to our apartment. We didn't have intercoms, so we'd leave the phones off the hook so she could hear if the baby was crying." Around eleven P.M. Calvin would arrive at the Shermans' apartment to collect Jayne. "Hello," he would greet her. "Where's the coffee?" The Shermans noted that the couple never seemed to kiss. On weekends, Jayne had to wheel Marci out of the apartment in her carriage so that her crying would not disturb Calvin as he hunched over his sketches at the dining-room table. When the other young mothers would ask her where Calvin was, Jayne would sigh, "Oh, he's sitting at the table with his drawings." Etta Sherman recalled that the couple had frequent arguments and that afterward Calvin would feel contrite and guilty. "He'd send her flowers, or candy or wine," said Sherman, "or call her and say, 'Let's get a baby-sitter and go out to a fancy restaurant.' You know—money was going to take care of it all. And then he'd just go back to his designing, and then the same thing would happen again. I think she kept hoping it would be okay for all their sakes, but it just wasn't working."

Neither was Calvin's job at Halldon, which was slowly turning into another cul de sac for him. He tired of making fake-fur coats season after season, and no matter how much he was appreciated or how many perks they gave him, like frequent buying trips to Europe, he couldn't bear to stay on much longer. "One year we came back from Paris," said Louis Shlansky, "and Cal came to me and said he wanted me to back him in his own business." Shlansky discussed it with his partners, who were against the gamble, and Calvin was turned down. It was also gently pointed out to him that he had two years left on his four-year contract with Shlansky. In fact, Calvin's contract explicitly forbade him from free-lance designing for himself as well as for any other manufacturer: All designs that came from his sketch pad technically belonged to the Shlansky company.

As fate would have it, Calvin's old friend from Dan Millstein's firm, the patternmaker Abe Morenstein, had come to work at Halldon as well. Morenstein was a talented man with sparkling blue eyes and fiery red hair who was also burning with ambition. Although he was exceptionally well paid at his job, Morenstein always longed to go into business on his own, but he felt that his thick Polish-Jewish accent and lack of a cosmopolitan air would defeat him in the image-conscious marketplace. Over time he had become convinced that Calvin was the perfect front man for him, with Morenstein handling the technical end. Although Morenstein wasn't terribly impressed with Calvin's fashion ideas, they were youthful and good enough for a start, and months passed as they toyed with the possibility of going into business together. Since they were both employed by Halldon and would have been fired if anyone discovered their plans, they vowed to keep their pending partnership a secret.

To complicate the situation further, in the winter of 1967, Calvin unexpectedly received an offer for a new job that seemed perfect for him. A publicly traded sportswear company called Bobbie Brooks was launching its own outerwear division. The Bobbie Brooks executives heard all about Calvin and offered him a job as director of the new design department. The offer was tempting, but it still meant being an employee and designing the kind of clothes his bosses wanted. Calvin was considering the job when he told

Barry about it. "Don't do it," Barry said. "Open your own business. It's what you've always wanted. If you take this job, you'll just feel trapped again." Calvin turned down the job offer—much to the disappointment of the people at Bobbie Brooks—and went ahead with his plans to go into business with Abe Morenstein.

As time passed, Morenstein and his wife, Edith, a World War II concentration camp survivor, became close to Calvin and Jayne and began to feel like surrogate parents to them. Calvin became a regular visitor to the Morensteins' modest split-level house in Valley Stream, Long Island, only a ten-minute ride from his own apartment in Forest Hills. The two men set up shop in Morenstein's basement and began pricing fabrics and looking for a sample tailor. Frequently, on Sunday nights, Calvin and Jayne would bring Marci with them, and the little girl would play on the carpeted floor of the Morensteins' living room while Jayne and Edith made dinner in the kitchen and Abe and Calvin worked in the basement on samples for their new business.

Morenstein estimated that it would take at least $25,000 in cash to start up, including fabric and samples and several months' rent on a small showroom in the garment center. Since neither Morenstein nor Calvin had that kind of money, they decided to try to raise the capital on Seventh Avenue, a fruitless pursuit tried by hundreds every year. Among others, Morenstein took Calvin to a friend of his who manufactured buttons, Seymour Kerzer. After meeting Calvin, Kerzer took Morenstein aside and said, "Hey, what do you think? A little schnook like this, I'm going to put in money?" One by one, as more and more Seventh Avenue contacts began to refuse them backing, Calvin grew despondent. "You and I," he once told Morenstein, "are dead people." Morenstein told him to stop talking nonsense and keep his courage up. There was a touch of desperation in Calvin's voice as he began to approach his old friends from Mosholu Parkway to back him, but there were no interested investors anywhere. One day, after yet another refusal from a contact in the fashion business, a dejected Calvin was walking down the bustling streets of the garment center with Morenstein, dodging traffic and pedestrians, and he started to wax philosophic about how easily great dreams were dashed. He spoke to Morenstein tenderly about his father, Leo, and about how fate had relegated him to a job working in a grocery store for his wealthier brother. "How cruel life can be," Calvin said sighing.

Morenstein was thoughtful for a second and then surprised himself by saying, "One day you'll be cruel to me."

Calvin was shocked. "I'll never be cruel to you, Abe. Never. What a thing to say."

Eventually, Calvin grew so discouraged in his quest for backing that he considered giving up his career in fashion altogether. One weekend he went up to the Sundial Supermarket to have a heart-to-heart talk with Barry Schwartz about it. He spilled his guts out: He was only an employee; he had bosses who were making $10,000 a week off of Calvin's back, yet he couldn't break out of the mold, couldn't connect with the cash to start his own business.

His boyhood buddy listened to Calvin's lament and then shocked him with an offer. If Calvin was serious about quitting the rag trade, he could have one-half of the Sundial Supermarket if he wanted. Working as a team, Barry predicted, they would own a chain of supermarkets before long. Eventually, they would be bigger than the A & P.

Calvin was sorely tempted by the offer and said he would seriously consider it. When he left the Sundial Supermarket, he drove over to his parents' Rochambeau Avenue apartment to tell them about what Barry had suggested. "I didn't know what to do," Calvin said of that Sunday visit. "It was so *frustrating* on my job. . . . I was just miserable. It was one of the few times in my life that I went to my parents for advice. I was certain my mother would say, 'Stick to fashion'—she never wanted me to have anything to do with the supermarket business. And I was sure my father would say, 'Take Barry's offer, because who offers you half of something for nothing? And a partnership with your closest friend, what could be better?' *Instead,* my father said, 'I don't know anything about fashion or what you've been studying all these years, but whatever it is, I have a feeling that you haven't given it enough of a chance. An opportunity like Barry's may never come along again, but I think you'll be miserable for the rest of your life if you don't stick it out.'

"I was shocked. My father's a smart man. You know, I always thought I was so independent, that I never needed anyone's advice—but you *do* need advice. This was a serious time in my life, a really big decision, and coming from my father—I don't know, it just meant an awful lot to me. I was surprised and very moved. He convinced me and was responsible for my making one of the most important decisions in my life—making the commitment to stick with fashion."

Calvin called Barry and apologetically turned him down. After a moment's silence Barry said he respected Calvin's decision but that he would still help him out. He believed in Calvin's instincts so much that he would help bankroll Calvin's own business. "No problem," Barry said. "I'll finance it. I'll give you the money." There was a certain amount of cash from the Sundial, and he would let Calvin have it. It wouldn't be the full $25,000—Barry could only afford $2,000 at the moment—but it would be enough to buy the fabric to start making samples with Morenstein. When Calvin showed up at Morenstein's house with the money, the pattern-maker was amazed. Morenstein claims Calvin was evasive about where the funds were from and that he decided not to push him about it, but as the weeks went by and the money ran out, Calvin kept turning up with more. "I would run up to Barry's store in Harlem," Calvin would explain later, "and say I needed money for this sample or that fabric, and he'd take five hundred dollars out of the cash register so I could pay the sample tailor in Coney Island who had his sewing machine in his daughter's bedroom."

Over the course of several months, Calvin and Morenstein were able to put together a line in the basement of Morenstein's house in Valley Stream. As the line progressed, Morenstein was surprised to find that although Calvin was a whiz with ideas, he knew little about the actual construction of a garment and the simple facets of tailoring, so Morenstein spent many hours in the small basement room teaching Calvin a craftsman's tricks of the trade. As they went along, Calvin fixed and refined each garment, giving them more attention than anything he had produced in his career. He took each garment, put it on a stand, pinned it, pulled the collar away from the neck, and steam-ironed it, giving each piece a living look. Upstairs in the split-level Jayne whiled away the hours pouring her heart out to Edith Morenstein about her increasingly barren home life as the sympathetic housewife cooked them all dinner.

After many months the two men completed close to what

Morenstein remembered as a dozen samples. All in all, each of the garments cost upwards of $800 to make, and they were far beyond the quality of everyday samples, the mating of brilliant style and fine craftsmanship. Those who saw this first "collection" remember it as being superbly beautiful, like highly styled Balenciaga classics and the work of a true genius.

By the end of 1967, Morenstein was growing anxious to have Calvin incorporate a company and draw up partnership papers. Yet for some reason that Morenstein could not understand, Calvin seemed tardy in doing it. According to Morenstein, Calvin had some excuse about having to go down to city hall in Manhattan and wait in line for hours to file certain papers. The official formation of a partnership between Morenstein and Calvin began to drag out over many months. One reason may have been that without Morenstein knowing it, Calvin had already approached a lawyer, Robert Schindler, who was a neighbor in his building in Forest Hills, and paid him $200 to incorporate a company—with Barry Schwartz as a 50 percent partner. There was no mention of Morenstein at all in the incorporation papers. However, it was neither Barry's nor Calvin's intention that the former take an active role in the business. Time and time again Barry told Calvin that he had no interest at all in the garment center, that the grocery business was his trade. "I never expected Barry to be a *working* partner," Calvin said. "But I told him, 'Your money is as important as whatever talent I have. If you're willing to put up the money, then you certainly deserve half the business.'" On December 28, 1967, using the name Calvin Klein Ltd., the company was officially incorporated.

Meanwhile, an unsuspecting Morenstein set up an appointment to show the samples to more potential backers. One Thursday night in early 1968, Calvin and Morenstein were working in Morenstein's basement, and the patternmaker said, "The samples are going to be ready soon. You're supposed to show them next week. Do we have a name for the company?"

Calvin said, "I already have a name."

Morenstein looked at him in surprise. "What name did you give it?" he asked.

Calvin stared down at the floor and muttered, "It might as well be 'Calvin Klein.'"

Morenstein couldn't believe what he was hearing. The disingenuousness of Calvin's statement infuriated him. Morenstein flushed with anger but kept quiet for the moment. The following Sunday, however, after stewing about it for a few days, he summoned Calvin to his house and demanded to know how Calvin could name their company with his own name without first asking Morenstein. It was then that Calvin finally admitted that he had incorporated with Barry Schwartz as a silent partner.

Morenstein shook with rage at the revelation. "How could you do a thing like this?" he demanded.

"Abe, what are you worrying about?" Calvin said. "If this gets off the ground, it's going to happen for all of us. You're going to make money, too."

"But you *lied!*" Morenstein said. "I expected to be in business with you, and you lied to me!"

"Abe, *please*," Calvin implored, "I don't want to lose your friendship."

"My *friendship!*" Morenstein sputtered incredulously, "My *friendship?* Just take everything and get out!" He began shouting. "Take the samples, take everything, and get out!"

Calvin was silent for a moment, staring at the floor with eyes wide with hurt. Then he asked Morenstein quietly, "Will you help me get everything out to the car?"

"Yes," Morenstein said, "I'll help you get out." Stoically, Morenstein helped deposit the samples he had slaved over into the trunk of Calvin's old Plymouth. The patternmaker stood on the street as Calvin wordlessly got into the car, pulled away from the curb, drove down the block, and disappeared.

It would be twenty-four years before the two men ever spoke to each other again.

According to Calvin, the day before he planned to quit his job at Halldon, he was called into the boss's office. "I hear that you've been working on your own," Calvin claimed Shlansky barked. "You have a contract with us, I want the clothes, and I will destroy you for this." Calvin said he burst into tears as Shlansky shouted, "Get the hell out, get right out this minute."

Shlansky remembered a less threatening drama upon their parting. "We weren't surprised," Shlansky said about Calvin's plans to leave. "Not even disappointed. We already heard in the market he was taking one of our patternmakers and going into business. It's a *very* small market." Still, Shlansky was not prepared to give Calvin up so easily. "We have a contract with you," he told Calvin, "that has two more years to run, and we expect you to stick with it."

"I know I have a contract," Calvin said earnestly, "but I also know what kind of people you are, and I know you won't hurt me, that you'll let me out"

Shlansky laughed. "He knew us better than we knew ourselves," he said. "So basically we let him out. Unfortunately, he left us right in the middle of a new season, and I thought, Oh, my God, how am I going to find a replacement that fast? So I personally started to look through all the French magazines that we kept for sketches for something to copy, and lo and behold, I found three designs that Calvin had already [copied.]"

Whichever story is closer to the truth, one thing is certain: At the tender age of twenty-five, Calvin Klein was his own boss.

3

The year 1968 was not the most propitious time to start a career in the fashion business. Although after World War II the American fashion industry was beginning to emerge from under the yoke of Paris designers, for most of the sixties the fashion world was on a financial roller coaster. The public went through mini-, midi-, and maxi-lengths, through transparent plastic raincoats, oriental tunics, and a caftan craze. There was a unisex dressing fad and a season when see-through minidresses, op-art clothing, and neckerchiefs for men were all the vogue. By the end of the decade, an utterly unforgiving style of short shorts for women, called "hot pants," was the rage. Annoyingly, for American designers, a great deal of this instability had been sparked not on Seventh Avenue but by "Swinging London," which had unexpectedly swept to the forefront as the vanguard of creativity in music, photography, and style. All America seemed to offer in fashion trends was the hippie movement, which the garment center reviled because by definition the hippie style was *anti*style and very bad for business, unless you were manufacturing cheap jeans and tie-dyed T-shirts. Indeed, the biggest fashion impact of the decade had been made not by a designer but by the Beatles' haircuts, and even Calvin had grown long "Beatlesesque" locks. Manufacturers of mass-market clothing were reeling. In this turbulent climate, mass taste was so unpredictable that to succeed in the business was scattershot good luck. Small companies went out of business as quickly as styles changed. The life of an apparel firm was on the average only five years, and foreclosures of small garment-center manufacturing companies rose by 30 percent in 1968.

A few days after leaving Shlansky, undaunted by the odds against him, Calvin rented a dingy one-room showroom on the sixth floor of the York Hotel at 488 Seventh Avenue, a run-down building mostly populated by out-of-town manufacturers who needed only temporary space to show their lines. The top two floors were still rented out as rooms, and transients and traveling salesmen crowded the dowdy lobby. Calvin's showroom featured one grime-encrusted window, a table and chairs, and a changing booth created by hanging a cloth curtain. Calvin moved the small line he had prepared with Morenstein into room 613, opposite the elevator, and hung the samples on a pipe rack. Every day he got on the phone and called every buyer and editor he had met over the years, imploring them to come see his wares. People came, some even took out their checkbooks, but nobody placed an order big enough to make a difference. Money was running out fast, and the drafty York Hotel was a dreadful, depressing place to be. In a sweet gesture of support, Jayne brought up an arrangement of artificial flowers to help spruce up the place. Once in a while she would bring along the baby and rock her in her carriage while the family of three sat in the showroom and waited. Slowly, painfully, a few more orders began to trickle in, but hardly enough to pay the rent.

In the meantime, Barry did not seem too worried about the success of the fledgling business. Calvin had lied to Barry and bragged that he had friends who were buyers at Macy's and Bloomingdale's who would buy the clothes. If Barry thought he was embarking on a precarious proposition, he did not show it. At the time, he was still determined to be a silent partner and not interfere in the business. Besides, Barry had juicier things on his mind than selling clothes. He had met an insurance agent's daughter from Rosedale,

Queens, on a blind date at Roosevelt Raceway. She was a warm and attractive young girl, with pouty lips and a nicely proportioned figure that captured Barry's heart at first sight. It disturbed the young woman's parents that Barry had taken her to the racetrack to gamble on their first date; it disturbed them even more when Barry took her to the track on their next three dates. After a brief romance, Barry proposed. It would have helped if his fiancée had liked Jayne, since the two husbands had just gone into business together, but that was never to be. The two women were like oil and water. According to Jayne's friends, she thought Barry's girlfriend was a "phony" and trying to live beyond her Queens background. "The weekend that Calvin opened his business was the middle of March," Barry remembered. "I got married on St. Patrick's Day, and he came to the wedding. I went on my honeymoon, and he went to the York Hotel to open a business the same weekend. Fortunately, some of the people who came to my wedding gave me checks, because I took all of the cash on my honeymoon and lost it shooting craps the third day."

For the next three weeks, Calvin hardly saw Barry as he sweated it out at the York Hotel. Then, on April 4, 1968, Martin Luther King was assassinated in Memphis, Tennessee, and Harlem erupted in riots. Thousands of black residents stormed into the streets, looting and burning blocks of Manhattan stores in what was, at that point, the biggest race riot in U.S. history. The police from the local station near the Sundial Supermarket called up Barry Schwartz in the middle of the night and asked him to come up and secure the premises. "You tell the mayor to go up to Harlem and secure the premises," Barry told them, and went back to sleep. Later, one of the Sundial's black employees called Barry and told him not to come anywhere near Harlem, that it was too dangerous for a white man.

Barry waited two days for things to calm down before he went to see what had happened to the Sundial. His heart sank. A lifetime of his father's work lay in rubble. It was worse than he ever imagined. The windows were gone, most of the food was looted, cans and bags of flour were crushed on the floor—it was as if a tornado had whipped through the store. "It was totally wrecked," Barry said. "They gutted the place."

Barry found a working phone and called his friend Calvin to tell him what had happened. Calvin started asking how much it would cost to repair the damage when Barry cut him off. "I'm quitting," Barry said. "I'm giving up."

"Are you crazy?" Calvin asked him. "What are you going to do then?"

Barry said, "You come up here and look at this mess and then tell me what I should do. You won't believe it."

An hour later, Calvin arrived at the Sundial to see for himself. "It looked as if locusts had run through it," Calvin said. "Everything was thrown off the shelves, bottles smashed, everything destroyed and looted." He and Barry walked through the debris, estimating that it would take at least $40,000 to restore the store to working condition before he could reopen. "Then Barry surprised me," said Calvin.

"Let's run up and down the aisles and knock over whatever's left," Barry said, a wild gleam in his eyes, "and smash everything. I've always wanted to knock over this fucking stuff, anyway. I've hated it for so long!"

Calvin said, "After all those years, we both had the same impulse to finish the place off. What a pleasure." The two ran up and down the aisles like children, clearing shelves with wild sweeps of their arms.

"Let's take some food!" Barry cried. They grabbed four large shopping bags and carried them up and down the aisles, stuffing them with food, mostly cans of sardines, which were Calvin's favorite. When they had packed as much as they could carry, they took the bags outside to their cars. Barry and Calvin stood on the pavement in front of the ruined store and took a good look at the old place.

"Then I took the keys to the store," Barry said, "and I threw them in the rubble."

Barry Schwartz never again returned to the Sundial Supermarket. Instead, on the following Monday, he and Calvin Klein were in the garment business together.

CHAPTER SIX

I was delivering *diamonds* to the stores.
—Calvin Klein

W hat happened next, said Calvin, "was quite by accident."
As the days dragged by at the York Hotel, and spring drifted into summer without his getting a substantial order, Calvin's concern about the business began to escalate into panic. Soon the coat-buying season would be over, and just as he had warned Barry, "The coat business is a six-month business with a twelve-month overhead." Each day, as it got a little warmer outside, the pressure inside room 613 seemed to mount. Soon it grew hot enough to prop open the door of the small showroom and let in some air—and as long as the door was open, Calvin figured, why not hang one or two of his better samples on it? Maybe somebody—anybody—would pass by and notice them.

It was at about four o'clock on a humid Thursday afternoon when Donald O'Brien, the distinguished-looking vice president of Bonwit Teller, the important Fifth Avenue store, and his assistant, Charles Thompson, were on their way to an appointment on the seventh floor of the York Hotel. Unexpectedly, the doors opened on a lower floor, and while O'Brien waited impatiently for the doors to close, he looked across the hall and saw a coat and dress hanging on the open door of room 613. In just that instant he was struck by the cut and the colors. The muted pastel shades were youthful and contemporary, yet the garments had a precise, classic line that appealed to him. "Go!" O'Brien suddenly barked to his assistant. "Go check those coats out while I go upstairs to my appointment. I'll meet you back here." Thompson squeezed out the door as it was closing.

The instant Thompson had announced that Calvin was about to be visited by a vice president of Bonwit Teller, adrenaline filled his veins. When O'Brien entered the cell-like showroom twenty minutes later, its proprietor was ready for him. Calvin rose to the occasion and in his most articulate yet deferential manner explained his small collection to O'Brien piece by piece, sounding exceptionally knowledgeable about their place in the market. He was obviously a smart young man who knew both the economics of demand and the fine points of design. O'Brien thought the samples were good, so good that he offered "Cal" Klein the shot of a lifetime, the kind of golden opportunity that usually seems to happen only in Hollywood movies. "I'd like very much for Miss Custin to see these clothes," O'Brien told Calvin. "Would you bring them up to her office on Saturday morning?"

Calvin's pulse rate took another leap as he said, "Of course."

Not even an audience with the queen of England could have been a greater honor for Calvin, because no monarch could have made him as big an overnight success as Mildred Custin. As the president of Bonwit Teller, she was an industry star maker of the first order, "*the* major force in fashion at the time," said Calvin, "the grande dame of the retail world!" She was a chain-smoking New England dowager in her fifties whose impressive career in the retail field included the presidency of Philadelphia's Wanamaker's. When she took over Bonwit Teller in 1965, retail sparks flew. She transformed the chain's image from a fuddy-duddy old store to one on the leading edge of fashion. From her offices on Fifth Avenue and Fifty-seventh Street, Custin had introduced no fewer than three of Europe's great couturiers to the American market: Pierre Cardin, André Courrèges, and Emanuel Ungaro. "Miss Retail," as the newspapers referred to her, also introduced the concept of designer boutiques. And—perhaps most important—Miss Custin had what people in the trade called "a big pencil," meaning that when she wrote an order, it was for all of Bonwit's twelve stores.

On the day of Calvin's appointment with Custin, he was in a dither. He finally settled on chinos with a dress shirt, his fashionably long hair was freshly washed and blow-dried. "I don't think of myself as a perfectionist," said Calvin, "but I drive myself crazy trying to make certain things as perfect as they can be. So, on Saturday, I *wheeled* the rack of clothes all the way uptown to Bonwit's. It was my insanity. I could have folded those clothes over my arm and gotten into a taxi, but if there was *one* crease in any of those clothes, it would have killed me. So I wheeled them into Mildred Custin's office." And not easily, either, for as he was navigating the crowded sidewalks, one of the wheels of the rack broke. Calvin wound up having to drag his wares the remainder of the twenty-three blocks uptown to Bonwit Teller. "The trip was a disaster," Calvin said with a sigh.

To add insult to injury, Mildred Custin was not in a receptive mood. Every morning, "Miss Custin," as all the employees of the store referred to her, was accustomed to having her hair and makeup done. Bright and early the top hairstylist from the store's own beauty salon along with a manicurist would arrive in her executive offices and tend to her blond hair and red nails. Finally, one of the store's cosmeticians applied her makeup. Only then was Miss Custin prepared to receive visitors. But that Saturday morning not one of her groomers had shown up, and when Calvin was ushered into her forest-green and Chinese-red office, pulling his broken rack behind him, he was greeted with the unsmiling visage of an unhappy middle-aged woman.

Although Calvin couldn't possibly tell from her scowl, Miss Custin liked him from the start. "He was young and charming and open and without guile," she said, adding, "He was *cute*." What enchanted her the most, however, was the samples he showed her. He had brought with him a small collection of beautifully hand-crafted items of a quality she had never seen on the market for such good prices.

Calvin recalled: "I held the samples up one at a time. She never smiled, just looked at them and listened as I gave her the prices of the clothes."

Custin said, "they were extremely salable for us at the moment, and we could do a great deal with them." After some thought she said to Calvin, "I will give you an order—for fifty thousand dollars retail."

Calvin's jaw almost dropped open when he heard the enormous

sum. Fifty thousand was his projection of revenues for all his customers his entire first year of business, if he was lucky.

"However," Miss Custin continued in her clipped voice, "as we
write this order, we want to give you ten dollars more for each
garment than you are now asking because I don't believe you can
deliver them in this quality at the price you're quoting." She paused
for emphasis and gave him a warning look he would never forget. "I
want to be sure we receive the quality we are looking at now. I want
the garments delivered to Bonwit's exactly the way these samples
are made."

Calvin flushed bright red. Custin remembered the amazement
on his face. "He couldn't believe it," Custin said, "because paying
more for your clothes than you've asked never happened to a manufacturer in retail history."

It didn't take long for Calvin to realize that Custin was just protecting herself. "Traditionally," he explained later, "the sample is
always better than the stock you deliver to the store, and she wasn't
taking any chances on having that happen."

Then Custin added sternly, "And in return for paying you more
than you asked, I want exclusivity."

Calvin slowly shook his head as he silently figured the odds.
"Miss Custin, that's impossible," he said apologetically, "Other
stores are interested, and Bonwit's walked in by accident before
anyone else saw the clothes. I'll give you anything you want, but I
won't give the clothes exclusively."

There was a long pause as Mildred Custin's expression became
even more dour. "She just looked me over slowly and carefully,"
Calvin said. For one awful moment he thought he had killed the
whole sale. Then Custin finally shrugged and snapped, "Okay."
She dismissed him from her office without much more except to
say that on his way out of the store he should stop on the eighth
floor to show the coat buyer and salespeople his samples. She
would alert them that he was on his way down.

Outside Custin's office, Donald O'Brien asked Calvin what he
thought of "our Miss Custin."

"Doesn't she ever smile?" Calvin asked.

After visiting the eighth floor, a dazed Calvin was out on Fifth
Avenue, which was teeming with Saturday morning shoppers.

Bursting with the news, he hauled the rack to the nearest pay phone and dialed Barry's number. Barry was at home, with his feet up, watching a football game. Breathless with excitement, Calvin shouted, "We did it! We made a *fifty-thousand-dollar* sale to Bonwit's! *Fifty thousand dollars!*"

There was a moment's silence before Barry asked, "What's a Bonwit's?"

2

Custin's order was a good omen. That June a staffer from William VanBuren, a New York buying service that scouted talent for small out-of-town stores, also stumbled upon Calvin's den at the York Hotel. The VanBuren staffer borrowed three outfits from him and included them in a show held at the buying service's offices for a crowd of out-of-town buyers. When it was over, the buyers couldn't wait to place orders, according to a VanBuren executive, who took Calvin's hand at the end of the day and predicted, "You're going to be the designer of the future." Next came Garfinckel's, the cream of Washington, D.C., department stores, with six locations in its chain.

As the initial thrill of writing orders began to subside, it was time to get down into the trenches. "The next challenge was raising the money to start *manufacturing* the clothes," said Calvin. According to Calvin, he and Barry approached Manufacturers Hanover Trust, where they were told that if Barry put in another $25,000 on top of his original investment, the bank would match the total amount. Barry bragged, "I never had any problem with credit from the first time I sat down with the bank in 1968, and I needed thirty thousand dollars, I felt, to get through the season." But Barry would never be through with the lenders. Like most manufacturers, he and Calvin were now prisoners in a cycle. Each season a bank or factoring company would dole out enough money to them to manufacture more clothing as all the while they scrambled to pay off the previous season's debt.

As soon as a line of credit was established, the two partners moved from the cramped room in the York Hotel, not to a chic showroom but to an even bleaker, albeit larger space where they could do everything, from cutting samples to shipping. Their new headquarters was located in a decrepit loft building on West Thirty-seventh Street near Ninth Avenue, on the fringes of the garment district. "It was dingy and dreary," said one visitor to the $225-a-month loft, "nothing more than a hole in the wall." Indeed, the loft was so infested with rats that one of their first employees refused to enter in the morning until someone else flicked on the lights, scaring them away. Calvin and Barry worked out of an office not much bigger than a walk-in closet, with a secondhand file cabinet, a phone on the wall, and a beaten-up, pull-out sofa on which they could take turns sacking out when they stayed at the office too late to bother going home.

There were, at first, problems that seemed insurmountable. "Despite the Bonwit Teller order," Calvin said, "I was absolutely no one. There are a hundred million things you have to do to deliver clothes. You have to sit down with banks, get fabric, establish credit, find a factory to make the clothes, deal with the unions—it's endless." In fact, Calvin discovered that many suppliers didn't want to take the risk of doing business with an undercapitalized company run by a couple of brash twenty-five-year-olds. When Calvin tried to buy fabric for the Bonwit order from the prestigious J. P. Stevens Company, Calvin claimed that a Stevens representative scoffed, "Mr. Klein, come to us at another time, when you're really producing more clothes, when you can afford to do business with us."

What Calvin needed was what they called in the parlance of the garment center a "rabbi," an industry old-timer of standing who knew the right people to call and the right buttons to press, someone not just to arrange for the raw materials but to strike agreements with the truckers and labor unions without whose cooperation nothing in the garment center got made or transported. Someone, in short, to teach Calvin and Barry the real nuts and bolts of the business. Calvin turned to Sydney Salenger, the former general manager of Dani Juniors at Dan Millstein's company. In his prime Salenger had been a behind-the-scenes power on Seventh Avenue, but now, in his late fifties and suffering with chronic arthritis, he was considering retirement. Calvin remembered that even a taskmaster like Dan Millstein held Sydney Salenger in high regard and that Millstein was mightily impressed with the efficient and cost-effective way Salenger ran the entire fourth floor. "Salenger was clever and tough," said Dan's daughter, Audrey Millstein.

Calvin had first approached Salenger for his help months before, when he was in the process of trying to raise money to start a company, but he met with a wall of skepticism. "Calvin kept telling me he wanted to go into business and would I help," said Salenger. "I told him it's not right, and he said with my help or not I'm going in." Now with a big order to get out and Bonwit's credit behind it, Salenger was more willing to be courted. Salenger distinctly remembered that Calvin and Barry informed him they had a mere $16,000 in start-up funds at the time, so it is possible the duo scaled the figure down when it gave them a negotiating edge. In any event, unknown to Calvin and Barry, Salenger decided to check with Dan Millstein to find out if the coat king would be offended if Salenger helped his former employee go into competition with him. "I want to help the boys get started," Salenger told Millstein. The manufacturer hooted that a *pishach* like Calvin Klein was no possible rival to him. Salenger was now Barry and Calvin's man, guided, he said, by his big heart. "I couldn't see them losing their sixteen thousand, so I took them under my wing, and we started a business," he said.

Whatever was in the deal for him—none of the parties involved have ever revealed its details—Sydney Salenger is the man who wove the very fiber of the business for Calvin and Barry. "Salenger was Calvin's 'manager' " was the way one observer saw his role, introducing Calvin to key jobbers, making contacts, and hiring employees. "Sydney Salenger did more for Calvin than anybody in the whole world," said Marjorie Dean, a buyer who knew them both. "Salenger taught him everything he didn't know, and he didn't know much when he came out of FIT." By Salenger's account, he had thrown a lifeline to two upstarts who were out of their depths. "Calvin was a designer and knew nothing else," Salenger said, "and Barry was just a grocery man. I taught Barry everything he learned. I found them the bank; I found them credit." And perhaps his most important contribution: "I settled the union prices."

Possibly Salenger's stickiest moment was "settling the union" for

Calvin. "You cannot be in the garment field," said Salenger, "unless you have the union 'settled' before you do anything." On a practical basis, what that meant was that someone had to sit down face-to-face with tough, experienced negotiators from the New York local of the International Ladies Garment Workers Union. Calvin was pleased when, in May 1968, Calvin Klein Ltd. signed an agreement under which his sample makers and production staff joined the ILGWU—and the company agreed to do its best to manufacture in unionized factories. The company would also be allowed to job out to nonunion "sweatshops," provided it forked over hefty penalties based on the number of garments ordered. This levy, or "fine," as the union preferred to call it, went into the ILGWU's health and welfare fund. Since penalties were paid per garment, some manufacturers craftily put in a "cutting ticket" for 100 garments, and the contractor would make 150 outfits in return for under-the-table cash payments.

Sydney Salenger left Calvin's employ soon after the business was off and running. He retired to Miami, Florida, never to be acknowledged again, at least publicly, by Barry and Calvin. "Calvin has been a total ingrate," said Marjorie Dean. Salenger's legacy included a skeleton staff, among them a sample maker who was a Polish concentration-camp survivor and talked incessantly about the atrocities he had witnessed. There was also a patternmaker who was an industry pro, able to suggest factories to make the clothes, and a fitting model not quite beautiful or tall enough to be a top runway model but whom Calvin liked to use because she had a "regular" body that would help ensure that his clothes looked good on the average American woman. There was no division of labor. Everybody pitched in, right down to hanging each garment on a satin-covered hanger, carefully shielding every piece of merchandise with plastic. Calvin would attack cartons of work with obsessive ferocity, and when the model wasn't fitting or selling clothes, she could be found sewing the labels of department stores into the garments before they were shipped.

"We did everything ourselves," Barry said of that first year. "Trial and error. We worked seven days a week. We pressed coats; we shipped the coats. We did everything. We swept the floor. There were nights when we would iron and pack till the early hours.

Sometimes we even went until three in the morning, and we slept on a convertible sofa." They transported fabric in their own cars to save trucking fees, and another designer remembered constantly seeing Calvin rushing through the crowded streets of the garment center, ducking the pushcarts as he carried a flurrying sheaf of patterns from a large hook over his shoulder. He and Barry existed on black coffee in paper cups and burgers sent in from a nearby luncheonette.

From the start it was Calvin who was out meeting people, building up the image that would make the public think of it as "his" business. Barry was smart enough to accept his back-room function with grace, content to be out of the limelight. According to Gail Osman, who worked for them the first year, "Barry is a brilliant, brilliant man. He's a sponge, and he's got an *incredible* memory. He never cared that Calvin was in the front row. It didn't bother him in the least."

"I loved it," attested Barry. "It was very gratifying for me just to be out of Harlem. I could work a hundred hours a week and it wouldn't matter. My whole life had changed."

It was about to change even more than he or Calvin could imagine due to Bonwit Teller.

3

During that long, productive summer, Mildred Custin was making her own plans for Calvin Klein. The kind of clothing Calvin designed and the price he was selling it at fit into a scheme Custin had long been developing for Bonwit's, which was to market more moderate-priced goods and display them on the eighth floor of the flagship Fifth Avenue store. It would give the store's regular customers a broader choice and at the same time help attract younger, less affluent women. Bill McCarthy, who was vice president of sales and in charge of advertising and window displays, remembered that Custin called him into her office and informed him that the store was going to promote a young designer she had discovered named Calvin Klein. She explained how fresh and simple and young he was—an "American Yves Saint Laurent"—and she ar-

ranged for McCarthy to go up to Calvin's dumpy workrooms and
see the merchandise. Like so many others, McCarthy was swept
away with "Cal" Klein, who struck him as "refreshingly ingenu-
ous." Repeating a by now familiar refrain, McCarthy added, "What
a young, *young*, good-looking guy."

The nascent sex symbol's premiere for Bonwit's, it was decided
by Custin, would begin with a window display that heralded the
opening of the autumn buying season, right after Labor Day. The
store's Fifth Avenue windows bestowed enormous prestige in the
eyes of the fashion media and advertising worlds. For an unknown
designer like Calvin to be chosen for a Fifth Avenue window was
honor enough, but his clothes weren't going to be displayed merely
in a single Fifth Avenue window; they were to be given unprecedented star treatment in all *eight* windows of the store. Word rip-
pled through the industry, said Daniel Arje, director of display for
Bonwit's at the time. "Bonwit's had a policy of *only* showing designer clothing from the sixth floor in its Fifth Avenue windows.
This was the first time that formula was ever broken."

Calvin was not going to risk having some sloppy contractor putting the finishing stitches on the samples destined for the windows,
and he loaded the outfits into his car and drove up to Rochambeau
Avenue, where Flo sewed on the buttons. "The buttons were *two
dollars and fifty cents* each," a family intimate remembered. "Calvin
wanted them to look *just so*."

Tradition had it that all store windows were changed on Tuesday
nights. After Bonwit's closed at six, shades were drawn against the
great plate-glass windows while window dressers toiled away, out of
sight. Then, after theater or dinner, *tout le monde* would take a
leisurely stroll up and down the avenue to see what had been unveiled for that week. Bonwit's featured eight mannequins—
sparsely assigned one to a window—each sporting a Calvin Klein
suit or coat, with a placard announcing "Calvin Klein, Miss Bonwit
Shop, 8th Floor." A thrilled Calvin and Jayne drove in from Queens
and just stood there and watched as people passing by stopped and
stared at the mannequins. The next day, customers started to flow
into the store and up the elevators to the eighth floor, where they
swooped down on the racks of Calvin's coats and suits. Custin
warned him to gear up for more orders. Virtually overnight he was

the talk of the coat-and-suit industry. "Is he the son of Anne Klein?" everyone asked.

Yet the prestige of a Fifth Avenue window paled against the impact Calvin felt the next Sunday, when Bonwit's followed up with the first of dozens of full-page advertisements for his clothes on page 5 of the first section of the *New York Times*. Bonwit's considered page 5 its most important promotional spot, and the store reserved that space for itself every Sunday of the year. It was estimated in the industry that a full-page ad in the *Sunday Times* from Bonwit's did as much for a clothing company's revenues as having fifty salespeople on the road. "Whatever was shown on page five of the *Times* on Sunday," said McCarthy, "you could expect buyers from other stores to be in the showroom on Monday morning. We would have manufacturers throw dollars at us to carry their lines and advertise them. They didn't care if we sold one dress, because if a Bonwit Teller advertisement appeared, the merchandise sold."

For the next few months Calvin Klein's small offices were caught up in a whirlwind of breathtaking intensity. "Everything shipped to Bonwit's sold instantly," said Calvin, "and word traveled fast." The phone started to ring off the hook as stores all over the United States tried to place orders, and the showroom was besieged with visits from buyers representing virtually every top women's retail shop or department store in the nation. "Everyone in the country was calling," Calvin said, estatic at what Bonwit's had done for him, "and there was no way that I could supply everyone. I left people hungry. It wasn't just the clothes. Bonwit's ran an ad every month for the first year in business, and we didn't contribute a thing [to the cost of the ads]." Even the recalcitrant suppliers were calling back, including the J. P. Stevens fabric company. "Six months later, people from Stevens were calling me and asking me out to lunch," Calvin crowed.

Not only were Calvin and Barry getting orders; they were getting them from all the right stores, including important out-of-town stores like John Wanamaker in Philadelphia and I. Magnin in San Francisco. And it certainly turned out to be prudent for Calvin not to have given Mildred Custin an exclusive in New York, because within the year Bergdorf Goodman and Saks Fifth Avenue were begging for his clothes as well. At the end of his first season in business, when the company's revenues were tallied, Calvin Klein Ltd. had grossed an astonishing $500,000. At the end of the first full year in business it would reach a million dollars.

Executives at Bonwit's coat department remember that Calvin often came by the store on Saturdays, concerned about what styles were selling best and how the clothes fit and about the customer's comments. He was a consummate salesman and in the beginning, at least, loved to interact with his customers. His goal, Calvin happily confided one Saturday to store employees, was to "retire by forty."

The growing company needed more space, and Barry and Calvin could now afford to move to larger, more pleasant headquarters. It was no simple coincidence—or small irony—that Calvin chose to house his new headquarters in a fourth-floor loft at 205 West Thirty-ninth Street, just seven floors below the offices of Dan Millstein. Calvin was obligated to share the fourth floor with a company called Fredrick Sport, and he made no bones about wanting to move to Millstein's floor and take over his former tormentor's entire lease. He would frequently run into Ethel Mirkin, Millstein's longtime employee, in the elevator and assure her, "I'm going to get to the eleventh floor, Ethel, some way or another."

4

Calvin soon expanded his staff to include an in-house publicist. He was astute enough to realize that a symbiotic relationship was crystalizing between designers and the fashion press, a relationship that could be tremendously profitable to someone with Calvin's communication skills. Since the beginning of the 1960s, American designers were becoming of interest to the public, even to women who could not afford their clothes. There was a small top echelon of famous couturiers with private, made-to-order customers, like Norman Norell, James Galanos, and Pauline Trigère, who were known to the public because they dressed movie stars and celebrities. Below them was a group of less well known "name designers" who made more affordable clothes, including Bill Blass, Donald

Brooks, Geoffrey Beene, and Oscar de la Renta. Traditionally, the names of those who designed mass-market clothing available off the rack had never been advertised, yet alone revealed, and only the name of the manufacturer or the retailer was promoted. Americans were happily accustomed to wearing "a coat from Sears, Roebuck" or a "MacGregor jacket." The anonymity of the designer also suited the fashion magazines just fine, because their big advertising dollars came from fabric houses like Du Pont or cosmetics firms like Coty.

But all that was changing in what *Vogue* fashion editor Diana Vreeland proclaimed a "star-stuck nation." The change was visible on the labels in the clothing. What had once been a dress tagged "Made by Maurice Rentner" became "Maurice Rentner by Bill Blass," which a few years later changed to "Bill Blass for Maurice Rentner," and finally, "Bill Blass." Bernadine Morris wrote about the trend as early as 1966 when she noted in the *New York Times* that "a turning point" had been reached in American design in which the designers were "emerging from the insularity of the back rooms." Morris went on to explain that designers were getting "involved with all facets of the business, from producing and shipping the merchandise to selling it. They leave the showroom where they meet only store buyers and take their collections to stores where they meet the women who wear their clothes. They are concerned with the practicalities as well as the esthetics of the fashion business."

The "turning point" was also the start of an unholy alliance between the designer and the sycophantic fashion press. In no other field did journalists get so far under the sheets with the same people they wrote about. There was not only an open exchange of gifts and perks between the designer and journalist in return for hyperbolic stories, but designer and reporter often became close friends, with the media heavies acting as unpaid consultants whose fashion advice was solicited and heeded. And what journalist would give a bad review to a line that was her own "inspiration?" Thus, the men and women of the press slowly became beholden to the designer. The more popular he became, the more powerful, and the worst punishment he could mete out to a member of the fourth estate was to limit his or her access to him or his fashion shows.

In America, the emergence of the fashion designer as a star was due, at least in part, to Jacqueline Kennedy, whose interest in fashion and design mesmerized millions of women when she lived in the White House. As fashion became more fascinating to the mainstream, newspapers began hiring society-cum-fashion columnists, who breathlessly covered high society and what it was wearing, a specialty in which Eugenia Sheppard of the *New York Herald Tribune* was a pioneer.

Perhaps the greatest proponent of the designer as pop idol was John Fairchild Jr., the mercurial and feared publisher of *Women's Wear Daily*. Founded in Chicago in 1890 by John Fairchild, Sr., *Women's Wear Daily* was one of a string of boring industry newsletters until his son took over in 1960. The younger Fairchild was a gregarious man who was just as intrigued by society gossip as he was by the dull facts and figures of the garment industry. Over the next few years he widened the focus of *Women's Wear Daily* to include the designers and the people who wore their clothes as well as the garments themselves. *Women's Wear Daily* began to develop a taste for scandal. Paparazzi were hired to photograph the comings and goings of high society, and gossip columnists were hired to chronicle their lives and peccadilloes. Scooping other publications in such esoterica as an exclusive sketch of some debutante's wedding gown became an imperative to *Women's Wear Daily*. As its clout in the fashion world grew, manufacturers' fortunes rose and fell with its assessments, and a good review from the trade paper became the single most profitable verdict a designer could receive.

"Bronx Boy Makes Good Overnight" was a natural story for the media, and in the spring of 1969 it fell to the responsibility of Gina Epworth to let them know about it. Epworth was a sophisticated, Old World, European-born woman in her forties, married to a wealthy Park Avenue attorney, Lincoln Epworth. A onetime sportswear buyer for Abraham & Straus, Epworth had met Calvin a few years previously when she was writing for the trade magazine *Merchandise Motivation Incorporation* and Calvin was toiling at Dan Millstein's. They had lunch a few times, and Calvin liked her polish and class. "It wasn't just a question of having somebody do his publicity," said Epworth. "Calvin needed somebody to do *everything*. I was in the design room, I did this, I did that. . . . I even went into the market with him to help pick fabrics. He was a nice young man, and to me he was almost like a child. I showed him how to go about things. Remember, he had no money."

Certainly Calvin did not pay Epworth very much. At first, he couldn't afford to, but Epworth got the distinct impression during the four years she worked for him that even when he was able to reward her better, he did not care to. Although Barry Schwartz ostensibly handled the financial side of the business, Epworth realized that Calvin was no fool when it came to money and that he was even tighter with a buck than Barry.

"Barry sounded the worst of the two," said Epworth, "but Barry was the nicest when it came down to it. Barry was loud—if you're not used to that kind of person, it can be very upsetting—but actually he had a better heart, and I think he cared more about people than Calvin. He was rude, and his manners were bad, but his heart was, I think, much better than Calvin's was." One episode that confirmed this belief, she said, involved Barry's newest gambling habit, the stock market. After Epworth worked for them for a short time, Barry told her that if she gave him $10,000 of her savings, he would turn it into a king's ransom by investing it in the stock market. "He swore he was going to make me a fortune," said Epworth, "and I said, 'All right,' and gave him the ten thousand. I ended up without a penny. It really went down to nothing. Every month a statement came for a couple of thousand dollars less." Finally, Barry was so embarrassed by the loss that, ever the big sport, he reimbursed Epworth the entire $10,000. Epworth remembered that Barry dutifully paid back the money with a company check.

The first problem Epworth had in getting Calvin press was that she didn't know any of the key media people. From the start she had warned Calvin that she had only written for a trade publication, but Calvin said he expected her to perservere, and she did. She found names on the mastheads of fashion magazines and began calling journalists cold to rave about how she was working with the "American Yves Saint Laurent," a sobriquet Calvin would later regret. It helped that Epworth, who was at heart a shy women, believed in Calvin. "He was definitely a boy on the way up; even then we knew it. I liked having him meet people in the magazines, because once he met them, he charmed them. He knew he wanted to make good, and he was very sweet to everybody." She had to phone some of the fashion editors a dozen times until they finally took her call. One early triumph was Eugenia Sheppard, who mentioned Calvin in passing in her powerful *Herald Tribune* column. Calvin was so grateful to see his name in bold type that he dispatched Gina Epworth to an Upper East Side antique shop to buy an old English porcelain jar as a gift for Sheppard.

One evening shortly after Epworth went to work for Calvin in 1969, she wanted to take him to a cocktail party that was being held at the Essex House Hotel for the out-of-town fashion press. Calvin wasn't in the mood to meet so many people at once, but Epworth took him into his office and lectured him: "Look, Calvin, I'm going because I want to, but you *must* go. You have to start meeting people." Calvin reluctantly agreed to accompany her, but no sooner did they get there and Epworth introduced him to a couple of lady editors than "I realized he didn't need me," said Epworth. "He simply took them over. They loved him—he was *so* young, *so* attractive. I didn't even bother to stay and say goodbye to him or to anyone else. I realized I was superfluous."

"I cannot tell you the number of women over the years who had crushes on Calvin," said one of the Bonwit executives who watched him operate.

One of the more important introductions that Epworth would facilitate was to Barbara Slifka, the coat-and-suit editor at *Harper's Bazaar*, who became one of Calvin's most influential supporters. Epworth brought the two together over lunch at Bill's, a pubby garment center hangout, and she so fussed over Calvin that Slifka kept asking, "Are you sure you're not mother and son?" After lunch she was invited up to the showroom to get an advance peek at the fall line he was planning and asked to borrow some of the samples to take up to the offices of "the *Bazaar*" and show them around. Slifka couldn't have paid him a better—or more useful—compliment. "In those days," said Slifka, "the magazines had very strong points of view as to what they wanted to show, and so we often came in with ideas of what we liked. We used to plan the issue, and we used to think 'pastel' or 'plaid' or 'double-breasted.'" It was no small feat on Calvin's part, therefore, that he was able to anticipate perfectly the magazine's taste. His coats, trousers, tops, culottes, and jumpers were featured in almost every issue of *Harper's Bazaar* for the next three years.

5

Among the many magazine editors who were helpful to Calvin in his early years was one who held special sway. She was Eve Orton, the fur and fabric editor of *Harper's Bazaar*. There are many who think that Eve Orton was more than a fan, that the fifty-two-year-old divorced fashion editor fell in love with Calvin. Acquaintances could see it in the adoring way she looked at him. "She went crazy about him," said Barbara Slifka, who introduced them at the magazine's offices one day as she was showing Calvin around. "Eve went absolutely *nuts*."

Calvin was by now used to psychologically seducing older women in the business, but he had never won a prize quite like Orton. She was style incarnate, a woman of a certain age with a lilting Viennese accent, striking oval face, high cheekbones, and dark red lips. Elected to the International Best Dressed list, Orton was considered a woman of "perfect taste," as *Bazaar*'s editor in chief, Nancy White, put it. She could wrap a raggedy bed sheet around herself and make it look like a Balenciaga gown by pinning a dime-store brooch at the shoulder. Her easy stylishness was so renowned that she was photographed almost daily by the paparazzi entering or leaving the more exclusive Manhattan restaurants and was a regular on the taste-maker pages of *Women's Wear Daily*. Professionally, as the fabric and fur editor of *Bazaar*, she had become a powerful and influential voice in the industry because of the access she had to the best suppliers in the world. Her desk was command central for the fabric industry, with manufacturers and designers from several continents making pilgrimages to seek her advice on color and fabric direction.

Orton held Calvin entranced for hours as she related her glamorous—and improbable—life story. Born in Vienna to a wealthy family, she defied her father by marrying so young that her governess had to go on her honeymoon with her. She immigrated to America with her second husband and in a mink coat disembarked at Ellis

Island. From there a limousine whisked her directly to a cocktail party. Later that night they departed for Hollywood. She returned to New York a divorcée three years later and married the suave multimillionaire menswear designer John Weitz. These were her golden years, and she and her rich, witty husband were one of the most popular couples from Newport to Palm Beach. But when the marriage to Weitz ended in 1964, Eve's social star dimmed considerably. In need of money as well as an identity, she plunged into a career as a magazine editor for *Harper's Bazaar*.

For Calvin, Eve was the most soigné woman he had ever hoped to meet, and being "taken up" by one of the great doyennes of style was as potent an endorsement as a Bonwit Teller window. Calvin followed in the prestigious steps of two earlier Orton protégés, Giorgio Sant'Angelo and Ralph Lauren. "Eve showed him the ropes," said their mutual friend and magazine editor Betty Ann Grund. For a time he was her most frequent companion, they seemed to enjoy each other's company so much. She included him at her famous chili dinner parties with a bitchy fashion in-crowd, after which Calvin would escort Orton to the bar at the Carlyle Hotel, where they would linger over drinks and listen to her pal Bobby Short entertain. On other nights Calvin would join her and her friends for supper at Elaine's, the East Side glitterati bistro. Orton was well known enough to get one of the five front tables, and Calvin would watch wide-eyed as the New York notables streamed into the restaurant and stopped at her table to pay court and air-kiss her.

As well as enriching Calvin socially, Orton's friendship was an abiding catalyst to his artistic growth. In the beginning, his clothes had been uncluttered to the point of blandness, and there were few accessories. She was the first in a series of editors, helpers, and muses who would give life to his. Over a period of several years Orton would come up to his showroom and review his collections with him piece by piece before they were put into production. She had a superb eye for detail and could often suggest just the tiniest change in a garment and make it sparkle. Eve was especially valuable to Calvin in preparation for his fashion shows. Nancy White, the *Bazaar* editor, recalled: "When Calvin started, the clothes themselves were very professional, but they didn't have any particular zip, which is the kind of thing that Eve would give them. Eve just pulled everything together and put the right scarf or muffler or earring or what have you to make the look very snappy and professional. She could do it for herself, and she did it for everyone else. She was a whiz."

Gina Epworth remembered that Orton contributed far more than just trimmings. "She would not only accessorize," said Epworth, "but talk about clothes and find that this wasn't quite right or that could be changed or a new color . . ."

"Metaphorically," said one of Eve's friends, "she taught Calvin Klein to understand chocolate brown."

During the bloom of their friendship, Calvin presented himself to Orton as purely heterosexual, and Orton, who was sweet on him, preferred to believe rather than question it. If this was what he wanted, then she wanted it for him, too. There were times, of course, when the pretense wore a little thin. Eve and Calvin were in Europe together during the biannual showing of the collections in Paris, and they were invited to a party being given in the lavishly appointed Left Bank apartment of André Oliver, Pierre Cardin's friend and bachelor socialite. The party was filled with the stars of Parisian haute couture, including the homosexual power network that ran the French industry. Calvin, in a newly purchased, French-cut Renoma jacket, was the center of attention of a group of older men who were "dying to spoon-feed" the newcomer in the business, said one observer. When Eve Orton saw this, she descended on all the predatory gay blades like a sheep dog protecting her prime lamb. She knew that wasn't what Calvin wanted. After all, she thought, her darling boy was as straight as an arrow.

6

Count Nicolas de Gunzburg also looked out for Calvin's interests. As the fur and fabric editor of *Vogue*, the count was not only "a very close friend," explained Calvin mildly, but "a particular inspiration in my work. He was truly the great inspiration of my life from the time we met. . . . He was my mentor, I was his protégé."

The way one business associate saw it, "Calvin became *obsessed* with the baron for years. It was like he wanted to *study* the baron, wanted to *be* the baron."

"I think he just liked saying his name," another said, smirking.

"Nicky," as he was called by his chums—who once included Cole Porter and Gertrude Stein—was considered by the international chichi set to be the "last great gentleman," "the most civilized man in society," or as his friend designer John Weitz described it, "a civilized homosexual in the manner of Somerset Maugham." Aristocratically thin and regally erect, he had an attenuated face that was set off by a silver mane of hair, meticulously parted to the scalp and slicked back with glistening pomade. Although the baron was already in his sixties when Calvin met him, he dressed in the height of that year's fashion: gray wool pants, double-breasted navy sports jacket, and black capped shoes. His influence as a fashion pundit was so powerful that when the baron deemed it was fashionable in the sixties *not* to wear socks when wearing loafers, the idea caught on like wildfire, endowing America with generations of sockless social climbers.

Calvin met the baron in the late sixties when he was the only male editor in the business. Babs Simpson, another *Vogue* editor, who shared an office with the baron, remembered that the responsibility for covering designers was randomly divided up between staffers and that Calvin was fortuitously assigned to Nicky. "He met Calvin, and I think he fell in love with him," said another *Vogue* editor. "He came back and he came into my office and I had to see Calvin—everybody had to see Calvin." said Babs Simpson, "He taught Calvin everything about how to dress and fabrics and all the rest of it. Nicky really got Calvin on his way to do the kind of thing he did in the beginning. When I say he taught him how to dress, I don't mean himself, literally—although that was probably part of it, too."

Calvin and the baron were most unlikely friends except for the coincidence that they were both Jewish. The baron was born in Paris in 1904, the son of the finance minister of the last Russian czar. He grew up in a magnificent apartment at the Ritz Hotel in which his family owned shares and was known for his wildly rococo parties attended by the cream of the Parisian literary and art world. When the baron's father suddenly died, legend has it that the family fortune vanished, rumored to be locked away in Swiss bank accounts of which only the deceased baron had knowledge. All that Nicky had left was his reputation, some family heirlooms, and whatever cash was left in his checking account. Upon moving to Manhattan in the thirties, he used his remaining cash to throw a grand ball to announce, *"Je suis arrivé."*

In the forties, Nicky embarked on a career at the top fashion magazines, first as editor in chief at *Town and Country*, then *Harper's Bazaar*, and finally at *Vogue*, where he played éminence grise to a pixilated Diana Vreeland. "He taught me everything," Vreeland would tell friends when she was in one of her rare generous moods. *"Everything."* However, Vreeland was not immune to Nicky's stinging wit, and once, when the grande dame asked him at a staff meeting to remind her of the name of the fashion designer "who so loathes me?" Nicky responded, "Legion."

Although over the years de Gunzburg was able to buy himself a modest country "dacha" in New Jersey, he never again achieved the life of grandeur his family money afforded him in Paris. When he met Calvin, "he lived in one room," said Babs Simpson, "but it was a huge room of beautiful proportions with an extraordinary bed and wonderful *objets. . . .*"

Nicky took Calvin under his wing. He often lectured him about his perfectionism and getting hung up on details. "Don't look at the small picture," Nicky would intone in his rolling French accent. "Look at the big one." Nicky also introduced Calvin to the finer side of New York. "He said that whenever we go the first time to a restaurant, he pays," explained Calvin. "Every other time we go back, I pay."

"Where do you want to go first?" Nicky asked.

Calvin didn't think for a moment before he said, La Grenouille, the elegant French restaurant where society ladies lunched each day under the watchful eye of *Women's Wear Daily* tipsters. They were sitting at the restaurant, finishing a brilliantly prepared and served lunch, when Nicky said, "Now Calvin, I want you to tell me what you think and what you see."

Calvin said, "God, Nicky, the flowers are incredible and the people look so beautiful and there's such elegance and the food is superb."

Nicky turned to him and said, "Just remember, in minutes it all turns to shit, anyway."

The baron was outspoken about Calvin's talent as well. He was the acid test for most every creative endeavor Calvin embarked on for the next decade. Nicky always came by the office to offer a final verdict on a collection. He would sit in a chair during the dress rehearsals for each collection and make suggestions and changes. "I would show him something and he would say, 'The color, the cut of the sleeve.' He would drive me crazy." During the shows he would be given a seat of honor in the front row and sit there, sockless, nodding in approbation, his hands clasped on the sterling-silver newel post of a cane. The baron was a fixture at Calvin Klein's offices for the next ten years and an employee when he was turned out to pasture by *Vogue*. "There isn't anyone I knew that well for that long a time," said Calvin. "I know lots of incredible people, but it was different with Nicky and me."

7

The growing prominence of Calvin's line made his fashion shows an essential stop for even the busiest editors. His first full-scale fashion show was held at the end of April 1970, for a cost of about $10,000, to introduce his prodigious fall collection of fifty pieces. In those days fashion shows weren't the multimedia, sophisticated productions they became as the seventies progressed. Budgets were small, and a designer was lucky if he was able to hire four models. The mannequins walked rather than sashayed their way down a runway, stiffly holding up cards with the order number of the garment they were wearing while a phonograph record played tinnily in the background. However primitive, showing his fall line was a crucial roll of the dice. All the major buyers and fashion press, including the *New York Times* and *Women's Wear Daily*, would be passing judgment. Many far bigger names than Calvin had fallen flat on their faces with a bad show and seen a whole season's worth of goods languish unsold.

The show was pulled together with love and spit. Sixty folding chairs, all that would fit in his showroom, were rented for the audience. There wasn't enough money to have a real runway built, so Calvin borrowed mover's pallets, arranged them down the center of the room, and camouflaged them with a cheap rug. A folding table was set up, with Jayne enlisted to man the coffee urn and cookies, while the shipping room was curtained off as a changing area for the models. Calvin proved himself to be very fussy about his models from the start. He wanted them tall and thin—rail-thin. He wasn't interested in exotic beauties, either, but fresh-faced, all-American types who would complement his clothes. He flirted with the models, too, in a cute sort of way, and playing into this, they worked harder to make his clothes work.

Three days before the show, Calvin began a psychological ritual that would continue four times a year for the rest of his life. As time drew near, he went without sleep, fueled by gallons of black coffee, offset in the early hours of the morning with sips of vodka. His blood pressure soared, he turned nasty and sarcastic, his stomach began to cramp, and he began losing several pounds a day. Twenty-four hours before the show he was a nervous wreck. He had gone over every detail a hundred times. He even wrote up three-by-five file cards with instructions for each outfit: "Wear with black shoes" or, for the rainwear, "Spray model's face with glycerin." But no matter how many times he ran over it, he was still not happy with the collection. Nothing seemed to look right, and no matter how beautiful the brown and burgundy clothes were, there was no pizzazz to them.

Exasperated, he turned to his fashion godmother, Eve Orton, who limoed over to his office thirty minutes after his call with shopping bags filled with scarves, bracelets, brooches, and shoes. After the models put on the outfits, Eve went over the merchandise with him stitch by stitch. Pouring Stolichnaya vodka straight into a glass, she matched blouses with suits, shoes with coats, and added or deleted belts, buttons, and bows. She even loaned the girls her own panty hose in a rainbow assortment of hues, according to one employee who watched her magic wand transform Calvin's line. "Eve made the $69.75 coats work," the employee said.

Eve's editing and accessorizing went on into the small hours of the night, until she started to fade and demanded to be taken to Elaine's for a snack and a nightcap. Unable to look at another suit, she begged, "Calvin, darling, this *must* end!"

Calvin gave her his puppy-dog look and implored, "Just one more, Eve, please! I have to make it into a group."

Eve groaned melodramatically and agreed to stay just a little while longer to indulge her darling Calvin.

The morning of the show, Calvin received a telegram from Orton that said, simply, *"Merde,"*—the French scatological equivalent of "break a leg." He tried to appear calm on the surface as the buyers and press representatives—*Women's Wear Daily*; the *New York Times*—began arriving in the showroom, but when one of his models, Jenny Garrigues, arrived late, "Calvin was beside himself." People milled about for half an hour, nibbling on cookies and sipping coffee, and then each took a seat, and the show began. Backstage it was all a blur, and he worried he would disgrace himself, so bad were the pains in his stomach. Calvin described the show as "a mess" and remembered that the stereo equipment jammed mid-show and he had to jump up on the runway and dash across the showroom in front of the audience to fix it. One other thing that Calvin remembered was that Model 721, an unassuming, eight-button pea coat in three-quarter length, drew a rapturous round of applause from the audience. After the show everybody congratulated him and went home. A few of the buyers promised orders, then there was a one-day wait for the reviews.

Gushing is perhaps the only appropriate description of the *Women's Wear Daily* report. It was an unreserved coronation. "The Message": It proclaimed, "In just 50 pieces, Calvin Klein joins SA's [Seventh Avenue's] Big Names as a designer to watch." It cited him for "understanding the longuette mood" and for being "simple and direct." It thought his coats were "nifty" and raved about his broadtail and seal fake furs, made of "Scondia" and "Barana." The trade paper went on to announce dizzily, "It's a buyer's paradise. Calvin Klein is the fashion answer to this season's rising prices. If only there could be more like him."

The line took off like a rocket. His melton trench coat was such a smash seller that in its own self-fulfilling prophecy, *Women's Wear* put a sketch of it on its front page on June 9, 1970, with a banner headline that declared, "Best Seller on SA." The bold-faced subhead continued; "A Best Selling Calvin Klein Coat to Be a Classic." His clothing was so successful that there were times the stores literally couldn't keep the stock on hangers. That July, when Bonwit Teller ran an ad for his fake seal "Longuette" coats, "the first fabulous fakes to get designer Calvin Klein's seal of approval," the store's entire shipment sold out in one week—quite an amazing feat, considering it was broiling summer outside. "We're really not surprised," insisted David Long, assistant to the president at Bonwit's. "The fur is a great fake that's confined to Calvin Klein. It has every bit of fashion interest. Yes, we have sold coats and please add three 'esses' on the word coats." The following month, Calvin's number 509, a gray flannel jumper at $42.75, was another smash hit at the cash registers: Joseph Magnin reordered forty-five pieces, Saks "special ordered" thirty, and Maison Blanche in New Orleans begged for twelve more.

The style singly most associated with Calvin's early success was his pea coat—a brainstorm which Eve Orton claimed to have suggested to him. Calvin's interpretation of this classic coat was so stylish and well made that there are still men and women who have them in their wardrobes twenty-five years later. Calvin, of course, did not invent the pea coat. The Dutch have that honor. (The word *pij* describes a rough woolen fabric made into a hip-length, double-breasted jacket worn by fishermen and sailors.) In the 1920s, Chanel adapted the shape for women's jackets, and nearly half a decade later, in 1962, Yves Saint Laurent popularized the look with a navy blue pea jacket with gold buttons that became his trademark garment for a time—until Calvin appropriated the silhouette and virtually made it his own. His pea coat was such a bread-and-butter business staple that he kept it in his line year after year, updating and refining it with some clever, small twist like fewer buttons or different piping on the collar. Beginning in the fall of 1970, with his roomy, eight-button, slash-pocketed, high-collared, three-quarter length version of the coat, he sold twenty thousand copies at $59.75 wholesale to the stores. The second year, now priced $65.75 wholesale, he shipped thirty thousand of the coats, which had become so wildly popular that Bloomingdales' sold three thousand of them in a month. By 1974, he was selling thirty thousand pea coats a year at $65.75 wholesale, and finally, in 1975, he shipped another thirty thousand coats sold at $69.55 each. In total, nearly $8 million worth.

People in the business were sitting up and taking notice of Cal-

vin Klein. "I remember the first time," said his publicist, Gina Epworth, "that I was able to get Bernadine Morris, the fashion columnist of the *New York Times*, on the phone. My God! I thought I was
in seventh heaven." This was because although Morris didn't quite
have the absolute clout of, say, the *Times's* drama critic, the very
fact that a designer could *transcend* from the pages of fashion
magazines to the "newspaper of record" was in itself a milestone.

On May 12, 1969, Calvin accomplished this feat by appearing in
an article entitled "Keeping Fashion High and Prices Low." He was
photographed for it, rather dashingly, crossing a busy Manhattan
intersection with two models wearing his coats, their arms linked
behind them, laughing and looking sophisticated and smug in the
sunlight. Calvin was cited by Morris as Seventh Avenue's premier
newcomer, a designer whose appeal was "to give customers lots of
style for little money"—an appeal that Calvin would shortly es-
chew. The twenty-eight-year-old arriviste philosopher was quoted
as spouting virtual fashion heresy. "I don't think women should
spend hours deciding what they should wear," he told Morris, "and
frankly, there are more important things to do with their money
than putting it all into clothes."

Here, for the first time in print, was also espoused the Jewish
Horatio Alger tale that would become part of the Calvin Klein legend in the coming years: A poor boy from the Bronx, he had started
out just the year before with (this time) only "$2,000, a few sam-
ples cut on a kitchen table and made in his tailor's bedroom." Hard
work and belief in the American dream paid off. Now, rhapsodized
Morris, "seven hundred stores have sold close to one million dollars of his designs." And Calvin wasn't going to be limited to coats
and suits. His touch seemed so golden that he might branch out at
whim. "Who knows?" he said cockily. "We might make bathing
suits next year."

Epworth remembered that after this preliminary interview Morris seemed mightily impressed. "How *nice* it is," Morris confided to
her, "that there's a young designer in the business who has a wife
and child and isn't homosexual."

Morris was so taken with the young, straight designer that only a
month later she journeyed to his "modest Forest Hills apartment
. . . 10 minutes from Manhattan when traffic is right," as she de-

scribed the outing in an article about "Fashion Designers Who Shun the Fashion Scene." The piece, which also featured designers Victor Costa and George Nardiello (neither of whom would make it to the Pantheon), claimed that the three were "family men . . . who go to their jobs on Seventh Avenue as other men go to Wall Street. . . . Shunning the snobbery, hyperbole and flamboyance of the fashion business. . . . " Morris painted a scene of domestic bliss at Calvin's small Queens apartment, and the *Times* even ran a generously sized photograph of the family: Calvin's Prince Valiant– length locks gave him the appearance of a teenager as he sat on the floor next to Jayne. Her bleached-blond hair was teased into a fashionable bouffant, and there was a smile on her face as she watched cherubic two-and-half-year-old Marci building a toy house out of bleached-wood blocks. If the picture was disarming, so was the way Calvin cleverly put his career down: "Sometimes," he said, "people look at a coat I made and scream, 'It's great!' and I wonder, What can be great about designing fashion? Being a doctor, now that's great." But Morris noted that when Calvin the Great walked the crowded streets of the garment center, veteran manufacturers nudged each other, no longer wondering if he was Anne Klein's son but enviously whispering, "Calvin Klein, look how young."

At the close of 1971, Calvin Klein Ltd.'s volume was a staggering $5 million. The two partners were beating away offers for takeovers from entrepreneurial garment-center figures, all of which were not only refused but barely considered. The business was expanding by gigantic leaps and bounds, including an international licensing deal that Barry cut for Calvin to design coats and jackets for Begged D'Or, a pricey Israeli company known for its expensive animal skins. By now Calvin clearly needed more space than just his meager half of the fourth floor at 205 West Thirty-ninth Street, and he became more determined than ever to take over the entire eleventh floor—the one that belonged to Dan Millstein.

Time had not been good to Dan Millstein. His two brothers, who worked for the manufacturer for many years, had finally deserted his tyrannical reign and retired. Millstein himself had been diagnosed with cancer of the jaw, and he knew that he was destined to die a painful, disfiguring death. This did not in the least diminish his courage or tenacity when Calvin made known his expansion plans. Calvin elected to deal personally with his former boss in his negotiations to buy out his lease. Millstein intentionally quoted Calvin an impossibly high figure to discourage him and was astounded when his suitor remained implacable in his determination to get the deal. "He *only* wanted to sit in Dan's office," Mirkin said. "That was Calvin's goal, to sit in Dan's office."

And Millstein was equally determined to thwart him. "It got so bad with Dan that I had to let Barry take over," Calvin said. After months of haggling, a deal was finally struck that included certain pieces of furniture that Millstein agreed to sell to Calvin. Before the moving men carted Millstein's personal belongings away, Calvin arrived on the eleventh floor to claim some of the things he had bought, he said. "There was an old-fashioned oval floor mirror," said Ethel Mirkin, "that the boys had given me after I was at Millstein for ten years that Calvin wanted to take. I said, 'No, not that, it's mine," and he said, 'No it's not!" Both Mirkin and Calvin persisted until Mirkin threatened to break the mirror if Calvin did not allow her to keep it. Finally, Millstein called her into his office and said, "Ethel, give Calvin the mirror, what do you care?" Almost in tears she handed the mirror over, "because Dan was already ailing," she said, "and I didn't want him to be upset."

Now Calvin actually *was* sitting in Dan Millstein's office.

But that was not the last altercation between Calvin and the Millstein family. The King of Suits and Coats lingered on long enough to see at least the greater part of Calvin's success, dying finally at age eighty. He passed away shortly before Calvin lambasted him in the pages of *Playboy* magazine in 1980, labeling Millstein a "monster," among other sobriquets. Millstein's daughter, Audrey Goodman, was outraged that Calvin could so blithely defame her dead father. She wrote the designer an excoriating letter telling him exactly what she thought of him and had the missive hand-delivered to his Manhattan apartment. To this date, she has not received a reply.

CHAPTER SEVEN

Calvin Klein is a very easy man to get along with if
he gets exactly what he wants.

—Barry Schwartz

T o an outsider, Jayne Klein had everything: a rich and successful husband who put food on her table and a roof over her head, an
adorable child, beautiful clothes, a Mercedes automobile, and a
rented summer cottage in the Hamptons—a far cry from Rockaway
Beach. She was the envy of all the other young mothers.

To Jayne, however, Calvin's success was as much an irony as it
was a blessing. "She was in what at the beginning looked like a
wonderful marriage," said Gina Epworth, "and suddenly she had
no part." While before she might have suffered from lack of attention, by now she was beginning to feel downright shut out. At least
in the old days when Calvin buried himself drawing sketches for
Millstein at the dining-room table, she knew where he was at night.
Now he sometimes didn't come home at all—or only after she was
long in bed. What had first been at least a marginally satisfying
physical relationship had turned perfunctory, and when they did
make love, she complained he was "insensitive."

Socially, he went out with his lady-editor friends as much as he
did with Jayne, and Jayne sat at home when magazine editor Barbara Slifka took her husband to his first Coty Awards ceremony in
1970. A surrogate wife even appeared with Calvin in *Women's
Wear Daily* when he was photographed, dressed in black tie, going
out on the town for the evening, not with Jayne but with his house
model, Bianca, who was pictured kissing Marci good-night wearing

Calvin's full-skirted black coat with a luxurious silver fox hood and cuffs. The photo caption read "When Calvin Klein steps out for a night on the town, he does it with glamour." But not, obviously, with his wife.

Even Marci seemed an encumbrance to him. Although he clearly loved his daughter and tried to make time for her, his hyperactive, wound-up mind was always tuned somewhere else—on fabric availability or a lapel that didn't lie flat.

Yet there was something else, something more subtle than just a feeling of abandonment that made Jayne unhappy. It was an intuitive unease that nibbled away at her. Calvin was changing in ways that frightened her. Sometimes it was just some small thing he did, like a new, slightly jaded inflection in his voice, a sudden affinity to vodka cocktails, or the languid way he began to hold his cigarette between the tips of his long fingers, the smoke curling toward the ceiling as he talked. He began to dress more theatrically as well, in white bucks and tennis sweaters, as if he were putting on a costume for a role, the part of a preppie, clean-cut, happy husband and father on his way up, up, up.

Jayne tried not to resent him for it. She told herself it wasn't that he was becoming a phony; he was just breaking loose from the last vestiges of their common upbringing, trying to grow and savor the taste of the rich cultural and social life his financial success and publicity were offering him. The only really boorish thing he did was to begin to mock the Bronx and everything dreary it represented to him. He hated Bronx accents and Bronx-looking furniture, Bronx hairdos, and—suspected Jayne—his Bronx wife.

Even Calvin's Bronx complexion was on its way out. With the increasing frequency his photograph was appearing in magazines and newspapers, he became more sensitive about his skin than ever. The scars from his chronic acne showed only faintly around his mouth in close-ups, but to Calvin they looked like craters. He already had several Rolodex cards filled with the names of dermatologists and plastic surgeons, but no one could solve his dilemma until he was recommended to Dr. Norman Orentreich of Fifth Avenue. Orentreich was the newest rage among the youth-fad cognoscenti of the New York fashion industry. His reputation was as a magician who could fill in ugly craters and age lines with a few pricks of his ultrafine syringe filled with silicone. Socialites and Hollywood stars waited months to see him, only to be ushered into a warren of little rooms where Orentreich injected tiny balls of silicone into the scar pit or wrinkles with fine surgical needles, slowly filling out the depressions. It could take hundreds or more of these painful injections given during repeated visits, and the doctor's waiting room was invariably filled with people as Calvin came back time after time to have the scars around his mouth and cheekbones filled in.

Next, he tried to soften his thick Bronx accent by taking elocution lessons, without much success in the long run. There were other changes as well. Whereas a short while before, a major evening's entertainment for Calvin and Jayne was going to a neighborhood movie or a concert at the nearby Forest Hills Music Festival in Queens, Calvin was now consumed with being seen at the right Manhattan restaurant (Orsini's or La Grenouille for lunch—*never* Bill's, the garment-center hangout) or learning what the right schools were for Marci to attend (Dalton) and in what neighborhoods in Manhattan he and Jayne should live (the Upper East Side, Manhattan's Silk Stocking District) and what was the "in" dog to own (a large sheepdog named Snoopy). His new "hobby," as he called it, was reading the *New York Times* real estate section from cover to cover each Sunday, hunting for a good investment for his very new money. The couple's domestic geography would begin to read like a road map of Calvin's evolving bourgeois consciousness; they changed residence four times in eight years of marriage, each move to a slightly bigger, tonier apartment building and eventually to Manhattan's Upper East Side. "I've started collecting some things," Calvin told Elsa Klench, a writer for *Women's Wear Daily,* "old lithographs, posters. But I don't intend to keep them the rest of my life. I want to constantly change things. If I had everything I wanted, I would be a bore."

Unfortunately, said a friend close to them both, "it was at a time when his business was really moving along and Jayne didn't want to play the game. If the business was going to boom, Calvin had to create a personality and be a star. Jayne just wasn't right for the image." Said another in their inner circle, "Jayne just couldn't make the transition. She didn't have a bad bone in her body, but she just couldn't keep up with Calvin. She still had the Bronx accent, and she still dressed like she was from the Bronx."

Calvin was frequently appalled at how provincial she was. She sometimes forgot to wax her upper lip and intimates remember that after just one drink her voice changed in timbre and pitch and carried around the room. Calvin's new Manhattan friends were amused when at a dinner party Jayne served them "déclassé" hors d'oeuvres—"franks in blankets" and little egg rolls—purchased in the gourmet freezer department. She seemed to lack a certain worldliness. "When Calvin got tickets to the opening of the Broadway musical *Jesus Christ, Superstar,*" said a friend who went with them, "he had to explain the life of Jesus to her before they got to the theater." Intimidated by Calvin's fast-lane friends, criticized and belittled, the poor woman didn't know what to say half the time. One night, Jayne was giving Calvin's design assistant, Charles Suppon, a tour of their new Manhattan apartment, and when they got to the master bedroom, she pointed to the bed and told him, "This is where Calvin Klein fucks his wife."

Or didn't. "She told me once," said her friend Jane Sternberg, "that Calvin thought of her as 'really his best friend.'"

Jayne wanted more. She wanted to be lover and wife as well. She tried to grow with him, to be perfect like him, but there was no catching up, no pleasing Calvin. Success had become rocket fuel to him, and he was on Mars. In love and in hate with him, frightened and confused she was losing him, Jayne did the worst possible thing: She became desperate and clinging. The more Calvin pulled away, the tighter she tugged the reins. "She gave him very little movement," remembered Epworth. "He'd get to the office by seven-thirty and she was already on the phone five minutes later." The smothering and the guilt caused an incendiary buildup between them. Now the arguments were so vindictive that Calvin had to ask Gina Epworth to intervene. "Talk to Jayne," he'd implore. "She'll listen to you. See if she'll get a job. She'll be happier if she works."

But Jayne would not get a job. Jayne wanted to run a household. She had even told Bernadine Morris of the *Times* that she had given up her career as a textile designer because "I don't want any maid bringing up my daughter." Epworth said, "Jayne was a very neurotic young woman, and I think Calvin felt getting out of the house would help."

Their move in 1971 to 136 East Seventy-sixth Street in Manhattan was more of a turning point in their lives than either of them realized. "We moved here because we knew the building would probably go co-op," Calvin said, hoping to get a discounted "insider's price" when the apartment went on sale. The building was an undistinguished carbon-copy red-brick affair with a uniformed doorman and a small, burnished metal marquee. Calvin and Jayne's apartment, however, was not so ordinary. They rented a two-bedroom apartment with a terrace on the seventh floor and were able to create a huge living room by also renting part of the apartment next door and knocking down the adjoining wall. An additional bathroom was turned into a wet bar, an important accessory, Jayne told a reporter in yet another faux pas, because entertaining for the young couple was "mainly booze."

No longer just a poor schnook from one of the boroughs, Calvin was now able to afford a decorator for his family's new Manhattan digs, a young, up-and-coming interior designer named John Stedila from the trendy firm of Raymond Loewy-William Snaith. Calvin had admired an apartment Stedila had designed in a clean, contemporary style and called him on the phone one day, complaining that everything else he had seen looked too "done." Calvin explained he wanted something fresh and different in his signature earth tones. He invited the decorator out to their old Queens apartment to see if any of the furniture there could be salvaged for the move to Manhattan, but except for Jayne's piano, Stedila's verdict was to take nothing. "Calvin knew what he wanted, and I was very impressed," said Stedila, who did a rendering of the apartment for Calvin's approval. "He's a big person, and he needed a lot of open space, with large pieces of furniture. Calvin was obviously the one who was going to make the decisions. He was the arbiter of taste."

With Calvin supervising his every move, Stedila put six months of painstaking work into the apartment. He was the most particular and demanding customer for whom Stedila had ever worked. The tiniest detail had to be executed to absolute perfection before Calvin was satisfied, even if that required redoing things half a dozen times, from the patina of the paint to the fit of the electrical-outlet covers. The apartment that emerged from the construction rubble was well worth the months of arduous work. It was beautiful yet starkly cold—the cutting edge of the seventies minimalist movement, a stage set ready for a drama. The expansive living room featured a sixteen-foot, U-shaped, brown-suede sofa that Stedila had designed and built to order. Backless but strewn with large, plump pillows, the sofa floated on a stainless-steel platform and white base, surrounding a low, square coffee table. In other seating areas there were pairs of Marcel Breuer chairs and stainless-steel cubes for occasional tables. A Polito original hung on one wall, but most of the art was fashionably leaned on low ledges. There were no Bronx *tchotchkes* anywhere, and the primary artifact on display was the bleached antlers on a tall black pedestal. Jayne's gleaming black baby grand piano stood out against the muted diaphanous backdrops of translucent panels employed as sliding window treatments. The existing narrow kitchen was camouflaged with white stucco walls and cabinet facing and butcher-block countertops. Only Marci's room was spared the monotone minimalism. The five-year-old's room had cutely "pickled" navy blue floors, white walls, and a sky-blue ceiling complemented by white furniture. Calvin and Jayne's bedroom was more sensual, decorated in deep browns, with a beige goat-hair carpet on the floor, dark wood furniture, and a king-sized bed. A railed terrace surrounded the apartment on two sides, affording an impressive view of the neighborhood. The finished apartment was so striking that it was given a multipage layout in the *New York Times Magazine* section under the heading "The Anticlutter Approach," an unusual honor for the apartment of a relatively unknown garment-center manufacturer, however swanky. "We've spent a lot of money fixing it up," Calvin said of the apartment, but "Jayne keeps kidding me that the minute it's completely finished I'll want to move."

Calvin was so pleased with Stedila's work that he hired him to redesign his showroom, this time in a brighter, sleeker style more conducive to the showing of youthful American clothes than the hip but oppressive environment he had created on the fourth floor. Still, in keeping with Calvin's earth-tone theme, the showroom had many brown and beige touches to it, and since Stedila had already worked with him on the apartment, he should have known how exacting he could be about color. Sure enough, the color of the paint on one wall wasn't the "perfect" color Stedila had promised, and Calvin was on the warpath. Stedila was out of town on a work assignment on an isolated island in the Caribbean where there weren't many telephones, and it infuriated Calvin even more to discover that the only way to get in contact with the interior designer was to leave a message with a gas-station attendant. Calvin was so seething mad when he got the gas-station attendant on the line that the message he screamed into the long-distance wires was "Tell him, 'Don't ever come back to New York, because if you do, I'll ruin your life!' "

Stedila returned, but Calvin didn't ruin his life. In fact, he hired the designer to do yet another job—a dream apartment for Flo and Leo and Alexis—who continued to live with her parents at home while she went to school. With all the money coming in, Calvin was able to do something every good Jewish son dreams of doing—taking his parents with him out of the ghetto. Flo and Leo and Alexis got to leave the Parkway behind—if not as far as Manhattan than at least to a building near the cooling breezes of the Hudson River in the nearby suburb of Riverdale. In a gesture worthy of a Moss Hart play, Calvin notified the threesome that they were moving out of Rochambeau Avenue and leaving behind everything they owned, every stitch of it, all the second-rate Bronx furniture and antiques and appliances. Calvin was going to get them everything brand-new, the best money could buy. "Flo wasn't allowed to take one thing from her Rochambeau apartment," said one of her astonished mah-jongg partners, Laura Schwartz. "She got all new things. He had a decorator fix it up." The only problem with the decorator was that while Calvin wanted Flo to live in an apartment with Stedila's fashionable new look, Flo really wanted her fussy, faux-French furnishings from Rochambeau Avenue. "At first," said Stedila about the decorating process, "as long as there was a mah-jongg table, Flo didn't care. She set it up in the living room, and the ladies came and they played daily." But after most of the apartment was complete, problems began to develop. "It was a nightmare," said Stedila. "Flo couldn't get it. It was all very pale beiges with beige industrial carpet. The couch had pale beige fabric, and that was a point of contention with Flo. Calvin was paying the bills and we were doing a Calvin look and in the end it was disastrous. All of a sudden Alexis called to say the furniture was uncomfortable and they couldn't live with it, so I was fired. I think it was just a big shock to move into what was a very classy area."

Unabashed, Calvin even tried to gussy his folks up a little physically. He sent Flo to the $5,000-a-week La Costa Health and Beauty Spa in San Diego to get "streamlined," according to Laura Schwartz, who remembered, "Her [old friends] were completely dismissed." A few years down the road Flo could have anything she wanted, including an apartment in Sunset Lakes, Florida. Leo loved the Florida apartment, but Flo didn't like the heat, and she certainly didn't care for being away from her only granddaughter, Marci, upon whom the sun rose and set. Calvin even bought his mother's sister, Aunt Sylvia, an apartment, and sent Alexis to school to become an accountant.

Still, all his generosity didn't mean he wanted his Jewish relatives around the showroom. One day when Calvin was out to lunch, his Aunt Sylvia dropped by, and an employee had her sit in a chair in the showroom while she waited for him to return. Although he loved his aunt greatly, "she was fat and not well dressed," said someone who witnessed the event, "and Calvin returned screaming at the top of his lungs. He sent Sylvia to the back of the workroom and said to the woman who let her in, 'How dare you let them in the showroom? Put them in the back!' " Technically, this treatment didn't extend to his beloved father, Leo, who, although he, too, wound up in the back room of Calvin Klein Ltd. was at least employed there, as a bookkeeper. By now Leo was a needle-thin man with a stooped neck who reliably wore one of three sports jackets he owned to work every day over a print shirt. Employees remembered that when Leo was with Flo, he seemed more quiet and withdrawn than ever.

There was one family member Calvin was not able to help, and that was his older brother, Barry Klein. Barry was still living at home and working at his uncle's grocery store, eking out a living, and he resented it. Many people expected that with Calvin's newfound success he would hire his brother and give him a well-paying job in his growing organization, but Calvin didn't want to have Barry Klein anywhere near his business. Barry Klein's compulsive gambling continued apace. Barry told friends that after Calvin's initial monetary success his brother helped him out of a financial bind one time and never again. He said it wasn't because he didn't love Barry but that giving Barry money was just feeding his disease. To prove that he loved him, he happily paid for his older brother's wedding when he married in 1972 in Calvin's East Seventy-sixth Street apartment.

Barry and his new wife moved to an apartment in Manhattan, but the gambling continued apace, as did the phone calls to Flo for bailouts of money. Instead of being angry, Calvin decided to help. He began to understand that his brother's gambling was a compulsive disease over which he had no control, and that just like any other disease, you had to realize you were sick before you could heal yourself. Calvin went to the trouble to find out the names and phone numbers of three therapists who specialized in treating people with compulsive gambling disorders and met with his brother to give them to him. In an emotional moment he promised Barry that he would pay the entire therapy bill for as long as Barry was in treatment, no matter how long it would take, if only Barry would agree to get help.

But Barry lived in total denial, and his answer to Calvin was "Not me, I don't need treatment." Calvin never forgot that refusal.

It must have been rather irksome to Calvin that despite his disapproval of his brother's habit he couldn't dissuade his own partner, Barry Schwartz, from gambling with him. In the early seventies, just after Barry Schwartz struck it big with Calvin and bought a house in the New York suburb of New Rochelle, he would frequently invite Barry Klein and his wife to his gray colonial home for a Sunday of gambling. The two men's families would spend all day in the backyard, while the two Barrys bet with bookies on various ball games or horse races, sometimes doubling and tripling their bets or using complicated gambling schemes to parlay their money. They spent the afternoon glued to the TV and radio, listening for sporting results. One Sunday, according to intimates, the two Barrys ran their winnings up to $90,000. According to these confidants, the money came in handy, because it was at just one of those times that Calvin Klein Ltd. was expanding and temporarily tight on cash flow. Barry Klein claimed that Barry Schwartz asked to borrow $35,000 of his winnings to put into the business and that in a foolish show of bravado, he loaned Schwartz the money. A few months later, Barry Klein was back in the hole again and needed his $35,000 back, but every time he asked Barry Schwartz about it, he was stonewalled. Finally, Barry Klein complained to his brother, Calvin, about it, saying he wanted the $35,000 that he had loaned the business.

"What the hell are you talking about?" Calvin asked his brother. Calvin swore that Barry Schwartz had never told him about the money, that he had no idea he had made a "business loan," and that he would see to it the $35,000 was soon returned to his brother. When Barry Klein did get the money back, he lost it all yet again.

Barry Klein continued to pester Flo for frequent loans to pay his gambling debts, and "This is the last time" became a constant refrain. Although Calvin forbade it and Leo disapproved, Flo continued to secretly shell out money to her eldest son to pay his gambling debts—money she got from Calvin. It was Alexis who eventually discovered that her mother was surreptitiously funneling money from Calvin to Barry. Indignant, Alexis told Calvin about it, who put an instant stop to the charity.

"Then something incredible happened," said their old school pal Don Guerra. "Barry Klein [claimed he] hit on an enormous amount of consecutive wins, like eighteen baseball games in a row. He kept doubling up the money he bet so if he won $200, he made it $400, until it got to where he won, as I remember it, $135,000 or $150,-000. The bookies called up and said, 'Could we come and deliver the cash? We've never seen anybody hit these many games in a row. We'd like to meet you.'" Barry Klein told Guerra that two men came up to his place with a suitcase loaded with bills and counted them out on the bed. "I sat there looking at it, and I cried. I just cried," he told Guerra, "I don't know why. I always wanted a score like that, and there it was, and I didn't have the slightest idea what I was going to do next. I just ran my hands through the money and stared at it on the bed for a day before I made up my mind. I called up my uncle and told him, 'I quit, and you can take the job and shove it up your ass.'"

Then Calvin called him. "What are you doing?" Calvin demanded. "You can't *quit*. It's a family business. Uncle Ernie is very hurt by this. What are you going to do the rest of your life?"

"I'm going to bet baseball," Barry said.

Calvin said, "That's interesting. We'll see how long *that* lasts!"

Barry Klein eventually was able to buy a New York City cab medallion for approximately $43,000 in 1972. He has one son and continues to drive a taxi in New York City. Calvin and his brother rarely speak to each other and meet reluctantly face-to-face only on family occasions that involve Leo and Flo. Indeed, many of Calvin's closest friends don't even know he has a brother. Barry remains close to Flo, who long ago gave up working on a truce between her sons.

2

There remained one last convention of his Bronx background to be shed.

During the summer of 1970, while leafing through a fashion magazine, Calvin spotted a photograph of a young craftsman in his late twenties that was almost palpably compelling to him. There was something about the way the dark-haired man looked into the camera, his languid slouch against the bookcase, that drew Calvin back to the photograph over and over again. The man's name was Reginald Peters,* and not only did Calvin find him physically attractive, he was intrigued by his craftsmanship as well. For nearly a year Calvin kept the magazine in his possession, taking it out every now and then to stare at the picture of the handsome young man. Then, one day when Calvin and Jayne were preparing to move to their new apartment in Manhattan, Calvin decided to call Peters and ask to meet him under the pretense of hiring him to do some work in the apartment. Perversely, or perhaps as a defense, Calvin arranged to meet Peters for the first time in Jayne's company at the new apartment on a Sunday afternoon.

Peters remembered that Sunday quite clearly. It was hot and sunny, and when he rang the bell to the apartment, Calvin swung

---

*A pseudonym at the request of "Reginald Peters."

open the door and stood there smiling. The sun was streaming in the windows, silhouetting Calvin in his white linen pants and blue oxford shirt. "Jayne was sitting on the windowsill in the kitchen," Peters recalled, "very slim, very pretty, wearing a white blouse and khaki shorts." Although Calvin presented himself as a married man, interested in Peters only for business, the craftsman had his doubts. "I sensed an instant attraction between us," he said, and for a while the two of them pretended it did not exist.

The relationship developed slowly and cautiously over the next two months. Whenever Peters went to see Calvin on business, Jayne was always present. Peters didn't mind this at all, because he liked Jayne—almost more than he liked Calvin. She was chatty and warm, a good-hearted Jewish girl who liked to have a good time over a bottle of wine, which Peters shared with her on the many occasions the young couple asked him to dinner. He was enjoying his friendship with both of them when, one day, Calvin asked to meet him at the new apartment alone. Peters was only mildly surprised. He remembered an expectant tension in the air that day, and sure enough, when Peters tripped on some construction material on the floor, Calvin caught him by the arm, and the two exchanged a shy, embarrassed look. Then, according to Peters, the grip on his arm became an embrace, and in another moment the men were kissing. "The relationship began that day," said Peters, "and continued for another year and a half, nearly two years."

Much to Peters's growing chagrin, it was not a dreamily romantic liaison. "I thought I was in love," said Peters, "but I don't know what he thought. I don't know what goes on in people's minds. Calvin would always talk about how much he really loved his daughter. In that way, there was a marriage. He really loved Marci—he said it all the time—and I think she adored him."

Calvin seemed to enjoy the sex, at least physically, but distanced himself from his partner emotionally, so much so that Peters said he felt no personal guilt that Calvin was married, nor did he think of himself as a home wrecker. Indeed, Calvin's marital status only seemed to add to the excitement of the relationship. Calvin also let Peters know that this was not the first of his extramarital dalliances, confessing that he had experienced other gay encounters without Jayne's knowledge, but always in Europe, when he was on business trips. "He said he had 'Sex in Europe,'" said Peters, "but that he didn't dare do it in the United States for fear that anyone would find out." As for Calvin's sexual technique, Peters said, "he was hardly inexperienced."

The great majority of assignations between Peters and Calvin took place on Wednesday nights at Peters's uptown apartment. "Wednesday nights Calvin and Jayne both had off," said Peters, "no questions asked." There were also rare occasions when Jayne was out of town with Marci when Peters was invited to share Calvin's own marital bed, but that was only when Calvin was absolutely certain there was no possibility they could ever get caught. He dreaded discovery. "One weekend," remembered Peters, "friends of mine—a married couple—loaned us their house in Connecticut so we could get away and spend a romantic two days in the country. Jayne thought Calvin was going away on business." However, the couple who owned the house returned inexplicably the second day. Calvin stormed around the house a beet-red color and generally behaved as if he had been caught red-handed having a "dirty weekend." Within a quarter of an hour he insisted that Peters make his apologies to their hosts and leave with him at once and return to Manhattan. "I think Calvin was very discreet in what he did," said Peters. "He was in the windows of a lot of stores at the time, but it wasn't his image that was the issue. It was more 'Let's not tell Flo and Alexis.'"

The ruse worked well enough. "I'm sure Jayne didn't know I was having an affair with her husband," Peters insisted. "Her father was so obviously gay that to her the way Calvin acted was just normal for a man." In fact, she grew to be quite fond of Reggie Peters over the years and always included him in her social plans. "Why don't we have Reggie for dinner?" she would ask Calvin, or, "I'm going to my mother's house, why don't you and Reggie go out to a movie together?" One pal of Calvin's assumed that Reggie was Jayne's friend, not Calvin's, they seemed so close. Peters was also their houseguest at their rented Hampton cottage one weekend during which the two men could not help but pass furtive smiles. Still, Jayne finally came to suspect at least that Peters was gay. One night, when Calvin was unable to attend the party of a designer who lived on Park Avenue, he asked Reggie Peters to be Jayne's escort. Peters is uncertain what transpired at the party to make Jayne wonder about his sexual preference, but the next day, Calvin called him on the phone and laconically told him, "Last night Jayne asked me if you were gay."

"Oh, my God," Peters said. "What did you tell her?"

"I told her no," Calvin said, and the two men laughed. Even if Jayne didn't realize her competition was another man, she sensed something was wrong. "There was tension," Gina Epworth said. "Jayne became suspicious of every moment he was out of her sight." Once, remembered Epworth, when Calvin went to Paris on business, Jayne tried calling him several times at his hotel over the weekend, and he wasn't there. "She began calling me every fifteen minutes," said Epworth, "asking, 'Do you know where he is?' "

"He doesn't report to me, Jayne," Epworth told her. "Did you try his hotel?"

Jayne said she tried his hotel several times but he was never in.

"Well, you know, it's a weekend," Epworth said, trying to calm her. "Maybe he went south; maybe he flew to Cannes or to Nice. Maybe he wanted to see what was going on. You don't find anything out just by sitting in a hotel room."

Epworth came into the office on Monday and told Barry what she had told Jayne over the weekend. "My God," Barry said, "all she'll think of is he's somewhere playing around on the Riviera." Calvin brought back for Jayne some exquisite costume jewelry that he had found in Paris to smooth over his disappearance, and things calmed down—for a time.

In retrospect, said Epworth, "Maybe Jayne *was* aware of what was happening. I look back now and I think she may have sensed something was wrong."

3

Another signal something was wrong might have been Calvin's new friendship with forty-one-year-old Chester Weinberg, the debonair dress designer and dapper darling of the Ladies Who Lunch set. Jayne liked Chester well enough—everybody liked charming Chester, but Jayne knew in her gut that Calvin's new closeness with

Chester Weinberg was another step further down the line to losing her husband. Indeed, those who knew the ballad of Calvin and Chester say that Chester either gave Calvin the key to life or led him down the path to destruction. A few believed that at first Chester was nothing more than another addition to the retinue of taste-makers Calvin was collecting. "Calvin recognized early in his career," said a close observer of the two, "that there was a lot to learn and few excellent people to learn from. In a sense he created somewhat of a Renaissance environment with people like Chester." Others felt that Chester was different from the start and that Calvin and Chester really loved each other, a deep, abiding, platonic love that strengthened over decades of personal history. Either way, said an intimate of them both, "Calvin didn't begin to live, to exist, really, to have any personality, until he became friends with Chester Weinberg."

Chester was a compact man with a wide nose, black hair, and brown eyes, quick to show a warm smile and perfect rows of pearly white teeth. He might have met Calvin through Eve Orton or, as Gina Epworth remembered, on a press junket to Chicago in early November 1969, where Bonwit Teller was inaugurating a store in the newly opened John Hancock Building. Mildred Custin herself had handpicked two dozen of her favorite designers—"all of Seventh Avenue in one fell swoop," as a Bonwit executive put it—to attend the gala opening party. Included on the junket were Halston, Oscar de la Renta, Bill Blass, Geoffrey Beene, James Galanos, Chester Weinberg, and Calvin Klein, who was elated at being included in this cosmos. By the time he came home from that short trip, he was so smitten with Chester that he couldn't stop talking about him. Later, he appeared at Chester's showroom with Jayne in tow and announced, "You're the only designer I want to dress my wife."

Calvin brought Jayne with him as a shield, because from the moment he met Chester, he sensed that the older man was attracted to him, and while Calvin didn't want to encourage the attraction, he wanted to use it. Indeed, Chester practically melted every time Calvin leveled his light emerald eyes at him. But while Calvin wanted to take advantage of Chester's interest in him, he wanted to keep the relationship platonic. Calvin's first defense against Chester's infatuation was a living demonstration of his status as a loyally married straight man—Jayne. Chester later giggled with his friends and asked, "Who does he think he's kidding?"

Chester well knew who Calvin was kidding because he had kidded himself most of his life. He, too, was a gay man who fought tooth and nail against his homosexuality. He was brought up on Manhattan's hardscrabble Lower East Side in a family not all that different from Calvin's; his parents owned a newsstand near the White Turkey Restaurant on Madison Avenue. Drawing and art were a marvelous escape and pacifier to him as a boy, and he developed a near photographic memory for patterns and paintings and architectural design. A brilliant scholar, he held degrees not only from the High School of Music and Art but from the Parsons School of Design as well as a bachelor of science from New York University. After years of anonymous work on Seventh Avenue he obtained backing for his own business in 1966, and his soft, pretty dresses, with their trademark ruffles, became a favorite with fashionable socialites, including automobile heiress Charlotte Ford and stockbroker's wife Jane Holzer. The women who bought from him were as taken by his charm and witty small talk as by his dresses, and before long Chester was taken up by fashion society and himself considered one of Manhattan's "beautiful people."

Chester fascinated Calvin. He was a man who understood the subtleties of a finer life. He lived in a sumptuously decorated East Fifty-seventh Street apartment that boasted paintings by Chagall and Miró, whom he counted among his friends, as well as a Rodin head. Chester slept in the robber baron Jay Gould's very own antique bed and employed a Savile Row tailor to make his impeccably styled suits. He wore Turnbull and Asser evening shirts, which he had laundered in Paris, and he visited a Madison Avenue barber once a week to tend his thinning black hair.

Chester had been in psychotherapy for most of his life to try to convince himself he could be "cured" of homosexuality. In the fifties and sixties the American Medical Association as well as most mainstream therapists considered homosexuality a "disease," and Chester spent torturous years in treatment for his alleged sexual dysfunction. He had several women friends with whom he would dutifully go through the motions of sex—to no avail. Chester could no more change his sexual orientation than a heterosexual man could force himself to become gay. But whenever he strayed, sharing a few hours with another man, his psychiatrist threatened to end therapy, thereby consigning Chester to what he believed would be a life of doom.

Doom it seemed to be for many years. In the late sixties Chester was arrested in a gay club for dancing with an undercover cop. When he finally did summon the courage to settle down with a live-in lover, he arrived home one night to find the man bludgeoned to death, probably by an anonymous trick he had picked up. As if discovering his lover with his skull bashed in was not bad enough, the police held him overnight until they were convinced of his innocence. To make Chester more unhappy, even when he eventually came to terms with his sexuality, he secretly felt he never really fit in the gay world because he wasn't pretty enough. It wasn't that Chester was so unattractive; it was that Chester wasn't perfect in a world where perfection and youth held such great value. "Because he felt physically ostracized in the gay world," said an intimate of Chester's at the time he met Calvin, "he always needed someone heroic in his life. . . . Calvin became the embodiment of everything he wanted for himself."

And so they were perfect for each other, the odd couple, the seductive young heartthrob and the brilliant but unattractive Polonius who would teach Calvin about the world, both the elegant and seedy sides. Chester's favorite role was mentoring younger men. It not only gave him some sense of control, but he was excellent in the part as well. He had the uncanny ability to communicate the philosophy behind good taste. In later years he became a valued teacher at Parsons School of Design as well as a guest lecturer at art and design schools around the country. But his mission with Calvin went beyond fashion lessons. "It wasn't just that he was his mentor in terms of clothing," said Karen Mann, Chester's cousin and friend. "He was his mentor in terms of everything about life, everything beautiful. When Calvin first met Chester, his taste level was nowhere." On Saturday afternoons, Chester would walk Calvin up and down Madison Avenue on a combination constitutional and tutorial, bringing him to galleries and antique stores, where he would point out *objets d'art* and discuss their significance. He would visit Calvin's apartment and say, "Honestly, Calvin, you've got to get rid of that chair," or, "Lose that terrible lamp," or with a withering glance and a raised eyebrow wonder aloud, "Calvin, did you know those pants make you look like you have no waist?"

Chester liked to tell the story of how one day he was picking out a service for eight at the shop of the exclusive flatware maker James Robinson. As Chester's purchase was being wrapped, the proprietor unctuously remarked that Chester had chosen excellent silver plate.

Chester said to unwrap the flatware immediately, that he didn't want the service if it wasn't real silver.

"Oh, but our silver plate is excellent," said the man. "No one will know."

"Oh, *I'll* know," said Chester. Instead, he bought one place setting in sterling silver and over the years built it to a service for eight, including coffeepot and Queen Anne candlesticks.

Like everyone else, Jayne was taken by Chester at the start, even as she watched Calvin being spun into his web. Chester and his lover, Michael Datoli, became friendly with Calvin and Jayne, and Datoli quickly sensed the strain in their relationship. He compared Jayne's role to that of the wife of a Hollywood movie star. "She was sort of left out . . . she was 'just the wife' and you get tired of that. . . . She's a person, too." Datoli remembered that when Calvin was off charming editors and the magazine people, Jayne began to seek out other people who also felt left out. "I don't think she tried to just stay by his side and just be the little wife," Datoli said. On occasion, Datoli would be her default companion at parties while Calvin and Chester were off networking, and he and Jayne would dance and drink up a storm in the corner, having their own good time. After the party they would go back to Calvin and Jayne's apartment, and Chester and Calvin would complain, "Damn it, you guys had a lot of fun. We had to be serious and talk fashion. . . ."

As time went by, Chester discovered that Calvin wasn't just hiding his gayness; he was in some unfathomable state of denial about it. Chester was appalled at this lack of self-knowledge. He was an opinionated man whose own credo was "Be true to thyself." "Doesn't he *know*?" he would ask his friends about Calvin. But many people who knew Calvin believed he was really straight and wrote off Chester's cynicism to sour grapes because Chester wanted every attractive man to be gay. Calvin continued to do everything possible to imply to Chester that he was a blissfully wedded man. It is of particular note that throughout Chester's decade-long friendship with Calvin, he was never aware that Calvin cheated on Jayne with Reginald Peters.

Chester was Calvin's tour guide in another crucial aspect of his journey: the use of social drugs. Calvin had already adopted vodka as his favorite drink (after discovering that scotch gave him a hangover) and was beginning to get dependent on alcohol as a way to loosen up in social situations. But as far as drugs were concerned—even marijuana—Calvin was still completely naive and more than a little afraid to experiment. Chester, however, was a great explorer of the unknown, and years before, he had fallen in love with marijuana and become its ceaseless proponent. For him, a grass high had magical liberating properties. He enjoyed conversation more, he felt more creative, sex was better. Over the years Chester had gone from taking one or two tokes on a weekend night to smoking joints throughout the day. In Chester's mind people were divided into two classes; those who did and those who did not smoke it. "He didn't trust you if you didn't smoke grass," said a close friend. For the longest time, Calvin resisted Chester's attempts to persuade him to try some. Calvin was brought up to believe that only the lowest of lowlives fooled around with drugs.

Then, in 1973, on one of his many nights out without Jayne, Calvin broke down and smoked some grass at the home of a respected magazine editor with whom he frequently socialized. They were having cocktails before going on to a business party at the Park Avenue apartment of a vice president of Loehmann's, one of Calvin's important accounts. In the familiar surroundings Calvin felt confident enough to have a few puffs. He was pleased to discover that the effect was much more benign than he had believed, and he doubted it would turn him into a raving junkie. He found himself feeling lighthearted and giddy when he was high, albeit a little intense. However, when they left the secure confines of the editor's apartment and arrived at the noisy, business-oriented party, Calvin thought he would go out of his mind, he felt so out of control. "He was really getting paranoid," said the editor. "He kept asking me, 'Do they know I'm stoned?' and, 'Do I sound like a jerk?' " They finally had to leave the apartment and go someplace quiet till Calvin came down.

However, that wasn't the end of it. He tried it again and soon found how to deal with the paranoid feelings the marijuana gave him along with the high. He smoked a joint if it was passed to him and eventually bought some of his own. The grass had opened up a Pandora's box that it would take him twenty years to slam shut.

4

In its second year in business, Calvin Klein Ltd. had a 50 percent increase in sales. Practically overnight enough money was coming in for Barry and Calvin to easily siphon off fat six-figure salaries— sums only dreamed about on Mosholu Parkway or at the Sundial Supermarket.

Success turned out to be even more consuming than the striving for it had been. It was a heady, intoxicating time for Calvin and Barry, a period they would remember with great affection for the rest of their lives. The two of them displayed a tireless dedication at the start. They often slaved seven days a week, from early in the morning till late at night, and they relished every second of it. "There isn't any job in the place I haven't done," said Calvin, "and I'm really proud of it. It's really true that if you're going to be successful you have to work at it hard. I'm completely disorganized about everything except my business." He bemoaned that "I should exercise. Some morning my back kills me just bending over to brush my teeth. But I don't have the patience. Two years ago I joined a gym. I was so exhausted the evening I went that I took a cab from Thirty-ninth to Thirty-fourth Street. I paid two hundred dollars but never went back."

Barry was no less a workhorse. He immersed himself in the arcana of the garment industry, discovering that the rag trade was not much different from running a Harlem grocery store—dog eat dog, survival of the fittest. The cutthroat aspect of the business was a challenge to Barry, and he was determined to become the meanest, toughest son of a bitch on the block. The way Barry explained his business tactics was "I don't cultivate people. It's easier if people don't like you. It's true that I hold grudges. What's more, I have total recall. I don't forget it when I'm crossed." The adrenaline rush of the season-to-season gamble was almost better than the track. In this race you were betting on yourself.

Although Barry and Calvin thought they knew each other like brothers when they first went into business, even they were surprised at how smoothly their partnership meshed. "If you were good for Calvin," said one employee, "Barry could be terrific." As the years progressed, their trust in each other became legendary. "It's very unusual to find someone like Barry Schwartz who is willing to completely subvert himself for someone else and just tend to the business aspects," said a chum of Calvin's. Indeed, Barry wasn't the type to find satisfaction in seeing his picture in *Women's Wear Daily*. Barry's big kick was becoming known as the mailed fist behind Calvin Klein. It was a phenomenal feat to be in such synch, considering the tensions of the business and how different they were. Barry was thinking about collecting stamps and buying racehorses as an investment, and his idea of a weekend out was to take his two children, a son and a daughter, to an Adirondack Mountain amusement park where the family would compete in rowdy skeetball tournaments. Just to see their offices was a mark of their differences. Barry's was decorated with dark wood furniture and plants and photos he had taken of his family and of wildlife on an African safari vacation with his wife. Calvin's office was clinical white, with a large white table instead of a desk. Yet there was a path in the carpet worn between the two offices as the two men became more dependent on each other in business.

Barry never made a fashion suggestion to Calvin. The most he would say upon seeing a coat or dress was "That's a meat-and-potatoes item." According to one of Calvin's assistants, Barry "adored" Calvin, and from the start the two partners made a pact never to allow anyone to drive a wedge between them. If an awkward question came up that pertained to business, Calvin *always* said, "Ask Barry," or, "What does Barry say?" In fact, "What does Barry say?" or "What does Calvin say?" became company policy. Calvin couldn't have been more confident: "I give Barry my collection" was the way Calvin described the relationship, "and he turns it into money."

The creative chores of Calvin Klein Ltd. quickly became too nu-

merous for any one person to handle, and like almost every designer in the business, Calvin hired a "little designer" to help him
generate ideas. His first professional assistant, whom he hired in
1971, was a twenty-two-year-old student named Charles Suppon
whom Chester had highly recommended. Chester first met the Illi-
nois-born apprentice when he was guest lecturing at the Institute
of Art in Chicago. Suppon idolized him, and when he moved to
New York to attend Parsons, he yearned to work for him, but Chester was experiencing some business hardships and couldn't afford
to hire him at the time. The guy to work for, enthused Chester, was
Calvin. "Trust me," he told Suppon, "he's gonna do okay. He's *real*
aggressive." Calvin hired the novice designer totally on Chester's
say-so. "I didn't know where to get accessories," said Suppon, "I
didn't know how to sketch, but Calvin hired me, anyway." Suppon
also remembered that once he got the job, Chester would drop
hints to him that he would like to get to know Calvin more inti-
mately. "Don't you think Calvin and I would be good friends?" he
once asked.

For the next four years, almost uninterruptedly, Charles Suppon
shared an office with Calvin and observed his life. A tremendous
amount of responsibility fell to young Suppon, who slowly became
responsible for the nuts-and-bolts designing while Calvin slipped
easily into the no less taxing role of inspiration and editor. Suppon
quickly learned that he was working for a taskmaster and perfectionist who plied his craft with a passion. Suppon was expected to
be in the office no later than nine and sometimes to work ten- or
twelve-hour days if there was a collection to get out. More than
anyone, Calvin set an example with his long hours, and Suppon
noted that he was so driven to success that he would not go to the
bathroom until after 5:00 P.M., when the phones quieted down and
he would lock himself in a private toilet for a half an hour. That he
developed hemorrhoids became a crude office joke.

Suppon also discovered that just as time was saved, so was every
penny. If men's clothing had to be bought for use in a fashion
show, it was later resold to Calvin's friends. Samples and showroom merchandise were sold as well, and Calvin Klein Ltd. began
to develop a very good "Saturday business." This was cash-flow
icing on the cake. "Every Saturday," said Suppon, "they'd sell

wholesale to women, little Jewish women who go on Saturday to the closed garment center." These shoppers would go from building to building, whispering to the elevator men, "Who's selling wholesale today?" These were the same type of goods that Calvin's mother used to buy at Loehmann's—overruns, returns, and damages. "The salesgirls added ten dollars [to the price] and kept it," said Suppon. Eventually, the Saturday business was so good that "they hired a woman who did nothing but that."

Although it had previously been the company sales pitch that Calvin was the "American Yves Saint Laurent," Suppon was more than a little disillusioned to discover just how much Calvin borrowed from the superstar Parisian designer. Suppon quickly learned that the roots of Calvin's line were sometimes grown overseas at an Yves Saint Laurent boutique. Saint Laurent was moving away from being a rarefied couturier and shifting his attention to street fashion—tailored, tasteful clothes that appealed to women with careers. Calvin sensed that the look was just the thing for the millions of American women who were forcing their way out of the secretarial pool and becoming geographically mobile professionals. "Calvin, number one, wanted to make money," said Suppon, "and had no qualms about copying Yves Saint Laurent's pleated pants or Saint Laurent's trench coat. Yves Saint Laurent charged two hundred and fifty dollars, and Calvin charged only ten dollars, but the garments were identical right down to the four-hole mannish buttons." Suppon remembered that during the years 1971–75, he would frequently travel to Frankfurt and Paris with Calvin, just as Calvin had schlepped to the European fashion capitals with Dan Millstein. Calvin always stayed at the Bohemian left bank L'Hotel and rarely socialized with Suppon except on daytime clothes-buying sprees. "Calvin would go to Paris to shop on his way back from the fabric fair in Germany," said Suppon. "Only he would never buy fabric there, but get samples to be knocked off cheaper in the Far East. In Paris he would go to the Saint Laurent boutiques and go through the merchandise and buy clothing by the dozens to bring back with him. He'd hold up a jacket and say, 'I know I can really sell this in the Midwest.'" Back in New York, Calvin's staff patternmakers would make copies of the garments he brought back with him. The samples would be revised to Calvin's taste for the

American market and put into the line. Eventually, the similarities in designs did not go unnoticed by the press and buyers, who, said Suppon, would refer "under their breath to the clothing as 'Calvin Saint Laurent.' " Calvin soon decided that he should no longer be referred to as the "American Saint Laurent." The comparison had grown too dangerous.

Up until the fall line of 1972, Calvin had been making mostly two-piece suits and coats. As much as he wanted to branch out into other apparel, there was resistance among buyers and retailers. In the early seventies the fashion business was most comfortable pigeonholing designers, who were not expected to stray beyond their original forte. Calvin was pegged strictly as a coat-and-suit man. Determined to change that image with his fall 1972 line, Calvin presented his "coatless collection," as it became known, although Charles Suppon, who helped put the show together, remembered a coat or two sneaking out on the runway. Drastically minimizing this money-making section of his previous collections shocked the press and buyers into the recognition that Calvin was moving on. It was also in this collection that his theories about the American woman's ideal wardrobe began to crystallize, emphasizing the interchangeability of sporty separates that could be mixed and matched for day and night. In this collection he showed slacks, · sweaters, blouses, dresses, and skirts, retaining his use of earth tones and classic fabrics. "Women can no longer be dictated to," Calvin declared. "Their lives have changed, and there is little time for wardrobe planning." Nor, he said, was it realistic to expect women to throw out their entire wardrobes and start again each year. If Paris wanted to try to continue to persuade them to do this, let Paris take the losses.

Yet it was not until May 14, 1973, that he really set himself apart professionally with the premiere of a seventy-four-piece fall collection that defined a personal "look" which would become as much his signature as his natural fabrics and muted colors. There was a sensibility to these clothes that was inevitably described as "uniquely American." During Calvin's career millions of words would be written about his contribution to fashion, most of them in an attempt to describe the "look" that pervaded his best work, but ultimately it was too ephemeral to be pinned down. "Clean" is the adjective most frequently used, referring not only to the clothing's lack of frills or gimmicks but to the simplicity of the lines and the way the clothes draped on the body. Within a year or so of this collection he would be known on Seventh Avenue as "Mr. Clean" or "Calvin Clean." Another marketing brainstorm apparent in his new line was that "sportswear can be very, very sensual." The "whipped cream" and polyester of earlier years was gone, replaced instead with checkered British wools, luxuriously soft gray flannels, as well as buttery meltons. The prices were higher now, too, because the natural fibers he was using were more expensive than the synthetics he had slipped unobtrusively into his initial collections. "Polyester feels slimy," Calvin announced. "It represents everything I hate. It's synthetic, it's fake, it's cheap."

Aside from his latest version of the pea coat, the highlight of Calvin's 1973 fall line was a double-breasted "big coat," so voluminous and warm that it was fit for an officer in the Siberian army. There were also several classic shirtdresses, one of them shown in a series of clinging matte-jersey versions for evening. Evening wear was something new for Calvin and "very dramatic" according to Elene Zeltner of Bonwit's, who promptly placed an order. Bloomingdale's Richard Hauser called the seventy-four pieces "one of the most exciting collections I've seen."

The fall 1973 collection had another impact on Calvin's reputation even before the sales figures came rolling in. On Thursday, June 21, 1973, just a month after the collection was shown, actress and socialite Dina Merrill tore open a sealed envelope in front of an audience of the international fashion press assembled in New York and read Calvin Klein's name as a recipient of that year's "Winnie," the Coty American Fashion Critics Award. Along with the black designer Stephen Burrows, Calvin was being singled out because he had established his own "school" of fashion, the "crisp and classic." Said a Coty official, "A fine designer's work is as recognizable by its unique 'brush stroke' and color palettes as that of a top painter."

When a *New York Times* reporter called Calvin to tell him, he was so dazzled that all he could think of to say was "*Wow*." After he caught his breath, he added, "I bet Barry will be pleased." So was Flo Klein. When Calvin phoned her bellowing, "We won! We won!," all her neighbors knew in ten minutes. She was so proud of him that she rushed to Cartier and bought him a tank watch with a congratulatory inscription. Calvin treasured the watch and swore to wear it always.

The attention-starved fashion industry liked to compare the Coty Awards to the Academy Awards' Oscar, which was like comparing a softball game on a sandlot to the World Series. The Cotys were begun in 1943, when the war cut off imports from Paris and American designers took center stage by default. Until the awards were stopped in 1988, it did not seem to bother many people in the fashion business that Coty Inc. was a perfume and cosmetics manufacturing company with its own partisan interests in the awards. In point, Dina Merrill was not only mistress of ceremonies of the announcements but a vice president of Coty as well. The award was supposedly kept honest because the voting committee consisted of fifty-seven independent fashion editors and reporters who made the nominations and four hundred other press members throughout the country who voted. Of course, most members of the nominating committee, like Eve Orton, Barbara Slifka, and *Vogue* editor Nicolas de Gunzburg, knew Calvin personally, as did many of the press corps. Indeed, the chairperson of the 1973 selections committee was Bernadine Morris, from the *New York Times*, whose daughter Cara was embarking on a modeling career and whom Calvin felt obligated to use in his shows. Morris even wore a Calvin Klein dress to the awards ceremony. Still, back scratching or not, the Coty was all the fashion industry had, and it was a ticket for Calvin into an aristocracy populated with giants like Norman Norell and Claire McCardell. The cachet it lent could be attested to by the stream of celebrity clients who suddenly appeared at Calvin's showroom, including Faye Dunaway, Lauren Hutton, and Calvin's most devoted celebrity customer, actress Alexis Smith, who was appearing on Broadway in *Follies* and graciously agreed to be one of Calvin's models at the Coty presentations.

That October, nine hundred of the fashion and social elite assembled in dinner jackets and gowns at Alice Tully Hall to witness Calvin and eleven other designers receive awards for excellence. During the two-hour awards ceremony each designer was given a few minutes to parade the most eye-catching pieces of his collection. In Calvin's two successive scenes he showed a smooth, fitted topcoat with a rich fur collar and then a big-pocketed suit and a sleek black "smoking" jacket (which Saint Laurent had recently popularized) with satin collar. Unfortunately, Calvin's sophisticated little show won only a restrained round of appreciation from the crowd. Audrey Smaltz, the fashion editor of *Ebony* and chairperson of the presentation committee, remembered there was ill-hid disappointment in the audience. "Calvin's clothes were all *gray*," said Smaltz. "It was *dull*, uhhhh. Dull. He did gray and camel hair. Oh, it was dull." It was newcomer Steven Burrows's brilliantly colored, skin-clinging jerseys that stole the evening. But while the crowd may have screamed the loudest for Burrows, they knew in their pocket books that it was Calvin Klein whose clothes were going to set the cash registers ringing around the country. Thus, it rankled Calvin even more that the following month it was Burrows, and not he, who was asked to exhibit his clothes at a joint international fashion show at the palace of Versailles to which the "best" French and American designers were invited. Halston, Oscar de la Renta, Bill Blass, and Anne Klein received invitations as well, and it burned Calvin that he wasn't included. He let everyone in his office know it. "He was furious for days," said Suppon.

Although some Coty winners were never heard from again, the award certainly lent a recipient a fleeting high gloss with the buyers. It brought with it sudden new visibility not just in the industry but with the public at large, and it became necessary for Calvin to upgrade his publicity office. Gina Epworth could no longer handle the task herself. Indeed, Epworth got the distinct feeling she was not wanted anymore, and Calvin made it clear to the middle-aged woman that he was marketing youth. "Calvin commented that he couldn't stand having old people around him," Epworth said, "and then he turned to me and said, 'Of course, you're an exception.'" Epworth refuses to discuss the final moment of her parting, flushing an angry red when asked why she cleared out her desk and quit. Barry was a gentleman to the last, said Epworth. He looked doleful and said with a sigh, "I thought you'd be with us all your life." Calvin did not feel so generously disposed to his first publicist. After she had left, he stalked into the model's dressing room where Charles Suppon was fitting an outfit and warned everyone, "I never want to hear Gina Epworth's name again."

Age was certainly not a consideration when Calvin hired his next public relations executive, because Eleanor Lambert was already in her mid-sixties when he became one of her many clients. This fluttery little lady with sea-blue eyes and perpetually blond hair was the great doyenne of fashion-business publicists, a charming and determined woman of humble background who had come to New York, married a multimillionaire publisher, and became the most desired and powerful fashion publicist in the business. Lambert was also a great innovator of promotional ideas, and she is credited with inventing both "market week," to bring out-of-town buyers to New York at the same time, and the Coty Awards, which she ran for two decades. Perhaps her most famous annual project was officiating over the International Best Dressed List. She had clout, class, and plenty of her own cash, and Calvin was lucky to be taken up by the lady who could help elevate his career a notch or two.

Lambert has one striking memory of her early days as Calvin's publicist. The two of them were lunching together at La Grenouille. Lambert seemed to know everyone in the room, and Calvin was duly impressed. During lunch she tried to feel him out about what he wanted from his career, what image he wanted to project, and what he hoped she could accomplish for him.

He was grasping to verbalize his vision for himself when the haute couturier Halston entered the restaurant and a frisson rushed through the room. Every well-coiffed head turned to see society's top dressmaker make his way to his table, looking like Darth Vader with his mirrored sunglasses and all black attire. All the magazine editors and billionaire's wives seemed to be vying to catch Halston's eye, swooning with pride if he deigned to stop by their table and say hello.

"*That*," said Calvin, watching Halston. "That's what I want."

CHAPTER EIGHT

It's the Citizen Kane syndrome. Calvin is just a little boy who never expected any of this to happen.
                    —an anonymous pal of Calvin's

It was the perfect start to the perfect career, and the perfect designer could not be openly gay, at least not the Best Little Boy from
the Bronx. Gay liberation was a fragile social force in the early seventies, and many of the mainstream Americans to whom Calvin
sold his clothes reviled homosexuality. Calvin continued to cultivate the image of himself as a happily married heterosexual. He was
careful to sprinkle references to Jayne and the baby in interviews,
observing, "My wife Jayne has superswell color taste. We fight." Or
proudly mentioning that Marci was old enough to "recognize my
stuff at fifty feet." Calvin could hardly not have noticed that in a
recent *New York Times* article by his friend Bernadine Morris, he
was singled out along with designers Ralph Lauren and Ilie Wacs
for the manner in which their clothes reflected "the way most people live today. . . . Perhaps not incidentally, each is married and has
children."

But no demand of propriety by the public put more pressure on
Calvin to be heterosexual than his own regrets. He was disappointed with himself for his furtive dalliance with Reginald Peters,
and as he grew weary of the sexual titillation, he began to feel dirty
and ashamed. After eighteen months he wanted to scrub clean and
head back to the straight and narrow where he really belonged.

As for Reginald Peters, he was privately surprised their relationship had lasted as long as it did. Since the time Calvin initiated

135

their affair, Peters felt he never really got to know him as anything more than a bedmate. Guarded and distracted when they were together, Calvin never furthered the relationship beyond that of a sexual partner. Therefore, it did not come as a big surprise to Peters when one night, about a year and a half into their affair, Calvin matter-of-factly told him, "I can't come back here anymore." Stunned by the cruel casualness of the proclamation, Peters protested little as a composed Calvin said goodbye and walked out the door. Calvin was true to his word. Although Peters and Calvin's paths would continue to cross in ways neither of them could have imagined over the coming years, that night was the end of their physical relationship.

It was Peters's distinct impression that Calvin was calling it quits not just because he feared for his reputation but because he was desperately trying to save his failing marriage. He had married the Best Little Jewish Girl in the Bronx, and he had an obligation to honor his vows. "I think," said one of Calvin's close friends, "that he was a very middle class Jewish guy who felt the marriage should work." And it wasn't just for Jayne's sake, either. It was for Marci. He had never known he could love anything as much as he loved that sweet little seven-year-old girl with the upturned nose. With every passing day he felt more responsible for her happiness.

Already, Marci was aware of the discord in her parents' life, and Calvin worried about her behavior. She was shy and withdrawn, and one night, while Calvin and Jayne were entertaining some business associates at a dinner party, she walked into the dining room in her pajamas and burst into tears, crying, "You're all talking about me! I know you're all talking about me!" Calvin and Jayne jumped up from the table and assured the little girl nobody was talking about her and put her back to bed. Calvin also told friends that sometimes he awoke in the middle of the night to find Marci standing next to their bed, a ghostlike waif, staring at him and Jayne.

But as much as Calvin's better instincts drove him to patch up the marriage, there was a chance it was too late. Miserable beyond bearing, Jayne no longer tried to play the perfect wife. "The marriage was bad by 1972," said a friend of Calvin's, "because I'd invite them to dinner and more than once Calvin would come by himself.

. . . There were excuses about why he was going out alone, like 'Jayne's not feeling well.' " Grasping for some way to persuade Jayne he was serious about salvaging their relationship, Calvin asked her to go into therapy with him with an Upper East Side psychologist. But that, too, fell apart. "Jayne only went once," contended her friend Jane Sternberg. Whatever Jayne heard at that first meeting convinced her that there was no point in trying to save the marriage. Some friends figure that Calvin was so convincing and compelling in telling his side of the story that Jayne felt she would never get a fair shake from the doctor. Jayne's women friends admired her for dropping out of therapy and believed she was taking a strong—and justified—position. Calvin, however, continued to visit the therapist, seeing him on and off for nearly the next twenty years.

As the acrimony mounted at home, Jayne's morale crumbled, as did her self-esteem. Desperately in need of affection, many friends believed that Jayne began to have her own affair in the summer of 1973 when she was living in their rented beach cottage in Amagansett, East Hampton. The friends say she took as a lover a blond and muscular local fireman whom she had met at a club. He was, said friends, about as far away in type as you could get from an effeminate women's clothing designer. Many close to Jayne believed that this dalliance was a revelation to her. Her virile fireman-lover was a restorative no therapist could have provided. According to one friend, he gave her "a pretty good sense of herself as a person. Until then she blamed herself for the problems of the relationship. [Now] Jayne realized it just wasn't all her fault . . . the other relationship helped her see there were big problems that weren't resolvable. . . . She just didn't feel as much of a women in her relationship with Calvin, and she hadn't for a long time. In retrospect, Jayne realized Calvin was more homosexual than heterosexual. She realized she couldn't have the kind of intimacy of a man-woman relationship. . . ." In fact, Jayne was said to have been so thrilled by the sex with the fireman that she decided to memorialize it by taking a photograph of his large penis, a souvenir she carefully hid from Calvin. Foolishly—or perhaps intentionally—she confided in her sister-in-law, Sherry Klein, about the affair and showed her the picture of the impressive endowment. Sherry told her husband, Barry Klein, and on one of the few occasions that Barry felt superior to his younger brother, he made Calvin come to his apartment to tell him the news: Jayne was cheating on him, and taking pictures of it, too. Calvin rushed home to Jayne in a rage, but she denied the affair. For a time, Calvin kept his own counsel. He lived in a glass house.

The couple were heading for catastrophe, and it finally happened one night that same summer of 1973 in Amagansett. Marci and Jayne were staying at the Long Island resort full-time while Calvin worked thirteen-hour days in the city during the week, joining them on weekends. According to one version of the story, late one night Calvin arrived in Amagansett to find a pickup truck parked in the driveway. According to friends of Calvin's, he raced down to the moonlit beach and discovered Jayne with a man. He later said it was one of the most horrible moments of his whole life—the last thing he had expected from Jayne. Despite his brother's warning, he somehow thought that Jayne would be faithful to him. "He felt very betrayed," said a friend, "devastated."

Gina Epworth remembered it was a Sunday when her home phone rang. It was Calvin calling for her husband, Lincoln. "Calvin said it was urgent he talk to Lincoln about a divorce," recalled Epworth, "and Lincoln told him to come right over to the apartment to discuss it." Epworth decided to give Calvin and her husband some privacy, so she left the apartment for the rest of the afternoon. Later that day, after Calvin had left and Gina returned home, the phone rang again. This time it was Jayne wanting to consult Lincoln about a divorce. Jayne was shocked to be told by Lincoln that "Calvin just left here." Making embarrassed apologies, he told her she would have to find another lawyer to represent her.

That she did, hiring a T. W. Rubin, Esq., of Madison Avenue. Allegedly under advice from his attorney, Calvin projected a gentlemanly image and let Jayne sue him for divorce, but as the lawyers began to spar with each other for position, armed camps were drawn. The antagonism grew so fierce that the couple were unable to be in the same apartment together, and Calvin moved out, first to a stylish hotel and then, so he could be close to Marci, to a one-bedroom furnished apartment in the East Sixties, a few blocks away from his old home. The day Calvin actually packed his bags and left, Jayne was torn apart, seeing her childhood dream in ruins. Then the anger welled up, and her first instincts were to change the locks behind him. But, she told her friend Etta Sherman, her lawyer reminded her that "Calvin was making money, and she could get a large settlement" if she played her cards right. Her lawyer advised, Jayne elaborated: "Don't change the locks. Don't show that you are locking him out. If he wants to come in any time, it's still his home."

Calvin's assistant, Charles Suppon, remembered that Calvin and Jayne met in a restaurant for lunch to try and discuss the details of the settlement civilly but that Calvin returned to the office steaming mad, complaining that Jayne had flared up and made a spectacle of them both. After that incident, Calvin's attitude changed drastically; embittered, he began to collect a dossier of evidence against her, said Suppon, who speculated that he planned to try to get the family court to declare her an unfit mother. "Jayne ended up getting a terrible reputation while they were breaking up," Suppon remembered. "Calvin would get phone calls about her in the office." What didn't come to Calvin unsolicited, he sought out, calling their mutual friends to look for tittle-tattle he could use against her. One of the most unlikely recipients of one of those calls was Reginald Peters. "I was surprised when he called," said Peters, who had expected Calvin's farewell to be his final word. "There are different voices for different Calvins, and this was a friendly voice at the other end of the phone. He was trying to get dirt on Jayne to minimize his financial exposure. I was asked a lot of questions by Calvin about Jayne. He wanted a swift divorce, and he was asking everybody if they knew about her having affairs so he could make accusations and get out quickly."

The divorce became final on August 29, 1974. The actual papers were sealed by the court to protect a minor—Marci—and indicated that whatever accusations were made against each other by her parents were damaging enough to cause her harm if they were made public. The exact terms of the divorce are still known only to the couple and their lawyers; however, Jayne told friends that the terms were in a sense designed around Marci's welfare, not Jayne's, and that Jayne would fare well as long as Marci benefited. The agreement also allegedly dissuaded Jayne from remarrying. "The apartment was in Calvin's name," said Jayne Sternberg, "and the agreement was that she could only live in it so long as she did not remarry. I remember thinking that wasn't very nice for such a wealthy man. You know, she *is* the mother of his child. . . ." Some also remember that Jayne's ability to date after the divorce was compromised, and Calvin was adamant that Jayne not allow men to stay with her in the apartment. Friends figured that in some mysterious way Calvin still regarded at Jayne as his wife. Once, when a divorcée whom Calvin knew started dating, Calvin blurted out, "What does your ex-husband think of *that?*" He blushed bright crimson when the answer was "He has no say."

Other friends remember that Calvin was very generous to Jayne despite the restrictions. "It was the best divorce in history," said one of them. "He was wonderful to her after the divorce." The couple's childhood friend Molly Ann Acker was especially impressed when Jayne told her that if she needed a driver and car for Marci— to take her to a doctor, for example—all Jayne had to do was call Calvin's office and say, " 'I need the car,' " and a chauffeured vehicle would appear at her building. Others saw that as exactly the kind of controlling thing Calvin did that was so unfair. "Jayne felt the divorce was turning her into Marci's handmaid," said Reginald Peters. "Calvin adored Marci, so nothing was denied her. Jayne was just there. He wanted his kid to travel first-class, and if the kid traveled first-class, the governess [Jayne] traveled first-class." Calvin also worried that Jayne spoiled the child in some unspoken competition for her affection. Sometime after the divorce was final, Calvin and Jayne flew up to Maine together to visit Marci in summer camp on Parents' Visiting Day. Jayne arrived at the New York airport laden with "enough toys to take care of an army of kids," said another parent who rode on the plane with them, and "Calvin was livid that she had so much stuff."

Within a relatively short time the couple managed to get back on civil terms not only for Marci's sake but for business purposes as well. Jayne was aware that to hurt Calvin's image would only damage herself and their child. Besides, she began to find that without marital obligations, and with the divorce behind them, she liked him again. She remembered that he could be funny and genuine, and she also knew that in his own peculiar way, Calvin still loved her. Jayne reciprocated by loyally sitting in the front row of his fashion show and accompanying him to the 1973 Coty Awards—wearing a Chester Weinberg dress. After the ugliness of the divorce had passed, she told Etta Sherman, "We get along better now than we did before. I can talk to him, I can ask him things. Now we don't argue. . . ." Sherman said, "He was still giving her everything [financially], and she was not having to put up with his artistic tantrums. . . ."

In fact, Calvin was making so much money that he did not seem to care what his new household arrangements cost. Mistakenly, said a pal, Calvin initially sent Jayne weekly alimony and child-support payments instead of the monthly ones called for in the financial settlement. "He just signed the checks," said a friend. "There was so much [money] there, it just wasn't thought about. . . . She took the money for a little bit and then just couldn't handle it." Jayne eventually told Calvin about his mistake and offered to return the money. He unconcernedly told her to keep it and use it to look after Marci.

Impressed with what appeared to be the perfect parting, one of Calvin's colleagues came to him for advice about his own marital problems. Calvin blithely recommended the therapist he had gone to see with Jayne and then began wistfully reminiscing about the golden days of his marriage and fatherhood. "There was a bitter-sweet quality to it," said the man, who was touched by the tenderness in Calvin's face as he spoke of Jayne.

As for Flo Klein, she was heartbroken over the divorce. She loved her *hammischer* daughter-in-law and thought the divorce was a terrible mistake. Also, with her mother's instincts, she might have sensed that this breakup signaled more malcontent on Calvin's part than he was letting on. Yet, after a while, it was as if the divorce had never really happened. After all, Jayne was still the mother of her only grandchild, Marci, and she was the first love of her anointed son. "Flo still considers Jayne her daughter-in-law," a friend said. "Flo will *always* consider Jayne her daughter-in-law."

2

Some say that Calvin did not break up with Jayne because of his emerging homosexual bent but because he was infatuated with another woman, a woman whose mysterious sexual allure might allow him to postpone the moment when he would finally have to submit to leading a life as a gay man.

Lizzette Kattan was an exotic beauty from Honduras whose lustrous black hair, sloe eyes, and tawny skin, inherited from Arab ancestors, had earned her a successful modeling career. Her lithe, almost boyish figure was a familiar sight in glossy fashion magazines and runway shows in Paris, Rome, and New York. Lizzette was first sent to Calvin's showroom as a fitting model, but he was not even around when she walked through the door and she was sent to a workroom to meet his assistant, Charles Suppon. It was Suppon who fell in love with her first. "She was so special and incredible and had this sparkle," Suppon remembered of that first meeting, "one of the greatest gals I ever met." She was also upbeat and mischievous and not at all uncomfortable being around gay men. Her stylishness so turned on Suppon that before she left that day he went to Calvin's office and told him that he just *had* to meet this wonderful young fitting model.

Some would like to dismiss Calvin's relationship with Lizzette as that of a "beard," the kind of woman a gay man takes around town with him to hide his homosexuality. But Lizzette wasn't a ruse. She struck a chord in Calvin he had not even known existed. He had never before felt quite so at ease with a woman. "Puppy love" was the way Billy Tsoutsos, one of Calvin's assistants, described the way they acted together. It was certainly a different feeling from the loyal, protective love Calvin felt for Jayne at the start. He had dreamed of finding a woman like this, one whose beauty was unmarred by the traces of feminine artifice that made most women seem so smothering to him. Lizzette was tomboyishly playful, yet willing to keep her emotional distance. Calvin was physically attracted to Lizzette as well, and yet he did not have to hide his other proclivities. Indeed, there was a mature openness toward bisexuality on Lizzette's behalf—she was a worldly creature to whom no pleasures of the flesh were intrinsically sinful. In fact, she understood none of the provincial conventions of the Bronx that kept Calvin so boxed in and was determined to help free him. "He used to just work and work and work and work until I came along," said Lizzette, "and then I ruined him."

If this was ruin, Calvin could not get enough of it. Friends remember that he was so obsessed with Lizzette that soon after his divorce became final, there was talk of his marrying her. "She was really hot, really gorgeous," said Fran Boyar, who modeled with her, "and they really fell for each other." Within time, Lizzette moved her possessions out of the residential hotel where she had been living and into Calvin's furnished apartment on East Sixty-fourth Street. On and off for the next three years, throughout various relationships Calvin had with other men, Lizzette was the great female love of his life. "We lived together seventy-four, seventy-five, seventy-six," she said, describing their relationship as so "intimate" that "we have something we want to protect."

Lizzette loved to dance and loved the New York nightlife, and she was the perfect carousing partner for him, always ready for adventure. They both had a penchant for foreign lands, and they roamed the world together, including one memorable trip to Brazil in the winter of 1975. "Just the two of us," recalled Lizzette demurely, "just to play around." Calvin and Lizzette's mutual friends also remember that particular trip well, because it seemed to them that Calvin returned more relaxed and open to sexual experimentation than before he left.

As the years went by, however, it became clear that neither Calvin nor Lizzette was ready to settle down—at least not with each other. What had once been an open relationship with no promises was becoming more constrictive. Lizzette began to show a possessive streak, remembered Billy Tsoutsos, who traveled the club scene with them. If Lizzette caught him looking "at another boy or another girl, she would walk away and huff and puff." Lizzette says it is she who ended the relationship, but another friend remembered that the couple's cohabitation ended with Calvin's putting Lizzette out, dumping her suitcases and television set unceremoniously in the hallway. Refuting this version, she maintains, "I left. I was interested in other things. I wanted to develop my career. My mind was somewhere else. I was the young girl." By 1976, Lizzette's modeling career was taking her to Italy more frequently than she worked in New York, and she fell into the *dolce vita* of the wild modeling world in Milan.

Calvin still pined for Lizzette and kept in constant touch with her, jealous of all the fun she was having. Kattan blossomed in Milan. Too intelligent and ambitious to model for the rest of her life, she was discovered by publishing magnate Guiseppe della Schiava, who hired Lizzette to be a fashion editor of the Italian edition of *Cosmopolitan* magazine and later named her editor in chief of the Italian edition of *Harper's Bazaar*. Calvin continued to pursue Lizzette with phone calls, always managing to find her whether she was in Rome, Florence, or Milan. He still had tremendous pull over her as well. Once, when she was off in the countryside of Italy on a location shoot for a magazine, he tracked her down "and demanded she come to New York," recalled an Italian *Bazaar* staffer, "and Lizzette left her job and went." Yet slowly, with time and space and circumstance separating them, they lost touch. Today Kattan is a diplomat, holding the post of Honduran counsel to Switzerland. She divides her time between Zurich and a villa in Milan, where she lives with her husband, an Italian industrialist, and their two children.

3

Lizzette Kattan was still very much in the picture, however, in the summer of 1974, when Calvin spent his first weekend in a house in the Fire Island Pines. Calvin had been invited out by an old chum of his from high school, Howard Garfinkle* who rented a modest house with several other gay men. Garfinkle had never known Calvin to be openly gay, and he wasn't surprised when Calvin accepted his invitation for the weekend only on the condition that he could bring his girlfriend, the model Lizzette Kattan, with him. Garfinkle said that was fine with him as long as she didn't mind spending the weekend in a house with four gay men. Calvin assured him she wouldn't. So it was slightly disconcerting to his host when Calvin

*A pseudonym.

called the day he was due to arrive to say that Lizzette had "other plans" for the weekend and he would be arriving alone by seaplane.

Fire Island is a paradisiacal wisp of sand and pine barrens on the Atlantic, stretching thirty miles, like a bony finger, along the southern coast of Long Island. Only a few thousand feet wide in places, it is composed of a string of communities, of which just two—the Pines and Cherry Grove—are predominantly gay. It is accessible only by ferry or seaplane, and the dreamy landscape is without the intrusion of roads and cars. In the Pines, where Calvin eventually bought his own home, the thick pine trees and holly forests were interrupted only by plank boardwalks meandering among the tasteful beach houses. These magnificent homes of sun-bleached wood were in great part inhabited by some of the most brilliant minds in the creative arts, and the architecture and interior design of each and every house seemed more perfect than the last. Sheltered from the mainland by its inaccessibility and shunned by outsiders as a homosexual vacation spot, the Pines was a Shangri-la and coming-of-age rite for gay men in the seventies—Sodom by the sea.

While Garfinkle was pondering the significance of Calvin's coming to the Pines alone, he was even more surprised to discover that once Calvin settled in, he didn't seem the least bit uncomfortable in a household of four gay men. Though he didn't ogle boys on the beach like the rest of the crowd, he was animated and friendly as they sat on the deck of the modest beach house, passing a joint around before getting dressed for Tea Dance. It was then that Calvin surprised the group by announcing that he had been to Tea Dance once before, the previous year, with his wife, Jayne. There was an embarrassed pause before the group went on to another topic of conversation.

Tea Dance was a Fire Island ritual, the name satirically taken from Britain's 4:00 P.M. national-beverage break. It described an afternoon disco "appetizer" before the main event later in the evening as well as an opportunity for cocktails and cruising. "Tea" took place at the Botel, a large dockside motel and discotheque complex overlooking the bay where the ferries came in. Just opposite the Botel was a long, wide dock that all summer long was filled with lavish yachts from around the world. The complex's multileveled outdoor decking was furnished with umbrella-shaded tables and lined by sturdy railings where a thousand or so spectators could lean or sit and pose and stare. Many participants came directly from the beach, tanned and dressed in brief bathing suits or shorts and T-shirts. There was an occasional queen in a caftan or sarong. The popular drink that summer was a bright, baby-blue, crushed-ice confection called a blue whale, and the curaçao dye had turned thousands of tongues at Tea Dance neon blue. The crowd danced in celebration of sunset, and when all light finally faded, they drifted home to rejuvenate for the evening's revels. Calvin was transfixed by the scene—so many beautiful bodies and such uninhibited revelries. His host remembered that Tea Dance was also perhaps the most uncomfortable moment of the weekend. Calvin was clearly intimidated by the many men who tried to catch his eye and get a smile out of him. He deftly pretended not to notice and clung to his housemates. Later, back at the house, another tense moment transpired when one of the other houseguests, a handsome black man, let it be known that he and Calvin could share a bed that night. Calvin pretended not to hear.

On Saturday night all the members of the house were invited to a theme party. In this land of make-believe, where the architecture and landscape were so perfect, the people had to look perfect as well, and it was commonplace that color themes were established for parties. The theme that night was "Black and White," and Calvin, feeling a little foolish, obediently decked himself out. There is a photograph of him taken that evening with his arm draped in a comradely gesture around the shoulder of one of his weekend housemates, a tall, bare-chested, blond, mustachioed man with a surfer's build. Calvin is shirtless as well, dressed in soft black drawstring pants, a black T-shirt draped around his neck, from which dangled, necklace style, a cigarette lighter on a black cord. A carefree grin plays on his lips.

What happened the next day seemed like a sign from the wrathful gods. His treasured Cartier tank watch—the one his mother had given him on the occasion of his winning the Coty Award in 1973—"disappeared," said a housemate, "maybe from his bedroom." Everyone in the house was mortified as Calvin's mood turned dark and accusatory. He called all the other people they had visited over the weekend and asked if anyone had found his watch.

Alas, it was gone forever, and a dour Calvin left for the mainland on Sunday afternoon.

4

It caused nothing less than a sensation in the fashion press when, in October 1974, Calvin was presented with a Coty Award for the second year in a row, this time a "return" award, cited by the Coty committee as a "noted sportswear designer." Gone forever would be the curse of suits and coats. This time, during his moment in the spotlight at Lincoln Center's Alice Tully Hall before an invited audience of a thousand fashion professionals, instead of showing a monochromatic line, Calvin showed a brightly colored resort collection of eye-popping shades of bougainvillea and malachite green, as well as a *"carnevale"* look in oranges and limes. For the finale, he presented a line of cardigan sweaters coyly opened to reveal bikini bathing suits. Calvin beamed proudly backstage as the audience burst into cheers.

As the accolades grew, so grew his grosses. The phone began to ring incessantly in the offices the day the award was announced, and it didn't seem possible that Calvin could become much hotter or more important in his field. Business soared into the stratosphere on West Thirty-ninth Street. Revenues leaped from $3 million to $17 million by the end of the calendar year. The merchandise was flying out of the stores. During the winter of 1975, Bloomingdale's sold over three thousand pea coats and was still reordering them into the warmth of the spring. Saks sold seven thousand gabardine pants in one season, a figure unheard of in the garment business. All locations of four major chain department stores—Bloomingdale's, Saks Fifth Avenue, B. Altman, and Bergdorf Goodman—set aside windows for the exclusive display of Calvin Klein clothing and had implemented weekly major newspaper and magazine advertising campaigns as well.

Most stores were lucky even to get Calvin Klein merchandise. Barry and Calvin could pick and choose to whom they wanted to sell, and if a store was late paying bills or complained about the merchandise or—gulp—*dared* to try to return unsold goods, Barry cut them from his list, and they were banned. "In almost every major city there are stores we don't sell," Barry said, "and once we close an account, we never reopen it. I'm stubborn, I'm hard, but I'm also fair." Retailers did not always see it that way. Charles Suppon remembered that as soon as one buyer from a big account made a justifiable complaint about a shipment, Barry threw her out of the showroom and walked her to the elevator to make sure she got on. Barry had already pruned down to five hundred select stores in 1973, to four hundred stores in 1975, and to a goal of only three hundred of the most elite chains in America by the end of 1976. By 1975 the company employed the services of forty-one factories in New Jersey, Pennsylvania, Virginia, West Virginia, Massachusetts, Connecticut, and New York, and they still couldn't move the merchandise out fast enough. Calvin also granted the giant Toa-Bo Spinning Company a license to reproduce his entire line for sale in Japan. There were also extensive plans for their own in-store boutiques, at Bloomingdale's and Kaufman's in Pittsburgh, with plans for "at least a dozen shops open by fall," said Barry. "It's just a question of choosing what store we want in each city." Also: "The business had gotten too big to control manually," Barry said, and state-of-the-art computers were installed everywhere to handle the complexity. "We can easily see this becoming a thirty-million-dollar-business in the next three to five years," Barry bragged, never guessing for a moment just how low that figure would turn out to be.

The company had grown large enough to warrant taking over the entire fourth floor of 305 West Thirty-ninth Street as well as the eleventh. Calvin now had *five* design rooms, with three tailors and a patternmaker in each. There were assistants, secretaries, clerks, and bookkeepers. Calvin was far too busy to see most of the buyers himself, and an experienced sales staff took three duplicate collections around the country for "trunk shows" at the stores each season. As it was, Calvin was constantly on the move. In a one-year period from 1974 to 1975, Calvin made fabric-buying trips to Paris, Scotland, Rome, and Frankfurt, besides taking vacations in Egypt and South America, visiting the West Coast on business several times, and once, during Christmas vacation, he took Marci to Disneyland.

Calvin's days became so hectic and long that in addition to having his executive secretary, he found it necessary to employ a former marine corps corporal named Maxine Furstenberg as an "executive assistant" and factotum. "I find I have to have a staff to help me," said Calvin. "I can't be bothered." Corporal Furstenberg had an audience with him for half an hour once a day during which he assigned her her duties. "He has to be free to do other things, to concentrate on his designs," she said. "I take care of trivia," which included such chores as making sure his personal wardrobe was pressed and cleaned and that the florist had delivered fresh orchids to the office.

And yet, for all the modernization and computers and assistants, there was no real delegating of responsibility at Calvin Klein Ltd., because the bigger the business became, the more Calvin and Barry became determined to do it themselves. They mistrusted everybody else. They were not trained in management techniques and had no interest in learning them. "There was an attitude," said one executive who worked with them, "that everybody else was wrong and that Calvin and Barry were right. You were going to do it their way or you weren't going to do it."

Said another top executive with the company, "It was really run like a mom-and-pop operation. It was very unprofessional. Nothing could be done without Barry's permission. I was a vice president, and I didn't have my own key to the premises. I was trusted about the same as the lowliest mail clerk. It was the kind of place where the principals made *all* the decisions. I don't even think there was an office manager." This executive remembered that an air of suspicion pervaded the firm and that all the women employees had to show the contents of their handbags and shopping bags to a security guard before they left the premises at the end of the day to prove that they weren't stealing merchandise. "Taking over his father's grocery at such a young age," said the executive, "Barry learned [not] to trust anyone and to be tough with everybody, that everybody takes advantage of you and everybody is going to steal from you. It's a real ghetto store-owner mentality, so you must forgive him." However, not many ghetto store owners owned a growing stable of racehorses, went on private safaris to East Africa for summer vacation, or bundled themselves into the best bespoke suits to go to work every morning.

One way Barry and Calvin saw to increase revenues without adding to their work burden was to expand their already healthy licensing program. By 1976 licensing would be netting the company $6 million with relatively little investment of time or money. With licensing, Calvin could let a manufacturer with expertise in each individual field have the headaches of turning out the line and in return take a cut of the profits. Licensing fees could escalate anywhere from a few percentage points to, in rare cases, as high as 20 percent—depending on how good the sales were. In order to develop a roster of licensees, Calvin and Barry hired Hermine Mariaux, a former vice president and director of Valentino in America. Mariaux remembered that Calvin's philosophy about licensing was "I don't want to be there first; I want to be there when it sells." Since Calvin was selling a "total look" to his customers, it made sense for him to design the shoes and hats and handbags to wear with his outfits.

Mariaux's first action was to insist he retain one of the country's top attorneys, Charles Ballon, to handle licensing deals. The elderly lawyer's firm, Phillips, Nizer, Benjamin, Krim and Ballon, already represented many of the who's who of fashion as well as many corporate clients. One of Calvin's licensees remembered that the impeccably dressed Ballon was nicknamed "Mr. Ambassador." "He was like their father," said the business associate. "Charles Ballon would keep decorum. It was wonderful when Charles was in the room, because he was able to keep them calm. They would always defer to Charles and ask Charles his opinion."

Ballon reviewed the small print on their first megadeals, including one with Isetan, the upscale Japanese department store, which would reproduce every item in Calvin's repertoire, shortening the sleeves of his designs to make them fit the petite national build. The Canadian company of Omega was signed to manufacture Calvin Klein belts; Vogue Butterick would manufacture Calvin Klein patterns in the United States and Canada; Mespo Umbrellas agreed to turn out Calvin Klein bumbershoots for all of North America.

Perhaps most important to his image was Calvin's coup in landing as his very first licensee Alixandre, the famous furrier. Edwin Schulman ran the prestigious firm, which manufactured the most sumptous furs for the world's top couturiers. It was Schulman's job to bargain with Barry. "He's tough but he's fair," Schulman said, "and he speaks for Calvin, which means I always know who I'm negotiating with. Schwartz doesn't worry about stepping on your toes, but he won't put a knife in your back. He's a professional." Calvin joined two other designers who licensed their lines with Alixandre, Viola Sylbert and Hubert de Givenchy. The most expensive top-of-the-line creations were the realm of Givenchy, and Calvin was expected to design the "sportier," more affordable furs. At the June 1974 premiere of Alixandre's fall line, Calvin's startling collection of coats and jackets was the curtain raiser. A procession of haughty models sauntered down the ramp in slinky "tube" coats of coyote and fox, dyed in strikingly unusual tones, like cinnamon raisin. There were also full-cut minks with raglan sleeves and a Jazz Age–style raccoon that the *New York Times* pronounced perfect for blizzards. Naturally, there was also his signature pea coat—only this time it was made of sable.

5

It was a bittersweet irony that Calvin was now successful enough to become a patron of one of his idols in the business, the Baron Nicolas de Gunzburg.

The baron needed a job. By the mid-seventies, Diana Vreeland's grip on *Vogue* had been pried loose, finger by finger, by Condé Nast publications, and Nicky, too, was "let out," said the baron's friend John Weitz. "It was pathetic, because he was basically not a man who contributed anymore, but he was around, and everybody loved him." Not long after the baron was put on a Condé Nast pension, Calvin began to receive phone calls from the aging aristocrat, who was mortified to admit that he was slowly going broke. Said Charles Suppon, at first it was "a new set of tires for his car" or a "new sewer" for his New Jersey house, and Calvin always said of course, he would send a check right away, or perhaps the baron would drop by the office and give him some advice and he could pick up the check then. It pained Calvin to see his idol on the dole, but at the same time it was an opportunity. "Eventually," said Suppon, Calvin saw a chance to have a real-live baron and fashion star in his stable, and "the baron was hired as a consultant."

Having the baron's taste and opinion on call when Calvin wanted it was nothing short of a miracle for a designer like him, who was a better editor than he was an original thinker. As a consultant to Calvin Klein the baron was expected to go over the early stages of a line with Calvin, to help pick fabrics, advise on the procedure for fashion shows, or just chat about trends over lunch, but he was never required to keep to a schedule. Fashion was his life, and if it made the baron happy and gave him self-worth to be able to sit in an office one or two days a week and offer his opinion, Calvin was happy to oblige him. Slowly, however, the evolution of fashion to a new casualness passed the baron by, and rooted in the Old World elegance he so treasured, his advice became esoteric and rarefied. Even on the few days a week he showed up at Calvin Klein Ltd. there was little for him to do. On especially slow days, he would take a rag and clean the windows or dust the racks. Others remember the master of style vacuuming the carpeting before a fashion show. "It was the most frightening thing," said Charles Suppon.

One of the many things the baron advised Calvin to do was move from the furnished apartment to a place that was more appropriate for a man of his position. Prices were low on co-operative apartments, and Calvin went out looking with many brokers, sometimes taking Eve Orton or the baron with him as apartment mavens. The majority of the co-ops he saw were stuffy Park Avenue maisonettes. "I was looking for an old building with fireplaces in each room," Calvin said. There was one seven-room apartment on Park Avenue priced at $175,000 that Calvin seriously considered, but in the end he decided that he didn't really want the ambience of Park Avenue at all and that what he *really* craved was a room with a view. His life needed a new backdrop, and all of Manhattan was just about the right size for it.

That was the scene from the floor-to-ceiling windows on the forty-sixth floor of the Sovereign, a glass-and-stone residential monolith at 425 East Fifty-eighth Street. "When I came up here and saw the view," said Calvin, "I just freaked out." The Sovereign was big and impersonal, yet it afforded the same luxuries as a Park Avenue building. It had its own driveway encircling spotlit fountains where taxis and limousines discharged passengers into the care of liveried doormen. Inside there was an opulent two-story lobby with a concierge desk, banks of elevators, and a tiered chandelier half a story tall. Even with high-speed elevators, the ride up forty-six floors to Calvin's new apartment took a few moments of ear-popping patience. When one stepped inside, the apartment seemed to float over the island of Manhattan, with only the city's tallest spires high enough to punctuate the views. The reaction to the vista by one of Calvin's first guests stepping out onto the terrace was "My knees are shaking! It's *staggering.*"

Despite the panorama, for the approximately $3,000 a month rent that Calvin was paying, he was getting a rather ordinary flat without much charm, its boxy, featureless rooms arranged in a pedestrian layout. But that was not an insurmountable problem, since walls could be torn down and moved by a new young genius, Joe D'Urso, to whom Chester Weinberg had introduced him. For the next decade, D'Urso would become Calvin's court designer. Calvin had rarely met anyone before whose vision of interior design was such a perfect match to his own taste. D'Urso was a short, balding, patient man who had no qualms about Calvin's perfectionism. He was a disciple of the furniture maker Ward Bennet, who was one of the first to include elements of industrial design into his style. Emerging from under Bennet's wing, D'Urso became the ad hoc leader of a chic new movement dubbed "high tech," a stark look that implemented industrial-grade materials, such as gray carpeting, cyclone fencing, or hospital bathroom scales. While there was none of that at Calvin's new apartment, there were specially designed occasional tables of black rubber and a leather hammock under a ficus tree. The design and decorating price tag of nearly $100,000 represented an extraordinary investment in a rental apartment. D'Urso's first chore was to have the apartment walls torn down and replaced with curved lacquered partitions installed on tracks that rotated on an angle. In this way Calvin could convert the space into smaller, intimate segments or open it up for parties. All the fabrics were sensual and soft, and seating areas consisted of low pillows on which one had no choice but to recline and slouch. Everything in the apartment seemed to long to be touched, particularly the thousand-year-old fertility stone from India that guests invariably rubbed for luck. As sexy as the whole apartment was, there was no room more erotic than the master bedroom, in which the bed seemed to float center stage.

"In this apartment there are two things that stand out," said Calvin, "people and plants. Women especially look beautiful here. What happens with the contemporary environment is that instead of covering up people, it really exposes them. And flowers look so fascinating, too, because there are almost no colors." There was, also, a bedroom for Marci. "Calvin made a big deal about making a room for Marci to come and visit," said Suppon.

Calvin held the public premiere of his new digs the night of March 25, 1975, to coincide with the opening of his first in-store Calvin Klein boutique, which was being inaugurated that night at Bloomingdale's, as well as the simultaneous opening of a Calvin Klein boutique in Japan at the giant Isetan store. To give the event even more gloss, the boutique premiere would double as a benefit and fund-raiser for the Lighthouse for the Blind, a charity to which Calvin had no allegiance but whose chairperson, the actress Alexis Smith, was one of his most notable customers. After a small fashion show at the store, Calvin invited a select group of press and VIPs to a supper party at the Sovereign, turning what could have been a drab promotional event into one of the hottest tickets of the week.

Calvin had the Baron de Gunzburg advising him on this night every step of the way, from the color of the runway rug to the shade of the lipstick on each model and the placement of the scented Rigaud candles in his apartment. Even with "Mr. Taste" vetting his plans, Calvin was as much a wreck the night of the party as he was before showing a major collection. For one thing, because Bloomingdale's didn't close until 6:00 P.M., the workmen were unable to build the runway ahead of time, and Calvin, who usually left not so much as each step of a model's walk unchecked, would not have a chance to rehearse the show in the actual space. "It's not like on Seventh Avenue, where I can set up way ahead of time," he moaned as the workmen knocked together platforms and sound technicians set up a speaker system. Moments after the carpeting was laid on the ramp, the doors were opened and the bars and hors d'oeuvres were descended upon by hundreds of guests, including Margaux Hemingway, who sat cross-legged as she sipped a cola and surveyed the crowd. Since it was a stacked house of invited guests, there was practically a riot in the audience as Calvin's resort line came down the runway, and if cheers were any indication of how commercial the collection was, it would be a sellout. "The audience loved it," reported *Women's Wear Daily*. Aside from the cheerfully colored summer togs, the crowd especially oohed and aahed over the unique accessories in the show's finale: a live white dove, white roses, and a white Himalayan cat—imported at the suggestion of the Baron de Gunzburg, it would turn out. "You can rent anything in this town," Calvin nervously explained of his props, adding that white doves were only fifteen dollars a piece.

Behind him, the baron, lest anyone would think they could afford only one bird, intoned, "We could have had any number we wanted but thought one was enough."

Later, the elite of the fashion world made the pilgrimage to the summit of the Sovereign. The guest list included the top names from the mastheads of every fashion magazine in town as well as Bloomingdale's CEO, Marvin Traub, and a dozen or so gorgeous men and women lounging on the built-in pillow furniture, giving the view some competition. Calvin, proud as a kid with a new train set, spent the major part of the evening giving tours of the apartment—the view from the terraces, the special bedroom for Marci, his bedroom, the swinging lacquered walls that glided at the touch of a finger. It wasn't until after midnight that he finally took off his jacket and sat down to nibble a few bites of food.

The Sovereign was soon the setting for another celebrity-crammed soiree when designers from all over and a covey of industry tycoons and their wives assembled to help Calvin fete Carrie Donovan. The *Harper's Bazaar* fashion editor was leaving the writing business for an even more powerful position as vice president of communications at Bloomingdale's, and Calvin wanted to cement what was already a gratifying relationship. The guest list that evening included Calvin's great early design influence, Jacques Tiffeau, as well as Ricky and Ralph Lauren, Bill Blass, Oscar de la Renta, record mogul Ahmet Ertegun and his decorator wife, Mica, Henri Bendel's president Geraldine Stutz, jewelry designer Elsa Peretti, and—at exactly 8:00 P.M.—Halston, in an Ultrasuede jacket. When Pat Buckley, the reigning grande dame of New York society, made her entrance, she seemed breathless. "Do you realize we just made forty-six floors in something like thirty seconds?" she asked Calvin. "My ears are gone. One could get jet lag in this ritzy building."

Almost the same group, with the inclusion of Andy Warhol and Mamie Van Doren, flocked to yet another of Calvin's rare bashes in that period. By now he was getting quite a reputation as a party giver, and the evening was going full blast when the doorman rang up to say that Rock Hudson had just come in and was on his way up. As word spread of Hudson's arrival, an audible murmur rose through the party, for as celebrated as the other guests were, Rock Hudson was a legend. It was especially thrilling and gratifying for Calvin, who did not know the star and had not invited him. Yet there he was at the doorway, his arm draped over the shoulder of his longtime male lover. "He was very drunk," said one party guest.

Calvin pleasantly introduced himself, and Hudson explained tipsily, "We just got into New York and we heard you were having a party and hoped you wouldn't mind if we just dropped in."

"Of course not," Calvin said graciously, and invited Hudson and his friend inside, where the actor proceeded to get so plastered he had to be half-dragged, half-carried, out of the apartment.

Although over the years Calvin would give other promotional parties at the Sovereign, on the whole he preferred not to conduct business entertaining at home. The apartment was not created for publicity. It was his inner sanctum, a playground where he could relax and let down his guard. "Pre-Sovereign, Calvin was a pretty normal guy," said a pal. "Post-Sovereign, he was the millionaire. Things changed drastically. All of a sudden, after he became famous, he didn't want people calling him. There were people wanting things from him, and it became very difficult for his friends. You couldn't just call like in the old days and say, 'Hi, Cal.' You felt you were bothering him if you called. Everything had to be scheduled weeks in advance." Slowly, except for Chester Weinberg, all of Calvin's old friends began to take the hint and drift away, even Eve Orton, as he shifted into the fast lane.

CHAPTER NINE

The sweet smell of success.
                    —*The New York Times*

In a Byzantine twist of fate, around 1975 Calvin's assistant, Charles Suppon, became roommates with Reginald Peters, Calvin's former lover.

It turned out that although Charles was talented beyond what Chester or Calvin could only have dreamed, he was also a hopeless party boy. He was foolishly generous to his friends and lovers, and if he got his paycheck on a Friday, it rarely lasted through Sunday morning. Since moving to New York he had been evicted from more apartments for nonpayment of rent than he cared to remember. Suppon had met Reginald Peters several times at the Calvin Klein offices, and one night, after Suppon was evicted from his latest apartment, he called Peters and asked if he could spend a few nights on his sofa. A few nights turned into many, and eventually Suppon became Peters's full-time roommate. Calvin couldn't even imagine what his assistant and ex-lover were saying about him at night. However, as clumsy as the situation at first appeared, all three men managed to be adult and nonchalant about it. Over time, the arrangement came to feel so comfortable that Peters and Suppon even invited Calvin to one of their frequent all-male dinner parties.

Among the other guests one night was a thirty-two-year-old designer named Perry Ellis and his longtime roommate, Robert MacDonald. Calvin had heard all about the dashing young designer from the South who was making a name for himself by designing a women's sportswear line for Vera, a firm best known for its scarves and sheets. Ellis recently was getting a lot of press that predicted he was going to be the next young designer to pull away from the pack. While Ellis was no commercial threat to Calvin, he was at least as striving and ambitious. He also was impishly handsome and exuded the slow and easy, gentlemanly charm of a Presbyterian educated at private schools in Virginia. It was a charm that the Bronx-born Jew apparently found irresistible, and Calvin and Perry Ellis were in the same room together only five minutes when the sparks began to fly, according to Suppon and Peters. There was an animation to Calvin usually reserved for buyers with "big pencils."

Loosening up with a few vodkas, Calvin planted himself directly next to Perry Ellis on an oversized, twelve-foot-long sofa, knees touching. Throughout the party the two men chatted incessantly, hardly aware that anyone else was there, according to Suppon. "They were obviously smitten with each other," said Peters, not without a tinge of jealousy for his former flame. "They spent the whole evening together on my couch. It was obviously mutual." Peters said they were very physical with each other, if not overtly sexual. "They weren't making out," said Peters, "but it was one step below that."

For several months it seemed to Suppon, Peters, and others who were close observers of the situation, that Calvin was seriously besotted by Perry Ellis. This was of engrossing interest to Chester Weinberg, who wholeheartedly approved of Ellis as a mate for Calvin and let it be generally known that he thought Calvin had met "Mr. Right." Ellis initially also seemed charmed. Yet after flattering Calvin for a while he abruptly became unavailable to Calvin. Simply put, the way Peters saw it, "Perry dumped Calvin," after a dalliance that was never consummated.

One day many months later, Calvin was talking with a designer who coincidentally had had an affair with Perry Ellis, and Calvin asked him about it. Calvin listened in rapt silence as the designer went on about his unhappy experience with Ellis, which ended in stinging disappointment. Ellis had a habit of cultivating men who could help him with his career, then dropping them, the designer said. When the story was finished, Calvin shook his head dolefully in agreement, saying, "Boy, you and I were taken in," he said.

Usually, however, it was Calvin who broke hearts, not the other way around. Friends remember that one of his most ardent admirers was young Simon Press*, a twentyish, aspiring fashion illustrator who was highly regarded in the industry as a talented newcomer. Simon could paint, sing jazz, play the piano, and tell a funny story. He had a wry, theatrical pizzazz, never allowing himself a public down moment. "Everyone loved Simon," remembered a close friend of his when Simon dated Calvin. "Simon was a personality."

He was also movie-star handsome. When asked to describe Simon when he first met Calvin, one woman friend of Simon's said, "Oh, baby, he was Troy Donahue with blond hair and blue eyes, maybe six-feet tall, a cute figure, a very nice body, with a twenty-nine-inch-waist and major luggage."

Simon lived in a chic, high-tech studio apartment on the West Side, conveniently just cross-town from Calvin's Sovereign digs, where Simon was a frequent visitor. According to Simon's pal, when the pair were together they seemed "infatuated" with each other, and they even spent a romantic interlude together on a trip to Hawaii in 1975.

Simon was not only apparently in love, he was enormously proud he was dating the famous designer, and he bragged about his status as "Calvin Klein's lover" with friends and acquaintances rather indiscreetly. Said one accessories designer who knew Simon, "It became his calling card that he was Calvin's lover." After a time, when Calvin saw how serious the young boy was getting over him— and the "I'm Calvin Klein's lover" stories began to get back to him—Calvin started to shy away. Simon was an interesting divertissement, but Calvin wasn't about to settle down—or be labeled queer all over town. "All of a sudden," said Simon's woman friend, "Calvin said, 'Look, we can just be friends and don't call me anymore.' " Simon was at first so hurt he began to shrug off the relationship, telling one friend, "Calvin was the worst kisser that he ever kissed in his entire life." The sting of Calvin's rejection soon passed, however, and over the intervening years, Simon and Calvin have remained on friendly terms.

*A pseudonym.

Calvin's intimates also remember another brief infatuation around this same time with one of the first in a long series of houseboys who tended to Calvin's apartment. This particular employee, a young Frenchman who spoke only rudimentary English, captured Calvin's attention so completely for a while that the designer enrolled in a foreign-language school to learn to speak French.

In fact, none of these liaisons were serious. Calvin had no intention of dedicating himself to an entirely gay, *faygeleh* lifestyle. He loved women too much ever to give them up completely, and Lizzette Kattan was still in the picture, although disconcertingly caught up in her new life in Italy. Calvin continued to look for the right woman on whom to bestow his permanent love.

As time went by, Chester went against his own dogma, which was "Even if you suck only *one* cock your whole life, that still makes you a cocksucker." He slowly came to believe that Calvin was a rara avis indeed. Chester's friend recalled: "Chester said that Calvin was the only 'true bisexual' he had ever known." Another pal who made the disco rounds with him in those early years after his divorce saw his switchable sex objects as indulgent experimentation in his newfound freedom, like a kid let loose in a candy store. "If I wanted to screw a broad one afternoon, then I'm straight" was his friend's assessment of Calvin's attitude. "If I want to be gay the following night in a disco, that's fine. If the next day I want to do alcohol and drugs—in other words, you have got the world to play in and the environment is Play kid! Live it up! Live at the heights, you've reached the top."

Chester's lover, Michael Datoli, said, "I never got from him that it was a conscious decision to go from straight to gay. At that time it was more important for Calvin to be in the right place at the right time, at the right parties, the right disco. I don't think sex was that important. It was the thrill. Maybe it was experiencing being a bad boy."

"By 1975," said one friend who went dancing frequently with Calvin during that period, "he was going to clubs that were a little mixed." A "mixed" club was the hip new thing in New York in the mid-seventies—a disco where trendy straight couples mingled with a discreet gay male clientele who were often themselves accompa-

nied by women. It was perfect—one night Calvin could take Lizzette; one night, Simon. One of Calvin's favorite clubs was Les
Jardins—a rather ironic name, since it was located in the basement
of a seedy hotel on West Forty-fourth Street, just off Times Square.
Les Jardins, with its fanciful lattice partitions and palm fronds, was
the invention of former gay fashion model John Addison, who was
the first disco impresario to adopt a shirtless dress code for his
bartenders and put his busboys in white satin shorts. Calvin found
the atmosphere provocative and knowing. He loved the place, for a
minute, and made the scene there before he took a sonic jump in
taste to a club called Flamingo.

From the moment Flamingo opened its doors in December 1974
it was a sensation. Flamingo—"the" was never used—was a private
men's discotheque whose membership boasted several thousand of
the most handsome and muscular men in the gay world, so stunning "the pack can barely stand how handsome they are," one observer wrote. The membership list at Flamingo was so carefully
restricted that each new prospect not only had to be recommended
by an existing member, but he had to be personally interviewed by
the club's owner, Michael Fesco, to pass muster. Within a year of
the club's opening, memberships were selling for five hundred dollars on the black market, and Calvin wasn't happy until he got one
of his own.

Flamingo had mystique as well as great beauties. It didn't open
until midnight, and it was open only one night a week—Saturday—
in an event that turned into a gay tribal ritual, a celebration of flesh
and music that was expected to last into the next day. The club was
in a loft building on the northern edge of SoHo, without the benefit
of any sign or indication it existed behind the nearly hidden doorway. Up one flight, inside a loft that ran the length of a city block,
the scene each Saturday night was spellbinding in its ferocious energy. Beginning at midnight, Flamingo was a sea of writhing bodies—sweaty, shirtless men dancing to the powerful, imaginatively
mixed disco music, the deejay presiding over the dance floor from a
raised booth, bent over his turntables like a mad scientist.

If Flamingo was a shrine for the emerging gay culture, that culture worshiped not only muscle and sex but drugs, for no liquor was
served at the club. The customers were expected to bring any man-

ner of space-aged pharmaceuticals to get them high. Grass was smoked openly, cocaine was passed around in the open, revelers shared multicolored pills, and the dance floor reeked of amyl nitrate poppers. A few of the more extreme couples danced attached by an ethyl chloride–soaked rag that they clenched between their teeth. Up along a carpeted ledge that wrapped around the club, the more exhibitionistic in the crowd danced by themselves like erotic cheerleaders.

As Calvin wandered through the crowd at Flamingo, the body heat rushed through him like a revelation; this was the cutting edge. These men, these outlaws of society, the temperament, the clothing, the feel, the use of drugs as a propellent, this was what was coming in America: Disco would become the dialectic of the straight population as well. But most important, the men! The men at Flamingo had less to do about sex for him than the notion of portraying men as gods. He realized that what he was watching was the freedom of a new generation, unashamed, in-the-flesh embodiments of Calvin's ideals: straight-looking, masculine men, with chiseled bodies, young Greek gods come to life. The vision of shirtless young men with hardened torsos, all in blue jeans, top button opened, a whisper of hair from the belly button disappearing into the denim pants, would inspire and inform the next ten years of Calvin Klein's print and television advertisements. So compelling was this vision to him that there were nights he could not tear himself away from the crowds and stood for hours at Flamingo entranced until 7:00 A.M.

Calvin was so taken with Flamingo that he choose it as the venue of what would be his most important fashion show to date, the premiere of his 1975 fall line, which would be shown to the trade on May 6. Immediately, the choice of Flamingo became a matter of industry gossip, not because it was a mecca of gay culture but because collections were always shown in the garment center as a convenience to the press and buyers who rushed from show to show. In any event, Flamingo was so underground in reputation that very few of the critics and buyers from around the country knew it was a gay club. However, for thousands in the fashion and related industries in Manhattan—hairdressers, stylists, decorators, graphic artists, as well as the membership of Flamingo—it became a sensation that Calvin would be audacious enough to hold a fashion show on such sacred gay ground, and within a week invitations were scarcer then a dropped stitch.

Anticipation about the collection grew even more fevered as word spread that Calvin intended this to be the greatest fashion production ever mounted by an American designer. The budget for the forty-five-minute production was $250,000, which represented over $9,000 in modeling fees, plus the salaries of a behind-the-scenes crew of over fifty lighting and sound technicians, makeup artists, hairstylists, and design assistants who toiled to pull the show together. The show itself promised to be spectacularly mounted, and the lighting equipment Calvin wanted to use was so powerful that even with the massive amounts of electricity available to run Flamingo, there wasn't sufficient power. Portable generators had to be hired and kept in trucks on the street in front of the club, with bulky power lines snaking up the fire steps.

Calvin designed over fifteen hundred samples for the show—a long way from his days with Morenstein, when he could only afford to make six. The fifteen hundred garments were then whittled down to the best 350, constituting what *Women's Wear Daily* would still call a "giant sized" collection. Thirty-six models were rehearsed for the show, closely supervised by Calvin and a team of assistants led by Charles Suppon. Polaroid photographs were taken of each completed outfit and accessories, against which the models would be checked before being sent down the runway. Through the months of preparation Calvin was even more high-strung than usual, smoking one cigarette after another, haranguing the models, and drinking cup after cup of black coffee as he went over each garment with the same meticulous detail as he had used on the samples he brought to Mildred Custin. The tension mounted as a few days before the show the international fashion press descended on Manhattan.

It was not a good omen that on the Tuesday of the show it was pouring rain in New York and most of the audience arrived at Flamingo soaked to the bone and disgruntled. Perhaps even worse, the guests were surprised to discover a space that looked—without the benefit of a dose of LSD and the participation of a thousand half-naked men in tribal pursuit—like a rather ordinary loft. A team of carpenters had built a six-hundred-foot, pristine white runway down the middle of the room, and nearly one thousand white high-backed chairs were placed exactly five inches apart in five rows. Along the carpeted ledges of the room, huge white urns and fish-bowls were filled with giant white calla lilies. In the reception area there was cheap wine and an unappetizingly funereal display of all-white crudités in white baskets.

But the real problem, according to Pat Shelton, who covered the event for the *Chicago Daily News,* was that hundreds of young party crashers—"friends of the house," she called them—showed up early, and by the time many of the eight hundred invited guests arrived, the club was "wall-to-wall bodies." Local fire laws forced Flamingo's owner, Michael Fesco, to close the doors to the club, even though many of the buyers and press holding legitimate invitations were standing outside in the rain.

The pecking order of who sits where at fashion shows is of absorbing significance to the fashion world, and egos are often hung on such petty matters. Front row center, direct middle of the runway, is generally regarded as the place of honor, and importance fans out from there, with rank diminishing to sides and back. Only at Flamingo the all-important little place cards carefully set on the white chairs were mostly stolen or moved, so people had no idea where to sit. Unfamiliar faces were in some of the best seats. "Bernadine Morris told me that Paloma Picasso had my seat," said Pat Shelton. "We were stacked up against the back wall. We found ourselves standing behind a ten- or twelve-row-deep mob."

Invited at 6:00 P.M. and promised that the show would begin at seven, the crowded audience was ready for a lynching when the music had not yet started by half past. By that time even one of Calvin's biggest fans, Carrie Donovan, seatless, walked out, followed shortly by John Schumacher, the president of I. Magnin. "Your pal [Calvin] must be on an ego trip," he told his store's top executive, Bill McElree, reportedly forbidding McElree to buy the line. "It was a madhouse," said Schumacher, "I can't look at clothes in a carnival atmosphere. It was hard enough to get here in the rain, and then to have people spilling red wine and fighting for seats—it was too much."

"More of a Bash than a Show" was Pat Shelton's headline in the

Chicago Daily News. "Fashion's mob scene isn't for everyone" was her assessment, for which she was banned for life from attending any further Calvin Klein fashion shows.

But even Shelton liked the clothing—Saint Laurent–inspired separates in groups of browns and red, blacks and whites, and gray-blues and ivory, which she called "easy classics put together well." More important, the ultimate arbiter, *Women's Wear Daily,* called the show "Fashion plus Showmanship." The daily pointed out that Calvin dragged "people two miles out of their way after a normal workday, packed them, rainsoaked and water-logged, into a dance hall, kept them waiting 45 minutes and still managed to keep his audience applauding throughout an hour-long fall collection. . . . It's hard to find fault with a collection like this." Indeed, when the models finally sashayed down the runway, I. Magnin's Bill McElree liked what he saw so much he "beat his palms red with applause," reported *Women's Wear,* and he gave Calvin a large order despite his boss's alleged caveat.

The Flamingo controversy became part of Calvin's growing legend, and even his petulant revenge in banning Pat Shelton cemented his power with the press. This was not someone with whom you meddled. What was more, the line was not only a great hit with the buyers and press but with customers as well. Barry booked $5 million in orders directly after the show, and the total gross for 1975 would soar close to $20 million. If that was not proof enough that Calvin had created another hit, on June 26, 1975, it was announced that Calvin had been voted into the Coty Hall of Fame, at thirty-three the youngest designer ever to achieve that distinction. He was also presented with his third consecutive individual Coty Award, this time honoring his luxurious collection of furs licensed by Alixandre. Calvin was over the moon. "It's unbelievable," he said.

The national press now turned its spotlight on Calvin. Calvin exuded "The Sweet Smell of Success," said the *New York Times,* adding that "the homage of the fashion press . . . is paralleled by the nation's retailers who have been pouring into the firm's showroom." To *People* magazine, in October 1975, Calvin was the "The Freckle-faced Kid They Call Calvin 'Clean' and the King of S.A. *People* described him as a dashing young divorcé, who was never too busy to spend time "horseback riding and sailing with his daughter, Marci, age 8." This glowing assessment ran alongside an equally flattering photo of Calvin, boyishly debonair, surrounded by gorgeous models wearing his coats, Seventh Avenue teaming with street traffic, men bundling pushcarts in the background. And soon after, in November 1975, *Newsweek* magazine gave Calvin a full-page profile in its "Lifestyle" section. Fashion writer and editor Grace Mirabella, who wrote the article, explained Calvin's significance in the industry thusly: "If you were around a hundred years from now and wanted a definitive picture of the American look in 1975, you'd study Calvin."

His celebrity quotient soared. People recognized him walking down the street. In 1976 he was invited to the White House—twice in eighteen months—once to a luncheon given by Betty Ford and one time when Jimmy and Rosalynn Carter asked him to be part of a contingent representing the fashion industry at a fete honoring choreographer Martha Graham. Jayne laughed when she heard Calvin was going to the Executive Mansion to mix with foreign diplomats. "What would he talk about?" she quipped. "Fashion?" No, politics. "I thought there was power in New York," said Calvin upon his return "but the first time I went to the White House to a state dinner, I realized it's *there*. The power to control the world. Exciting. You feel as if you could do something, make a contribution."

One day Chester and Michael Datoli were chatting about Calvin's emergence almost overnight from obscurity. "You know, Calvin became famous *so* quickly," said Chester, "I wonder if he even *knows* he's famous? I don't think it's hit him. I think I'll ask him." The next time Chester saw Calvin, he remembered to ask, "Do you realize you're famous? I mean, nationally *famous?*"

Calvin thought for a moment, and then, with a mixture of pleasure and awe and apprehension, he looked wide-eyed at Chester and said, "Gee, you're *right*."

2

The success did not feel as good as it looked. Certainly Calvin loved the fame and the money, but he began to secretly doubt that he was *that* good. Surely he wasn't the angel the press was making him out to be. So he decided to go back into therapy to deal with this unexpected issue of his worthiness of success. Calvin also tried one session of est, the personality polish devised by Werner Erhardt. Chester was a rabid proponent of est for a time, and he dragged Calvin to a meeting one Sunday when Calvin got off a plane from the Rancho Spa, where he had been tending to his body. After one meeting Calvin never went back. "The man up there was saying we're all jerks. I couldn't relate to that. My life works." Later, he said, "What am I seeking? More awareness of myself, really understanding more about myself. Some of those things are not necessarily for me. I think a lot of people go through more than one method to try and understand themselves."

Calvin also had seen up close just how fleeting success could be. Just as quickly as his own star was rising, Chester Weinberg's career had taken a demeaning downturn. The business partners who owned his company had passed him over in favor of promoting other designers—particularly a newcomer named Donna Karan—and they eventually closed him out. For a time Chester went into business with his brother, Sydney, but that ended in bankruptcy and left Chester owing back taxes and penalties which he was painstakingly paying off by working as a "designer for hire" for various midrange dress houses, including Jones Apparel Group.

But something else was happening in Chester's life. He was not only coming out of the closet; it was becoming a crusade with him. By the mid-seventies, gay liberation had so raised the public's consciousness that being gay was not considered as cursed a thing as it had been in the past. By now the suicidal homosexual characters from the 1968 play *Boys in the Band* were a tired cliché—gays clearly weren't that miserable and didn't need to be. In 1973, even the heretofore resolute twenty thousand members of the American Psychiatric Association decided to change their opinion that homosexuality was a curable "disease" and in a historic vote declassified homosexuality as a mental illness. It was no small irony lost on

Chester. For years he and Calvin had suffered and tortured themselves because they were supposed to be sick in the eyes of society, and now, just by a *vote,* they were normal. Indeed, gay ideology became so encouraged that it was moving to the other end of the spectrum with the radical idea of "gay pride."

With society's permission, Chester's lifestyle began to reflect this new political consciousness. Now that he was no longer obliged to appease the darlings of the cocktail-dress set, he shed his effete suits and Madison Avenue barber for a more obviously gay style, a "Christopher Street clone," as it was known in the gay vernacular: mustache, short hair, button-fly blue jeans, a flannel work shirt, and a hooded sweatshirt topped by a lumberman's jacket. And like many Christopher Street clones, Chester became a "gym queen," obsessed with daily attendance at one of the dozens of gyms all over Manhattan that catered to gay men. "The gym helps psych your head," Chester explained, saying that until then the most exercise he got was a back kick in the showroom. "I have to be careful, because I'm not really tall, so I don't want to bulk up to the point where I look like I'm competing for something. . . . I was your average flabby guy who counted on custom-made suits from London. Now, if I go out dancing I can wear a T-shirt and pair of jeans and feel damn good about the way I look."

This public flaunting made no sense at all to Calvin, who could have cared less about gay pride or the gay political movement. First of all, he wasn't really gay, he wasn't really *anything,* he was a creature unto himself. And second, what fascinated him about gay life wasn't political. He sensed in an almost prescient way—his great talent—that gays were moving into the vanguard of art and fashion and music and design. Gay was where it was happening, gay was hot, gay was going to be "in," and that was where Calvin wanted to be.

In the summer of 1975, Calvin rented his own house in the Fire Island Pines, and Chester Weinberg fell into the role of staff social director, like a gay *tummler* from the Catskill Mountains. This is not to say that Calvin and Chester ran a party house with lots of traffic in and out. There were no big parties at all, and only a select few were invited for dinner, but Chester made sure that those few were the handsomest young men on the island and that the best drugs were on hand. Drugs were important to Chester and becoming more important to Calvin. Paradoxically, although Chester was making his body prettier on the outside, he was also pouring into it every kind of drug imaginable. Chester had progressed far beyond his round-the-clock joint smoking and was now totally immersed in the drug subculture that seemed inseparable from fast-lane gay life on Fire Island. It seemed that every day a new drug was being concocted with magical qualities and alluring names like Ecstasy and TT-One. But most important, there was cocaine. Cocaine was a panacea, an aphrodisiac, and slowly but surely a part of Calvin and Chester's everyday life. Cocaine seemed to be part of the wave of the future. Also that summer, for the first time, Calvin delved into hallucinogenic drugs, and he was not embarrassed to let people know about his hip new experimentation. One weekend, high on mushrooms or LSD, Calvin had an epiphany about some guy he met on the beach. When he he came to work on Monday morning, he excitedly told Charles Suppon about the drug revelation. "I met this guy who was really like the devil," he told Suppon earnestly.

Chester was also very helpful in finding young men for Calvin as well. Even as Calvin's fame made meeting young men easier for him, he was still paralytically shy, and if the boy was exceptionally handsome, he could hardly bring himself to say hello. Chester knew it was mostly out of fear of rejection. "I tell him to handle his romantic life like he handles the fabric cutters," said Chester, but he couldn't, and Chester would seek out the boys with swimmers' bodies for him and say, "My friend Calvin Klein wants to meet you." According to one close observer of Calvin and Chester that summer, "Chester would go out and get little goodies. 'Candy'—anything. Fun things. And he would also set up parties, too."

The frequency and availability of sex on Fire Island that summer was without limit. The message at that time was supposed to be liberation, but along with it came unhalting promiscuity; for once out of the closet, sex was so constantly available, there seemed to be no reason to deprive oneself. Between the Pines and its sister community, Cherry Grove, there was a spot among several miles of thick pine barrens known as the "Meat Rack," where men congregated for anonymous sex. Calvin found the environment surreal, a black-and-white moonscape where occasional orgasmic moans were punctuated by the sound of waves crashing on the beach nearby. Shadowy figures flitted between the pine trees, only the gray-white light of the moon illuminating the men kneeling or bending at the waist before each other.

That summer of experimentation took its toll on Calvin. By August he felt increasingly listless and began to shed pounds from his already bony frame. He felt so ill that he even thought to mention it to a reporter from *Women's Wear Daily*, saying that he just got over "the worst cold of the summer." Only it wasn't a cold. It lingered and made him even weaker, and eventually the color of his urine turned dark. Surprisingly, Calvin did not rush to consult a doctor. In fact, he could not admit to himself that something was drastically wrong until he found himself snapping at Barry. Only then did he go for a checkup. The doctor immediately diagnosed him with hepatitis, a disease of the liver that is frequently sexually communicated. It is also a dangerous and debilitating illness that thoroughly weakens the victim and ruins liver function. Calvin was rushed to Doctors Hospital, a small, posh, private institute on East End Avenue, where he was put in a private corner room with a view overlooking Gracie Mansion, the residence of New York's mayor. Calvin lay in bed for weeks, a sickly mustard-yellow color, so weak and nauseated that he couldn't even watch food commercials on television.

Calvin insisted it be kept secret that he was in the hospital suffering from a disease that many people found embarrassing because of its potential sexual connotations. However, word of Calvin's illness raced up and down Seventh Avenue. Within a week his room was filled with flowers and gifts from magazine editors and department-store executives and anyone who wanted to endear himself to him. There were very few visitors allowed, however, for he could hardly keep his head up—although Flo, for one, could not be kept away until she was told to let Calvin rest. The only other person who saw him on a regular basis besides Chester Weinberg was Charles Suppon, who had to carry on at the office in Calvin's absence. Calvin was angry to be bedridden, and he was determined that as sick as he was, he was going to pull a collection together for a sales presentation that had been promised to Ellin Saltzman, the fashion director at Saks Fifth Avenue. Calvin also needed to put together the show for his Coty Award Hall of Fame ceremony, looming September 24. Charles Suppon worked on the line in the office every day, and in the afternoon he brought his work to Calvin for his comment and direction. He would lay the sketches out on the floor, and Calvin would make suggestions. Eventually, Suppon made the presentation to Ellin Saltzman at Saks and pulled the Coty Show together as well. He was probably more exhausted than Calvin, who was released well rested from Doctors Hospital just in time for the Coty ceremony. At the awards he looked gaunt but handsome in his tuxedo. This time he was accompanied by Flo, Marci, and his sister, Alexis, in what the *New York Times* called "Coty Night: It Was Like a Family Night Out."

When the show was over, Calvin rewarded Charles Suppon for all his hard work by giving him a Cartier tank watch worth about $1,500. It was inscribed: "Thanks, with love, Calvin." Suppon tried to contain his rage until he got away from Calvin. It was an expensive watch, but there was something impersonal and dismissive about the gesture, "the kind of thing you give to someone after fifty years, when they're retiring," said Suppon, not the kind of gift you gave an employee who helped you pull chestnuts worth millions out of the fire. Charles never felt the same about Calvin after that, and he became determined to get away and start his own company—just the way Calvin had felt a decade before. A few months after the Coty Award presentation, Suppon didn't have enough money to pay Reggie Peters his share of the rent, so he gave Peters the watch instead. To this day Peters owns a Cartier watch that is inscribed "Thanks, with love, Calvin."

Suppon left Calvin for six months, came back, and eventually left again to start his own company. By then he and Calvin disliked each other intensely, Charles resentful that Calvin was the star and he was the workhorse. "When you know the secrets of the magician," Suppon said, "his illusions are only tricks."

"It was a very painful decision for Charles," said one of the assistants who watched the breakup. "There was such a closeness between him and Calvin, a very close relationship where it was hard to express independence, hard for them to express how much they needed each other. Anyway, Charles broke, and it was a very difficult separation."

Suppon started his own company only a few months after leaving Calvin. He found ready backing from manufacturers who wanted him to copy Calvin's women's-wear designs stitch for stitch, but Suppon went a classier route and began to develop his own, more daring style. Calvin remained so miffed with Suppon's departure (and the subsequent publicity he got from his association with Calvin) that he refused to go to Charles's first show. For a time it seemed that Suppon was going to be a smashing success on his own. In 1977 he won a Coty Award for his women's wear, but only a few years later he was out of business. He was no better a businessman with his company than he was with paying his rent. Eventually, he began to support himself with a small, private clientele for whom he designed extravagant articles of clothing, like snakeskin sports jackets. As Suppon's design income dwindled to zero, he became the personal assistant to one of his customers, the entertainer and songwriter Peter Allen. He worked with Allen for years as his wardrobe coordinator, designer, and sometimes gofer. Suppon also coauthored and designed the costumes for Allen's ill-fated Broadway show *Legs Diamond* before he became too ill with AIDS to continue working. He never spoke to Calvin Klein again. When he died on March 21, 1989, he was at work on a thinly disguised roman à clef about the life and times of Calvin Klein.

Calvin was not, however, without a senior design assistant. There was a twenty-six-year-old named Zack Carr waiting patiently in the wings. However, Carr would be much more than just an assistant. He became the heart and soul of Calvin Klein's designs, the genesis of many of the brilliant fashion looks that came out of Calvin Klein's design studios for the next decade.

For a talented designer, Carr hardly looked like a fashionable young man. He was an open-faced, unassuming fellow with such a thick Texas twang that he seemed like a hick—until he started talking about fashion. Carr was obsessively in love with fashion and fed on obscure detail about its world. But more than being just a font of trivia, Carr was a fashion scholar to rival Chester Weinberg, a man who understood the heritage of the great designers and how and why the business had evolved.

Using a small inheritance from his mother, who died when he was nine years old, Zack Carr graduated from the University of

Texas and studied at the Parsons School of Design before working for the venerated designer Donald Brooks. Even before Suppon's departure, Calvin was looking for a sketch artist with fresh ideas and heard through the grapevine that Carr not only knew how to draw but that he could take the slimmest idea and develop it into a complete look on his pad. Calvin asked to meet him during the summer of that year, and Carr arrived for the interview wearing his best sports outfit, an Yves Saint Laurent safari jacket and pants. "It sounds terrible now," Carr remembered, "but it was at the height of fashion then, and Calvin Klein was wearing almost exactly the same thing." Carr describes the rest of the meeting almost like the beginning of a love affair. "There was a bit of *fortification* in terms of our identity," he said. "Naturally, we just took to each other without really saying very much. We didn't want to say very much. He said he wanted me to work for him as a sketch artist, and I just sat down and sketched my life away and loved it."

Carr was the perfect "second" for Calvin, and he became something many sociologists call the "office wife." Explained Carr, "I was very, very, very quiet, and I was very shy, very sensitive—probably overly sensitive—and Calvin protected me. He let me have my own time to develop, to see how I would grow." Scores of employees associated with the company credit Zack Carr with being the vessel of interpretation of Calvin's creative wishes. This is an area where Carr treads with care. "Who do you really define as the designer?" he asks. "Is the designer the person that actually sits down and sketches and chooses fabric and its relationship and works out ideas and sees them put to work and then sees them go out into the audience? I consider that a designer. . . . Calvin and I had a very extraordinary relationship."

Over the next ten years, said Carr, "I never knew Calvin as the big man. . . . It was Calvin and me, so many times left out in the street in the rain, no umbrella, unable to get a cab. There were times when we would travel to Europe together and get on trains and handle the tickets [ourselves] and we would get lost on trains and find ourselves three hundred miles away from our destination, one day late. The credit card with the name Calvin Klein on it did not matter to anybody. We were like college kids traipsing around, and yet he was a multimillionaire and a very, very famous man. Yet for some reason, together we helped each other to remain grounded, yet we were very aware of the importance of what we were doing and that it would be noticed around the world."

"I imagine," said Carr, "that a lot of people would like to know the intimacies I shared with Calvin, but I really don't remember them except to say that we were very close, and I knew Calvin in a way that I don't think anybody else has ever known him except for his wife."

3

Giorgio Sant'Angelo did not want to meet Calvin Klein at first, but Eve Orton kept insisting. "You'll love this boy," she told Giorgio. "You'll be best friends." But Giorgio doubted it. Calvin was, after all, a manufacturer and a Jew—not that Giorgio was prejudiced, but after all, he *was* the Count Giorgio Imperatrice di Sant'Angelo e Ratti di Desio, one of the most talented—and eccentric—haute couturiers in the business. Calvin Klein just didn't seem his *type*. But, he gave in to Orton, and he and Calvin met one night over a chili dinner, served by her sassy maid, at Orton's Park Avenue apartment. Calvin quickly learned that in Giorgio's presence he was no longer the center of attention. Giorgio was clearly the star of his own universe. Waving an omnipresent, unfiltered Gauloises cigarette—or just as likely, a joint—he told wild, funny stories in a musically lush accent that melded his Florentine heritage with an adolescence spent on the Argentine pampas. The lure of a job as an animator with Walt Disney studios brought him to the United States, where Diana Vreeland flipped over the neon-colored jewelry he had designed on a lark from scraps of Lucite. Vreeland discovered that Giorgio was one of those rare Renaissance talents who could not only design jewelry but could cut and style hair, paint scenery, or design furniture. He became an overnight sensation with his American Indian look, which sparked an industry craze.

Giorgio was ten years Calvin's senior, a romantically handsome man with a perpetual suntan, compact and bursting with vigor and enthusiasm. He dyed his Botticelli curls blond so many times they occasionally turned orange, a hairdo he wore with no apologies. No apologies was what Giorgio was all about. Giorgio had always been completely at ease with who he was, and because he was able to love himself, it was easy for him to love others. He was a creature who fascinated Calvin. In the end, Giorgio's gift to Calvin was a simple maxim: "I like myself very much," Giorgio would explain, "and because I do, I cannot make a mistake, I cannot be mediocre."

Nobody who knew Giorgio could believe they became such good friends. "A lot of people felt Calvin was beneath Giorgio," said designer Martin Price, Giorgio's longtime companion. For one thing, while Calvin's life was filled with a lot of men, Giorgio was surrounded most usually by beautiful women, including model-turned-jewelry-designer Elsa Peretti; Saint Laurent's muse, Lulu de laFalaise, and her mother, Maxine; and models Naty Bascal and Marina Schiano. "People would ask Giorgio why he was hanging around with someone who was beneath him," said Martin Price, "and Giorgio would say, 'No, no, no. He's a good guy. I like him, I sincerely like him.'"

"I was surprised," said Michael Foley, Giorgio's business partner. "I didn't think Calvin Klein was in Giorgio's league. But somehow, they clicked as friends. Calvin was just beginning to license, and we were doing eight or ten licenses at the time, and Calvin would ask advice, like how much to charge for neckties." Calvin soon learned that knowing Giorgio gave him entrée into a new, faster, more sophisticated set. "Giorgio got Calvin Klein invited places," said Foley, and Calvin lapped along with him like a puppy, hanging on his every word. Before long they were jetting off together or carousing at all of New York's trendy spots.

In some ways, Giorgio was the jet-set version of Chester Weinberg. While Chester was able to show Calvin the auction galleries of Madison Avenue and London tailors, Giorgio showed Calvin the world. When they went away on vacation together, Giorgio took Calvin to Bali, where they dined with the prince and princess. Giorgio, however, couldn't stand Chester. Giorgio was all about high fashion and glamour and style; Chester was wearing jeans and T-shirts and was into gay lib. "Ooooh, that tacky person," Giorgio would say to Calvin when Chester was out of earshot. "Get rid of him."

In the summer of 1976, Giorgio and Calvin rented a house together in the Fire Island Pines. "Giorgio was in charge of that house, you better believe it," said Martin Price. It was a simple house, decorated in plain white furniture, but Giorgio made it look like heaven with a few sheets thrown over the furniture, a vase of flowers at the right spot, candles at the table. They hired a houseboy for the summer, who cooked and emptied ashtrays. Giorgio made every weekend magic. Calvin was so busy he only claimed to have made it out four weekends, but on those four weekends the fashion flock remember it being the most desirable house on the island. The great muses of fashion, like Lulu de Lafalaise, Elsa Peretti and Marina Schiano, would loll around the house while Giorgio cooked big pots of pasta. Late at night, very stoned and drunk, Giorgio, Calvin, and their houseguest Chester would talk for hours about color and fashion.

It was after sharing a house together that people began to assume that Calvin and Giorgio were lovers. Occasionally, they did things that reinforced the notion. Both Calvin and Giorgio attended a cocktail party Eleanor Lambert gave for *Times* writer Bernadine Morris. Calvin was on one side of the room cryptically saying he was going on vacation. "And I'm not telling anyone, and just alone, alone, alone, absolutely no one, and it'll be so wonderful." Andy Warhol later spoke to Giorgio who said he was going away to the Greek Islands for two weeks, "alone, alone, alone."

"Are you sure you're not going with Calvin Klein?" Warhol asked.

"Oh, you know everything," Giorgio snapped.

Although Giorgio was widely regarded as one of the most inventive minds in the business, his clothing was never considered commercial. Slacks of aluminum mesh or five-layered wrap skirts did not become fashion staples, nor can they be easily mass-produced. And what looked gorgeous on Lena Horne under a spotlight did not wear well for a well-heeled woman from Shaker Heights. Moreover, Giorgio never stayed with one style and built an audience. While his private clients and the press loved him, he didn't make enough to keep himself afloat from one year to the next. "He got praise but no big money," said Foley, and eventually, "he was embittered by the way the market works." He would ask Foley, "Why can't you do for me what Barry did for Calvin?" And Foley would say, "Because you don't do those kind of clothes."

Indeed, by the late seventies Calvin's interlocking line of women's sportswear and associated apparel had become one of the most popular brands in the United States. He had adjusted his draped, clean look to one slightly more romantic and closer to the body. It matched perfectly the rapidly changing view of the role of young American women in society, and an army of working women and mothers wore his fashions like a uniform. Many fashion critics think the last five years of the seventies were Calvin's most creative years, and some equate his creativity with his newfound sexual freedom and recreational drug use. They were productive years as well; even his resort collections contained more than 350 pieces. That did not mean Calvin was impervious to failure. His big fall fashion show following the one at Flamingo, at which he introduced his new, softer shape, was considered a small disaster. Ironically, while just the year before it was considered an imposition to travel out of the garment center to see a fashion show, now all the designers were vying for unique settings in which to show their lines. Calvin chose a small theater, Circle in the Square, for his May 10, 1976, showing of his fall line. "I wanted to do a big, splashy presentation," he said, "so I went for elaborate music that would go with lots of applause. Well, after the third girl came out, I knew the show was a disaster, you just feel it. And here was this ornate music that seemed to make everything worse."

"Calvin Klein Salable" read *Women's Wear Daily's* front-page headline, but it "lacks excitement." Although the show was coordinated and professional, it was "too subtly colored, too repetitive and showed an excess of outerwear and hard tailoring." They called his mid-calf skirts "difficult to wear and somewhat school marmish" and his evening stripes "pallid and boring." Friends who read the reviews were worried, and they decided to drop by the Sovereign later to cheer him up. What they found was not a disconsolate designer but Calvin and Barry totally unconcerned, confidently pricing the line. They were right, too. Despite the review, the orders from stores were the biggest of any season yet, and more important, when they shipped the next season, the line sold out to the piece.

As the name Calvin Klein became a household word in America, the gross revenues rocketed from $40 million in 1976 to $90 million in 1977. At the age of thirty-three, Calvin was paying himself a $4-million-a-year salary, as was Barry Schwartz, and this salary was presumably exclusive of whatever other profits the company showed at the end of the year, which of course was wholly paid down to Calvin and Barry. On Christmas, 1977, Calvin bought himself as a gift a burgundy-and-silver Silver Cloud Rolls-Royce for $135,000. "On Christmas I was very depressed," he said, "and I said, 'Screw it, I'm going to buy myself something special.' Then I said, 'What does every poor guy from the Bronx think about owning?' The answer came to: 'A Rolls-Royce.' So I went out and bought myself one. I started driving it around, and I felt like a chauffeur, not the owner. In truth, I was far more at home in my jeep. . . . I asked Barry when I bought the car if it was too pretentious or too old for my age. I was feeling guilty in a way, so I had to sit down and talk to him. He is the only one I can really talk to. If one day he wants to stop the business, I'm going to stop it, too. I cannot continue without him."

CHAPTER TEN

"A designer dresses not only for the eyes, but for
the other senses as well."

—Karl Lagerfeld

One autumn day Calvin was sitting in the waiting room of a
doctor's office on East Fifty-seventh Street, contemplating the
fashionably dressed matron seated across from him. The woman
was drenched in a new perfume Halston had recently launched on
the market, and Calvin tried not to breathe the permeating scent
too deeply, but it was inescapable. Truly inescapable—that sharp,
distinctive smell was *everywhere,* in restaurants and elevators and
waiting rooms, or so it seemed. Halston's perfume was the talk of
the town. It was the most successful new fragrance to be introduced on the market in years, a bona fide blockbuster expected to
gross *$100 million* by the end of its second year.

And Halston wasn't the only one cashing in on fragrance. Designer perfume was the hottest new trend in the fashion business.
Until then, only a scant few of the legendary haute couturiers had
their own perfumes, like Chanel's No. 5 or Lanvin's My Sin, but in
the past few years, with the advent of the designer-as-star, so-called
designer fragrances accounted for a major part of the yearly $660
million U.S. fragrance market. Designer perfume was the housewife's access to haute couture; while there were only an estimated
three thousand women in the world who could afford to buy a designer dress, almost every middle-class woman could afford a designer scent. By the late seventies, a recognizable scent was
becoming de rigueur in a woman's wardrobe and a designer hadn't
arrived until he had his own scent.

Not only was the perfume business prestigious, few businesses were as lucrative. Perfume was like alchemy; it cost only pennies to make—the liquid in the bottle was mostly alcohol—and it sold for hundreds of dollars an ounce, only soon to evaporate into thin air. And a fragrance didn't have to be redesigned four times a year like a line of clothing; a scent was "designed" only once and the task was over. Cosmetics was also a goldmine—makeup was colored talcum powder and lipstick was mostly wax, but the markup could run to 1,000 percent.

At the same time, the financial risk involved in launching a perfume was astronomical. Six out of seven new perfumes failed, and even successful ones didn't last more than three or four years on the market. With development costs, packaging, advertising, and promotion, just to set up shop could easily cost $10 million, and perhaps over $50 million during the ten-year period that it took to establish a line as a "classic." The only feasible way for a designer like Calvin to start a fragrance was to license a perfume to one of the giant cosmetics companies, like Revlon or Estee Lauder, who could handle the financial risk. Indeed, many of the big names in the business had already approached Calvin about licensing his own perfume, but Calvin had resisted. First of all, why end up with only 6 percent of the profits when you could have it all, and second, Calvin wanted "total control"—not just over what the perfume smelled like but over the shape of the bottle, the packaging, the marketing concept, the advertising campaign—*everything*, right down to the thickness of the cellophane on the package. And he was deadly serious about it. Lots of other designers licensed their name and let assistants do the work. But Calvin was a fanatic about quality and detail, and everything under his name had to be perfect.

Thus far no cosmetics company was willing to give Calvin absolute control. After all, it was their money, they were experts, they had to have *some* say. But no, Calvin was willing to wait until the right deal with the right company came his way. Only now the matter seemed more pressing. As an extra thorn in his side, Ralph Lauren was starting his own perfume with exactly the kind of deal Calvin was looking for. Lauren had announced that he was developing a new fragrance with an unusual partner, the behemoth media conglomerate Warner Communications, whose congenial CEO, Steven J. Ross, was a Lauren fan. Ross was backing Lauren with $6 million in start-up costs and another $100 million promised in the long term. Calvin felt left in the dust. Ralph Lauren was really beginning to bug Calvin. In 1973, the Bronx-born menswear designer had licensed his Polo line to a women's-wear manufacturer and had gone into direct competition with Calvin. Worse, Calvin was sick of the odious comparisons in the press between him and Ralph Lauren just because they both grew up on Mosholu Parkway and went to P.S. 80. Yes, they both dressed mainstream America, but Lauren's sense of fashion was based on reviving American styles of times past, while Calvin's clothing looked to the future as well as defined the present. But the press had set them up as rivals.

At least that was the way he felt that day in the doctor's office, inhaling Halston's perfume while he was waiting for his energy shot. Calvin had very little patience for waiting, but this was worth it. He had begun frequenting this East Side internist who had garnered a reputation in the fashion industry for his restorative injections of vitamin B_{12}. The doctor's other patients included Oscar de la Renta, as well at Kurt Waldheim, then Secretary General of the United Nations, and people swore by his injections for health and energy. Calvin always plugged into the newest youth fad, particularly where skin and aging were involved, and he had a whole Rolodex card filled in with doctors' names. At the first sign of the slightest little pimple he was out the door on his way to the dermatologist, and if he heard of a new concoction to reverse aging or aid in vitality, Calvin would be at the head of the line. This doctor was so busy that he didn't even give the shots himself. When Calvin was finally called inside an examining room, he was told to drop his drawers and bend over for a shot administered by the doctor's medical technician, Ruth Kohlenberg.

"Do you like the smell of Halston's new perfume?" Calvin asked Kohlenberg.

"I'm not crazy about it," the technician told him as she plunged the syringe into his rump. "Why don't you have a fragrance of your own?" she asked.

Calvin stood up and fastened his pants. "I'd like to," he said. "I've been thinking about it for a long time, but we can't find the right company to do it."

"Why don't you call my husband and talk to him about it?" Kohlenberg asked.

Calvin didn't understand at first. Then Kohlenberg explained that her husband was Stanley Kohlenberg, a name Calvin instantly recognized as one of the premier marketing men in the fragrance industry. A former president of Coty, Kohlenberg was currently domestic president of Revlon's Group III, an upscale line of fragrances and cosmetics. Kohlenberg was an easygoing, savvy fellow, admired in the industry as much for his wit and geniality as his expertise in women's facial treatment, which in part came from his background as a pharmacist on Coney Island Avenue in Brooklyn many years before. Calvin and Ruth Kohlenberg decided that their meeting was "kismet," and a lunch with Stanley Kohlenberg was arranged at the Plaza Hotel's Oak Room.

It was at this meal that Calvin outlined his "total control" demand. Kohlenberg shook his head. Revlon would love to bring Calvin in under its wing, and it would make many concessions to him, but he would never find a company that would chance spending tens of millions of dollars to get him started and let him run the show so completely. Fragrance and cosmetics was a very different business from the women's ready-to-wear business, Kohlenberg explained. It was a "packaged goods" business with a specialized selling philosophy and business techniques best left to experts. But Calvin would not budge: "total control" or no deal. Feeling frustrated, Kohlenberg returned to Revlon empty-handed.

But not for long. Several months later, Calvin ran into Kohlenberg at a party at the Metropolitan Museum of Art and asked him to lunch again. This time, Calvin and Barry had found a solution to the problem of "total control." "We've decided to do it ourselves," Calvin told Kohlenberg over lunch.

"Yourselves?" Kohlenberg asked, impressed. "Are you prepared to spend that kind of money?" he asked the partners and Barry and Calvin assured him they were. The pair went on to outline a plan in which they would commit as many millions as needed to start a cosmetics and fragrance business themselves instead of giving away over 90 percent of the profits. They were forming a separate company called Calvin Klein Cosmetics with its own capital. Then a licensing agreement would be drawn up between the new cosmetics company and the umbrella company, Calvin Klein Industries, because even though they owned both companies, they would have an "arm's-length agreement" to protect them in financial and legal scrapes.

"And we'd like you to join us," Calvin said.

Kohlenberg couldn't have been more surprised. He was a president of one of Revlon's most profitable divisions, highly salaried and with many perks. His influence was at its height, and his future at the company was unlimited. To leave Revlon at this point to start a company from scratch was a risky move. But Calvin and Barry insisted they would make it worth his while, and after weeks of secret negotiations they came up with a deal that lured Kohlenberg into their camp: simply put, 20 percent ownership. The only catch was that Kohlenberg could not cash out on his 20 percent until the company was operating in the black.

As Kohlenberg's employment papers were being readied to sign, he asked that his impending departure from Revlon be kept a secret until he was able to inform his superiors himself. He would give sufficient notice and leave the company in an orderly and dignified way. However, characteristically determined to be in charge of every last detail, Calvin himself leaked Kohlenberg's arrival to *Women's Wear Daily,* and on Friday, January 28, 1977, there was a front-page headline announcing that Kohlenberg was jumping ship from Revlon to start a new company for Calvin Klein that would introduce a full line of products, including a fragrance. "I'll apply the same taste level, the same standards of quality, to these products that I do to my clothes," Calvin proudly told the paper.

Kohlenberg was livid, but no less livid than his boss at Revlon, Michel Bergerac, who read about it over breakfast. When Kohlenberg arrived at his office, he was promptly escorted out of the building by security guards, and the very next day, Tuesday, February 1, the disgruntled executive reported for work creating Calvin Klein cosmetics and perfume.

His first day on the job was a depressing awakening for Kohlenberg. To save on start-up costs, it had been agreed that instead of pouring hundreds of thousands of dollars into offices on Madison

or Fifth Avenue—where most fragrance companies were located—
they would run the company out of the bowels of the ready-to-wear
business on the tenth floor of 139 West Thirty-ninth Street. "I had
never been beyond the showroom and Barry and Calvin's offices
until that point," said Kohlenberg, who was shocked at how grimy
and ugly the rest of the enterprise was. Kohlenberg found himself
consigned to a decrepit room with "an old metal desk with three
drawers hanging out, kind of broke," he said. Making the best of it,
Kohlenberg started to organize his new office when he opened a
desk drawer and discovered a pair of men's shiny black Oxford
shoes. "There are a pair of shoes in my drawer," he told Barry, who
shrugged, then said, "Oh, they belong to Nicky de Gunzburg. He'll
be using your office when he changes his clothes." When Kohlenberg asked for a key to the executive men's room, he was told there
were only three restrooms on the premises: one exclusively for the
use of Calvin and Barry; one near the showroom, reserved for the
use of buyers; and an unlocked common toilet that Kohlenberg had
to share with all the other men in the firm. When he complained
about the peeling paint and broken stall doors, Barry said, "It's only
a bathroom. What's wrong with that toilet?"

Kohlenberg began to form a team. An office staff was handpicked from the best people available in the industry and installed
in a little warren of rooms near Kohlenberg's office. Penny Irwin
was hired as head of product development; Tom Sedita was named
the new manager of operations; Nick Jordan was named director of
sales; Nick Mottola was appointed head of the sales staff; and Ted
Bocuzzi, who had been corporate production manager at Fabergé,
was hired to run a plant they leased in Kearny, New Jersey. Phyllis
Posnick, who was a beauty editor at *Vogue,* was hired as director of
merchandising and public relations. Dan Moriarity, one of the industry's top public relations men, was hired away from Max Factor
to take charge of promotion.

The newly assembled staff was soon to discover what Calvin and
Barry's other employees already knew: Nothing escaped Barry's attention. Barry kept a hawk's eye on everything that went on in the
company. One thing in particular he was concerned about was
stealing, and he had installed surveillance cameras all over the factory with monitors in his own office to stem employee theft. But

the cameras also allowed him to watch who was goofing off. One day when Barry spotted a shipping clerk on another floor loafing, he called the foreman on the phone and told him of the transgression. Barry watched intently on the monitor as the foreman gave the man hell in full view of the camera. The new staff also learned that it was not unusual to find Barry out by the elevators fifteen minutes before quitting time to see who was slipping out early. Also, there was only a nominal office manager, and every new file cabinet or box of paper clips had to get Barry's approval. And Barry had to sign every check for no matter what, and every penny that went out of the company was approved with his signature. Said another executive in the company, "The entire time I worked there I was never given a key to the place. Nobody was trusted enough to be there without Barry around. Barry was running the place like it was a Harlem grocery store—trust no one. But this wasn't Harlem, this was big business."

Penny Irwin remembers one episode that for her sums up Barry's relationship with his employees. Almost every day at a certain time when the racetrack results were broadcast on the radio, Barry would stop in Irwin's office and ask to borrow her inexpensive clock radio so he could listen to the racing results. Irwin never understood why Barry didn't buy his own radio, but she was happy to let him use hers. One night when the offices were being painted, her radio was stolen from her desk, and thinking that Barry might replace it—both because it was stolen from his premises and because he listened to the track results on it every day—Irwin asked Stanley Kohlenberg to mention the theft to him.

"What has her clock radio got to do with me?" Barry asked, affronted, and stormed off down the hall. Irwin had to replace her own radio, and Barry resumed listening to it.

2

There was a more fundamental problem than pettiness to confront at Calvin Klein Ltd. Many times Calvin wasn't sure of what he wanted creatively. The more successful he got, the more he was afraid of making a mistake. It took him a long time to make up his mind, and then he changed his decisions ad infinitum until scheduling forbade any more changes. Then, when he finally did decide on a color or a fabric or a cut, he was "an impossible perfectionist," said Kohlenberg. "He could almost physically not let go of anything that had his name on it that he didn't love. Even though he wasn't an expert in cosmetics and fragrance, he had some strong opinions about certain things. Where he didn't have strong opinions, he trusted his friends."

Calvin's "friends" in these matters were the Baron de Gunzburg and another maven of taste, Frances Stein, the former *Vogue* magazine editor. For years now Calvin thought the sun rose and set on Stein and her infallible good taste. Calvin would never forget that when he was in the hospital with hepatitis, Frances Stein had sent him a gift wrapped not in paper but in a beautiful scarf and grosgrain ribbon. He was so enamored of the editor and so positive of her "perfect" taste that Frances Stein was his companion when Betty Ford invited him to the White House. In August 1976, Calvin hired her as "director of the design studio," which ostensibly handled all the licensing, but Stein did much more. Installed in an office right next door to his, Stein became his litmus test for everything. "Frances Stein was his right hand," said one executive. "She was his taste mentor. After Barry she was the second most powerful person in the company."

And one of the most difficult. A skinny, nervous, dramatic-looking woman with bangs, she was a bona fide genius, and to "make things work" was her great gift, said a former assistant. She was a magician; she could take a simple shirt, the right pearls, a belt to set it off, and create a golden illusion of glamour. "I'm *horrible*," she once said about her perfectionism. "I can see one-eighth and one-sixteenth of an inch differences [in the way something is cut]." She worked in an office filled with her "security stuff" of handbags and fabrics and beads. "Piles and piles and *piles* of stuff that I never even look at," she said.

After graduation from Smith College she had applied for a job at *Harper's Bazaar* with Diana Vreeland, who at first sight grabbed Stein's hair and cried, "Russian hair! When can you start?" Vreeland helped "form her eye," according to Stein. "She taught all of us that there was no middle ground: either it was wonderful or it was just to be ripped up and put in the wastepaper basket." And rip things up is what Francis Stein did. She would shred clothing, stomp on belts, or hurl handbags at people who displeased her. She threw things at people "with force," remembered a colleague.

Her reputation for dramatic temper tantrums began at *Vogue,* when assistants would scurry from her sight, but the incident that made her notorious in the business was when a hapless delicatessen delivery boy walked into a conference room with a cardboard box filled with coffee cups and cold drinks just as Stein blew her top. She smashed the box right out of the hands of the startled boy, and the coffee flew all over the office and splattered everything. The employees named the brown blotches left on the wall the "Frances Stein Coffee Stain."

"She would definitely *lose control,*" said one of her employees at Calvin. Another executive said, "She was capable of anger that would remind you of a scene in *The Exorcist.*" She once ranted and raved after a coworker, down the hall, into the elevator, out onto the street, and to the door of a taxi. When the coworker said, "I don't appreciate being screamed at," Stein snarled, "I'm not screaming, I'm sharing."

The net result of this kind of temperament was that among Barry and Frances and Calvin "it was not a happy, productive place [to work], so much as a scary place," said one executive. "It was remarkable how frightened everybody seemed to be. People working in the office at levels high and low always seemed to be waiting for some kind of explosion or another." But Calvin was unwavering in his adoration, and at times Stein seemed equally besotted. Staff members recall one 1976 business trip to Paris when Calvin took everyone out to dinner at a posh restaurant. After five bottles of wine were consumed by Calvin and his party, Calvin was so drunk he couldn't feed himself. "He had his head cocked back like a bird in its nest," recalled a designer who was present, "and when the *framboise* came for dessert, Frances shoveled the *nougatine au chocolat* into his mouth."

Frances Stein and Calvin both had very definite opinions about women's makeup, in particular that Calvin would *never* carry blue eye shadow in his line. Calvin *hated* blue eye shadow—it reminded him of the grotesquely rouged and lipsticked faces of his mother and the other ladies from the Bronx and Brooklyn. No matter that blue eye shadow was the single most successful selling color in the country. By adhering to his high principles he was slashing his bread-and-butter profits. Calvin stuck to his art. "It would be dishonest to [carry] shades just because we think they will sell when we believe they're wrong," he said.

Another concept Calvin held dear was that the cosmetics colors should complement the colors of his clothing. He decided to develop five basic "faces"—lips, eyes, cheeks, nails—that would produce a total look to go with the seasonal colors of his lines. The problem was that Calvin's color taste was so neutral and natural that often what he liked in a pot looked sallow and unbecoming on the face. Frustrated and insecure even with the advice of the baron and Frances Stein, Calvin hired one of the foremost makeup artists of his day, Way Bandy, in an unusual consulting capacity. Calvin had great trust in Way Bandy's taste, because he had worked with him dozens of times on fashion shows and photographic layouts. Since Calvin would not need Bandy's help for more than a day to choose the colors and because the advice he gave on that day might result in a bonanza for Calvin, it was agreed that Bandy would be paid a special flat rate of $25,000 for the one day's advice. Bandy spent that day at Calvin's office playing with thousands of lipstick colors and consistencies and pancakes and foundation mixes, rouges and color charts, like a child with finger paints, until by late that night five faces were put together: a honey, coral, mauve, rose, and rouge face with a variety of lipstick and nail-polish colors with names like geranium and paprika. It was the most profitable day of Way Bandy's very profitable career.

Next, the line had to be bottled, packaged, and wrapped. Calvin wanted the perfume bottle and cosmetics cases to be unique, and he refused to buy stock cases and bottles. Calvin's signature shape was an elongated oval, a "racetrack oval," Barry liked to call it, and they decided to manufacture their own cases completely from the ground up despite the fact it would add three quarters of a million dollars to their budget to do their own tooling. But Calvin insisted the cases be perfect, smooth, gorgeously fitted, and crying out to be touched. Moreover, Calvin ruled that the glass perfume bottles had to be manufactured in France, where the clarity of glass bottles was the best in the world and the glass stoppers perfectly fit the seal. (Plastics later replaced the glass stoppers.) The one-ounce, French-made bottle he choose cost $1.50 to produce, twice the cost of most perfume bottles, but the crystal-clear glass oval was exquisite to look at, as were the accompanying burnt-red, Chinese-lacquered compacts and rouge pots that echoed the oval shape of the perfume bottle. At first, buyers worried that the lipstick would not stand up on end because of its oval shape—anathema in the cosmetics industry—but "It will look just as pretty lying down," Calvin insisted, and it did. Calvin hired Irving Penn, the dean of fashion product photography, who worked extensively for *Vogue,* to help design the print ad. Like everyone who saw the cosmetics cases, Penn was taken with the beautiful ellipses and the smooth indentations where they split open. Penn and Calvin spent several hours in Calvin's office playing with the Chinese-orange cases like boys playing with building blocks. They discovered that by gluing them together, they could build an improbably balanced but highly stylized stepladder of just the beautiful cases in an arcing sculpture, with the perfume bottle balanced precariously at the pinnacle.

Once Calvin got down to it, he had idea for dozens of other related products. He wanted to manufacture scented shelf paper, silk potpourri sachets for lingerie drawers, potpourri closet pomanders, and incense sticks and scented candles. Frances Stein helped invent a scented silk charmeuse furoshiki-style lingerie bag, and when it came to packaging, Stein would allow no synthetic coverings to be used, and only real silk and velvet fabrics could line the trademark deep red boxes. On and on it went for a year, with each product and the packaging passed on by Calvin and the baron and Frances Stein. And they still did not have the most important piece of the venture—the signature scent, the heavenly fragrance that would summon to mind the name "Calvin Klein" to millions of women around the world. They didn't even have a name for it. Around the office, employees had taken to calling it by the code name "Seventh Avenue" because it was so unusual to be developing a fragrance there.

The biggest stumbling block to finding a scent was Calvin himself. It had come as an unhappy surprise when Calvin's staff discovered that he actually disliked perfume. Perfume reminded him of his P.S. 80 schoolteachers or his mother's friends who came to play mah-jongg. Calvin never used cologne himself, and if there was one smell he liked at all, it was musk—an earthy, musty, natural smell which he found sexy. Calvin's predilection for musk was well-known by his apple-polishing younger employees, and "the offices downstairs smelled of it all the time," said Kohlenberg. "All the people who worked for him used to wear it, men and women." But musk was not a feasible scent for woman's perfume, and every time Kohlenberg tried to find out what smells Calvin liked, he kept insisting, "I can't tell you. Something floral but not heavy. Something that doesn't hang like a cloud over a woman or set off the sprinkler system."

To find a fragrance that would please Calvin was clearly a daunting proposition. Perfume is comprised of thousands of kinds of essences and oils in an alcohol base, distinguished by their "top notes" or immediate impact of the fragrance. Top notes generally fall into families like "single floral," the scent of one flower in particular, or "floral," the smell of a bouquet of flowers, or "Orientals," which include the intense scent of jasmine, or the "green" families, which evoke pines and other woodsy smells. These families are mixed and matched into literally millions of possibilities, with new combinations invented chemically every day.

Faced with Calvin's inability to find anything he wanted at the laboratory stage, Kohlenberg devised a plan. He went to Bloomingdale's and purchased a bottle of every last perfume sold in that store. Then he masked each bottle and disguised the shape so Calvin could not be prejudiced by name and brand. For three days running Kohlenberg spritzed Calvin with the perfumes, asking him to rate the scents from zero to ten in the hope this would establish a pattern. "After spritzing all the fragrances in the United States," said Kohlenberg, "none of them did better than a five with him, except for musk, so I knew I was in trouble."

For professional help Kohlenberg turned to International Flavors and Fragrance (IF&F). Located in Union Beach, New Jersey, IF&F was the largest creator of fragrances in the world, a billion-dollar global company that supplied the formula for fragrances, perfumes, soaps, and cleansers. They were reputed to have the best "noses" in the business—account executives with gifted senses of smell—as well as chemists who could re-create virtually any scent or flavor under the sun. Almost weekly different essential oils and potential perfumes were sent to Calvin and his taste team to smell. Many months went by without satisfying them. If a perfume appealed to Calvin, Frances would take one whiff and wail, "This is *pissvasser!*" If Frances didn't mind one scent, the baron thought it was "garbage!" Finally, after Calvin and his crew rejected dozens of scents from IF&F, the chemists happened to formulate a new smell that everybody fell in love with. It was very "in your face," yet dreamy and easily identifiable. Bob Foster, the IF&F account executive, brought it to Kohlenberg's office, and he and his staff loved it. "There was nothing like it on the market," said Penny Irwin. "It was *so delicious,* everybody loved it." Kohlenberg told Calvin he was positive they had finally found a "winner" for "Seventh Avenue" and asked to make a presentation to the taste mavens. On the afternoon of the meeting Frances Stein, the baron, as well as the *New York Times* fashion journalist and pal Carrie Donovan were assembled. Kohlenberg spritzed them one by one. As the mist settled, "Nicky de Gunzburg wrinkled his nose," said Kohlenberg, and Frances Stein "made a funny face. Calvin looked at the baron and Frances Stein, and *he* made a funny face."

"We can fix it," Kohlenberg said hopefully. "We can lighten the top."

"Why bother?" the baron said grandly.

"That killed it completely," said Kohlenberg. Dejected and more than a little angry, Kohlenberg went back to his office and called the IF&F account executive, Bob Foster, and said, "We lost it. We'll have to start from scratch."

Foster said that he also happened to be the account executive for Ralph Lauren, who was still looking for a fragrance himself. Since Calvin had turned the new discovery down, would they mind if it was offered to Ralph Lauren. Kohlenberg said, "Sure, why not? It's a dead issue over here," and didn't give it a second thought.

In the interim Frances Stein went to Paris on business and stopped into a small, exclusive *parfumier* that specialized in made-to-order fragrances for private customers. Stein had the boutique meld together a rosy brew she favored and brought it back to Cal-

vin. He took one whiff of the stuff and started raving about its
"deep, romantic scent with lots of jasmine and attar of roses." He
sprayed half the staff with it before calling Kohlenberg into his
office and ordering him to have IF&F analyze Stein's perfume and
"make us this fragrance." Kohlenberg took the bottle back to his
office and smelled it. It had no "cleavage," as they said in the business, no sex appeal. "Mildly inoffensive" was his verdict. "It
smelled something like Cashmere Bouquet. It had no distinction at
all."

"It was tacky," said Penny Irwin.

But Calvin and his coterie strongly disagreed. Women would
love it, Frances said. It was chic and classy and light and oh, so
Calvin.

It was also very expensive to have IF&F's scientists break down
and analyze the contents and then reproduce it exactly. The top
note turned out to be from one of the most expensive kinds of rose
oils in the world, which would cost sixty-five dollars a pound versus
twenty-five dollars for a typical oil. This in turn would raise the
retail price per ounce to eighty-five dollars, making Calvin's new
fragrance one of the most expensive ever to enter the market, more
costly even than Norell's or Halston's.

Not only was Calvin going to break the rules about price, color,
and smell; he was going to make some innovations in the business
end of the cosmetics industry as well. For one thing, there was to
be no "gift with purchase"—a marketing technique widely used in
the cosmetics business as an inducement to try the line. But Barry
and Calvin would be damned before they were going to give away
umbrellas or rain hats to get customers to buy something. After all,
they did not give away belts to women who wanted to buy pants.
Second, they would take no returns. "It was against [Barry's] reli-
gion," an executive noted. "Returns were Barry's *enemy.*" But in the
cosmetics business the manufacturer always allows the store the
courtesy of "revolving" their stock for newer merchandise. "One of
the rules of the cosmetics business," said one company executive,
"is that merchandise is always for exchange if the product doesn't
sell." But Calvin and Barry didn't give a damn how the cosmetics
business worked. They were Calvin Klein, they didn't take returns
on clothing, stores were clamoring to carry their name, and they

would have it their way or not at all. Word went out that Barry would only take returns on damaged stock or shipping errors.

In any event, Barry and Kohlenberg assured the stores that there would not be any returns, because not only would the line sell out, but the stores would never overstock. Barry was pioneering a computerized reordering system that would infallibly send the stores balanced amounts of product as needed. The buyer at each Calvin Klein counter would simply fill in the stock control sheet and send it back. The computer would do the rest. And in yet another break with tradition, the counter people were going to be paid less than most other companies paid, but in return their commission was being raised in what Barry believed would be an incentive to sell. In addition, the markup was raised by 5–10 percent from the industry-wide 40 percent standard in the hope that the counter girls would push those items harder. Another rule they made was not to break up the fragrance and cosmetics line—a store had to sell both or none at all. And, to boot, Calvin was demanding that any store carrying his line give him twelve feet of sales space—two counters' worth—in every cosmetic department.

Finally, after a year in the making, the launch was set for late February 1978. It was of no small annoyance that Ralph Lauren had chosen exactly the same time to launch his own new fragrances (and perhaps no coincidence as well). Word on the street was that Ralph Lauren was supremely confident that his perfume was going to be a big hit. Warner Communications was rolling out massive promotional artillery for the launch, including four full pages in the *New York Times,* store appearances, and television commercials. It would dwarf Calvin's own launch, which he was backing himself. Barry and Calvin couldn't wait to smell Lauren's perfume, and the week before it was due in the stores, Barry got his hands on a bottle and brought it into Kohlenberg's office. Kohlenberg took one sniff and smiled.

It was the fragrance from IF&F that Calvin and Frances Stein and the baron had all turned down.

After that, anything that Calvin heard Ralph Lauren had planned for his launch Calvin refused to do. Ralph was going to appear in his magazine and newspaper ads; Calvin refused to be photographed in connection with the fragrance or cosmetics. Calvin wanted to launch his perfume at Bloomingdale's flagship New York store. The cosmetics and fragrance departments on its main floor were some of the most prestigious and beautiful in any department store in the world. But in discussing the launch date with Bloomingdale's president, Marvin Traub, Calvin was told to "avoid" the last week in February, because that was when Ralph Lauren was launching his scent there. Calvin canceled Bloomingdale's altogether. "I couldn't follow another designer into the store," he said huffily. He choose instead to launch at Saks Fifth Avenue, which was anxious for him to appear in a major television campaign it would help finance, as well as a series of in-store appearances at Saks locations across the country. But that was too similar to Lauren's plan, and Calvin refused to travel or appear in TV commercials. Eventually, a March 6 launch date was decided upon, at which Calvin reluctantly agreed to appear in the New York store, followed by a West Coast launch in Los Angeles at I. Magnin, to be tied in with a luncheon for a local charity event.

Finally, there was one last important detail left unattended to. The fragrance needed a name. They couldn't continue to call it "Seventh Avenue," after all. And so, after much deliberation, they decided it might as well be called "Calvin Klein."

3

As if starting his own cosmetics company, fulfilling the demands of eleven licenses, and designing four women's wear collections a year wasn't task enough, in March 1977, Calvin announced a historic venture which had the fashion industry "agog," according to the *Daily News Record.* He was going to design and license a complete menswear collection, a staggering range of suits, sport coats, top coats, trousers, shirts, sweaters, leisure wear, ties, belts, and eventually a hosiery and underwear division. It would be the first time that any designer, from any country, would try to enter the men's field with such a huge and diversified line. If Calvin succeeded in capturing a lion's share of the men's market as well as maintaining his existing women's-wear stake, it would make his America's premier designer label perhaps the most important sportswear design label in the world. If he failed, it would badly hurt his reputation as one of the country's most savvy young entrepreneurs.

But this was not a project likely to fail. Department stores had been begging Calvin to expand into menswear for years. Bloomingdale's even offered to put aside a budget to manufacture the line for him, if he wished. His soft, pared styles seemed perfectly adaptable to men's clothing, and the timing was ripe. He was keenly aware that most men rely on their wives and girlfriends to help them pick out clothes, and his name had tremendous recognition value among women. Moreover, in the status-hungry late seventies, men were increasingly using the way they dressed to help define themselves and were becoming aggressively style-conscious. Calvin had experimented at making clothing for the male models who enlivened his women's-wear shows, and in the fall of 1973 he produced a tailored men's pea coat for Saks Fifth Avenue that was enormously popular with customers. Saks also offered to back a menswear boutique in its New York store for him, but it was too much work to design a line just for one store. He was either going to go into it in a big way or not at all. The only problem was that the start-up costs for a menswear line made the capital launching a cosmetics company seem like play money. A venture on the scale that Calvin envisaged could easily eat up $30 million, and not many companies were going to sink that kind of money into one man without a say in what was going to be sold. Over the years he had serious discussions about licensing a menswear line with Larry Leeds, president of Manhattan Industries, with the Bridgeport, Connecticut, clothing conglomerate Warnaco, and with Irving Selbst, head of the huge Bond Industries, with whom he almost closed a deal. But all of the discussions fell apart over that old bugaboo, Calvin's insistence on "total control." No CEO in his right mind would put up $30 million and relinquish control.

Except for Maurice Bidermann. A short, barrel-shaped man with lips that seemed permanently poised in a playful smile, this forty-three-year-old Frenchman didn't care about total control. Pugnacious and street-smart, he had been working with big-time designers long enough to figure he knew his way around their fickle daydreams. Dangle the prospects of huge grosses in front of them and they would soon forget their dictum about quality and construction. Cardin. Saint Laurent. Hechter. They were all made by Bidermann's factories. Anyway, $30 million would not break Monsieur Bidermann, who was a hundred times as successful as Calvin in his own business. He was the mastermind of one of the largest manufacturing networks in the world, with thirteen thousand workers in thirty-four factories. His plants in France, the United States, and Hong Kong churned out nearly $200 million in designer duds each year. Bidermann commuted between Paris and New York almost weekly, and he not only drove a Rolls-Royce; it was a *classic* 1961 Silver Cloud. To give further cachet to Monsieur Bidermann, he was the brother of Regine, the jet-set nightclub owner of New Jimmy's and Regine's, in Paris and New York.

For all of Bidermann's European affectations, Calvin found that he was just like any other Jewish garment-center kingpin, only with an entourage and a fancy accent. Bidermann was, in fact, born Maurice Zylberberg in Brussels and grew up in the poor Jewish quarter of Paris. At fifteen he ran away to join the Israeli army. With little formal education, he went to work at his uncle's menswear factory in 1955. He proved to be a cutthroat competitor and ended up taking over not only the factory but his uncle's name as well. Each year he hunted down manufacturing plants in financial trouble and bought them up, until he was soon one of the largest producers of men's clothing in France. His production of Pierre Cardin and Yves Saint Laurent suits had made him famous in the United States, but still, his factories were too big and varied to be kept busy at all times, and Bidermann needed to land a name like Calvin. Bidermann approached Calvin because, he said, "I thought Calvin Klein was talented." He believed Calvin would fill a growing gap in the U.S. market between cheaper, off-the-peg, nonfashion clothing and the $800 *prêt à porter* by the existing designer names.

Negotiations began in August 1976. Calvin, Barry, and Monsieur Bidermann were the perfect match for one another, haggling over each point like *zaydas* in the rag trade. Barry would snarl and threaten to walk out, and Calvin would ask for more approvals and control than any designer had ever demanded before. He wanted to dictate at which factories and in which countries the clothing would be made. He wanted to decide the quality of the thread and the stitching, the size of the needles used to stitch it. Bidermann fought every concession by not giving an inch on his royalty offer. Negotiations were made even more laborious because Bidermann said he did not speak English well enough to negotiate without a French interpreter. Everything that was said in the room had to be translated from English to French and vice versa, causing confusing lapses in the heated bargaining. This, claimed Stanley Kohlenberg, who sat in on several meetings, was a brilliant ploy by Bidermann, whom Kohlenberg believed understood and spoke English quite well and who used the tedium of translation to break everybody down.

Michel Zelnick, the boyish thirty-four-year-old president of Bidermann in the United States, helped hammer out the final deal. Zelnick was a fashionable young Frenchman, educated in America, with a matinee idol's looks and a temperament as highly strung as a violin. He would be directly responsible for the day-to-day running of Bidermann's American companies. According to Zelnick, it was Calvin who dragged out the negotiations, not the language barrier. "Barry is a very rough character, but I think Calvin is much rougher in a different way," said Zelnick of the nine months it took to conclude a contract.

One niggling concern Bidermann had about signing with Calvin was that Yves Saint Laurent, with whom he had a long and most profitable relationship, would be angry. After all, Calvin had widely been criticized for copying Saint Laurent. Bidermann tried to keep the negotiations with Calvin quiet, but in the middle of the bargaining he was obliged to invite Calvin to Paris for a tour of some of the factories where his menswear would be made. While he was in Paris, Bidermann promised Calvin *une grande soirée* at his sister Regine's nightclub to which he would invite *tout le monde* from French society. With party invitations sent out, Bidermann could no longer avoid telling Saint Laurent and his business partner, Pierre Bergé, about his pending deal with Calvin. But fate took the sticky task out of Bidermann's hands. By chance, Pierre Bergé was on the same flight to Paris as Calvin, and Bergé's chauffeur and Bidermann's chauffeur found themselves in the same limo line at the airport in Orly. Bidermann's driver mentioned that he had been sent to fetch the American, Calvin Klein, who was Monsieur Bidermann's newest designer. And so it passed that Pierre Bergé learned this delicate news from the lips of his chauffeur.

Eventually, a five-year licensing deal was signed inaugurating a newly formed company called Calvin Klein Menswear Inc. The contract was renewable by Bidermann as long as the manufacturer reached certain volumes in sales. There was no advance of dollars to Calvin, but Bidermann was committed to building an entire business for him from the ground up. In return Calvin got a royalty increasing to over approximately 7 percent, depending on "volume and minimum guarantees," said Michel Zelnick. "It was an interesting amount of dollars."

When the deal was announced to the press with much attendant hoopla, Calvin was quick to point out that the menswear line would not be the work of a dozen drones but would bear the imprimatur of the master. "I don't believe in lending my name for royalties and walking away. Maybe other designers feel they can do that, but not me," Calvin said.

With that clarified, the enormous undertaking was under way. Joe D'Urso was hired and given a $1 million budget to build one of the most spectacular and unusual showplaces ever seen in the fashion industry. Located not in the grimy confines of Seventh Avenue but in the prime midtown business district in the Celanase Building on the Avenue of the Americas with a spectacular view of a skyscraper canyon, the showroom and offices occupied over half of the thirty-second floor. Beyond a reception area, where Calvin's name was displayed in giant, brushed-aluminum letters, was a white-and-gray showroom with glossy white walls that floated on tracks and could be dismantled or moved to form smaller and larger spaces at will. The floors were coated in black Perelli rubber tiles, and merchandise and fabrics were shown to buyers on black vinyl tabletops in arcades resembling miniature storefronts, complete with floor-to-ceiling windowpanes. The sleek sample cabinets were modular, designed so they could be emptied and laid end to end on their sides to form a long runway down the middle of the showroom. Above the runway was a six-foot-wide mirror, positioned so that buyers and press not seated in the front rows could look at the reflection of the clothing planetarium style.

Determined to shake up a sleepy industry dominated by middle-aged salesmen, Calvin hired a staff of executives in their twenties who were so young in comparison to other companies that one observer referred to them as the "Youth Crusade." The sales force largely consisted of lissome women with Farrah Fawcett hair and in slinky Calvin Klein clothes, the music was turned up loud in the showroom, and the staff always seemed to be laughing and having a good time. "It was beautiful people having fun" was the way executive Edward Jones III described the showroom. "Calvin's idea was to make it the place to be, and it *was* the place to be."

Calvin also put a team of designers in place, led by the talented Bill Robinson, a former rising star at Anne Klein and Valentino. But no one doubted where the design buck stopped—Calvin's desk—even if, as some executives quietly grumbled, he was out of his depth. He had devoted all his life to making *women* beautiful. He himself was hardly a candidate for the Best Dressed List. His own favorite clothing was a mélange of sweatshirts or T-shirts and jeans, with a few ordinary Brooks Brothers suits and an occasional bespoke suit from Savile Row. Calvin seemed uncertain of the right look for his new enterprise, the signature of which would be the shape and silhouette of the suit jacket.

"We went through all sorts of shoulders," said Zelnick. "No roll. No soft. Modified Brooks Brothers. Traditional shoulder. One day European, one day Ralph Lauren. Then he was concerned about the growing popularity of Armani." What could have been completed in one month took nearly a year. Eventually, recalled Bidermann executive Stephen Wayne, "we found a suit from Canada at Paul Stuart [a tony Madison Avenue men's shop], and that's the silhouette we agreed on." Calvin's stroke of genius was to intentionally cut the suit roomier, to allow for the American male's tendency to a paunch. Bill Robinson said, Calvin realized that "a little bit of innovation could go a long way." They ended up with what Bidermann executives summarized as "American with British leanings." Said Stephen Wayne, "Calvin was fussing over minor distinctions. In menswear there isn't a lot of design. The fabrics were what made the suits authentically Calvin Klein."

The fabrics were mostly tweeds from Great Britain. There were a few additions from Far Eastern mills, but no lightweight wools, let alone poly blends to pamper to the sweaty Sunbelt market. In that period, fast-growing southern states like Florida accounted for

one-third of all sales, but "Calvin didn't want to hear about it," said
Wayne. Calvin's design team was told to submit prototypes of each
garment and fit them on Calvin, who acted as his own model. He
would strut and twirl and posture in front of a full-length mirror
before passing judgment. The final samples also had to pass muster
with Frances Stein. Calvin would sit on the floor at development
meetings, looking boyishly innocent, said Bill Robinson, "and let
her be the hit man." Invariably, Stein would "hate everything everybody did," he recalled and send them back to the drawing board.
Often the slightest detail would send her off. Once, when she did
not like the way samples were pressed, she tossed them to the floor
and bellowed, "You call this ironing?"

Calvin was finally ready to unveil the collection on January 26,
1978, at a fashion show almost as spectacular as his new showrooms. The line contained a mind-boggling 799 fabrics and thousands of articles of clothing, including 500 suits, challis and
Egyptian cotton day shirts, "the perfect evening shirt" (in handker-
chief linen), tweedy, British-looking sweaters, khaki and flannel
pleated pants, leather bomber jackets à la Christopher Street, and a
cashmere sweater designed to look like a sweatshirt that would
become one of his biggest sellers. The applause at the end of the
show was thunderous and sincere; a brilliant menswear designer
had been introduced. Amid the kisses and congratulations on the
gorgeous new showroom, buyers placed $10 million worth of or-
ders. The next day, based on projections, it was estimated that the
company would gross $40 million its first year. After the show,
though, Calvin seemed pensive. He scolded his public relations
woman for not having enough "superimportant" people in attendance and seemed more worried than relieved. "He went around
snapping at his staff," recalled Bill Robinson. "Everyone felt very
upset and alienated." It was almost as if the spectacular showroom
had outdone the clothes. "That was it," said Robinson. "We never
had another fashion show there again."

CHAPTER ELEVEN

Dionysus became a publicity hound.
                              —*Fame* magazine

What was this? Calvin wondered in amazement as he turned
the corner with his friends. It was nearly two in the morning on a
warm May night in 1977, and West Fifty-fourth Street between
Eighth and Ninth avenues—a neighborhood heretofore best
known as the male-porn theater district—seemed like the vortex of
Manhattan.

On a typical night there were several hundred people pushing
and shoving to get under a black marquee whose silver art deco
logo read *Studio 54*. The crowd was an eye-popping, unpredictable
assortment of humanity, as if an open invitation had been sent out
for a Federico Fellini casting call. Fashionable young men and
women in disco garb mingled with society couples in dinner jackets
and cocktail dresses. There was a West Point cadet in full-dress
uniform with his girlfriend in a prom dress, and a six-foot-two fairy-
princess drag queen on roller skates blessing everybody with her
Lucite wand. There was a woman with smudged eye makeup in a
pants suit and a man in a radish costume and two Mafioso types in
cheaply tailored tuxedos with red carnations and on their arms
even cheaper-looking blond girlfriends. Just outside the crowd
stood two hookers in hot pants and spike heels and bouffant wigs,
nervously smoking cigarettes, pacing, waiting. The throng swelled
and compressed, like an amoeba, twenty deep, pouring out into the
street and blocking traffic, already a tangle of double-parked limousines and yellow cabs. Police barricades held the mob back so that

cars could get by, and to make the scene even more surreal, paparazzi restlessly scanned the occupants of every arriving car for celebrity prey, their strobe flashes freezing the night in a hot white tableau.

On scores of nights Calvin plunged fearlessly into the mob, so tightly packed that it threatened to lift him off his feet and carry him to and fro. He pushed his way toward the marquee, where three lengths of red velvet ropes held back the crowd as efficiently as Moses parting the Red Sea. Of course, the five menacing bouncers standing on the other side of the velvet ropes, as hulking as they looked mean, reinforced the message not to cross them. This security force was protectively watching a small, skinny man with sad blue eyes and a prominent nose who paced beneath the marquee like a nervous cat. He seemed an unlikely choice for so much attention, dressed in a faded Lacoste shirt, worn-in jeans which hung on his hips, and white Nike tennis sneakers, but the crowd at the velvet ropes were calling his name in a cacophonous chant like hungry birds crying to be fed—"Steve!—Steve!—Steve baby!—STEVE!—Steve Rubell, remember me?—STEVE!"—pleading for his eyes to rest on theirs for just one moment, but instead, his wide stare passed them by, anxiously searching the crowd until it finally halted upon a face that he liked, a pretty face or a sexy face or his favorite kind of face, a celebrity face.

Calvin Klein!

Steve Rubell's face lit up like a klieg light.

"Calvin Klein!" he shouted excitedly, pointing Calvin out to the bodyguards. "It's Calvin Klein!"

As word of his presence spread through the mob, Calvin could hear people saying, "It's Calvin Klein! Look, it's *Calvin Klein!*" and strobe lights went off in his face, *pop* flash, blinding him as the pushing and shoving got worse, and suddenly a bodyguard had him by the arm and whisked him beyond the velvet ropes and through a set of blacked-out doors and down the rabbit hole into wonderland.

Or so it seemed.

It was dark inside, a wide entrance foyer of an old theater lined with mirrors, infinity reflected, and it took a moment for Calvin's eyes to adjust. The air was filled with the pulsating sound of disco music so deafening that it seemed to carbonate the air. "Oh, Calvin

Klein! I'm so excited to meet you!" Rubell shouted in a loud, nasal voice he had perfected to be heard over the din. Sometimes, late at night, with a little booze and a Quaalude or two, Steve Rubell's voice sounded just like a phonograph record being played a speed too slow and an octave too high. "I'm such a big fan of yours," he whined on, looking up at the designer with true adoration in his eyes. "I'm *honored* you're here in my club. *Anything* you want is yours," he told Calvin as they walked along, "anything, any*body*. Here, here are free drink tickets." Rubell pressed a half-dozen gold-and-black cards into Calvin's hands, good for free drinks. "But you won't need them," he went on, "because I'm buying you and your friends all champagne. *Calvin Klein!* I'm so happy to meet you!" Even as Rubell marched him forward into the vast cathedral-like main room of the club, he kept frantically imploring anyone within earshot, "Guess who just walked in? Calvin Klein is here! *Calvin Klein!*" completely unembarrassed to be saying this right in front of Calvin. Whether artifice or not, it was this self-effacing delight that gave Rubell his power to charm, a trait that would serve him well over the next twenty months as he would become the social arbiter of all New York.

Inside, the club was controlled mayhem, like Mardi Gras and New Year's Eve combined. A former cavernous opera house and CBS television studio from which they used to broadcast *What's My Line?* The orchestra had been ripped out to create a 5,400-square-foot dance floor above which five thousand individual lights blinked and throbbed in the most elaborate and stunning series of lighting effects ever created for a disco, including a man in the moon who snorted cocaine from a spoon and a giant amyl nitrate popper that showered confetti. On the main floor was a huge circular bar manned by bare-chested bartenders in tight jeans. Upstairs, in coed bathrooms at least as popular as the dance floor, the booths were crowded with couples having *soirées privées*. Up another flight of steps into the dark, steep second balcony couples of every combination of sex, race, and creed indulged in public displays that were sometimes more appropriate for the balcony of an X-rated movie theater than the world's foremost discotheque. Last but not least, Rubell took Calvin to the club's inner sanctum, the restricted domain of the "playground" room in the basement, so called be-

cause of the Astroturf on the floor and the pinball machine and
leftover children's toys used as props at a party. Located almost
directly beneath the jungle-like pounding of the massive dance
floor, the playground was a place where "things go on that you
wouldn't even believe," Steve Rubell promised.

For the next twenty months, until it was shut down by the Internal Revenue Service and Steve Rubell was shipped off to jail for tax
evasion, Studio 54 became an addiction in Calvin's life. It mixed
the wildness of a gay disco—manic dancing, drugs, beautiful party
people—with the respectabilty of a straight nightclub. Every night
there seemed to be some new titillation: Ryan O'Neal and Margaret
Trudeau bickering on the rear staircase. Diana Ross in a black
gown in the shadows of the disc jockey's booth. Cher and a girlfriend combing their voluminous hairdos in the mirrors of the coed
lounge. The members of the Yale wrestling team dressed in running shorts, stomping around the dance floor with their girlfriends
while only a few feet away from them an oblivious Robin Williams,
drenched in sweat, eyes closed, danced shoulder to shoulder with
an Italian princess and her female lover. On the banquettes Mick
Jagger had fallen asleep on Mikhail Baryshnikov's shoulder, and
Cheryl Tiegs was nibbling Peter Beard's ear. And there was Mrs.
Vreeland and Richard Bernstein and Halston being kissy-poo with
Truman Capote after his face-lift, who was being kissy-poo with
Liza, who sat next to a rigid-looking Andy Warhol, whom nobody
touched. Once a marching band in full dress uniform crisscrossed
the dance floor at midnight, and on another occasion the local
Hell's Angels rode their motorcycles in the front door and out the
back. A naked black man rode on a white horse for Bianca Jagger's
birthday, and for Steve Rubell's party the place was turned into a
giant playground, including basketball courts and sets of swings.
On New Year's Eve, 1978, the floor was covered a foot deep with
gold glitter. At the club's first anniversary party, so many people
were trying to get inside that the mob overran the velvet ropes and
bouncers and started to smash down the front doors.

Calvin found the club and all its treats so compelling that he was
unable to tear himself away for more than a few days. It was a
spectacle unlike any other on earth, and on summer weekends,
even in the splendor of the Fire Island Pines, he worried that he

was missing something and kept in touch with the club's manager, so he could hop a seaplane to get him back for a "good night." In 1980 he bought designer Angelo Dohngia's Key West house for $300,000 as a winter weekend retreat, but Studio 54, even two thousand miles away, preyed on his mind, and he reserved a small private plane at the airport to fly him back to New York at a moment's notice if he heard by phone that the club had an especially pretty crowd and the stars were out and the boys were hot.

Of course, Calvin was not alone in his Studio 54 addiction. Gaining admission to Studio 54 became a nightly imperative for international society. "I turned away sixteen hundred people tonight," Rubell would brag. It made some of them angry, too. One man punched him to the ground twice when he wouldn't let him inside his playground. But he didn't want swarthy Iranians at his party. He didn't want the "Bagel Nosh" crowd, or "Garmentos," or "bridge and tunnel" people who came from the suburbs to gawk at the stars. And no men with manicured nails or wearing wing-tip shoes or Rolex watches or any jewelry at all around the neck. Sometimes Rubell toyed cruelly with those most desperate to get in. One young man had to consent to allow Rubell to burn a cigarette hole in the collar of his suit—Rubell disapproved of the fabric—before he was allowed through the magic portals. Some petitioners at the velvet ropes had the temerity to offer Rubell money, waving hundred-dollar bills in front of his face as a bribe, but that was the last way to get in. Rubell loved money sure enough—his mother sat in a basement office counting out as much as $600,000 a week in cash, and one night, the sight of $80,000 in cash in a shopping bag excited him so much he spread it on his bed and masturbated on it—but you couldn't buy your way into Studio 54.

Had Rubell arrived at the velvet ropes himself, he would without doubt have turned himself away. He was the five-foot-five-inch gay son of a postal worker who grew up in a three-room apartment in Canarsie, Brooklyn. His handsome older brother was a six-foot-tall tennis player who became a prominent doctor, and Rubell had a lot to prove right from the start. After attending Syracuse University and working as a Wall Street runner, he borrowed $13,000 from his parents to open a small chain of family-style restaurants called Steak Loft. But the food business held no glamour for Rubell; there was no star shine to lift him above his humdrum life. Restlessly looking to move into the big time, Rubell hooked up with an old college pal, Ian Schrager, a fledgling attorney. Rubell had a bit of a crush on his handsome partner, and although Schrager was straight and very much the ladies' man, the two of them clicked together in a spontaneous synergy—much as Calvin and Barry. One of their first ventures together was a popular gay bar on Lands-downe Street in Boston, after which they opened a Douglaston, Queens, discotheque called the Enchanted Gardens. This club was a solid financial success, but its clientele was mostly youngsters from Long Island, without a celebrity in sight. The big time and public recognition lay across the river in Manhattan, and after two years in Douglaston, they leased a disused, cavernous old theater on West Fifty-fourth Street. With $400,000 of borrowed money, they built in only two months what would turn out to be the great-est nightclub of all time. Steve Rubell, a schlemiel from Canarsie, would overnight not only become an international social arbiter but Calvin Klein's new best friend.

2

Revisionists contend that Studio 54 was a destructive, malevolent place, a septic tank that glorified drug use and promiscuity and that Steve Rubell was the devil. But Studio 54 wasn't a cause; it was only an effect, the physical embodiment of one of the more de-bauched periods of social history. And if Rubell was a personifica-tion of a dark force, it was Dionysius, not Satan, who hired a press agent and made Studio 54 his clubhouse.

By the end of the seventies, helped along by two liberal mayoral-ties, New York City was headlong into a period of extreme sexual permissiveness, unusual even for "the city that never sleeps." It was not so much an amoral period as a time when reasonable and so-phisticated people believed they could toy with social drugs and casual sex, without ever having to pay the piper, waiting in the wings. By April 1977, when Studio 54 opened, glittering Manhat-tan was already serving up an array of every kind of hedonistic plea-sure imaginable. Prostitutes in black lace underwear and red raincoats were as common as lampposts on midtown street corners. Higher-class, high-priced call girls advertised openly in magazines or on cable TV channels, where the broadcast of pornography was permitted under federal freedom of access laws. Not to be left out, male prostitution—once considered a seedy profession practiced only in midtown alleyways—had gained considerable prestige and glamour, and several gay madams with exclusive stables of men for sale were prospering heartily. On the Upper East Side there was also a male "hustler" bar where hundreds of sellers and buyers competed with one another. Scores of gay and heterosexual bathhouses and swingers' clubs like Plato's Retreat and the St. Mark's Baths were operating at capacity. These kinds of places became so commonplace that it seemed plausible when it was widely rumored that Jacqueline Kennedy Onassis had visited a back-room bar called the Anvil in the meat-packing district with Andy Warhol to watch an American Indian boy dance with a snake and not much else.

They are all gone now, for the most part wiped off the face of the planet by the fire of AIDS, yet to many, such endeavors did not seem particularly dangerous or even immoral at the time. Perhaps the social use of drugs and alcohol blurred not only good judgment but good taste. Life in the fast lane was, after all, fueled by cocaine. It seemed a logical—and harmless—accompaniment to the excesses of the times. Yuppies regarded cocaine as an acceptable *tira misu,* just like a demitasse of espresso. Many a hip young Wall Street broker and Park Avenue attorneys with pretty young wives would feel positively déclassé if they were caught without an emergency half gram in their Crouch and Fitzgerald wallets. In the banquettes of hip New York restaurants, people snorted openly, if discreetly, over their coffee and cigarettes. When Studio 54 first opened, the Betty Ford Center didn't even exist, and only the worst alcoholic reprobates and junkies went to rehabs—or so people thought. Therefore, it was not particularly shocking that when Steve Rubell sent a limousine to pick up a celebrity, there was often a gram of cocaine wrapped in tinfoil slipped under the back armrest as a gift. For Rubell to be dispensing drugs to celebrities and friends was regarded as a rather harmless gesture, no more villainous than the host buying you a drink.

It was Calvin's gift and his curse to be on the cutting edge of everything that was new and in and hot, and at the end of the seventies that was sex and cocaine. Not only was he using cocaine regularly, but now Quaaludes had been added to Calvin's drug regime as well. Quaalude was Steve Rubell's favorite drug, and he handed out " 'ludes" to friends at the club like candy. They were chunky chalk-white tablets, made at the time by the pharmaceutical firm Rorer Incorporated and sold by prescription only—and on the black market for five to ten dollars each. Quaaludes were classified as a "hypnotic" sleeping pill, and while it was possible to fall asleep on one, the light, uninhibited, rubbery feeling it gave the user was too pleasant to miss by falling asleep. And although it was easy to get sloppy or overaffectionate on them, the right combination of cocaine and Quaaludes was perfect for a night at Studio 54. It made Calvin feel less shy, and the slippery, glimmering sensation the drugs gave him perfectly matched the quality of the club. Thus began Calvin's daily seesaw of vodka and drugs.

By the wee hours of the morning, Calvin would be in a dreamy, rolling, anesthetized stupor. With his judgment thus impaired, he began to behave publicly in a way that he most certainly would have found unacceptable had he been sober. On one particularly embarrassing occasion, the guests of attorney Roy Cohn's 1978 New Year's Eve party, including some judges and prominent attorneys, arrived en masse in a fleet of limousines at Studio 54's back door and were ushered down a hallway where, according to one of the crowd, Calvin was involved in a moment of passion. Calvin hardly seemed to notice the group, he was so involved, and they turned and scurried away as quickly as possible to offer him some privacy. At another time, Calvin and a friend were in a clinch on the Astroturf in the VIP playground while Andy Warhol, playing the pinball machine in the corner, tried to ignore them.

Calvin frequently stayed at the club long after it closed at 4:00 A.M., too wired on cocaine to go home to sleep and unable to tear himself away. "A couple of times after closing," recalled handsome, long-lashed bartender Rod Nevs, Calvin was so lost for something to occupy himself with that "he helped me count the money [from the cash register] after I closed the bar. And he counted it wrong, and I was told off because I didn't bother to double-check it. He was probably high."

Calvin Klein (left) with best pal and future business partner, Barry Schwartz, both at age nine. They already dreamed of making a fortune together. (NYT Pictures)

Calvin (second row, center) in his ninth grade class photo. At fourteen, he left his Bronx junior high school for Manhattan, where he would begin studying design and fashion.

Five years into what seemed like a storybook suburban marriage, Calvin and his wife Jayne (front right), attend the bar mitzvah of a friend's son. (© Walter Teitelbaum)

Calvin and Jayne in their apartment in Forest Hills, New York, with daughter Marci. To an outsider, Jayne appeared to have everything—devoted husband and an adorable toddler. (NYT Pictures)

A carefree Calvin on a weekend trip to Connecticut in the early seventies. (© Michael Datoli Photography)

In 1977, Calvin was introduced to the glittering disco scene of Studio 54, which he found so compelling that he was unable to tear himself away for more than a few nights at time. (© Rose Hartman)

Calvin with Frances Stein, his magically talented design director whose dramatic temper tantrums were legendary. (© Rose Hartman)

The Viennese-born doyenne of style, Eve Orton, who introduced Calvin to the gilded inner circles of international high society. (© Rose Hartman)

Calvin at his first all-male weekend in the Fire Island Pines, dressed up for a "black and white" theme party.

Calvin's beach-front house in the Pines, which he bought in 1977. He had the pool built so he could watch model Roland Hall do his morning laps.

Calvin and his mentor, dress designer Chester Weinberg, who introduced him to the gay fast-lane set. (© Michael Fatoli Photography)

Calvin sunbathing in the Pines with avant-garde fashion designer Giorgio Sant'Angelo.

Kidnapper Dominique Ransay after his arrest for the abduction of Calvin's daughter, Marci. (UPI/Bettmann Newsphotos)

Moments after rescuing Marci, the shock registers on Calvin's face as he realizes *Daily News* photographer Tom Monaster had been trailing him. (Tom Monaster/*New York Daily News*)

Calvin made headlines around the world when the FBI gave a press conference announcing his heroism. The $100,000 recovered from Marci's kidnappers is spread before him on the table. (UPI/Bettmann Newsphotos)

One of the central figures of the disco era, Calvin parties at Studio 54 with actress Ali McGraw and friend—as well as the club's owner, Steve Rubell. (© Robin Platzer, Twin Images)

Calvin at the 1981 reopening of Studio 54 with (from left) Andy Warhol, Brooke Shields, and Steve Rubell. (© David McGough/DMI)

Calvin posing with one of his models whose exotic beauty lent allure to his simple, yet sexy, designs. (Dustin Pittman)

Calvin in 1981 making the scene with supermodel Iman. (© David McGough/DMI)

Kelly Rector, age 16, when she was a student at an exclusive Manhattan private school. (© Gerard Malanga)

A radiantly happy Calvin, 43, and Kelly, 29, as they emerge from Rome's City Hall after their wedding in 1986. (Reuters/Bettmann Newsphotos)

Calvin and Kelly weep after the 1989 funeral of Steve Rubell. (Albert Ferreira/DMI)

Kelly with fellow guests, including writer Fran Leibowitz (with cigarette) at Malcolm Forbes's seventieth birthday extravaganza in Morocco in 1989. (Albert Ferreira/DMI)

Calvin with David Geffen, his best friend and advisor who bailed his company out of impending financial disaster in 1992. (© Rose Hartman)

Calvin with another stalwart pal, Hollywood mogul, Barry Diller. (© Rose Hartman)

Marci Klein (left) with Tatiana von Furstenberg at a party for the launch of Kelly's book *Pools.* (© Rose Hartman)

Barry Schwartz, Calvin's longtime friend and loyal business partner, and his wife, Sheryl, greet Donna Karan (left) at a Metropolitan Museum of Art gala for the Costume Institute. (© Rose Hartman)

Calvin with British model Kate Moss. Critics worried that her emaciated frame, made famous in Calvin Klein advertising, set an unhealthy example to young women. (© Rose Hartman)

Calvin and Kelly at the Hamptons annual horse show. (© Rose Hartman)

Calvin and Kelly's beach-front mansion in the exclusive Long Island retreat of East Hampton. (© James J. Mackin/South Fork)

Tanned and healthy Calvin and Kelly at a fundraiser in the Hamptons. (DST Photos)

The newest incarnation of Calvin Klein—clean, sober, and content.
(Albert Ferreira/DMI)

Ironically, by day Calvin was a hypochondriac, and he worried constantly about the damage he was doing to his body putting all those poisons into it. As a countermeasure he now became obsessive about his physique and exercising, as did many in the gay community. By the end of the seventies, definied muscles were basic currency in the gay world, and pectorals and biceps were worth their weight in gold. Calvin was so determined to bring his skinny body up to par, he had his own gymnasium in a room right next to his office. Seven gleaming, hulking weight machines were installed that isolated for biceps, triceps, quadriceps, and so forth. Every morning before work, Calvin met with a trainer for a ninety-minute workout. Considering that he often had little or no sleep and was regularly hung over from drugs and drink, these workouts were no small chore. However, no price vanity. "Keeping the body in shape is more important than fashion," he told the *New York Times*. Anyway, later in the day, when his fitting models came in, he'd boast, "Look at my muscles," and proudly ask them to squeeze his biceps. He even posed shirtless, working out on the lat machine, for *People* magazine.

3

With Steve Rubell as the glue, Studio 54 was also the backdrop against which Calvin formed a tight bond with three new pals. Only these new pals were not exactly hanging out at the corner candy store, harmonizing under a lamppost. They worked and played hard, a little club so rich and powerful—and so renowned for their steely toughness in business—they became known by wags in New York and Los Angeles as the "Velvet Mafia."

The Velvet Mafia was comprised of Steve Rubell, Calvin, and other moguls who were already good friends from the West Coast, including the balding, gap-toothed, thirty-five-year-old Paramount Pictures chief Barry Diller, who was a frequent companion of designer Diane Von Furstenberg; the 5-foot-7½-inch record-company founder and onetime boyfriend of Cher, thirty-four-year-old David Geffen; and the boyish personal talent manager Sandy Gallin. This group had many uncannily striking similarities in their histories. They were all aggressive Jewish boys, each uncomfortable enough with his sexuality to disguise it for business purposes, each overcompensating for the hurt and humiliation of being different with a burning determination to be the brightest and the best at what they did—and they were. "Killer" Barry Diller became CEO of Paramount Pictures when he was only thirty-two years old, before he got bored and left to run the 20th Century-Fox Entertainment corporation, where he was responsible for assembling the fourth television network, Fox TV. David Geffen, a combination record-business entrepreneur and movie and Broadway show producer, became the first man in show business to become a billionaire, and by the time Sandy Gallin was thirty, he was the mastermind of an elite coven of entertainment superstars that included Dolly Parton, Cher, and Michael Jackson. Like all powerful men, they had many detractors and enemies, but at the same time, they were inspirations and role models to a legion of young gay males who were afraid their sexuality would limit their potential to rise to such exalted states in business.

Calvin's friendship with these men was a revelation to him. For the first time in his adult life he found a loyal and sympathetic circle of friends of his own caliber who enjoyed the same level of accomplishment as he. "While most people in the world can have their choice of fifty friends," said one of the group's acquaintances, "there weren't that many other gay [or bisexual] men in the world who could comfortably be Calvin Klein's friend except for these guys." Now if Calvin felt like renting a jet plane on whim to go to Key West for a Saturday night, there was someone who could afford to go along with him. This was also the first time that Calvin had a confidant other than Chester Weinberg. It was an unusual pleasure to be able to pick up the phone and gossip with David or Barry or Sandy, who understood not only the problems and complications of his personal life but were gifted business advisers as well. To the others, Calvin was a cynosure of glamour. He brought stardom and class to their circle, for although their Hollywood world seemed glamorous to outsiders, in its own way it was a small, claustrophobic, mostly straight world where gay or bisexual executives hid their proclivities lest they be seen as a weakness in business. To them, Calvin was a *star* and in some strange way an innocent compared to David Geffen and Barry Diller, who were wiser and more savvy about the world. Together his friends formed a protective and supportive shield around him. "Calvin is a force among his friends," said Chester Weinberg. "When Calvin's sad, we're sad; when he's up, we're up." Together the Velvet Mafia came to his fashion shows, sat in the front row, and applauded fiercely, and he went to their movie premieres and raved about their films. Some of them had Sunday brunch together and took Sunday walks in the park or attended the muscle-man contest held by *Blueboy* magazine at the Felt Forum. Some rented vacation homes in St. Bart's and took with them dates each more beautiful than his predecessor. One young man remembered being so star struck at being taken on vacation with Steve Rubell, David Geffen, and Calvin Klein that he spent the morning wading in the surf on the private beach in front of their rented house singing "If my friends could see me now" to himself. Calvin and his chums once held a contest among themselves to see who could land the most attractive date on a Saturday night, and one enterprising member of the group recruited a porn star and flew him in from Chicago for the occasion. Sometimes, recalled David Burns, one of New York's top call boys, if they found a young man they thought was especially amusing, they would send him down the line. "It was like the food chain," said Burns.

Among them all, Calvin's friendship with short, skinny David Geffen was the strongest. Geffen and Calvin were like Mutt and Jeff, so different and yet so much alike. Geffen grew up in Brooklyn's Borough Park, a sociological mirror-image of Mosholu Parkway, in a three-room apartment with an older brother, a distant father, and an overpowering mother, Batya, who sold brassieres out of the living room. After flunking out of two colleges, he moved to Los Angeles and took a job in the legendary mailroom of the William Morris Agency, where he met Barry Diller, the son of a wealthy Jewish builder from Beverly Hills, who had dropped out of UCLA. While Geffen formed his own record company, Diller, a self-described "Brillo pad" of toughness, moved briskly up the corporate ranks to a top programming job at ABC-TV before he became the CEO of Paramount Pictures. Geffen, too, tried his hand at running a studio, but he lacked the sanguine personality needed to put up with corporate politicking. In fact, his reputation was as much for being a vengeful hothead as it was for a sensitive discoverer of talent. "David Geffen is an atomic weapon," said agent Swifty Lazar, "and you're lucky if you're not in his sights." As reported in GQ magazine, Geffen was powerful enough to help depose the president of CBS Records, Walter Yetnikoff, after he heard that Yetnikoff said he'd like his girlfriend to get lessons from Geffen in "sucking cock." At the time Calvin met him, Geffen was temporarily retired from active business; two years before, he had been diagnosed—incorrectly as it would turn out—as having a cancerous growth in his bladder, and believing that he had only a limited time to live, he was indulging himself in life's pleasures. "I started to want to get laid a lot," Geffen said, and Studio 54 was the perfect place to do it.

Alas, Calvin's new buddies merely tolerated Chester Weinberg, for he was hardly in their league. Chester couldn't compete on any front, and he had to hang on fast to Calvin's friendship. The kind of life Calvin was suddenly living—trips to London for the day or weekends in Key West—was too expensive for Chester, and if he was to be invited, Calvin had to pay for him. Still Chester remained a mainstay in Calvin's life. They would have dinner together once a week, and Calvin would pour out his heart to his wiser friend and ask for advice. And when Calvin's new friends were frequently out of town, Chester got Calvin's full attention. The night of Chester's birthday in October 1978, Calvin joined a group of friends at Chester's apartment. "We smoked lots of grass, and there was lots of coke," one participant remembered. "We were going out dancing later to Studio 54, and we were joking about finding Chester some hot number for his birthday."

Calvin said, "Let's call for one on the phone."

Calvin dialed the number of a local gay madam he happened to have handy and dutifully recited Chester's special requests. "Tonight we want blue eyes and blond hair, white guy, well endowed and circumcised."

Within an hour Chester's phone rang; it was the hustler. Calvin took the call, asked the young man what he looked like, and told him that he would be required to perform in front of the party guests before visiting privately with Chester. The boy agreed. The scene that followed was "wild," said the friend, "wild and funny. I'd never seen such a thing in somebody's home. And then we left the guy with Chester. That was Calvin's present. He paid for it. He was often generous where that was concerned."

4

People came up to Calvin all the time at Studio 54. Women flirted with him and told him they loved him and his clothes. So did boys. People asked him for jobs or fashion advice or gave *him* fashion advice. Some just wanted to shake his hand or buy him a drink. Calvin, who was shy with strangers, was reserved and patient with these intrusions unless the person lingered too long, and then, with a few shots of vodka and a couple of hits of cocaine in him, he would explode, spittle flying, in a rage that made Dan Millstein's temper tantrums look like an Easter sermon. One night soon after Studio 54 opened, Calvin was leaning up against the central circular bar at 4:00 A.M. He was going to Frankfurt the next day and decided to stay up all night and get some sleep on the plane. He'd had a few drinks when some character came up and introduced himself as Peter King, a garment-center consultant who had another brilliant idea for him.

He should license blue jeans.

He had already tried making his own jeans the year before, in 1976, and they were a terrible flop. He manufactured them himself in small lots, very tailored in a straight-legged style, of good-quality denim, but the production cost him a fortune, necessitating an unprecedented retail price of fifty dollars a pair. The jeans had been unveiled at Bloomingdale's amid much press fanfare, only to sit unsold on the shelves for months.

Nevertheless, the guy at Studio 54 had a point. Recently, the country seemed to be blue-jean crazy. Blue jeans had been a staple of American dress since the 1850s, when Levi Strauss introduced denim overalls to the gold miners of San Francisco (although denim was originally a French invention, made from blue-and-white cotton twill manufactured in Nîmes, France; hence, the name *de Nîmes*). In the late 1960s and early 1970s, jeans had been given a fashion spin with bell-bottoms and brushed and dyed styles

manufactured by companies with hip-sounding names like Faded
Glory and Jordache. But selling at about twelve dollars a pair,
denims were still considered proletarian work clothes, and the idea
that blue jeans could be high fashion was unthinkable.

Improbably, it was poor-little-rich-girl-turned-designer Gloria
Vanderbilt who changed all that, along with a Brooklyn-born marketing genius named Warren Hirsh. Hirsh, forty-five, was a former
salesman and garment-industry veteran who was president of the
American arm of Murjani International, a large but undistinguished Hong Kong–based manufacturing company. One day,
while walking through a department store, it occurred to Hirsh that
Murjani's huge manufacturing capacity could be put to use manufacturing mass-market clothing with the status of a designer's
name on the label. Blue jeans seemed like a perfect place to start,
and Hirsh set out in search of a name designer. Hirsh was rebuffed
by several designers, including Pierre Cardin, before the idea came
to him to use a name from "American royalty," like the Rockefel-
lers. They didn't need to know how to design anything—that would
be done by a professional team. All they had to do was lend their
name for a hefty fee. Hirsh not only approached the Rockefeller
family; he had the audacity to ask Jaqueline Onassis to put her
moniker on blue jeans. After several more rejections, he wooed and
signed the heiress Gloria Vanderbilt, widow of conductor Leopold
Stokowski, ex-wife of director Sidney Lumet, and great-great-
granddaughter of Cornelius Vanderbilt himself. Treacly-voiced
and aristocratic of bearing, Vanderbilt had recently realized some
success selling her own line of home furnishings. It was also
Hirsh's stroke of genius to use Vanderbilt as her own model, a ful-
ler-figured woman to attract an older, more suburban customer.
Vanderbilt's elegantly scrawled signature above the insignia of a
swan would appear on the right hip pocket of every jean, the first
time ever, Hirsh claims, that a designer's name appeared on blue
jeans. He filmed an inexpensive TV commercial which consisted
mostly of Vanderbilt wearing the jeans as she danced across the
screen in white limbo, and with only a limited budget he gambled
by spending most of his money to put the ad on the air in ten major
cities during the 1976 Academy Awards presentation.

The jeans exploded like a cork out of a champagne bottle. Seventh Avenue had seen lots of unexpected success stories, but the impact of Gloria Vanderbilt jeans on the fashion industry was breathtaking by any standard. Well-dressed women everywhere were wearing jeans, and Vanderbilt's brand became so popular with women that sociologists, along with Madison Avenue, began to ponder the trend. Whatever their "meaning," Murjani was selling $150 million a year worth of jeans, and Warren Hirsh was hailed as Seventh Avenue's latest genius. Bud Johns, of Levi Strauss, commented, "It's said there are forty million pigeons in the United States. Thirty million are birds, and the rest are buying designer jeans."

Quicker than you could say "bandwagon," it seemed as if every designer on the block was announcing his or her intention to manufacture blue jeans, including Anne Klein, Geoffrey Beene, and Bill Blass. One of the few who resisted was Halston, who sneered, "Only a pig would put his name on blue jeans." Calvin had been called worse.

But that night at Studio 54, the guy wasn't suggesting that Calvin manufacture his *own* blue jeans, which was expensive, but that he license them to someone else, somebody named Carl Rosen, who owned the giant dress company Puritan Fashions.

On the surface, it was a thoroughly improbable idea. Puritan was a cow—a cash cow but a cow nevertheless. It was the largest low-priced dress manufacturer in the world—"dresses for masses with fat asses," they jeered in the business. Puritan manufactured and sold over forty different, mostly schlocky clothing lines, backed by a small army of salesmen out on the road pushing their $10.95 retail dresses to millions of overweight Sears, Roebuck customers. Mostly the company had become famous in the fifties when Carl Rosen persuaded European designers like Pierre Balmain and Givenchy to design dresses for him to retail below fifteen dollars. As far as advertising went, Puritan's idea of promotion was to sign Gloria Swanson to a lifelong contract and advertise the laughable "Gloria Swanson's Mother's Day Dress." It wasn't surprising that Puritan had lost money three of the last four years.

However, Puritan was still a very rich company, and they didn't call Carl Rosen "the King" for nothing. Of all the monarchs in the garment industry, of all the titans with the Midas touch, Carl

Rosen was the biggest and richest. *Meaner* than Millstein, *classier* than Seymour Fox, Rosen was more than a star; he was a whole constellation unto himself. He was a short, bull-like, hawk-nosed man, perpetually tan, with thick, wavy hair and deep-set eyes that glowered at employees. Everybody in the business knew whose gold Rolls-Royce it was waiting for him in front of 1400 Broadway, and when the windows shook in showrooms up and down Seventh Avenue from the roar of a helicopter, they knew it was "the King" rising over the canyons of the garment center in his own private whirlybird, on his way to see one of his thoroughbreds run at the track. While Barry might have started to dabble in owning racehorses the last two years, Carl Rosen had been investing and breeding horses for *twenty* years and owned whole stables filed with champion thoroughbreds, including a Triple Crown winner.

In fact, Rosen was everything Barry aspired to be, but double. Barry owned a Rolls-Royce; Rosen owned *two* Rolls-Royces, both painted gold, and the one he kept at his Palm Springs estate once belonged to the queen mother of England. There was a gold station wagon as well for the staff at his twenty-five-acre estate in Massachusetts overlooking the Charles River. The restless manufacturer also kept an Essex House duplex, a Miami Beach Jockey Club co-op, and a Park Avenue pad where his mistress was installed.

Although Puritan was started by Rosen's father, Arthur, in 1912, the company was not handed to him on a silver platter. He started as a bundle boy at the Boston, Massachusetts, firm and worked his way up to president, displacing several relatives from their jobs along the way. The name Puritan was also an ironic joke in the garment center, for the company was associated with a reputation for hanky-panky among the salesmen; reportedly, divorces were rife, and Carl supplied hookers and dirty weekends to Las Vegas for the buyers.

In recent years Puritan might have suffered some losses, but Rosen had survived hard times before by seizing upon trends; he was the first to license Beatles merchandise in the sixties, and he invented the successful "now" clothing chain of Paraphernalia stores. He had also signed tennis star Chris Evert to a licensing deal, and he had done so well with her sports line that he named his Triple Crown winner after her. Rosen believed Gloria Vanderbilt's stunning success with jeans was not an isolated phenomenon and that soon all merchandise would have to be associated with a status name to generate sales. He was convinced that the future of Puritan was in phasing out the chintzy dresses and coats and moving into upscale, designer sportswear. If, said his emissary that night at Studio 54, Calvin and Barry would consider giving Puritan a blue-jean license, Rosen would make them an offer they couldn't possibly refuse.

One million in cash, up front.

For that kind of money, Calvin said, he was sure he and Barry would meet with Carl Rosen. The next day, Calvin called Barry from the airport and told him to expect a call from Puritan. Ten days later, he returned to New York. "I had forgotten about the whole jeans thing," said Calvin, "but Barry said, 'You know, I think we've got a live one here.' "

For Barry, negotiating with Carl Rosen was like being a contender for the world's heavyweight title, and by the time he sat down in Rosen's paneled conference room, surrounded by trophies and photographs of Rosen's horses in the winner's circle, Barry was loaded for elephant. Determined to beat the master at his own game, Barry spat out certain basic rules, including "total control." Rosen smiled. He was relaxed and confident, a polished, pampered man who exuded power, from the way his salt-and-pepper hair was brilliantined back from a small widows peak to the nails manicured by a girl who got a fifty-dollar tip. "The first time I met Barry," said Carl Rosen, "I found him to be irritating, sharp-tongued, dictatorial, and overpowering." "He's the toughest kind of negotiator because he doesn't seem to care if he makes the deal or not." Calvin was no pushover, either. Rosen decided that "Calvin and Barry are two beautiful people. Calvin is beautiful-beautiful, and Barry is ugly-beautiful." In the end, Rosen declared that Barry was a much nastier negotiator than himself, which is perhaps why he gave Barry a deal that was more advantageous than anyone had ever heard about in the garment industry. Rosen proposed that aside from the $1 million cash advance, he would guarantee them a minimum of $1 million every year for the life of the contract, on top of which he would pay them an unprecedented royalty of one dollar for every pair sold. The only hitch was that, technically, Calvin and

Barry had signed away the right to make men's jeans to Maurice Bidermann, and he had to be brought into the negotiations. Among the Frenchman, Carl Rosen, and Barry Schwartz, the meetings turned into a sideshow of one-upmanship until it was finally agreed that Rosen would pay Bidermann a dollar for every pair of men's jeans he sold as well as a dollar to Calvin Klein.

The deal was signed on Wednesday, June 29, 1977, when Calvin announced to the industry that Puritan Fashions would produce indigo-dyed, 100 percent cotton denim, straight-legged jeans, some prewashed, to be manufactured in seven Puritan plants in Texas. The cost to manufacture would be about $7.50 a pair. Shipping and advertising would add about $5, and Puritan would sell the garments wholesale at approximately $20 each. The retailers would add another 100 percent to get a $40 in-store price. The jeans would be sold exclusively at the three hundred stores that already carried Calvin's ready-to-wear collections—and not just in the Calvin Klein boutiques, but on the racks right next to Levi's and Lees. Barry, in what he probably thought was a rosy exaggeration, predicted they would sell a million pairs of jeans that first year, which were going to be shipped to stores in early 1978. Calvin said he expected these jeans to be even better than the ones made by his own company, because, he said, "when you're mass-producing something, costs come down, and very often quality improves. The production people who are making a style repeatedly eventually will make it perfectly."

Unlike the torture he went through designing his menswear line, the design of the jeans was relatively simple. Calvin knew what he wanted. He had watched enough attractive young people with good bodies in tight jeans dancing at Flamingo and Studio 54 to know that the "basket" and the behind was what gave jeans sex appeal. Calvin sent his assistants out for several pairs of jeans, including the classic five-button Levi's, and cut them apart to see how they were made. Then he cut the "rise," or area from the waistband to under the groin, much shorter to accentuate the crotch and pull the seam up between the buttocks, giving the behind more shape and prominence. The result was instant sex appeal—and a look that somehow Calvin just *knew* was going to sell.

5

In 1977, in the first summer Studio 54 was open and Calvin found it so difficult to tear himself away, he bought a beach house called Nimba in the Fire Island Pines. It was the same house he rented the year before, and he was afraid *not* to buy it lest it get away from him. There were bigger, more impressive houses in the Pines, but Nimba had a simple perfection to it, clean, contemporary lines built out of cedar left to weather naturally, with architectural ellipses and semicircular decking in a style so complementary to Calvin's taste it could have been made to order for him. Designed by noted architect Horace Gifford, the two-story, five-bedroom house overlooked the beach at the end one of the most western walks, Driftwood, before the community ended in a tangle of pine barrens. If one were to look back at the house from the beach, it would appear to be a giant eye of glass, perched on the dunes, staring at the Atlantic crashing to the shore. Calvin bought the lot and another, nondescript house behind it as well so he could tear it down and build a pool, but initially he changed his mind. "It was too much fun to jump off the deck onto the dunes and run to the beach." An open staircase lead from the towering glass living room to the master bedroom, which shared the same panoramic view along with a private deck and chaise longues. One of the four guest rooms included a bed that was built into a semicircular mirrored alcove. There was also a hall shower complete with a stainless-steel anal douche and a peephole the size of a ship's porthole disguised by a hinged photograph in the hallway. When word spread that Calvin Klein had bought the house, it instantly turned into a landmark attraction, even by the standards of the enclave's existing homes of the gay and famous. Suddenly, the plank boardwalk that ran adjacent to it became the most popular route to the beach on the island. Passersby found that by walking on tiptoes it was just about possible to see over the fence and get a glimpse of what was happening inside. Calvin was able to lie in the sun on his front deck and survey the tanned sun worshipers in their Speedo suits as they lingered by his gate, hoping for an invitation.

It was around that time that Calvin began a lengthy infatuation with a model from Queens, New York, known only by the name of

Alphonso*. With his chiseled, rock-hard swimmer's body, curly hair, monosyllabic answers, and the swagger of a street kid, Alphonso was a sexy enigma. Friends remember that Calvin met Alphonso through Giorgio Sant'Angelo, who passed Alphonso along after having a brief affair with him. The sketchy biographical information about him—which he evasively would neither confirm nor deny—was that he was a New Jersey or Brooklyn working class kid who married and fathered a child, then five years old, with his high school sweetheart. They lived in a shack of a house in the marshlands of Queens, waiting patiently for the day he returned. Giorgio's friends also remember going to a squalid apartment in Spanish Harlem to visit Alphonso. Alphonso was the most significant and tortured in a series of unrequited love affairs that Calvin embarked upon with allegedly straight boys, relationships that strained the patience of his other, more prescient friends. Alphonso was tolerated by Calvin's friends, even though he was supposedly as dumb as a post. "He had a nice, hard ass," remarked one of Calvin's staffers, "but not as hard as his head." Alphonso seemed available to wealthy gay men, although quite clearly he was filled with disdain about it. He was archetypal homosexual "trade," a straight boy who would allow himself to be had in exchange for gifts or money. Whatever the motive in Alphonso's mind, he was given prominent modeling jobs in Calvin's menswear collection, and he was Calvin's constant shadow. "He seemed to me to be a guy," said one of Calvin's design staff, "who was looking at Calvin as a cow to be milked. He was a hustler, you know, the worst kind, because Calvin seemed quite smitten and I heard rumors that Calvin gave him a car." Calvin might not have given Alphonso a car, but he did loan him his own when Alphonso said he had an errand to run. Calvin didn't realize, however, that Alphonso was going to pick up drugs, and driving the car home high, Alphonso badly damaged it in a traffic accident. Calvin was furious, but he could never be furious with Alphonso for too long. One look from those dark eyes and Calvin was lost. When Chester would tell Calvin that Alphonso was only trouble, Calvin would say, "Who am I going to settle down with? A thirty-year-old author with patches on his sleeves?"

*A pseudonym.

Indeed, Calvin's romantic fixations seemed to inevitably revolve around the most unobtainable straight men. Calvin would have sex with gay men, but the only boys that he really seemed to fall in *love* with were straight. Perhaps this was the paradox Jean Genet wrote about, that the homosexual's search for an ideal man is doomed to defeat, because as soon as another male returns his affection, he is no longer ideal. And that is what Calvin was after, a real man with whom he could fall in love. "The real truth," said his assistant Zack Carr, "is that underneath, Calvin is a very romantic man. And to meet someone and to fall in love and to give [his] heart away . . . is something that Calvin would like very much to do. . . . I remember . . . people who Calvin thought he loved—I think he *did* love—that didn't turn out to be as loving to him and only hurt Calvin that much more because they made Calvin terrified that he would only be loved for money."

Naturally, his pursuit of men most likely to reject him proved frustrating. Worse, he was ill suited to his role of aggressor and still felt uncomfortable in his gay status. One summer day in Central Park, Calvin by chance ran across a heterosexual but naive aspiring model named David Chapman who had just come to New York from Ohio to find fame and fortune. The blond, blue-eyed young man was surprised to get a message from Calvin the next week inviting him to bring his modeling portfolio for Calvin to see at his Sovereign apartment. "We were sitting on the couch," remembered Chapman, "and I showed him my portfolio, but he didn't really seem that interested in it." Chapman let it be known in the course of conversation that he was heterosexual. "We started talking about where I was from and how much we both liked Key West, and then he began telling me how good-looking he thought I was, and I started feeling very uncomfortable. I said to him, 'The one thing I don't like about the modeling business is that I don't like being hit on by gay photographers and people. . . . I don't like feeling pressured.' "

"Well," said Calvin, stumbling for something to say, "I think that in New York, in this day and age, I don't think you should think of yourself as being gay *or* straight. You ought to think of yourself as doing what you want to do and be your own man. Flesh feels good no matter what it is."

Chapman told Calvin he once tried some minor homosexual experimentation and that it "repulsed" him. "He started getting really irritated," said Chapman. "He kept asking me if I wanted drinks. I don't recall how it ended, but he knew he wasn't getting anywhere, and I just left." Chapman never worked for Calvin Klein.

Steve Rubell was unluckier in love than Calvin. As much as Steve Rubell procured dates for other people, he got to enjoy very little of it for himself. "By the end of the night," said one employee, "he would be so fucked up with seven Quaaludes in his mouth and coke up his nose that he didn't know what he was doing and he was always about to fall over. So if he took anyone home, he would fall asleep." There are hundreds of paparazzi photos of him nodding out on the banquettes toward the end of an evening, and for those hearty enough to stick it out until 4:00 A.M. closing at Studio, it was not unusual to find Rubell stumbling around, bumping into walls like Charlie Chaplin's little tramp.

Calvin was not far behind on some nights. "I was with him a lot," remembered Allen Tucker, president of Calvin Klein's fledgling menswear company, of those nights in Studio 54. "He would fall in love with beautiful people all the time, both men and women. I mean, he would just go gaga over them. But he was very concerned about that image—he didn't want the public to know [the gay stuff], and he was never sure what he was. He had a lot of psychological problems. He obviously didn't know who he was or wanted to be, personally, sexually, the whole thing. It wasn't easy for Calvin. He couldn't just snap his fingers and say this isn't the kind of person I want to be anymore. He went along with the fads of Steve Rubell and the gay rights, but he never really thought about what he was doing or who he was."

Helen Murray, Calvin's in-house publicist during the Studio 54 period, remembered one weekday night at the club when she had overindulged herself in the many intoxicants available and she was leaning on the center bar, off in a contemplative netherworld watching the lights change, when an inebriated man standing next to her bumped her with his elbow. As their eyes met, Murray realized the man was her boss, Calvin Klein, and an embarrassed moment passed until they chuckled with each other conspiratorially. Still, Murray felt uncomfortable about having Calvin see her a little tipsy at three in the morning on a work night, and she became resolved that the next day she would be in the office half an hour earlier than usual to show Calvin how professional she was. The following morning, when Murray arrived a little after eight, Calvin was already in his own office working away.

Perhaps that was because there were times he didn't even go home to sleep after Studio 54. "I mean, Calvin was at fucking Studio 54 day and night," remembered Allen Tucker. "He would be at the office at eight A.M., work until eight at night, then sleep from eight until eleven or twelve and go to Studio 54, where he would stay until six A.M. Then he would go home, change clothes, and come to work. You just can't live like that."

But Calvin did live like that. On weekend nights especially he would go on drug and alcohol binges and stay up till dawn. On Saturday nights, coked up until his pupils were like tiny specks of carbon, Calvin would arrive at the club past midnight and stay until it closed at 4:00 A.M., when he and a friend, usually Chester Weinberg—and Rubell, if he was still conscious—would take a limousine down to Flamingo, which was at its peak arrival time. More coke, a 'lude, maybe a designer drug, would keep Calvin bouncing off the walls, watching all the cleavage at Flamingo till 6:00 A.M., and by then, if he still couldn't find somebody to go home with, he was off to the notorious Mineshaft on the fringes of Greenwich Village in the deserted meat-packing district. Leaving his brown leather bomber jacket in the backseat of the limousine while the driver waited with the motor running, Calvin shivered in his thin white T-shirt and jeans as he stumbled toward an unmarked door beyond which he climbed a dimly lit flight of steps. At the top Calvin was scrutinized by a doorman with a checklist more rigid than Steve Rubell's. After being deemed macho enough to be allowed inside—no cologne or Lacoste shirts, only work clothes and leather allowed—Calvin passed through a dimly lit bar and checkroom into a duplex of rooms dark enough to offer him complete anonymity. The warren of rooms was crowded with men, many openly having sex, as Calvin wandered by, hardly seeing, heavy-lidded, certain they did not recognize him. Calvin stumbled down a concrete staircase to a lower level, where a curly-haired man with a mustache took hold of him firmly by his belt and maneuvered him up against a grimy wall. Calvin closed his eyes, leaned back, and succumbed, too stoned and drunk to resist. A few minutes later he stumbled out the front door and took big gulps of the clean night air before climbing into the backseat of his limousine. The sun was already coming up as he told the driver to take him back to the Sovereign. The car slipped silently through the deserted city streets as Calvin stared out the window, unseeing.

He could have anything he wanted in the world.

And he chose this. As far away from love as he could go.

Was this what he had bargained for?

CHAPTER TWELVE

One way or another my life is starting *now*.
                                    —Dominique Ransay

On the morning of February 3, 1978, the same day 200,000 pairs of Calvin Klein blue jeans were flooding the market, a month before the launch of his cosmetics company and three months before his menswear line hit the stores, Marci Klein was standing on the southeast corner of Madison Avenue and Seventy-sixth Street waiting for a public bus to take her to the Dalton School. She was dressed in mittens and a down ski parka so big it dwarfed her small frame, and in her hands she held a white shopping bag containing candied apples for the Dalton School bake sale.

Marci Klein's daddy may have been rich and famous, but that was nothing out of the ordinary at the Dalton School. More than any other private school in New York, Dalton was a bastion for children of the rich and famous, a protective and spoiled fortress away from the savage Manhattan public schools. The competition to get into Dalton—only sixty or so new students were accepted each year—was the subject of many conversations on Central Park benches among distressed mothers watching their preschool toddlers play. Not only was Dalton a major status chip in New York social circles; it attracted a precocious intellectually elite group of "children of the arts" (not to mention the children of multimillionaire stock traders). At one time or another Marci's schoolmates included Ralph Lauren's two children; Barbra Streisand and Elliot Gould's son, Jason; Tom Brokaw's son and daughter; Barbara Walters's daughter; Hal Prince's children; Gloria Vanderbilt's son,

Carter Cooper; and the children of Robert Redford, whose wife, Lola, was on Dalton's board of directors. And at Dalton there was no demure modesty displayed over a parent's fame. In fact, at one point a banner was hung in the lobby of the school that read "Come See Dalton Parents Robert Redford and Barbra Streisand in *The Way We Were.*" And the year Hal Prince's daughter, Daisy, graduated, he arranged for the school play, *Oliver!,* to be held at the Shubert Theatre on Broadway, with the graduation party later at Studio 54. None of this necessarily boded well for these privileged children, for as one graduate noted, "If we have a class reunion, it should be at Hazelden [a drug rehabilitation center]."

Of course, the children of the rich and famous had the same capacity as any children to be mean, and over the years Marci's famous father had become the subject of a great deal of gossip in the school. Classmates of Marci had heard their own parents telling tales in their twelve-room Park Avenue apartments, and the talk was that Calvin Klein was gay. Word spread, and before long Marci was being taunted with "Your father is a faggot" from one catty student in particular. And she was so stung by it that she kept asking grown-ups over and over, "Is my daddy gay?" She asked Chester Weinberg, and he said, "Ask your father." She asked her mother, and she asked her aunts, "Is my daddy gay?" And all the adults said, "Of course not," and looked away uncomfortably, and Marci knew. Yet no child at the Dalton School adored her father more fiercely than Marci Klein, because he *needed* her more than most daddies and because she also knew that Calvin loved her more than anything else in his world, loved her more than life itself, and she felt safe and secure in this world, no matter what they said about him.

Within the last few years, a difficult situation had developed between Calvin and Jayne regarding Marci. Like many little girls her age, she resented her mother and became rebellious; with her daddy, on the other hand, everything was light and laughter. Calvin rarely had to discipline Marci, and she was certainly never subjected to his bad moods. He was a devoted father who lavished love and gifts and attention on her, and Marci made it no secret that she would have preferred to live with Calvin rather than Jayne. She certainly wanted to stay with Calvin that February night in 1978 instead of staying with a babysitter at her mother's apartment. Jayne was away on vacation all week, the houseguest of friends in Fort Lauderdale, and Marci was being supervised by a baby-sitter, Lily Voss, who stayed with her in the apartment. Marci had called Calvin Thursday night to ask if she could come to the Sovereign to stay with him, but Calvin told her that his housekeeper had left him a sardine dinner and that it had made him so violently ill "I thought I was going to die." Marci laughed at her daddy's silliness and went to bed. At 7:00 A.M. Friday morning, February 3, she awoke, ate breakfast, and was escorted to the building elevator, where she was met by yet another baby-sitter, who walked her to the bus stop. From there, unattended, the child would ride a public bus to school.

As Marci stood waiting on Madison Avenue, two buses trundled up the street and arrived at the stop at the same time. She boarded the first one and took a seat toward the back. Two blocks farther north, a tiny woman named "Christine" Paule Ransay Lawrie, twenty-four years old, paced back and forth on the street as she watched Marci board one of the buses. Because of the perspective, it was impossible for Christine to tell which of the two buses Marci had boarded. Perhaps, Christine thought, that was a sign.

She had been looking for signs all morning. Just a few minutes before, Christine Ransay Lawrie had been in church, praying for direction, consumed with doubt over what she was about to do. Dressed in a thin cloth coat, a colored turban on her head, a cheap plastic pocketbook in her hands, Christine struck a small, forlorn figure, five feet tall and ninety pounds, with light cocoa-colored skin, gaunt features, and thin eyebrows. A French-speaking native of the French West Indies, she had moved to New York with her parents in 1971. Since that time the best job she was able to find was as a lunchtime hostess at a midtown restaurant called La Potagerie, and it was a monthly struggle to make the $140 rent on her sixth-story walk-up apartment.

Confused about which of the buses Marci had boarded, Christine decided to let fate play its own hand; if she got on the wrong bus and Marci wasn't on it, she would simply go home and forget about it. But no such luck. When she entered the first one, there was Marci.

The eleven-year-old was surprised to see her sometime baby-sitter—yet again. Marci really didn't know Christine that well, but recently she had been popping up everywhere. Christine worked at the busy Fifth Avenue restaurant owned by Jayne's present boyfriend, fifty-year-old Kenny Sheresky, and on the few occasions when Marci's regular baby-sitter couldn't watch her, Sheresky asked Christine to sit for Marci. Two days before, Marci found Christine waiting in the lobby of her apartment building when she came home from school. "She said she just wanted to say hello," Marci recounted, "so I told her to come up to the apartment." Upstairs they talked about school for a while—the name of the school and where it was located—and when her mother would be home from vacation. And again, the day before, Marci ran into Christine just outside her building, which Christine passed off as coincidence. And yet now again, out of the clear blue, Christine appeared on the bus.

Only this time she was crying. "What happened?" Marci asked her, thinking something terrible must have happened to Christine.

"It's not about *me*, it's about *you*," Christine said, choking back tears.

Marci's eyes opened wide as a ball of thorns began to spin in her stomach. "What is it?" she whispered. "Is something wrong with my mother?"

"No, it's your father," Christine said, her eyes brimming over. "Your father is very, very sick. He might die."

Marci instantly burst into tears. "Die!" she wailed, "My daddy dead!"

"Your mother called me from Florida," Christine continued hurriedly, "and told me to get you from school. Your father is in Mount Sinai Hospital and we're going to see him."

Marci was sobbing so loudly at this point that everyone on the bus was staring. Christine knew that drawing attention to them was one of the worst things she could do, and, a little embarrassed by the loud wailing, she told Marci to follow her down the aisle and off the bus at the next stop.

Out on the street Christine hailed a taxi, and Marci piled into the back after her. "Mount Sinai Hospital," Christine told the driver.

"What about my father?" Marci asked. "He called me last night and said that he wasn't feeling too well." Marci remembered the sardine sandwiches that had made her daddy sick and that she had laughed when he told her, "I feel like I'm going to die."

"I guess that's that," Christine answered glumly. Twenty blocks farther north she told the driver to pull over at the corner of Ninety-seventh Street, paid the fare, and got out of the cab, with Marci following behind her.

Marci looked around. They were in a very bad neighborhood, she thought. It was a forgotten block, on the edge of Spanish Harlem, lined with tenements with fire escapes covering the front of the buildings like filigreed prison bars. It was scary in this neighborhood, Marci thought, and she was afraid of the people on the street. "Where's Mount Sinai Hospital?" she asked Christine.

"I'm looking for a phone booth to call the hospital and ask if you're needed," Christine said. Then, with an alacrity that terrified Marci for fear of being left alone, Christine took off down the street so fast that Marci couldn't keep up with her.

"Christine, *wait!*" Marci called.

But Christine didn't slow down. Instead, she yelled over her shoulder, "Hurry up! Come on!," and Marci ran even harder. When the child finally caught up with Christine, she was out of breath and panting. "Where are we going?" she gasped.

"We're going up to my apartment," Christine told her. "I have to make a call to see if you're old enough to go into the hospital." With that, Christine sprinted up a stone stoop between two faux Roman columns covered in graffiti and disappeared into the forbidding gray tenement. With her heart pounding wildly, Marci followed up the steps after her.

Inside, the building was dark, and the air stunk with the overwhelming smell of insecticide and garbage. Christine was sprinting up the steps so fast that she had already reached the top landing when Marci was only on the third, out of breath and panting. Marci caught up with her just as she was about to turn her key in the lock.

Suddenly, from behind, there were loud footsteps on the stairs, and a dark figure loomed over Marci, enveloping her. She began to let out a terrified shriek when at the same instant her face was shrouded with something scratchy that smelled like medicine, crushed into her nose and mouth by big hands, suffocating her.

Her nose started to bleed and her braces tore into the inside of her lips as blood poured down over her chin.

Marci managed to let out a panicky squeal, and the man pressed harder on her face with the muffler and shoved her through the open door to Christine's apartment. Christine began begging the man, "Please don't hurt her! Please don't hurt her!"

The man let up his grip a little, and Marci managed to plead, "Please! I can't breathe! Please put your hands over my mouth, not my nose!"

"Be quiet!" the man snarled, half-carrying, half-shoving, the child through the living room and into a small bedroom to the left. "Face the walls!" he shouted.

"Do as he says!" Marci pleaded with Christine. Then to the man she begged, "If you want money, I'll give it to you."

Without answering, the man grabbed her small hands behind her back and tied her wrists together with white electrical cord. Then he tightened the dirty muffler around her eyes, enclosing her in a claustrophobic blackness that increased her panic tenfold. She began to whimper loudly.

"Shut up!" the man warned her, his voice rising in pitch and more threatening. "I've got two sex maniacs here if you don't shut up."

Marci's heart almost stopped. She choked back sobs as best she could.

The man shut the bedroom door behind them and went to a phone on the kitchen wall.

Taking a deep breath, Dominique Ransay dialed Calvin Klein at his home to demand his ransom. Calvin sounded "shocked," just as Ransay had expected, and by the time Ransay put down the phone, his heart was pounding. So far, so good, he thought. Although it was just the beginning of a long day, Ransay was not worried; he had planned long and well.

At nineteen years of age, Dominique Ransay was just a kid "who saw no way out," said one of his teachers, "who just kept running up against walls." Six feet tall, 150 pounds, thin but firmly built and with a feral-looking mustache and goatee, he also had an omnipresent sneer, and when he moved, he assumed the swagger and arrogance of someone much older. It was an attitude won on the hardscrabble streets of New York, an attitude he copped after being cheated—by circumstance, he thought—of all the good things in life.

Born in Martinique in the French West Indies—as was his half sister Christine—Ransay was the son of a mother who cleaned houses and a father who worked for Con Ed in New York. After being expelled from a series of schools, Ransay was able to pass the high school equivalency exam and enrolled at State University of New York at Potsdam. However, by age nineteen, after racking up a record which included driving without a license, possession of a firearm, shoplifting, and possession of stolen property—for which he served six months in jail—he was back home living with his mother and father in a cramped apartment. Christine got him a job working at the same restaurant as she, La Potagerie, as a dishwasher. "I had nothing," Ransay said. "I figured that money would help me." What he wanted, Ransay said, was enough cash to "have a stepping-stone to the world," and now that stepping-stone was tied up with electrical cord in his half sister's bedroom.

The idea to kidnap Marci Klein first came to him in late November, when Christine showed him pictures of herself with the famous fashion designer Calvin Klein in a magazine. One night a few months before, Jayne had asked Christine to help her take a dozen of Marci's school friends out to dinner and to see *Beatlemania,* a Broadway show, in celebration of Marci's eleventh birthday. That night, Christine was standing in front of 136 East Seventy-sixth Street with Marci and Jayne when Calvin arrived in a taxi to pick them up.

"Who's *that*?" Christine blurted out, surprised at how tall and handsome the man was.

"That's my ex-husband," Jayne said, a little amused.

"He's a *really* good-looking guy," Christine commented.

Later, at the restaurant, they met up with Marci's birthday guests and some of their parents. Calvin was at his dazzling best for the other parents, and Christine watched him in awe. However, just before dinner, Calvin made some excuse and left the restaurant, to rejoin the party later at the Winter Garden Theatre, where he promptly fell asleep in his seat next to Jayne and snored loudly throughout the performance. Later, as they were all leaving the theater, a *paparazzi* rushed up and took several pictures of Calvin Klein and Marci with Christine in the background. A month later, the photographs turned up in a Spanish-language magazine, which Christine proudly showed to Dominique.

Dominique was fascinated that his half sister had such close access to a man as rich and famous as Calvin Klein. Ransay hatched a plan, which in his mind was so ingenious it even had a name, the "Fifty-five Day Plan." It had three segments. The first was to learn everything there was to know about Calvin by spending hours in the periodical room of the Forty-second Street library, staking out Calvin's apartment building and showroom—sometimes hiding in doorways with a camera—and taking over fifty photographs of Calvin as he went about his daily business. The second part of the "Fifty-five Day Plan" was to learn everything about Marci, and she, too, was followed and photographed. The third part of the plan was an intricate and complicated scheme to lure Marci off the street, into a car, and get $100,000 for her in ransom. For this part, dozens of public pay-phone numbers were recorded, routes mapped out, timetables set, and alibis prepared. Since Christine didn't even have a phone in her apartment, one was installed just a few days before the kidnapping. Ransay was so meticulous that the night before the kidnapping, he called Calvin to make sure he had the right number. "Can I speak to Jones, please?" Ransay asked when Calvin answered the phone.

"Nobody by the name of Jones here," Calvin said. Ransay repeated the number he had dialed. "That's the correct number," Calvin said, "but there is no Jones here," and hung up on him.

Ransay still wasn't satisfied. He redialed Calvin's phone and again asked, "Can I speak to Jones?"

"There's *no* Jones here," Calvin said, and hung up.

Finally satisfied, Ransay burned all his notes and photographs and flushed them down the toilet.

Prepared as Ransay was that day in February, the morning already held some unexpected surprises. To begin with, the night before, he had gone out to a disco and didn't arrive home until 4:30 A.M. After only two hours' sleep, he dressed in jeans, a striped shirt, and a rust-brown leather jacket and went across the street to wake his accomplice, Mousie, whose real name was Cecil Wiggins.

Mousie was a tall, skinny twenty-five-year-old with a short Afro who lived on the same block and worked in the corner supermarket as a stock boy. Just two weeks before, Ransay had gone to Mousie's apartment to enlist his help. He showed Mousie the pictures, explained how rich Calvin was, and asked Mousie to get a car. The plan was that Christine would lure Marci into the car at the bus stop; then Mousie would drive her to Christine's apartment and help watch Marci during the day. In return he would receive $25,-000 of the ransom money. Mousie tentatively agreed to help, but when Ransay knocked on his apartment door the morning of the kidnapping, it was Mousie's girlfriend, Anette Evora, who answered the door. Anette had some bad news. The night before, Mousie had run a red light and was arrested for driving while intoxicated. The car had been impounded, and Mousie was in the drunk tank. Actually, Mousie was sound asleep in the next room, having decided he didn't really want to be involved in a kidnapping scheme.

Furious with Mousie, Ransay went back to Christine's apartment and told her she would have to handle the abduction by herself. Her alibi was going to be that she had been forced into it under threat of death by two strange men.

And it had worked.

Now, in the other room, Marci Klein sat tentatively on the edge of the bed, her nose and lips still dripping blood.

"Can she have a tissue?" Christine called out to her brother. "Her nose is bleeding!"

Ransay dutifully got a roll of paper towels from the kitchen and handed them to Christine through a crack in the door. Christine started to wipe Marci's face. "Marci, I lied to you," Christine told her, weeping softly. "Your father is okay, nothing ever happened to him."

"What do you mean?" Marci asked.

"I told you a lie," Christine answered. "I told you a big lie."

The little girl was bewildered.

"They came to me last night and made me do it," Christine said. "These people, three men, they came to me and said to me, 'If I don't get you, they were going to kill me.' So I had to get you." Christine wept louder now. "They told me, 'We saw you with Mr.

Klein and Mrs. Klein.' I told them, 'I have no idea of what you're talking about.' They told me, 'Don't lie to us, we have photographs.' " Christine went to a drawer in the dresser and showed Marci the published photographs from the night of her eleventh birthday celebration, but Marci had no memory of the photographs being taken.

Slowly, things began to fall in place. Her daddy wasn't dying! He was well! And if he was okay, he would come save her no matter what the kidnappers wanted. Her heart filled with naive forgiveness, Marci tried to comfort Christine. She hugged her and said, "It's all right, Christine, it's *okay*."

In the living room, Ransay dialed Mousie's number. No answer. If Mousie didn't show up, Ransay wouldn't be able to leave for work and have an alibi. He called Mousie yet again. No answer. Well, he couldn't wait any longer. He went to the bedroom door and through the crack he said, "I've got two guys taking over. I'm paying them well to watch you—not wait on you. They speak only Spanish, so don't bother them. The best thing for you to do is to be quiet and everything will be okay."

Then Ransay shut the door tightly behind him. In the event that Mousie might finally show up, he left the front door to the apartment firmly shut but unlocked. Then he went across the street and took the subway to work at La Potagerie, where he tried to act naturally. Thirty minutes later, he tried Mousie's number yet again from a basement pay phone. "Where the hell you've been?" Ransay shouted when Mousie finally answered. "I went ahead without you, and everything's all right. Get over there and I'll speak to you later."

Mousie took his time getting dressed and walking over to Christine's building. After the long climb to the top floor, he was surprised to find the door unlocked. Inside, the apartment was deathly quiet, and Mousie perched on a stool and waited, wondering what to do. After a while, the bedroom door cracked opened, and Mousie saw Christine standing there. "Then I saw the other girl [Marci]," Mousie said, "and . . . that's when I realized that . . . they . . . somehow got the girl there . . . I just stayed in the kitchen . . . I just sat there by the door."

Now Mousie was in charge of Marci's life.

2

That most hideous and confusing day of his life, Calvin was certain about only one thing.

He was going to get Marci back. He was going to save her. A hundred thousand or a million, he was going to get her back. Nobody would endanger her life in order to catch the kidnappers. Not the FBI, not anybody.

By the time two FBI agents, Damon T. Taylor and Fredric V. Behrends, arrived at Calvin's house a little after 9:00 A.M., Calvin was distraught. "He often paced," remembered Agent Taylor, "his hands trembled, his voice wavered, and sometimes he stuttered."

Although the two agents had been alerted that the case was supposed to be "high profile," Taylor and Behrends were not really sure who Calvin Klein was. "I didn't even know he was a multimillionaire," said Behrends, "or how famous he was. All I knew was he was a designer." Behrends remembered how surprised he was when Calvin answered the door. "He was a good-looking kid, very neat, very pleasant," he said, "who was only concerned about the safety of his daughter."

The two agents ran through several scenarios with Calvin until "I was literally hysterical," Calvin said. "I became hysterical because I felt terrible guilt. They started asking me questions like 'Who's her doctor?,' questions that I didn't have the answers to because she wasn't living with me, and I suddenly felt very guilty." The agents in particular wanted to know if Calvin had any enemies. Since $100,-000 was not a tremendous ransom, considering how rich Calvin was, what if the kidnapping was only a hoax and Marci was being used as bait, the real target being Calvin himself? Or maybe Calvin would pay the ransom and they would kill Marci, anyway. Or the kidnapper could discover that Calvin went to the FBI and kill them both. Calvin said, "They told me that my daughter's safety was in my hands and that if I led the kidnappers to believe that I had informed agents or that there were people following me, if I cracked under pressure, there was a good chance Marci wouldn't live through the day." The agents suggested that Calvin use a double and they would substitute an agent to go in his place. But Calvin insisted he rescue Marci himself.

As usual, it was Barry who handled the money. Barry arrived at Calvin's apartment somber but stoically supportive. Barry had children of his own and could well guess how Calvin felt. The only thing that Barry could do for him at the moment was to get the $100,000. An FBI agent escorted Barry to the Manufacturers Hanover Trust branch on Eighth Avenue and Thirty-seventh Street where Calvin Klein Ltd. did much of their banking. Barry withdrew $100,000 in cash in hundred-dollar bills from one of the company's accounts and was then escorted to the sixth floor "counting room" of the East Sixty-seventh Street FBI headquarters. The money was then counted and photographed, and each bill was sprayed with an invisible chemical so that the kidnapper's fingerprints would show up if he touched them. Then the cash was wrapped in twenty brown-paper packages which Barry Schwartz took back to Calvin's apartment.

By that time several interviews had already been conducted at the Dalton School, where a classmate of Marci's, Jenny Semel, told agents she had seen Marci leave the bus with a woman. When Jayne was interviewed over the phone in Fort Lauderdale by New York FBI agents, she was able to identify the woman as Christine Ransay by Semel's description. Jayne told the agents that Christine worked for her boyfriend, Kenny Sheresky, at La Potagerie, and fifteen minutes later two agents arrived at Sheresky's East Side home. Sheresky told them he had no idea why Christine would take Marci off a bus. Jayne, in the interim, frantic and helpless, boarded the next plane for New York.

At the same time, teams of FBI agents began arriving at Calvin's office, some disguised as phone repairmen, and a pall fell over the showroom. "We knew something was terribly wrong, but we weren't sure what," said Beth Luttinger, a saleswoman. "You could tell from just looking at them that they were cops or FBI agents. Two of them began to take apart the switchboard." The plan was to trace the next ransom call, but the FBI quickly realized they had their work cut out for them when they discovered that between 1:37 and 2:30 P.M., a staggering sixty-four phone calls were logged to Calvin Klein Ltd.—more than one a minute.

None of the FBI's work was for naught, however, since Ransay had set Mousie the task of finding out if Calvin had reached his office with the money. Mousie called Calvin's office several times, and each time, when Calvin's secretary answered the phone and told the caller Calvin was not in the office, Mousie abruptly hung up. At exactly 2:43 that afternoon the agents were able to "trap" one of the calls originating from apartment 34 of 60 East Ninety-seventh Street, and teams of undercover FBI agents as well as New York City detectives from the Major Crime Squad began to discreetly spread out on Ninety-seventh Street and surround that building.

Calvin was already en route to his office with the $100,000. In case he was being watched by the kidnapper or his confederates, elaborate precautions were taken to make it look as if he were unaccompanied. He was seen leaving the building by himself and getting into his Rolls-Royce limousine. That day, however, his usual chauffeur had been replaced by crack FBI driver Ralph Ianuzzi. When Calvin climbed into the back seat he was surprised to find a second FBI agent crouched on the rear floor of the car, covered with a leather auto blanket. Ianuzzi drove Calvin his usual route to his offices and dropped him off. When Calvin arrived upstairs, an FBI agent asked him if he knew anyone at 60 East Ninety-seventh Street. Calvin said no, but the number stuck in his mind all day.

At three, Dominique Ransay walked to Grand Central Station and dialed Calvin's office from a pay phone. As the phone began to ring on Calvin's desk, he took a deep breath and picked it up. Opposite the desk from him sat an FBI agent with earphones and a monitoring system, taping the call.

"Mr. Klein?" Ransay asked.

"Yes."

"Is everything ready?"

"Who is this?" Calvin said, pretending he didn't know, then, "Ah, ah, yeah," he said. "Hello."

"Do you have the money?" Ransay asked. "All in twenties?"

Calvin's heart dropped. "You didn't tell me all twenties," he said.

"What did you get?" Ransay asked.

"I got all different bills," Calvin said. "I got hundreds . . . But, ah, I mean, does that matter? I mean, you didn't tell me what, you know, how, you know, what kind of . . . twenties, tens . . . "

Suddenly, Calvin sounded strange to Ransay, who was hit by a surge of paranoia like an adrenaline shot. "Did you call the police?" Ransay suddenly snarled, his voice rising.

"What?" Calvin asked with half a breath, trying not to sound guilty. There was a look of panic in his eyes as he glanced at the FBI agents standing in the office with him.

"Did you call the police?" Ransay growled threateningly.

"No!" Calvin barked out, trying to sound indignant. "Are you kidding? Listen, all I'm worried about is my daughter."

"Look, look, look," Ransay said, interrupting. "You will not see her unless I have the money and I'm safe. Okay?"

"I have the money," Calvin insisted. "You tell me what you want me to do. I have it all in hundreds, the bank is closed now, it took me a long time to arrange this thing. I mean, I just want to make sure that you don't fuck this thing up. Because I'm only concerned about my daughter and nothing else."

"Very well, then, very well," Ransay said. "You have a brown paper bag?"

"Yeah, I have a brown paper bag."

"Okay. You have twenty minutes to get on Forty-second Street and Lexington Avenue. Okay?"

Calvin pretended he was slowly writing down the directions as Ransay told him to go to a cluster of phone booths at a corner of the intersection.

"Now just be there and I'll call you," Ransay said.

Calvin quickly interjected, "Now wait a second, let me speak to Marci. I—"

"She's not with me right now," Ransay said.

"Where is she?" Calvin asked.

"You won't talk to her until I have the money," Ransay warned him again.

"How do I know that she's okay?"

"She's okay," Ransay said blandly.

"How do I know that?" Calvin said, his voice rising in anger, "I mean, you—"

"You take my word for it, okay?" Ransay snapped.

"But—!" Calvin sputtered.

"You be there in twenty minutes, all right?" Ransay shouted.

"You're asking me for a hundred thousand dollars," Calvin shouted right back.

"You—!" Ransay snarled menacingly.

"And you—!" Calvin growled back, his anger boiling over.

"Look!" Ransay said, "I have no—look, I—look, I don't want to harm your daughter, okay? She's worth nothing to me but a hundred grand, okay? And that's all I want. Now what the hell would I want to hurt her for? Okay? You'll speak to her, okay? As soon as I have the money, you'll speak to her, and I'll tell you where to get her when I'm safe, okay?"

"You'll tell me where to pick her up?" Calvin asked.

"Yes. Just . . . go by the phone. I'll call you."

"Wait," Calvin said, stalling for time. "Now let me get it straight one more time."

"No. Goodbye," Ransay said firmly, and slammed down the phone.

Even before Calvin put down the receiver, dozens of FBI Agents were flooding into the area of Forty-second Street and Lexington Avenue, some dressed casually in jeans, some as businessmen. By now, over a hundred agents were working on the case. Meanwhile, on the ninth floor of the *New York Daily News* building on West Forty-second Street, the day-shift photo editor was routinely monitoring the open radio frequencies of the FBI when a "kidnapping in progress" call went out in code. Something was about to "go down" at a phone booth at Lexington Avenue and Forty-second Street. Kidnappings, naturally, were big news, and the editor instantly dispatched a crack staff photojournalist, Tom Monaster. When Monaster got there, he immediately saw the phone booths and ducked into the nearby doorway of Howard Johnson's restaurant to wait.

Back at his offices, Calvin was waiting for the elevator when his assistant, Zack Carr, came dashing into the waiting room. He had just discovered what was going on and blindly ran out to the elevators to see Calvin. Just by looking at his mentor Carr could tell "he was mustering up whatever ounce of courage he could [find]. He was in a state of shock, moving on pure instinct." Unable to find the right words to say, Carr flung his arms around Calvin and held him tightly until the elevator door opened and Calvin got inside.

In another moment Calvin was in the backseat of his Rolls-

Royce on his way to Forty-second Street and Lexington Avenue, the blood pounding through his head as Agent Ianuzzi wove in and out of heavy traffic. When the car finally arrived at the corner, Calvin was incensed to discover that there weren't *three* phone booths on that corner as the kidnapper had insisted, but *two*. Across the street Calvin saw a cluster of three and headed toward them. Even as he approached, the middle one began to ring. Such timing made it clear that the kidnapper was watching him at that very moment.

The voice on the phone said, "Now walk directly to Fifth Avenue and Forty-second Street and you will see on the same side of the street several telephone booths. You will receive further instructions there."

Annoyed that there was still more to this mean game, Calvin hung up the phone, walked back to his car, and got in. "Listen," he told Ianuzzi, speaking very rapidly, "this guy told me to walk to Fifth Avenue, and I don't think you should drive me."

Ianuzzi looked at Calvin in the rearview mirror. Calvin was pale and sweating. "He struck me as a man who might panic at any moment," Ianuzzi said. "He was clutching the paper bag so hard that his hands were shaking. I told him, 'Do whatever you feel is best.'"

Calvin walked briskly to the next set of phone booths, where he recognized Special Agent Behrends in one of them. Almost immediately the phone in the next booth started ringing and Calvin hurriedly picked it up. It was Ransay. "I want you to run," Ransay said, "*run*—not walk—*run* up Fifth Avenue to Forty-fifth Street, then *run* down Forty-fifth Street until you get to the Pan American Building. There are two pairs of escalators. Use the ones on the right side, and when you get to the top, drop the money over the right side of the rail."

"When do I get to see my little girl?" Calvin asked.

"When I have the money and I am safe. When you drop the money, go back to the *first* telephone booth where I called you. Okay, wait five minutes and start running."

Calvin hung up the phone, ready to jump out of his skin. If he ever got his hands on this guy, he would tear him limb from limb. Calvin started pacing angrily on the street and staring at his watch as the seconds went by. Meanwhile, right under the noses of the

FBI, the kidnapper, and Calvin, *Daily News* photographer Tom Monaster was snapping hundreds of pictures. "I was across the street," Monaster said, "when I spotted Calvin walking in and out of a phone booth with a paper bag under his arm. Later, I found out it was a hundred thousand dollars in ransom. I started taking pictures like I was a tourist, knocking off frames with my motor drive."

After two minutes had passed, a man on the street in a trench coat came up to Calvin and asked him for a light. Calvin was about to say, "No," when the man whispered to him, "I'm giving you a transmitter so that you can speak to the FBI during the rest of the day. We won't be able to speak to you, but you can let us know what is going on." The man passed Calvin a small, thin instrument in a leather case that looked like a pocket calculator and then just walked away.

Calvin waited three more minutes, and then, not knowing or caring what people thought, he bolted down the street like a maniac, as if he were running for his life.

3

Marci Klein, exhausted by her ordeal, had fallen into a troubled sleep in Christine's bedroom. When she awoke after an hour, she was disoriented and frightened again, and Christine got her a ham sandwich and turned on the TV. As she watched the sun get lower in the sky over tenement rooftops, her hope began to wane. "It became later," Marci said, "and I was getting very worried and scared."

"Where *is* he?" Marci asked Christine. "Where is my father?"

"Don't worry, Marci," Christine told her. "He's going to come. Just relax."

Marci sat in silence for a while, and suddenly the phone rang in the other room. There was a muffled conversation, and then Mousie came in. "Look, I'm going to have to tie you both up because Mr. Klein is coming to bring the money."

Marci, in relief, began to sob loudly.

"You've got to be completely quiet," Mousie warned her, "and no one will hurt you."

When Mousie left the room, Christine tried to console the child.

"We're going to be okay," Christine whispered to her, and they both cried aloud.

As it happened, Calvin was so panicked he left the money at the wrong place. When he got to the Pan Am Building, which towered over Grand Central Station, Calvin got confused. The lobby of the forty-six-story skyscraper was teeming with people. "I entered the building on the wrong side," Calvin said, "and found an escalator. I wasn't sure if I should leave the bag there. I looked around, and I decided I would drop the money." Calvin just let go of it, plop, $100,000, onto the marble floor, and walked away.

Meanwhile, Ransay was waiting by the other escalator when it occurred to him that maybe Calvin went to the wrong one. He could have tossed $100,000 over the railing where anybody could pick it up and walk away. So, as calmly as possible, Ransay took off for the other side of the Pan Am Building, weaving his way through the busy concourse, until he reached the opposite escalator. The money wasn't there.

Ransay started back toward the original bank of elevators when he suddenly realized that the man just ahead of him was Calvin Klein. "He looked extremely confused," Ransay said, "in a dazed state," and, Ransay saw to his horror, he was no longer carrying the brown paper bag. Klein must have dropped the money on the floor someplace. Ransay made a sharp U-turn and headed back to the escalator. There, on the floor, was a small brown paper bag. Ransay scooped it up, and walked out of the building. Quickly ducking behind a granite pillar on the traffic promenade, he ripped open the bag. It was amazing to see—$100,000 in one little packet, one thousand hundred-dollar bills! The sight made him giddy. It was all he could do not to jump for joy as he hailed a cab. "Look for a phone booth," he told the driver as he got inside. In the backseat he thumbed through a packet of hundred-dollar bills lovingly. "Ha-ha!" he laughed aloud. "You won't believe me," he told the driver proudly. "I just came into one hundred grand!"

The driver congratulated him and pulled over to a phone booth at Thirty-seventh Street and Madison Avenue. There Ransay called Calvin.

"Did you get the money?" Calvin asked him frantically.

"You did fine. We got the money."

"Thank God," Calvin said. "Now where's my little girl? I have to speak to Marci. I've trusted you. I've done everything you asked me to do. But you still haven't let me talk to Marci yet."

"Stay there," Ransay said. "Marci will call you in five minutes." Ransay slammed down the receiver and then dialed Christine's apartment. *"Bingo!"* he cried when Mousie answered the phone. "I got the money. You call Klein and tell him the address to pick up the girl. Now get the hell out of there."

Ransay got back into the cab and smiled all the way uptown. When he got out, he gave the driver a five-dollar tip.

4

Calvin waited breathlessly by the pay phone until it rang again. This time it was a new voice, a man who whispered so quietly it was almost impossible to hear him say, "She's at Sixty East Ninety-seventh Street, apartment six F.' "

Calvin demanded to speak to Marci, and they put her on the phone. He almost broke down and cried when he heard her shriek, "Daddy! Daddy! Please hurry up and come here!"

"I'll be right there, honey! I'm coming! I'll be right there!"

He hung up the phone and looked around him. He decided he had had enough of the FBI for the moment. If Marci was okay, that's all he cared about, not catching the kidnappers, not getting his $100,000 back. He decided to ditch the FBI. Paranoid that any taxi waiting at the curb might be a plant containing another under-cover FBI agent, Calvin hailed one just dropping someone off and dove inside. The driver, Rafael de Jesus, turned around to see who had plunged into the backseat. Calvin thrust a twenty-dollar bill at him through the partition and shouted, "Sixty East Ninety-seventh Street. It's between Fifth and Madison."

DeJesus, who had been pushing a hack for years, started out in traffic and said, "No, I think it's between Park and Madison."

As the taxi fought rush-hour traffic on Madison Avenue Calvin studied the back of deJesus's head. "Somehow I felt I could trust him," Calvin said, "and . . . I started to talk to him because I thought of the possibility of me going into that building and not coming out alive myself." Calvin explained to deJesus that he was about to do something very dangerous to save the life of his child. He wrote his name, his phone number, Barry's name, and the names of the FBI agents on a business card and handed it to deJesus. "Leave me at the corner of Park Avenue and Ninety-seventh Street," Calvin told him, "and if I'm not down in five minutes, then call this telephone number and tell my partner or the FBI that you've dropped me off there."

Then Calvin took the transmitter out of his pocket and gave it to the driver in case he was frisked when he went inside. "Just hide it in the taxi," he told de Jesus, who slipped it under the front seat.

As Calvin was about to get out of the cab, de Jesus looked at him in the rear view mirror. "I have a feeling it is going to be okay," he said. Calvin was silent as de Jesus turned around in his seat and added, "Have faith in God."

DeJesus watched as Calvin disappeared down the block and went inside a building. He sat studying his watch carefully as the minutes ticked by. When six minutes passed and there was no sign of Calvin, de Jesus bolted from his cab and ran to the corner phone booth. But when he picked up the phone, it was dead.

5

When Calvin got inside the building, he almost went mad. There were no letters on the doors, only numbers, and he had no idea where Marci was. In desperation he started wildly banging on every door in sight, screaming, "Marci! Marci! It's daddy!" He went from floor to floor, shouting at the top of his lungs.

Up on the sixth floor, Marci finally heard him calling and ran to the apartment door screaming, "Daddy! I'm up here! Up here!"

Suddenly, the door flew open, and there was Calvin. Father and child fell into each other's arms and Marci sobbed hysterically into his neck. Calvin hugged her hard for a moment. Just beyond them stood Christine, sobbing as well. "At that moment," said Calvin, "I thought the woman [Christine] was another hostage. Marci had the presence of mind to pick up her schoolbooks and tell me to take the rope [they had tied her up with] for evidence. There's no question that she was more in control than I, because she knew she hadn't been physically harmed. I didn't. . . ."

In a few more heart-pounding moments they raced out of the apartment, and holding Marci by the hand, they bounded down five flights of steps two at a time and bolted out the front door of the building. Calvin looked toward the corner, and there was deJesus, waiting for him next to his cab. He began to rush toward the waiting taxi, holding Marci by the hand, when, in a move so swift it shocked him, a woman passing by on the street grabbed Marci away from him in a steel grip.

"Daddy! Daddy! Daddy!" Marci screamed as she was dragged away from him.

Calvin reached for her and tried to shout, but before he could utter a sound, Marci was tossed like a bag of flour to a strange man passing on the street and *BAM!*, three men threw Calvin headfirst up against a brick wall and crushed him to it so hard he thought all of his ribs were broken.

Calvin tried to cry out to Marci, but the sound was cut dead in his throat by the hard steel of a revolver barrel viciously pressed against his skull. Dozens of men and women now seemed to swarm over them from nowhere. Then Calvin felt himself being roughly frisked, and somewhere off behind him he dimly heard a man say, "That may be her father." In another second he realized these were not kidnappers; they were FBI agents and police. He would later learn that nearly sixty agents converged on the block at that moment and jumped on him, uncertain whether he was Calvin Klein or one of the kidnappers.

Calvin, Marci, and Christine were whisked to the FBI offices on East Sixty-ninth Street in a procession of cars. Marci's personal physician was summoned to the FBI offices, where he examined her and determined that she had been neither sexually nor physically abused. Jayne was midair when a stewardess rushed down the aisle to call her to the cockpit, where she learned over the plane's radio phone that her daughter had been recovered unharmed. Jayne went directly from the airport to the FBI offices to be reunited with Marci and Calvin.

In another room, on another floor, Christine Ransay doggedly stuck to her prepared alibi: The night before, as she was entering her apartment, she was pushed inside by a gunman who tied her up, in the process ripping her pants and shirt, which she was prepared to produce for the police. She was threatened with death by unknown assailants unless she lured Marci to her apartment. But the FBI wasn't buying it. Why didn't she try to run away and call for help when she was on the bus? Why didn't she tell the bus driver? And if she was alone with Marci in a taxicab, why didn't she ask the driver to take her to the nearest police officer or station house?

But Christine would not be shaken. She insisted there were men who would have found her and killed her had she not brought Marci to her apartment. Even after she flunked a lie detector test, she stuck to her story. "She was a hard nut," said Behrends.

At ten o'clock that night, FBI agents interviewed Dominique Ransay at his parents' apartment. He said he wasn't close to his stepsister and could tell them little. He was at work, he knew nothing, and seemingly satisfied, the FBI agents left. Later that night, Ransay went to celebrate his good fortune at Studio 54 with a gram of coke.

Calvin Klein would not be there that night.

That night, at the Sovereign, he and Marci and Jayne all slept under the same roof together for the first time in four years.

6

The next day, Saturday, February 4, at 2:30 P.M., two FBI agents picked up Dominique Ransay at La Potagerie and took him to FBI headquarters for further questioning.

From the room where Christine was being interrogated, the FBI agents intentionally allowed her to see Dominique being escorted onto the floor and led into a holding room. As they had hoped, she jumped to a fatal conclusion: The FBI had arrested Dominique, and he was confessing. Relieved that the charade was finally over, Christine announced to the agents that she "might as well confess." A tape recorder was set up for her, and as soon as she began to incriminate Dominique, the agents marched across the hall and informed him that his half sister was implicating him in the kidnapping of Marcia Robin Klein.

At 6:10 P.M. Saturday night, Dominique gave the FBI a full and detailed confession on tape, bragging to them about the meticulousness of his Fifty-five-Day Plan. Later that night, as he was taken downtown to the Tombs and booked, he had one statement to make: "Tell Mr. Klein I'm sorry."

In one last odd twist, *New York Daily News* columnist Jimmy Breslin had learned from his police contacts that Christine Ransay once worked as a cashier at the Pioneer Supermarket on Ninety-sixth Street and headed over to talk with the owner, Seymour Lehman. Lehman couldn't remember Christine, but he suggested the stockboy might. His nickname was Mousie.

Breslin was directed down the egg aisle to where Mousie was stacking condiments. Breslin talked with Mousie, who admitted he knew Dominique and Christine. When Breslin suggested to Mousie that kidnapping was a terrible crime and that Christine could get twenty-five years for it, "the linen supermarket apron remained motionless while everything inside it revolved," wrote Breslin.

Mousie said he could be of no further help, so Breslin moved on.

Later that night, Breslin was hanging around the FBI offices when they brought Mousie in. "From now on," Breslin declared in his next day's column, "Mousie shall be known as 'Cecil the Rat.'"

CHAPTER THIRTEEN

It's time to get back to fashion.

—Calvin Klein

Nothing could have prepared Calvin for the hot blast of publicity that followed his daughter's kidnapping.

"Cops Closing in on Kidnap Gang," screamed the front page of the *New York Post*.

"100 Grand Paid for Girl," blared the front page of the *New York Daily News*, "Fashion Designer Child Safe."

"Calvin Klein's Child Abducted, Then Freed for $100,000," cried a three-column headline on the front page of the usually sedate *New York Times*, where the story made page 1 news three days in a row. The news of the kidnapping was also carried by the Associated Press, United Press International, and Reuters wire services, as well as the BBC and every American television network. Suddenly, men and women all over the world who had never given a hoot for fashion or even heard of Calvin Klein before knew about the designer who rescued his daughter from kidnappers. Calvin inadvertently added fuel to the fire when on Saturday afternoon he agreed to appear at a press conference at FBI headquarters to help the agency announce the capture of the kidnappers as well as to praise its efforts on his daughter's behalf, a generous gesture considering that an overzealous agent had nearly blown his brains out. At the press conference, Calvin vociferously complained about the photographs Tom Monaster took during the kidnapping, saying that if the kidnappers had noticed a photographer during the ransom process, it could have endangered Marci's life. The *News* had run a series of Monaster's poignant shots: Calvin waiting in the Forty-second Street phone booth with the brown bag containing $100,000 under his arm; the agents mobbing Calvin and Marci on East Ninety-sixth Street; and, most intimate, one of Calvin and Marci in the backseat of an FBI sedan, Calvin's arms wrapped protectively around her, his right hand caressing her head as he pulls her toward him, hugging her so many times that the caption reads "Overjoyed father can't stop hugging his daughter as they begin trip home." The FBI and the New York police launched a full-scale investigation to find out who tipped Monaster off, but the *News* refused to divulge its source, and the authorities never discovered it was from something as simple as monitoring the police radio band. No one else was going to get a chance to reproduce the offending photographs, though. The negatives have mysteriously disappeared from the *Daily News* photo library, and the photographs reproduced in this book had to be copied from existing prints.

By now the tabloid press and international paparazzi had descended upon Calvin's life like a pack of wild dogs, chasing him through the streets to taxicabs, camped out on the sidewalk in front of his house, until he and Marci and Jayne had to hole up for several days in the Sovereign, "in seclusion," as the newspapers put it. Locked away behind closed doors, the family was having a long-delayed heart-to-heart. For the first time, Calvin went out of his way to explain the reasons behind the divorce to Marci in a way she could understand. Sitting the little girl down, he said "[The divorce] is what I thought was best, and I'm really sorry that I wasn't there for you." He assured her, recalled a family member, that from now on they were going to have the closeness he missed with his own father. Calvin told Jayne that he wanted to buy her and Marci a new and larger apartment, with a maid's room, so that Marci would never have to be left in the care of baby-sitters again. Both parents agreed that it was important Marci get back to school and her regular schedule as quickly as possible, and within a week she was back at Dalton.

It was perhaps just as important to Calvin that he get back to work. That was the only way that he knew how to find his center again. As far as he was concerned, "It's amazing. You go through something like this, you just want to get back to work." However,

when Calvin appeared at 205 West Thirty-ninth Street a few days
after the kidnapping, his presence had the most unexpected effect.
There was no feeling of relief or jubilation. The horror of the situation was appreciated by those who worked with him, especially
those who shared the fear and tension when the FBI agents had
dismantled the front switchboard to put in phone taps. It was almost as if someone had died rather than been saved, and when
people came face-to-face with Calvin in the hallway, there was no
backslapping or congratulations, just a murmured "I'm sorry," to
which Calvin would respond with a mumbled "Thank you."

There was plenty of work to keep him busy. Few enterprises in
business history have experienced the kind of wild popularity that
overtook Calvin Klein Industries within the next few months. "It
was unbelievable," recalled Dianna de Martino, vice president of
sales for Calvin Klein jeans. The explosive sales figures read like
passages from the *Guiness Book of Records*. Within one week of the
kidnapping, 200,000 pairs of blue jeans at thirty-five dollars each
were snatched up by customers in stores across America. Saks
Fifth Avenue's New York store reordered its entire stock of 30,000
pairs after only six business days. Stock boys couldn't replenish the
supply fast enough, and customers milled about empty shelves
waiting for them to be refilled. Calvin wanted to go to Saks and
watch the buying frenzy himself, but a Saks executive begged him
not to show up. "They'll tear your clothes off," he was warned. "It
will be like Elvis showing up."

Over the next year, gross-revenue estimates tripled, and Calvin
Klein jeans became the second-largest-selling designer jeans, behind Gloria Vanderbilt, with a 20 percent share of the market. Of
Puritan's $80 million in sales that year, nearly one-third came from
Calvin's jeans. Carl Rosen would make more money on them than
on any other single product in the history of Puritan. The factories
in Texas could hardly keep up with the demand, and Carl Rosen
hurriedly sold off one of his less profitable dress divisions and
closed a sportswear company so he could get his hands on enough
cash to lease even more production facilities and buy tens of thousands of yards of raw denim to keep the plants running at full capacity. In February 1979, Calvin and Puritan added jeans for men,
and sales jumped another 30 percent. Calvin and Barry took some

of the royalties and immediately bought up 175,000 shares of Puritan stock, giving them a 7 percent stake in the company. Their business looked so rich and ripe that the communications giant International Telephone and Telegraph came courting to buy Calvin Klein Industries in its entirety. They backed off when the trial figure floated was $100 million.

On Monday, March 5, less than a month after the kidnapping, Calvin emerged from his self-imposed purdah and made his first public appearance. A three-page ad in the *New York Times* heralded his presence on the main floor of Saks Fifth Avenue at 2:00 P.M. that day to inaugurate his new cosmetics line. Aside from the press conference set up by the FBI, this was his first public appearance since he had rescued Marci. "Turmoil" was the way Saks's president, Bob Suslow, characterized the event. By noon of that day, over four thousand women had poured onto the main floor of the store, jamming the flow of traffic and disrupting business throughout the building. When Calvin was ushered through the crowds by security guards, the women nearly rioted to get close to him, smashing several cosmetics counters in the process. A record three thousand samples of his perfume were given away in two hours. Suslow declared it "the most successful launch in Saks's history" and immediately doubled Saks's orders. In its first six weeks on sale, Calvin's fragrance sold $2 million worth nationally.

In perhaps the greatest honor of his career so far, on May 8, three months after the kidnapping, Calvin appeared on the cover of *Newsweek* magazine, one of only a handful of fashion designers ever to make the cover of a national news magazine. It is still perhaps one of the most flattering photographs ever taken of him. The serious set of his angular face, eyes lowered in thought, was softened by the tantalizing presence in his arms of a sultry blond model. Says the cover line, "Soft and Sexy—Designer Calvin Klein." The five-page-long coronation of Calvin, written by no less than Susan Cheever Cowley, novelist John Cheever's daughter, acclaimed him as "Fashion's Golden Boy." This was "the year of Calvin Klein," she wrote. "His name is everywhere, his approval fiercely sought, his judgment final." Calling the kidnapping a "dubious seal of his celebrity," the article said Calvin represented the "coming of age of American fashion," extolling him as a crucial player in seizing the fashion initiative away from European couturiers.

The very week that *Newsweek* was published, over seven hundred buyers and press were turned away from Calvin's fall fashion show. His staff had to lock the doors in the showroom to keep people out. The ones who did get in placed $28 million in orders within forty-eight hours of the show, and that wasn't just because he was hot. The new line was inventive, soft, and romantic. *Women's Wear Daily* called the handkerchief linens and charmeuse satin clothing "superbly shaped," "the best of the bunch," "applaud winning," and "great." Soon after, when his menswear collection premiered at a celebration to mark the opening of the new gray-and-black Saks Fifth Avenue Calvin Klein shop on its sixth floor, seven hundred guests, including Joel Grey, Prince Egon von Furstenberg, Francesco Scavullo, Sam LeTulle, Count Lorenzo Atolico, and Xenon discotheque co-owner Peppo Vannini showed up.

Things had just started to quiet down a bit when, on May 8, the pretrial hearings for the first-degree kidnapping opened in the New York Supreme Court building in lower Manhattan before Justice Harold Rothwax. Usually the family of a crime victim demands the maximum penalty from the district attorney prosecuting the case, but not Calvin and Jayne. Explained the thirty-two-year-old bespectacled and balding assistant district attorney Thomas Demakis, to whom the case was assigned, "They asked me to do whatever plea-bargaining was possible. They wanted to avoid having Marci testify." Cecil "Mousie" Wiggins pleaded guilty immediately and was sentenced to two years, but Christine and Dominique Ransay had a surprise in store for Calvin. On the second day of the pretrial hearing, a sobbing Christine dropped a bombshell in the hushed courtroom.

She was Calvin Klein's lover.

In a sensational turn of events that once again produced international headlines—and left insiders aghast—the baby-sitter testified that not only had she and Calvin had an affair but that he put her up to the kidnapping for the publicity it would generate for his new cosmetics and menswear companies. Christine said that Calvin had promised her she could keep the $100,000 ransom, plus she would be paid an additional $100,000 after the kidnapping. He also promised, she claimed, that if she got into trouble, he would hire a lawyer to defend her. In open court, Christine rambled into a lurid but laughable story about meeting him at *Beatlemania,* where he allegedly made a pass at her before visiting her at her East Ninety-sixth Street apartment on three separate occasions. On the second visit, she vividly described to the court, they lit scented candles before making love in a scene straight from the pages of a bodice ripper. Calvin then gave her $1,300 in cash and left. Christine said she would produce witnesses from the neighborhood who would say they had seen Calvin go into the building several times prior to the kidnapping.

This accusation made Calvin so angry that his hands shook outside the courtroom as he talked to a mob of reporters. "It is the most outrageous, despicable set of lies that I have ever heard," he spat out. "If I had my way, she would get *more* than a life term. My wife and my daughter and I are very strong people, and we will get through this as we got through the other horrible things she has done." (Throughout most of the courtroom drama, Calvin invariably referred to Jayne as his "wife.") He accused Christine of a "desperate and despicable attempt to save herself by trying to destroy my daughter after all the horrible things she put her through."

"I Was Klein's Lover," the *Daily News* headline boasted, with other newspapers following suit. Calvin's alleged affair with Christine Ransay became the talk of the town. There was nothing the fashion industry liked more than a good scandal to pick over at lunch, but this time the cognoscenti were agog. The *idea* that Calvin would sully himself with a female baby-sitter sent the Fire Island queens rolling on their sisal in hysterics. Of all the dumb stories for Christine Ransay to think up! It would have been more believable if Dominique said *he* was having the affair with Calvin! In fact, the whole story was another of Dominique's dumb ideas. When Dominique Ransay was asked why, of all the stories he could come up with, he gave Christine the alibi of having an affair with Calvin, the kidnapper shrugged haplessly and said with a grin, "We didn't know he was gay."

Although Marci was never called to testify, the ensuing trial that September in Supreme Court in Manhattan smeared Calvin's name so indelibly that even to this day some people vaguely remember that "he put the baby-sitter up to it." Just as Christine had promised, she produced two neighborhood witnesses who claimed to see Calvin enter her building on various days prior to the kidnapping. Calvin, managing to conduct himself with controlled dignity, took the stand to deny emphatically any involvement with his sometime baby-sitter. Finally, after the trial dragged on for eleven days, the five-man, seven-woman jury retired to deliberate the case on Monday, September 25. They were sequestered overnight at the Golden Gate Motel in Sheepshead Bay, Brooklyn, and by the second day the vote was eleven to one to convict. The only holdout was a black woman who said she believed that Christine was telling the truth. However, she also believed that the FBI was bugging her phone and that she was the subject of a conspiracy of unknown persons who had the ability to make her ill and give her headaches. Justice Rothwax felt he had heard enough to be forced to declare a mistrial. It was delicately announced to the press that the juror's health was "impaired." The other members of the jury were furious, but no more than Calvin and Jayne and Marci, who worried about the damage to Marci now that they had to start all over again.

A second trial was scheduled to start two days later when the defense attorneys made an unexpected announcement in court. Christine and Dominique were prepared to plead guilty in return for a lenient sentence. Dominique said that along the way somebody tipped them off to the improbability of Christine's alibi. After conferring with Calvin, Assistant District Attorney Demakis let it be known that no such plea bargain would be allowed unless Christine Ransay withdrew her allegations that she was Calvin Klein's lover. And so, on November 1, 1978, Christine retracted her claim, and she and her brother offered their formal apologies to the Klein family for all the trouble they caused. The charges were reduced to second-degree kidnapping, for which they would get the maximum of twenty-five years, but only serve a minimum sentence of eight years and four months before being eligible for parole. "As a happy by-product" of Christine Ransay's confession, said Assistant District Attorney Demakis, "Calvin Klein's reputation has been cleared."

2

The Velvet Mafia listened intently as Calvin told the story of his heroism, from the first horrifying phone call to racing up the steps of the tenement calling Marci's name. They listened to how he sprinted through the streets of Manhattan and dropped a hundred grand on the floor of the Pan Am Building, and they listened to how the phone booths weren't on the corner where they were supposed to be. His friends listened politely the first time and the second and the third, until sometime later they couldn't believe he was telling the story again. "If I hear Calvin tell that story *one more time* . . ." one of his good acquaintances said under his breath. But Calvin dined out on the story of the kidnapping for years to come, until he could finally no longer bear to hear it himself.

Marci liked to tell the story as well. When she got back to school, the attention focused on her was tremendous—and perhaps more unhealthy for her than the crime. Part of her release was to answer questions about the kidnapping, acting it out, taking all the parts in a dramatic presentation that ended with her father's heroism. But then it turned into a cottage industry. For a while at Dalton, Marci Klein *became* the kidnapping. She had become such a celebrity that the newspapers reported that she made her "first public appearance" at Calvin's spring fashion show, where she was treated like a starlet by Bob Evans and Ali McGraw. Then, just as suddenly as it came, the heat of attention died down, and Marci became unruly and disruptive in class. The chorus of teasing resumed as well. This time it was one of Calvin's print ads of a bare-chested male model that had her classmates in paroxysms of "It's Marci's father's boyfriend." At the end of eighth grade, one of Marci's teachers said, Dalton's administrators asked her parents to transfer her to another school. Her father would always be her hero, and one weekend she had a photographer make a beautiful portrait of her as a surprise thank-you to Calvin. Still, the damage was done, and some of Calvin's more cynical friends nicknamed Marci "scar baby" behind Calvin's back.

One afternoon, Chester Weinberg's cousin, Karen Mann, got an unexpected phone call from Calvin. Mann was a mother of two who was a great believer that most everyone stood to gain from therapy, children included. Calvin said, "Chester suggested I speak to you because he has so much faith in the way you've raised your children. Do you think Marci needs therapy?"

Karen Mann answered, "Calvin, after the kidnapping, I think that would be beneficial." Then she added, "Look, Calvin, if I had a child and her father was Calvin Klein, I'd automatically take her for help."

There was dead silence on Calvin's end of the phone for a moment; then he forced himself to make some small talk and hung up.

An hour later, Karen Mann's phone rang again. It was her cousin Chester. "What did you say to Calvin?" Chester demanded, "He's beside himself. You know what he told me? He said that you told him, 'With a father like *you,* of course Marci needs therapy.' "

In retrospect, Mann smiled philosophically. "That was the way he interpreted it," she said with a shrug.

If Calvin overreacted to Mann's observation, perhaps it was because he was feeling a little guilty. Less than two weeks after the kidnapping he was back to his usual habits. A twenty-two-year-old, handsome Italian stallion for hire, Sal De Falco remembered meeting Calvin shortly after the kidnapping at a gay discotheque called the Ice Palace on West Fifty-seventh Street. De Falco was a dark-eyed beauty with a washboard stomach that was a product of thousands of hours spent at the gym. Calvin shyly engaged him in conversation, and the two of them had a few drinks at the bar before Calvin asked him home to the Sovereign. De Falco wound up staying at Calvin's apartment for the entire week, a period he vividly remembered. "It was *great,*" said De Falco, who loved being in the apartment so much he seldom left except to go to a nearby gym. "It had walls that moved. The maid would come in and feed me and do my laundry." De Falco also remembered that on "one side of the bed was Quaaludes and the other side was cocaine." De Falco spent most of the week in Calvin's bed, making "lots of phone calls to let everybody know where I was staying." At night, about eight, said De Falco, Calvin would come home from the office, and immediately want to have sex. De Falco was also quite impressed with Calvin's resilience, claiming it was normal for him to want to make love several times each night. At the end of a week, Calvin politely asked him to leave. There were no hard feelings, said the young man, for he never expected anything more from Calvin.

3

To add to the sensation the jeans were causing, it was decided that an easy advertising and promotion ploy would be to rent the massive Artkraft-Strauss billboard on Broadway and Forty-fifth Street, high above the hurly-burly of Times Square, in a space occupied for many years by a Camel cigarette sign that puffed real giant smoke rings. The billboard would cost Puritan $60,000 rent for the year, but they believed the investment could be returned many times that with the right ad. In early 1978, Calvin asked several photographers, including Guy Bourdin, Chris Von Wangenheim, and Charles Tracy, to submit ideas to him for the billboard. Charles Tracy, previously best known as the house photographer for Saks Fifth Avenue, was the wild card of the group. Calvin assigned him a test shoot with model Patti Hansen, an amply built, brassy blond girl from Queens, New York, who a few years later would have the distinction of being married to Keith Richards of the Rolling Stones for three years. According to Tracy, one beautiful sunny afternoon, Patti, her hairdresser, "and a shirt and the jeans" arrived at his eighth floor studio at Nineteenth Street and Fifth Avenue. Presumably, because Tracy was a relative unknown and a long shot to get the job, Calvin hadn't even bothered to send an art director along on the shoot. The look of the ad was left entirely to Tracy. The only guidance he got, he says, was to "produce a bottle of vokda, because someone told me Patti liked vodka." Patti sipped her way through two drinks and "we just fooled around," said Tracy. Then "all of a sudden she got on all fours and threw her head back and I said, 'That's it!' "

"That" was the famous shot of Patti on her hands and knees, her derriere sticking receptively up in the air, her honey-colored hair flailing around her, the Calvin Klein label on her right hip visible like a beacon. "It was like magic was happening in the studio," said Tracy of the shot, and magic for the cash registers it was. The rectangular billboard, seven hundred feet long and two hundred feet wide, made Calvin Klein jeans so famous it stayed up four years running. Calvin refused to have Tracy's name on the ads, and years later, when *Photo District News* asked Calvin who photographed his famous billboards, he said he couldn't remember.

"All of a sudden," said Calvin Klein Cosmetics' president Stanley

Kohlenberg, between the kidnapping and the publicity generated by the billboard, "the jeans went right through the roof. It was the most amazing explosion I ever saw in my life, with Patti Hansen's tushy sticking out all over Broadway. And here we were, the cosmetics line, just beginning to chug along. It began to look like an awful lot of work for very little money. The fashion industry is dominated by instant gratification. You know within six months if your line has made it or not, and it was very difficult convincing someone who spent his whole life worrying about the next four months that he has to wait for a payout in cosmetics for five years." By the end of its first year, the cosmetics business lost several million dollars on grosses of $4 million, and although the next year's shipments were expected to increase by a third, the company would still be bleeding money. The single biggest problem was the lightweight, rosy perfume. It never caught on with the public. "It had no tenacity," said Kohlenberg, and in the cosmetics business, where the fragrance must anchor the line, Calvin's fragrance accounted for only 30 percent of overall sales.

Barry Schwartz didn't like the cosmetics business to begin with. He just couldn't understand why, if in the garment business the buyers could come to you, in cosmetics you had to pay a lot of salespeople with big expense accounts and airplane tickets to go to the stores. He went through every expense report with a fine-tooth comb, and paychecks sometimes took months to arrive. "Barry was so good at what he did he didn't let a dime go by without being involved," said Kohlenberg. "Barry had to sign *all* the checks." Again, to save money, instead of opening a separate accounting office for the cosmetics company, the bookkeeping load was added to the apparel division accountants, who began to drown under the huge volume of bills and paperwork. They fell behind a year in settling disputes about damages and returns, and to get a check signed by Barry often took a month after it was drawn up. "We lived constantly without money," said Kohlenberg.

To add to the chaos, the computerized reorder system was a bust. Most of the counter help were too intimidated by the complex forms. Half of the 550 buyers in retail outlets ignored the computerized forms altogether, and the ones that bothered to fill them out were frequently shipped merchandise they didn't want. One hapless soul mistakenly filled out a form to indicate $17,000 in sales instead of $7,000, and the store was shipped thousands of dollars in unwanted goods. "We don't have Ph.D.s behind the counter," complained a merchandise manager at Wanamaker.

To exacerbate the financial problems, the atmosphere at 205 West Thirty-ninth Street was not conducive to running a happy, efficient company. Calvin's flash-point temper was more evident than ever, unleashing a string of invectives and four-letter words worthy of a seaman when he was displeased. It was also commonplace for Barry to be "pounding desks and slamming doors," and employees "froze in their tracks" when he passed by, said Kohlenberg. "He was like the angel of death in that place." One stunned executive watched Barry tear up an order that hadn't met his expectations and "put it in his mouth and spit in on the floor." The staff turnover was dramatic. In February 1978 the director of merchandising and public relations of the beauty line quit after being on board only three months, and in October 1978 the national sales manager left. Rumors of Kohlenberg's own resignation to become president of Max Factor were so rife that in June 1978 he received over two hundred phone queries from concerned sales help and suppliers. Retailers worried that they were investing money and counter space in a line destined for the junk heap, and Barry was forced to invite reporters up to the offices to see for themselves that business was being conducted as usual. "I'm very happy where I am," Kohlenberg woodenly told reporters.

Perhaps the most talked about parting at Calvin Klein Ltd. during that period was Frances Stein's unexpected departure on June 29, 1979. *Women's Wear Daily* snidely asked, "Quitting Time?" More likely "firing time." The circumstances surrounding Stein's leaving the company have become an evergreen in the gossip annals of the garment center, and she has refused to comment for this book. First, it irked Calvin when one snide journalist took note of her large contribution to Calvin's line by calling it the *"Frances Klein* collection." But according to another frequently told version of her departure, Stein was fired by Calvin after she threw a drink in the face of a very proper Japanese gentlemen from Isetan and told him to go "screw himself." In any event, Stein was gone, in the blink of an eye. She went on to work for several name designers in

Paris, where she continues to live and manufacture a successful line of accessories.

In August 1979, Kohlenberg wrote a letter to Barry and Calvin saying that it was obvious they weren't really dedicated to making a go of it in cosmetics and, in effect, to either put up or shut up. "You're not putting any money in," Kohlenberg wrote to them. "We have no plans for the next year, and here it is August, no budgets." Most pressing of all, Kohlenberg wrote, was that they had to introduce a new fragrance on the market to replace the stinker and that they had to do it *fast*.

There was a long, sweaty pause that August and September before Barry and Calvin announced they had given it careful consideration and that they were going ahead. They were going to build the cosmetics business no matter what it took, including money, and they were in it for the long run. Ted Bocuzzi, the director of operations in the New Jersey plant, said, "They really wanted to blow this thing and make it into another huge company." At that point they started hiring some "really big guns," said Bocuzzi, including Marty Danielson, a vice president at Aramis, and, with great press fanfare on November 12, 1979, Frank Shields, the father of teenaged actress Brooke Shields, as executive vice president of sales. Shields's immediate task was to recruit a crackerjack national sales force, and he began hiring the best talent he knew in the business away from jobs at other companies. At the same time, Kohlenberg was given the financial green light to launch a men's fragrance, and in an encouraging change of policy, Barry and Calvin agreed to a "gift with purchase" in which a small vial of cologne would be given away with every pair of jeans. Perhaps, Calvin indicated, he would relent and even make personal appearances at stores across the country. "The whole business began to take on a new complexion," said Bocuzzi. "The machinery was getting into place to make a real aggressive effort." Out at the warehouse/factory in Carney, New Jersey, "they were cranking," said Bocuzzi.

Ten days later, the Tuesday before Thanksgiving, 1979, Kohlenberg was summoned to Barry's office, where he was surprised to find a grim-faced tax accountant waiting. "We're closing the cosmetics company," Barry said gruffly. "We're getting out."

"Closing it?" Kohlenberg gasped. He looked around as though somebody were going to laugh.

"We can't afford the tax loss anymore," Barry said.

"How much time do I have?" Kohlenberg asked.

"Today," Barry said emotionlessly.

"Today!"

Barry nodded. "Today. Fire everybody, close the warehouse. Send telegrams to everybody in the field saying that they're fired. Send telegrams to the stores saying that they can't send any returns back to the warehouse, it's closed."

"But why?" Kohlenberg asked. "Why are you doing this?"

"My father told me," Barry said, "that your first loss is your best loss, and I'm *out*."

"But what about the twenty percent of the business I own?" Kohlenberg asked him.

"What twenty percent?" Barry snarled. "We *lost* four million dollars."

Later that day, Ted Bocuzzi had to break the news to the warehouse workers. "I had a real lump in my throat. It was around eleven-thirty in the morning, two days before Thanksgiving, and I called everybody in and told them they didn't have to come back after lunch. They got no severance. Nothing. Zero. They were paid up to that Friday. I told them, 'All I can ask is that you take your check, put on your coat, and leave.' After they were gone I just sat there and looked at an empty warehouse and it looked like the neutron bomb had hit because nothing was really destroyed. It was just empty. There were bottles of perfume standing still on the production line, it was like everything stopped in mid-air."

The following telegram was received by 250 Calvin Klein accounts: "Calvin Klein Cosmetics, Inc. will discontinue operations on December 31, 1979. . . . Our warehouse is now closed. No returns can be accepted. All sales are final."

Kohlenberg's final chore at Calvin Klein was to break the news to Frank Shields, who had just left a well-paying job at Helena Rubenstein two weeks before. When Kohlenberg told Shields the company had been shut down, he was astonished. "You'd have thought they would have thought of that before they hired me," he said. Shields maintained that he had a valid employment contract with Calvin Klein Industries and that the company would have to continue to pay him his salary or pay off the contract. He determinedly continued to come to the office every day. Then, at Christmastime, he took a ten-day vacation without Barry's explicit permission, and Barry contended this was just cause to fire him. Shields was outraged and sued Barry and Calvin for $1 million each in state supreme court, claiming that they "acted in concert to trick and deceive" him and that the precipitous shut down of the company had "the effect of aborting the plaintiff's promising career."

Kohlenberg sat out the days of his contract reading magazines in his office. After leaving Calvin Klein, he founded Sanofi Beauty Products, a cosmetics and shampoo line that made him a millionaire many times over. He is now semiretired and dabbling in the high-stakes casino and gaming business.

4

The cosmetics company had barely been shut down a month when, in January 1980, Calvin got a phone call from Robert Taylor, the president of a little-known soap and potpourri manufacturer called Minnetonka, headquartered in Chaska, Minnesota. Taylor said he had just read an article in a cosmetics trade magazine saying that Calvin Klein was going to declare his cosmetics company "bankrupt" and that he couldn't believe it. Calvin Klein was one of the biggest names in the world, Taylor said. There were millions to be made in cosmetics and fragrance using Calvin's name. "Rather than you closing the company down," said Taylor in a Chesapeake twang, "let's talk about me buying it."

Robert Taylor, forty-four, was a most unlikely suitor for a business marriage with Calvin Klein and Barry Schwartz. His heart and soul were far away from the garment center. Married, with two children, he was a handsome man in an open, midwestern sort of way, blond, blue-eyed, with a calm but direct manner. Raised in suburban Baltimore, he worked his way through Stanford University before becoming one of the top salesman for the behemoth hospital supply company Johnson & Johnson. Taylor left in a few years to start his own company, Minnetonka, with a partner from Minnesota. The fledgling company had been moderately successful in gift shops and drugstores selling a variety of potpourris and fancily packaged "soap balls" which Taylor first rolled by hand in a rented garage. But it was only in 1979 that the company burgeoned to $100 million a year in revenues by beating Procter & Gamble to market with a liquid soap in a pump dispenser—Softsoap as it was named—as well as a bestselling toothpaste in a pump dispenser. Taylor was suddenly cash rich and looking for investments; a Calvin Klein fragrance looked like a good bet to him.

For Barry and Calvin, Taylor was both a godsend and a fool; he would take the cosmetics mess off their hands and pay them to do it. They invited Taylor to New York to hammer out an agreement with a team of lawyers from Charles Ballon's firm, Phillips, Nizer, Benjamin, Krim, and Ballon. The negotiations were unusually tedious and cantankerous, Taylor thought, but he didn't really get a taste of what was to come until the very last, late one night at Charles Ballon's law offices. The royalty rate had still not been settled, and it had become the deal breaker. Taylor insisted that he would go no higher than 5 percent of gross profits paid to Calvin and Barry or the deal was off. Barry, in the interim, had gone off to dinner with friends and left instructions with his attorney that the royalty had to be substantially higher. When his lawyer tracked him down in a Long Island restaurant and told him that Taylor wouldn't budge, Barry demanded to speak to him. "I don't give a shit what you say!" Barry shouted into the phone. "Five percent is not acceptable!"

Taylor was amazed. Nobody in business had ever talked to him that way before. "You'll take the 5 percent or I'm packing up and leaving for Minnesota tonight," he said quietly.

Barry caved in—and never forgave himself.

On January 30, 1980, an unusual agreement was signed in which, Taylor hoped, he had "stolen the company" from Barry and Calvin. Taylor bought the company lock, stock, and accounts receivable. He bought all the inventory, leases, tools, dies, fixed assets, equipment, know-how, formulas and processes, and future licenses to perfumes and cosmetics. In return Calvin Klein Industries was to get a paltry $506,000 in cash, $256,000 payable on signing and another $250,000 in a year, plus interest. In addition, they would receive thirty thousand shares of Minnetonka stock then worth $510,000. (Several years later the Minnetonka stock split and became worth $3 million.] Naturally, Calvin would have complete and ultimate authority over anything that carried his name. The agreement was renewable every five years as long as certain minimum thresholds were met, *in perpetuity*.

Several clauses in the contract delineated Taylor's responsibilities in the collecting of accounts receivable. Barry claimed the department stores still owed the company $1.5 million for merchandise, and all that money was just sitting out there, waiting for Taylor to collect it. Once Taylor hauled it in, he would first pay off the accumulated debt and then share the profits with Calvin and Barry. But when Taylor started talking to the retailers, he discovered that stores were stuck with large amounts of unsold merchandise they wanted to return. Taylor realized his first job in resurrecting the cosmetics company would be to reestablish good relations with the stores, and he obliged the disgruntled retailers by taking back all of the merchandise, thereby reducing their debt. What's more, Taylor was not pleased to discover that Calvin Klein Cosmetics itself was laden with debt. It turned out that the company owed the in-store demonstrations people commissions for *eight* months, according to Taylor, in some cases even more. Salespeople had been stranded out on the road when the company was abruptly shut down, and they were owed money for plane tickets home. Taylor paid these debts and hundreds of others. Eventually, some $2 million in accounts receivable was eaten up in this manner, and the way Taylor did the addition, after deducting the $250,-000 he paid Calvin and Barry up front, "between what we paid out and what was returned, they owed *us* over a million dollars." Taylor sent Barry an accounting, and at the end of the reimbursement period, he called and said, "You owe me one million two hundred thousand dollars. When might I expect that check?"

"Never," Barry said.

"What do you mean?"

"You are totally irresponsible," Barry screamed at him, "You gave away our money. You didn't ask permission. You are too fucking easy with department stores. You accepted returns and now you expect me to pay you? Fat chance! Sue me!"

Taylor yelled right back, "I'm going to take you all the way to the mat, you *asshole. Fuck you!*"

Taylor stuck to his word and brought the issue to arbitration. It took two years of lawyers and depositions to resolve. Furious that Taylor had the audacity to sue them, Barry and Calvin developed a deep, abiding hatred for him. To pour salt on the wound, Stanley Kohlenberg, who sometimes conferred with Taylor about the moribund company, claimed that Taylor called Barry and Calvin "kikes" in front of him. Taylor vehemently denies this. Nevertheless, Barry and Calvin believed he did, because Kohlenberg told them. Now there was an unspoken issue of besmirched honor.

One of the many bills Taylor had to pay was to Frank Shields. After suing the partners for a million each, all Shields won was a reported $23,200 in severance pay. Just before the lawsuit was settled, Shields had lunch with his fifteen-year-old starlet daughter, Brooke, in a Manhattan restaurant. During lunch, Frank Shields told her he was suing Calvin, and his daughter lowered her eyes and seemed uncomfortable for a moment before murmuring, "I know, Daddy." A few minutes later, when Shields asked his daughter what her next modeling assignment was, she said, "I wish you hadn't asked that, Daddy. I'm shooting six thirty-second TV spots for Calvin Klein. He makes the only designer jeans I like."

5

It wasn't Calvin Klein but Richard Avedon, the dean of high-fashion photographers, who choose Brooke Shields for his new TV commercials. "Avedon had just photographed fifteen-year-old Brooke for *Vogue*," said Calvin, "and he showed me the shots, and they were incredible." What was incredible was Brooke's allure, that of a nymphette, pure as the driven snow but smugly erotic. Brooke had come to international fame three years earlier at the ripe age of twelve when she appeared as the barely pubescent daughter of a New Orleans prostitute in the Louis Malle movie *Pretty Baby*. In the film, the child is auctioned off to a photographer who is obsessed with deflowering her. The movie caused a sensation at the box office but outraged feminists and morality crusaders. The notoriety followed Brooke over the next three years as she developed into one of the fashion industry's top print models—with her raven hair, pouty lips, and endless legs. The fee Calvin negotiated with Brooke's controversial manager-mother, Teri Shields, for her to appear in a series of six commercials was an unremarkable $20,000—quite a bargain at the time for a hot model. But Brooke's mother smelled a winner in the wind. Calvin and Avedon spelled magic.

Calvin had consulted with Avedon because he was fanatic about having his TV commercials look different from all the other jeans commercials and he believed the high priest of fashion photography was one of the few who could do it. The fifty-six-year-old photographer was a celebrity in his own right, so beloved in the fashion industry that he was the model for the romantically debonair photographer played by Fred Astaire in the 1957 movie *Funny Face*. He had been the staff photographer for *Harper's Bazaar* for twenty years before moving on to *Vogue,* where his photographic style brought its pages a cutting-edge look. The inventive artist liked to capture models in exotic and unusual settings, like a NASA launchpad or in a tenement yard, in crisp, clearly lighted photographs. Perhaps his best-known photograph was of film star Nastassja Kinski reclining nude with a live boa constrictor wrapped strategically around her breasts and groin. Avedon had only recently begun to work on TV commercials with a languid, low-key spot featuring the beautiful French actress Catherine Deneuve pitching Chanel perfume. The commercial was so beautiful and unique, Avedon was now demanding $100,000 just to come up with a concept, whether it was used or not.

For several years Calvin had been against making any TV commercials at all. He loathed the crass kind of jeans advertising he was seeing on TV, and he was afraid it would cheapen his overall image. "In the jeans area," said Calvin, "[TV advertising] has been so saturated, so boring, and so tasteless, I didn't want to become part of it."

But by the start of 1980 he was getting clobbered at the box office by a host of new jeans companies. "Our lack of television advertising has not helped our salability at point of sale," Carl Rosen told *Women's Wear Daily.* With the success of Gloria Vanderbilt and Calvin Klein jeans, the market had became flooded with imitators—twenty-seven status-jeans companies, by Calvin's own count. These businesses opened and closed overnight in the volatile market, but those that managed to stay in for a few seasons made small fortunes, with the aid of names like Bonjour, Jordache (which sounded like a designer but was actually an acronym made up from the first two letters of the names of four Israeli brothers), and Sasson (which had nothing to do with the famous hairdresser Vidal Sassoon but meant "happiness" in Hebrew and was owned by Paul Guez). Yet the company that was really hurting Calvin Klein jeans (and Puritan) was Murjani, still run by Warren Hirsh, who started the whole craze. Hirsh was not only booking TV ads non-stop; he was doing at Murjani exactly what Carl Rosen wanted to do at Puritan: corraling a host of stars to endorse clothing lines. In the past year Hirsh had signed rock star Debbie Harry, tennis player Billy Jean King, and baseball player Reggie Jackson to his stable, and Murjani was pulling down $200 million a year in sales in comparison to Calvin and Puritan's $60 million.

The objective of Calvin's TV spots, said Avedon, was to lend "the Calvin Klein image to jeans and not a jeans image to Calvin Klein." With the help of free-lance copywriter Doon Arbus, the daughter of photographer Diane Arbus, Avedon decided not to shoot just one commercial and have it shown over and over again but to keep viewers entertained with a series of twelve different spots, ten and thirty seconds long. Avedon not only filmed the spots, but he directed and coached Brooke Shields in what some think is the most memorable performance of her career.

Visually, the results were unlike anything previously seen on American TV. Absent was the loud jingle or identifying music that most advertisers liked so much. It was all low-key, with a repetitive twist that would "melt" Calvin's name into "your brain," as one media watcher put it, by calling the product not "jeans" but "Calvins." Each spot featured Brooke playing a character type whose life was in some way enriched by her "Calvins." The lens lovingly explored Brooke's body, in various limber and suggestive poses, against a white limbo background. The camera slowly and luxuriously panned up her legs to her face, almost imperceptibly lingering on the inseam of her crotch. Doon Arbus's script for the spots were so brilliant they are still remembered by millions of people, like lines from a classic play. Her dialogue mingled girlish fun with sophisticated come-ons and double entendres. Each commercial had a title. There was the "Giggler" spot in which Brooke tries to recite a limerick and falls backward, laughing as she cries, "Help, I'm going to split my Calvins!" Then there was the more sexually implicit "Flirt" spot in which she relates that her mother has warned her about boys who only want her for her "Calvins." In the "Bookworm," Brooke contends that "reading is to the mind . . . what Calvins are to the body." The enigmatic "Teenager" commercials feature Brooke singing a few bars of "After the Ball Is Over" and saying, "I've got seven Calvins in my closet, and if they could talk, I'd be *ruined.*" In the "Fashion Freak" she was irresponsible but lovely: "Whenever I get some money, I buy Calvins. And if there's any left, I pay the rent."

Yet if there was one commercial that burned its way into America's consciousness it was the one Avedon called "Feminist II" in which Brooke, all doe-eyed innocence, uttered the classic line "Do you know what comes between me and my Calvins? Nothing."

Calvin, Avedon, and Rosen could only guess what the commercials would bring them. A heavy air schedule was planned for the spots, over $3 million worth, blanketing three networks and putting them head-to-head with all the other jean companies. The massive assault was readied to kick off on August 11, 1980. Calvin had only one reservation. He confided to Avedon that he had "never liked" his first name—a peculiar and rigid appellation—and he wondered how millions of Americans would react to it.

6

While the Brooke Shields commercials were sitting in the can, waiting to be aired, Carl Rosen stunned the business community by raiding the competition.

On Wednesday, July 23, 1980, in a manner befitting the style in which he did things, Rosen called a press conference at the Four Seasons restaurant and made a shocking announcement: He was turning over the reins of Puritan's day-to-day business to Warren Hirsh, the president of Murjani, who had invented the designer-jean craze with Gloria Vanderbilt. It was a typical Rosen coup: He was crippling the competition, leaving them captainless, and getting their trade secrets in the deal to boot. Yet to insiders it made no sense. Yes, Murjani would certainly be hurt by the defection, but how could Carl Rosen *ever* give up control of his precious Puritan?

A few weeks earlier, Rosen had invited Hirsh to lunch at Le Cirque. Across the starched white tablecloth and centerpiece of fresh pink flowers, Rosen confided that he was retiring in two years. At age sixty-one he wanted more time to play golf and be with his family, and Hirsh was the perfect choice to continue signing celebrity names for Puritan. If Hirsh came to Puritan, Rosen said, he would guarantee him complete autonomy plus enough Puritan stock to make him a real player in the company, not just an employee, as he was at Murjani. Rosen would even write his own retirement date into Hirsh's contract so Hirsh would be assured that "the Chief" would really abdicate for him. "Are you coming with me?" Rosen asked Hirsh over coffee.

"You can't afford me," Hirsh told him. Hirsh was already making $500,000 at Murjani, plus perks.

Rosen reached into his suit jacket and took out his checkbook. He opened it to a blank check and pushed the leather folder across the tablecloth toward Hirsh. "Here," Rosen said. "Fill in the yearly salary you want."

Hirsh took the book, thought for a second, and wrote in it "$1,000,000."

By the time negotiations were through, not only would Hirsh be given the title of president and chief operating officer of Puritan Fashions Corp and $1 million a year in salary but also additional cash-bonus incentives of $500,000 a year, depending on sales, plus 100,000 shares of Puritan stock, the use of a company-owned black-and-tan Rolls-Royce, and the rent on his $2,000-a-month, three-bedroom apartment on the Upper East Side. His forty-one-year-old brother, Peter, and twenty-one-year-old son, Mark, were also hired by Puritan as part of the deal. Hirsh fired a warning shot about his authority from the start. "If anybody ruffles my feathers," he told *People* magazine, "I'll leave."

There was only one caveat, Rosen told Hirsh. Barry Schwartz and Calvin Klein had to give Hirsh their seal of approval. They were the tail that wagged the dog. They not only had bought up 7 percent of Puritan stock by this point, but as it stood, Calvin Klein

represented 40 percent of Puritan's income, and Rosen wanted
them to be happy. The next day, Rosen called Barry Schwartz and
hyped Hirsh's abilities to the hilt, and Barry reluctantly agreed to
meet with him in Rosen's office. Hirsh was brazen and full of himself that day, and there was some tension in the air, but at the end
of the meeting, Barry gave Hirsh his blessing. Curiously, Hirsh did
not meet Calvin until the day of the announcement at the Four
Seasons. This was particularly ironic because Hirsh also lived at
the Sovereign. Since it was a convenient way to get to know each
other, Hirsh and Calvin began sharing a limousine to the office
together each morning.

Hirsh's first attempt to assert himself as the dauphin did not
bode well. He demanded that Rosen vacate the president's office,
and when Rosen refused, Hirsh was relegated to a smaller one
down the hall. His progress on the marketing side was more successful when he added a "tops" line to the jeans company; it would
manufacture inexpensive western-style shirts and jackets under the
Calvin Klein label. When the new Brooke Shields TV commercials
were proudly screened for Hirsh, he thought some of them were a
little too sensuous but reserved judgment for the moment. He did,
however, feel strongly that the "time buy" for the commercials was
all wrong and rescheduled the spots to run heavily during the airing
of the NBC miniseries of James Clavell's epic novel *Shogun*. The
high ratings of that show seemed a cracking endorsement of
Hirsh's marketing savvy. When the commercials started airing in
mid-August, they caused a sensation in the industry, and sales immediately jumped in the stores.

On the whole, however, Warren Hirsh's personal style affronted
Calvin. His defection from Murjani brought with it extensive media
coverage, including a four-page spread in *People* magazine in
which Hirsh crowed about his plans for Puritan and his absolute
power there. Also, one of Hirsh's new ideas for the company was to
put the Puritan name on all advertisements for Calvin Klein jeans,
to enhance Puritan's status. This enraged Calvin, who refused to
have his product associated with Puritan. "In Calvin's eyes," said a
Seventh Avenue source, "that put him on the same level with Sasson and Jordache."

But push did not come to shove with Hirsh until the Central

Park incident. One of the clever marketing ploys that Hirsh had instituted at Murjani was for the company to sponsor free rock concerts in New York's Central Park. Not only was it excellent national publicity; it created goodwill and a philanthropic reputation for the firm. Shortly before Hirsh moved to Puritan, he had been negotiating with Elton John's management for him to do a free concert in the park as part of the Murjani series. The contracts were never signed, however, and a few weeks later, Hirsh got a phone call from Calvin saying that Elton John was a friend of his and that Elton was prepared to switch the sponsorship of the concert to Calvin Klein jeans. Hirsh was delighted at the change, and the concert that September drew nearly 500,000 people, who cheered uproariously as Calvin appeared onstage, who in turn asked Hirsh to come out and take a bow. Later, after the concert, the press reports credited Hirsh for bagging Elton John, since he started the idea at Murjani. This irked Calvin, who felt it was *his* friendship with Elton that initiated the concert. Calvin didn't like the way Hirsh was bragging, and he was just waiting for the right moment to put him in his place.

That moment came on September 19, when Hirsh was called by gossip columnist Claudia Cohen of the *New York Daily News*. The Brooke Shields commercials had been running for a month by then and were already one of the most talked about ads ever to run on television. Cohen had been tipped off that WCBS and WNBC in New York had rejected some of the ads when they first reviewed them during the summer and that they were showing some of them only in restricted, "adult" viewing hours. Hirsh told the columnist that he thought the commercials were "silly" and that although they had signed Brooke Shields to do another set of six spots, he was going to change the format. The following morning, Hirsh was at the Gray Advertising agency on business when Carl Rosen tracked him down by phone. "Have you seen the *Daily News*?" Rosen demanded. When Hirsh said he had not but there was no reason to be so upset, Rosen shouted, "Barry and Calvin are furious with you! Get over to their showroom *now!*"

"I don't work for Calvin Klein or Barry Schwartz," Hirsh barked back. "I'm the president of this company, and when I'm finished with my meeting, I'll come over." Hirsh got to Calvin's showroom an hour later and found what he called an "inquisition" waiting for him. Barry and Calvin were sitting on one side of the white table Calvin used as a desk, Carl Rosen was in a third chair near them, and an empty chair situated by itself stood waiting for Hirsh.

"Did you see this article?" Barry demanded, brandishing the *Daily News* in the air.

"I didn't see it, but I heard about it, and I was misquoted," Hirsh said, his temper rising.

"I can't work with you anymore!" Calvin shouted.

"What the fuck am I going to do now?" Rosen demanded of Hirsh.

"I have a contract," Hirsh said.

"Fuck your contract!" Barry shouted, and threw the newspaper he was holding in Warren Hirsh's face.

Hirsh was a tough Brooklyn boy himself, and he jumped out of his chair and lunged at Barry Schwartz, who came toward Hirsh, his hands poised as if to strangle the executive. Carl Rosen jumped up and threw himself between the two, holding Hirsh back, crying, "Calm down! Calm down!" to both of them. In another minute Rosen had escorted Hirsh out into the hallway and toward the elevators. "What am I going to *do*?" Rosen called after Hirsh.

Hirsh turned. "I have a perfect suggestion," he said. "You want me to leave? Write me out a check for $7.3 million for my contract and I'll leave today."

Warren Hirsh had his check within seventy-two hours. Only it wasn't $7.3 million, but a $1 million settlement, plus the Rolls-Royce. Still, not bad pay for nine weeks' work. There was, of course, a catch: Hirsh had to sign an agreement saying he would not go into a competitive business for a minimum number of years.

One week later, Hirsh ran into Calvin for the last time in the elevator at the Sovereign. Both men nodded but didn't speak all the way down to the lobby. Since Hirsh's settlement with Puritan prohibited him from going into the jeans business for a proscribed period of time, he dabbled in other fields, including office-supply sales and a fashion marketing–consulting company with whom he signed a license to make Michael Jackson clothing. Hirsh is retired and living in Boca Raton, Florida.

7

The Brooke Shields jeans campaign exploded into the public's consciousness with the force of a tsunami. The ads were a sensation, so popular with the public that viewers would watch for them and collect them until they had seen all the different ones. Suddenly, Calvin's name was lifted yet again in media prominence—to the pantheon of one-named superstars like Cher or Liz.

It didn't seem possible to be more in the public consciousness until during the second "cycle" of the commercials, in the early fall, about three hundred righteous viewers began to complain about the content of the ads to local TV stations across the country. The single phrase that caused the most protest was "Do you know what comes between me and my Calvins? Nothing." As the weeks went by, the idea that Brooke Shields wasn't wearing underwear on TV as the camera traced her inseam began to incense increasing numbers of conservative viewers, and by mid-November of 1980, station KNXT, a CBS affiliate in Los Angeles, put four of the spots "on hold," meaning that after they were through being aired in this cycle, they wouldn't show them again. Soon after, KGO-TV, an NBC affiliate in San Francisco followed suit, as did WFLD in Chicago, while several Boston stations moved the commercials to late-night slots. Finally, even officials in New York—Sodom and Gomorrah—succumbed. After receiving 150 phone calls and letters, WNBC, the network's flagship station, banned both the "Feminist" and "Teenager" spots. The complaints, said a spokesman, "were thoughtful, not from cranks."

"ABC Drops Commercials," cried the front page of the *New York Daily News,* accompanied by a full-page photo of Brooke Shields. Calvin couldn't believe it. The Dow had broken 1000 that day for the first time, but his jeans commercials were bigger news. Now all hell broke loose. *Time, Newsweek,* and *People* all did stories. Newspaper columnists, sociologists, and eventually militant feminist groups like Women Against Pornography (WAP) began to chime in. The commercials were meticulously dissected and analyzed. The "Teenager" ad, about the seven jeans in the closet that could ruin Brooke's reputation, was a poorly hidden endorsement of sexual promiscuity, wrote one sociologist, and "in the closet" was a place where "secret sexual behavior took place." "The ads violate the taboo against children as sexual beings," wrote educator Mona Simpson in a paper presented at the International Society for General Semantics. But perhaps the biggest outcry came from the fashion industry itself. "I think it's disgusting," said Dick Gilbert, president of Zena Jeans. "It's getting to be who has the most lascivious commercial." Paul Guez, the president of Sasson Jeans, added, "You have to be desperate to do this—put sex into jeans commercials."

"People said we were taking advantage of a fifteen-year-old, which was not the truth," said Calvin. But when asked if the advertisements were not meant to be sexually provocative, he said, "Well, I like sex. What's bad about sex?"

But Gloria Steinem and WAP knew what was bad about sex. Gloria Steinem's view was that the advertisements were abusive to women and that they helped numb men into believing that women were solely sexual chattel, objects of submission and violence. WAP condemned the ads for "sexualizing a very young model as a matured, experienced seductress," contending that the "ad campaign . . . consists of an aboveground representation of child pornography."

"Fuck off!" was Calvin's response to Steinem and her ilk. "I really feel that *I've* been abused. . . . Oh! The letters, the threats, the accusations! It's like they have nothing else to do in their lives but complain about some goddamn commercials that really aren't all that important."

As for Calvin's competitors, they were furious. "I think he's creating [all the fuss]," said Zena Jeans' Dick Gilbert. "I think he's a genius."

"Maybe Calvin did start the whole thing," said a vice president at J. Walter Thompson.

His men's jeans commercials were no less provocative. One spot, filmed on a rooftop in SoHo, showed a shirtless model wearing tight Calvin jeans, the top buttons open to expose a trail of pubic hair as he leaned backward and touched his body onanistically. Calvin tried to get it approved by the network censors just before the Brooke Shields commercials started getting banned. At first, all three networks turned it down—until Calvin convinced them to run it. "Five days later the world is down on me for Brooke," said Calvin. "I thought, Well, I'd have to be on a death trip if I now run this. It never ran. I don't really love the idea that a woman at CBS says what the country can see." The commercial that finally did run, called the "Living Sculpture," caused enough of a commotion without excess skin when the male model told America, "A body is only a good-looking place to keep your brain warm."

But Calvin was fiercely proud of his advertising. "What I'm going to say may seem pretentious," said Calvin, "but twenty or thirty years from now, I believe someone may look at all the commercials I've done and view them as a vignette of the times, a reflection of what people were thinking, the moods of today."

Others weren't so certain Calvin reflected the mainstream. Calvin's ads "had strong homosexual ramifications," said George Lois, one of Madison Avenue's top advertising executives, "but a lot of people blinked at the homosexual stuff."

With the boost in recognition from the commercial, sales of Calvin Klein jeans now hit an unprecedented 2 million pairs a month. In 1978, Calvin Klein Inc. had received $1.2 million in royalties from Carl Rosen; in 1979 income had jumped to $3.8 million; by 1980 royalties would triple to $12.5 million.

The next set of Avedon/Arbus jeans commercials took a 180-degree turn. These were homey as apple pie, and what got people talking about them was that they were so puzzling. These hyper-realistic vignettes featured five young women whose names—Andie, Martha, Shari, Lauren, and Antonio—appeared momentarily in a corner of the screen to identify them. One of the women was Shari Belafonte, the daughter of the famous singer and producer. The women spouted monologues about their babies, families, horses— all totally irrelevant to the jeans. Avedon's goal, explained one of his aides, was to persuade viewers that Calvins were "so much a part" of the women's lives that they felt it was superfluous to talk about them. Some advertising experts railed that this was a ridiculous affectation. But the campaign became such a talking point around the country that *Saturday Night Live* spoofed it. "You can't buy that kind of publicity," said Avedon.

But perhaps the ultimate irony of the jeans advertising success was that they were probably the highlight of Brooke Shield's career.

So indelible was her association with jeans that a few years later she came out with her *own* line of jeans called "Brookes," manufactured by Batem Enterprises, owned by two ex-Puritan executives. When asked if anything still didn't come between her and her Calvins, Brooke sniped, "I have Brookes now. Why should I wear anything else?"

8

In the first two years that Studio 54 was open, Steve Rubell became one of the most powerful people in New York, with status and networking influence in the worlds of politics, entertainment, and the media. Most of all, he had the key to everyman's sybaritic dream: a good night out on the town.

But the more powerful Rubell became, the more he was hated. He was loud, drunk, and stoned most of the time. His discriminatory door policy was criticized as racist and meanspirited, and very quickly a Studio 54 backlash began to swell. First, the club was denied a permanent liquor license after it had already been open six months. There were also several lawsuits filed against the club over its discriminatory policies as well as the behavior of its bouncers, one of whom had kicked a customer in the groin so hard he crushed his testicles. In 1978, *New York* magazine ran a scathing article about the club entitled "Sour Notes at the Hottest Disco," which disclosed that Ian Shrager's father, known as "Max the Jew," was a loanshark and known associate of mobster Meyer Lansky (which only served to make Schrager and his partner seem even *more* glamorous). Also, Rubell got himself into hot water when he bragged to reporters and TV cameras, "What the IRS doesn't know wont hurt them," and told *New York* magazine, "It's a cash business, and you don't have to worry about the IRS." Indeed, Rubell and Schrager had such blithe disregard for the IRS, it was later revealed that in 1977 Studio 54 filed a tax return claiming only $47,000 profit on $1 million in revenues and paid only $8,000 in taxes.

On December 14, 1978, Studio 54 was raided by dozens of agents from the Organized Crime Strike Force (OCSF), a particularly hard-nosed division of the government well known for putting big-time drug dealers and tax evaders into prison for long sentences. Armed with subpoenas and search warrants, scores of OCSF agents descended on the club and seized everything in sight, including Rubell and Schrager. The OCSF was accusing Rubell and Schrager of skimming $2.5 million from their grosses by keeping two sets of books. The feds contended that early in the evening the partners were removing the cash-register tapes from each bar, emptying the cash drawers, and starting over again, this time off the books.

Searching the massive club from balcony to basement, the OCSF agents made several surprising discoveries, including two black garbage bags stuffed with money and hidden away in the rafters of the basement ceiling. Another surprise was locked away in the office safe: keys to a safety deposit box at Citibank which turned out to hold $900,000 in cash. However, the most disturbing discovery to Rubell's many pals was the seizure of a list of some of the most famous names in entertainment and politics, which appeared to be a record of complimentary drugs handed out to customers and the cost to the club. The price increment on this list was usually eighty-five-dollars—which coincided with the price of a gram of cocaine—and some names appeared more than twenty times. It appeared that Rubell was keeping tabs on the cost of getting his customers high, and now the federal authorities had a list of all the famous drug users who came to the club. "Those scumbags!" said one designer when he heard his name was on the list.

But not Calvin. Calvin stood steadfastly by Rubell as a friend. After all, Calvin wasn't a tax evader, but he had been at least as bad as his friend in other aspects of his life. Calvin gave Rubell moral support as the disco owner mounted a $1 million defense, employing a team of fifteen lawyers, headed by the notorious Roy Cohn. Rubell's side made a vicious counterattack on the government when it was claimed that Jimmy Carter's White House chief of staff, Hamilton Jordan, used cocaine at Studio 54, a charge which Jordan vehemently denied. But rattle the administration though they might, Rubell and Schrager and the stealthy Roy Cohn were unable to cut a deal with the feds—that is, until, to avoid spending the better part of his life behind bars, Rubell turned stool pigeon and gave information to the Feds that led to the conviction of four other businessmen in the disco business. Rubell and Schrager pleaded guilty to tax evasion and were sentenced to two and half years in prison. Rubell couldn't believe it when he heard the sentence. "I'm going to jail," he mumbled. "Greed and stupidity."

On the first of the year in January 1980, Steve Rubell and Ian Schrager went off to a minimum-security prison in Alabama to pay their debt to society. Shortly after arriving, the prison guards handed Rubell a pair of scissors and ordered him to trim the grass along the walkways. Later in his incarceration he would be promoted to the superintendent's driver; Ian, to busboy in the dining room. When Rubell was permitted, he made calls from a pay phone in the hall to his friends, among them Calvin Klein, who promised they would all be waiting for him to return.

CHAPTER FOURTEEN

Calvin Klein, the emperor of blue jeans. The king
of menswear. The prince of women's fashion. *The
president of the United States?*
                            —*Atlanta Journal-Constitution*

On January 18, 1982, Calvin Klein, media superstar, appeared
on the cover of *People* magazine, dressed in a white T-shirt and
painter's pants, with Brooke Shields literally astride his shoulders,
wearing his jeans. "Brooke and Calvin," said the cover, "Her bot-
toms-up commercials have made Klein the best-known name in
U.S. fashion."

It didn't make him any easier to deal with around the office. The
atmosphere at 205 West Thirty-ninth Street continued to be dark
and stormy. The person who got the brunt of Calvin's ire was Carl
Rosen. Carl Rosen might once have heatedly thrown a chair across
the conference room to make an indelible point, but for the most
part, he was a gentleman who eschewed scenes and prided himself
on being genteel. In any event, Rosen didn't need to cause a scene
to make an impression. One dark look from his craggy visage was
enough to wither the most hulking salesman. Calvin and Barry, on
the other hand, continued to behave like street fighters, shouting at
and insulting everyone in their path. Minnetonka's Robert Taylor,
who was no stranger to Barry's tirades, remembered being in Carl
Rosen's office when Barry called on the phone. "You'll have to excuse me," Rosen said with a smile, "while I take some abuse from
Barry," and then held the receiver away from his ear while Barry
cursed at him so loudly it could be heard throughout the room.

When Barry was spent, Rosen hung the phone up and said, "He just loves doing that. He just loves putting people down. I don't give a shit. I'm selling three hundred million dollars' worth of jeans. I can put up with some abuse."

Indeed, the sale of Calvin's jeans was responsible for nearly 95 percent of Puritan's quarter-of-a-billion-dollar volume, and neither side particularly liked the situation very much. Rosen hated being so totally dependent on Calvin and Barry, and he seethed when they didn't treat him with the respect he was accustomed to receiving. On the other hand, Calvin and Barry resented Rosen grossing $250 million on *their* product while they got a mere $15 million cut. "The Rosens actually believed the tremendous success . . . was something they had created," Calvin fumed: *"Bullshit."* Still, a dollar was a dollar as far as Rosen was concerned, and he wanted to expand the product range he was making under Calvin's label. But Barry and Calvin didn't like being associated with the Puritan image and refused to allow Rosen to produce two new, highly touted lines for them, an "activewear" collection, and a groundbreaking line—called "Classifications"—of sportswear, shirts, skirts, and pants that for the first time would introduce lower-priced, more mass directed Calvin Klein clothes for women. When Rosen asked why they wouldn't let him manufacture the Classifications line, which had projected sales of $50 million in 1984, Barry snapped, "Because we can do a better job."

Barry and Calvin resented, too, the way Carl Rosen spent all those big bucks they were pulling in for him. It was getting a little obnoxious—two of Rosen's sons and a daughter on the payroll, the hundred-dollar tips to elevator operators, a Rolls-Royce as a gift to a business associate, and the entourage of sycophants who clustered around him adoringly wherever he went. Rosen's racetrack winnings—from his own horses and from betting on others—ran to $11 million one year. He gambled so heavily at the track that one of his black employees, nicknamed "Peaches," would follow him around carrying the cash in a suitcase. Even Donald Trump, real estate tycoon and high roller himself, sighed and said, "That guy Rosen *really* has money."

By 1982, there was little about Puritan that made Calvin and Barry happy. They found Carl Rosen "arrogant." Calvin said, "We disagreed about everything; product, advertising, promotion, and distribution." Talk in the industry about Barry and Calvin's discontent with Puritan was so rampant that at one point Puritan's stock rose to a year's high of 26 on the rumor that Barry and Calvin would try to take over the company. But Rosen was too strong to take on. The last thing they needed was a bloody and protracted financial war, and all they could do was bide their time and wait.

Then, one morning in May 1982, Carl Rosen woke up with a sharp pain in his right side, a pain so penetrating that he knew it was no simple indigestion. Rosen began to consult a series of specialists. One by one, they began to hand down the same chilling verdict: Carl Rosen had bladder cancer, and this time the odds were against him. Even with aggressive therapy the doctors gave him only a year to live, if he was lucky.

But Carl Rosen was determined to beat the odds, just as he did at the track. He found the top surgeon in the field and underwent surgery, but when they opened him up, they discovered that the cancer had already spread. Stoically, he went for chemotherapy and radiation treatments at New York's Memorial Sloan-Kettering, one of the leading cancer hospitals in the world, where he endowed a chair in radiation therapy. He checked into the Mayo Clinic in Minnesota, where he endowed a urology professorship, but there was nothing they could do, either. He became a patient at Massachusetts General in Boston, where Harvard professors looked in on him, all to no avail.

After a few months of frantic searching, Rosen returned to New York. Quietly, pragmatically, he began to refer to his cancer as "my death sentence." The only noticeable change in Carl, said those who worked for him, was that he began to spend his vast fortune with even more alacrity than usual. He already owned a jet plane, but he bought a smaller, faster one, and when a friend asked him why, Carl smiled sadly and said, "I'm racing death."

Carl Rosen may have looked his own mortality in the face with more bravery than most men, but the one facet of dying that he could not make peace with was having to let go of his beloved Puritan Fashions. Though the company was traded on the New York Stock Exchange, management control had been in family hands for seventy years, nearly forty of them under Carl, and the thought of the family firm falling into the hands of strangers—in particular Calvin and Barry—ate away at Rosen as much as the cancer. The problem was that he had run the company as a sovereign state for so long, there was no easy heir apparent—although three of his four children worked at Puritan. His son Andrew, who was then titular president of the Calvin Klein men's jeans division, was only twenty-six years old, too raw to take over the company. Rosen had always hoped that someday Andrew would grow into the job, when he was more experienced and seasoned. Only suddenly there was no time, and grasping at straws, Rosen let it be known that Andrew would be his successor.

Calvin and Barry exploded. "If Carl thought I would stand for his putting a young kid in to run the company," said Calvin, "then he was a fool . . . and quite frankly, I begged [him], when he became ill, to consider my position."

"Calvin, you're absolutely right!" Rosen told him.

"Then he did nothing!" Calvin said furiously. "I suggested that Carl bring someone in who could teach Andrew and groom him for the position, but he didn't go for that. Up until the last few years, all the kid did was play golf every day. He didn't even complete his degree at the University of Miami."

Indeed, while Andrew was responsible in name for the day-to-day running of the men's jeans division, he made no secret of the fact that if he had his druthers, he would be out playing golf. A strapping, pleasant fellow with dark eyes and his father's wavy hair, Andrew played golf "pretty much every day," he said, and spent a good part of his childhood on the links at the Doral Country Club in Florida, perfecting his game and joyriding in the electric golf carts. After attending a series of elite prep schools and colleges, he joined the company in 1977 at his father's behest. After only eighteen months, he had been named president of the men's jean division. Slowly, young Rosen gained respect within the company, even from his father. In many ways, the two men were strangers. "I never knew him until about four years ago," Rosen said of his son. "I was never there when any of the children were born. I was always working."

In a gesture more practical than symbolic, the first step Rosen took in the speedy education of his son was to move Andrew's desk right into his office with him. For as long as Carl could hold out, Andrew would learn his father's job firsthand. Day by day he turned over the reins to his son, watching and listening as Andrew began to test his wings at administrating the multi-million-dollar concern. "He wanted to see how I handled myself before he did anything official or final," said Andrew. Within six months, Rosen was satisfied enough to name his son president of all Calvin Klein operations.

On another front, Rosen began to warm the Puritan board of directors to the idea of Andrew's succession. Since the company was publicly held, the board members were technically responsible to the shareholders, and Rosen had to square Andrew's succession with them. However, the ten members of the board were mostly men that Carl Rosen either appointed or nominated and over whose loyalty and patronage he held sway, including his trusted chief financial officer, Sam Rubinstein; his nephew, David Rosen, who ran Puritan's Winston Mills; Robert DiPaola, a lawyer whose firm billed nearly $800,000 from Puritan over the previous four years; Rosen's eighty-year-old longtime tax consultant, Bernard Pomerantz, who was paid nearly $200,000 for his services the year before; and Paul Gregory, an insurance broker to whose firm Puritan paid nearly $3 million in commissions over the previous few years. It was a board, critics charged, that was wholly dependent on Carl Rosen's wishes. Still, Carl politicked to get Andrew accepted. "I've had some physical problems, although hopefully they don't show," Rosen—looking thin and drained eight months after being diagnosed—said at a meeting of Wall Street stock analysts. "Latest scuttlebutt is I've got it beat, but I've arranged for the company to run without me. Sam [Rubinstein,] and Andrew work very well together. I would hope that relationship would continue."

Less than a month later, on March 18, 1983, Andrew was named president and chief operating officer of Puritan Fashions at a salary of $299,000 a year. Carl Rosen retained the title of chairman and chief executive. "He's earned the promotion," Rosen grumbled to critics, giving Andrew credit for business gains he had nothing to do with. "Since he came on board, he has taken the Calvin Klein's

men's division, then the smallest and fourth most profitable in the
company, and turned it into the largest and most profitable division."

Nobody was buying it, but Carl Rosen was a desperate man, and
he desperately wanted Andrew to succeed.

2

By the spring of 1983 it was clear that Barry and Calvin had very
little choice but to buy Puritan when Carl died, and a company
called Calvin Klein Acquisitions was formed specifically for the
purpose of a merger with Puritan when the time was right. They
also began discussions with their primary bank, Manufacturers
Hanover Trust, about borrowing the $60–$100 million that would
be needed to buy Puritan as well as pay off some long-term debt.

It was in the midst of these secretive and delicate negotiations
with the bank that one day Calvin came into the office ashen white.
"There is a rumor going on that I have AIDS," he said to Zack Carr.
His eyes were filled with emotion, more anger than hurt.

Calvin *hated* the word AIDS, hated the sound of it. It was the
most frightening thing he ever heard about—a disease that killed
gay men in a horrific, slow illness, eating them away with purple
skin lesions that covered their faces and bodies like the mark of
Cain or sucked the breath out of them with incurable pneumonia.
This whole AIDS thing was like a bolt out of the blue for Calvin.
Two years before there wasn't even anything called AIDS that anybody knew about. Scientists had only just discovered the retrovirus
that caused it, and there wasn't even a reliable test for it being
produced. Worse, people thought it was a dirty, sleazy disease that
only gays and hookers got by being promicuous, God's retribution
for being homosexual.

What a bitter irony for him. He had indulged himself in the gay
world, and there was a good possiblity it would kill him.

Calvin was scared silly. Although there were only three thousand diagnosed cases in the United States by 1983, in the fashion
industry people were dropping like flies. If the deaths kept up like
this—the models, the makeup artists, the photographers, and

designers—the industry would be decimated by the disease. Two of Calvin's houseboys were diagnosed, and although he felt sorry for them, he couldn't possibly continue to have them around as constant reminders of the plague. Calvin was already a confirmed hypochondriac, but now he lived in constant fear, every new blotch on his skin possibly Kaposi's sarcoma, every sneeze the onset of pneumocystis carinii pneumonia.

Zack Carr, at the advent of the rumors, remembered: "All I could think of was 'Well I hope its not true . . . I don't want it to be true. . . . ' " According to Carr, "The AIDS rumor was a very startling, very terrifying thing for Calvin to have to face. He didn't expect it, and it came at a time when . . . they were to borrow *sixty million dollars*. I could only tell one thing. Calvin needed to be comforted, and I wanted to comfort him. But the only way you could really comfort Calvin in a situation like this was for the rumor to stop, because this rumor was an extraordinarily huge, huge, huge, huge, *huge* rumor."

Thus began a trial by fire, a public mortification as the judgment of the world seemed to come down on him. "The bottom fell out of his world," said one close friend. "Calvin Klein has AIDS" became one of the most widespread rumors since the "Paul is dead" rumor that had plagued the Beatles. The most frequently repeated version of the story was that Calvin was undergoing treatment in either a Swiss or Parisian sanitarium or at a teaching college in South Carolina, where his blood was being "cleansed" of the HIV-III virus. Though there was no medical basis for such therapy, one doctor who vacationed on Fire Island insisted he saw the blood-changing machinery brought out to Calvin's beach house on a boat and that a nurse administered daily sessions. The list of hospitals in which it was reported that he was a patient was prodigious, including Memorial Sloan-Kettering, Beth Israel, and St. Vincent's in New York; the Mayo Clinic in Minnesota, and Massachusetts General in Boston—where the story went that he was in a room across the hall from Ronald Reagan Jr.

The rumor had its roots, in part, in Carl Rosen's search for a cure for his urinary cancer. "What really happened," explained Calvin, "was that . . . Carl Rosen was dying of cancer. It wasn't me. But every time he checked into the Mayo Clinic or Sloan-Kettering or the Massachusetts General Hospital, he would mention Calvin Klein so he'd get better treatment." Indeed, wherever Rosen went for treatment, his claim to fame was "I'm Calvin Klein jeans."

The rumor was also compounded because in 1981 Calvin was hospitalized for a disease deadly enough in its own right: viral meningitis—"a very dangerous illness," said Calvin. "Having meningitis was one of the worst experiences of my life. I had five spinal taps, which are both dangerous and extraordinarily painful. I had horrendous headaches for two weeks, and no matter what drugs I was given for the pain, nothing helped." Calvin spent four weeks in Lenox Hill Hospital recovering from this inflammation of the mensa membrane that covers the brain. "When I was in [the] hospital . . . people thought I was dying of *cancer,*" Calvin said; however, many people were convinced this was his first AIDS hospitalization.

Whatever the spark for the story, it spread like wildfire, and eventually journalists began to investigate it. One day author and columnist James Brady walked into the newsroom at WCBS-TV in New York and was told "by one of the producers that Klein was in Mass. General," explained Brady. "They even had a room number. . . . I called the hospital. Calvin wasn't there. That following Sunday night, I ran into Calvin at the Tony Awards. He was with Bianca and David Geffen. . . . Calvin didn't look as if he were dying."

Minnetonka's Robert Taylor remembered, "After . . . no more than a year in business with Calvin, we were getting phone calls [about the rumor]. [Someone from] Sloan-Kettering called and said, 'Just wanted you to know that Calvin's in here going through blood transfusions for AIDS . . . and that we just processed his blood. We think you should know about this.' Then we got a call from Boston," said Taylor. "Same situation, somebody working in the laboratory there says they have processed his blood and that we should know that he's got AIDS."

It was almost as if people *wanted* the rumor to be true, and there was a good reason why people were so willing to believe it. It was no small secret around town that Calvin had been wild. He even bragged about it that year to *Playboy* magazine. "I've fooled around a lot," he boasted in the *Playboy* interview. "I stopped at nothing. I

would do *anything*. I stayed up all night, carried on, lived out fantasies, *anything*. I did an awful lot. I'm not going to tell you everything, but I'll say that anything I've wanted to do, I've done. . . . I've
been real fortunate, because anyone I've wanted to be with, I've
had. . . . I think fantasies are for the birds. Anything I wanted to do,
I did. If there's something I want, nothing stops me. . . . Quite
frankly, my best sex had been with people who didn't know who I
was."

Fueling the rumors of Calvin's wild personal life was that Steve
Rubell was now back on the scene. He and Ian Schrager had been
released from prison in 1981 after a thirteen-month stay, and they
had made a remarkable comeback. When they were first released,
their million-dollar legal fees, plus the million dollars in fines due
the IRS, had left them nearly broke, and many of Rubell's old
friends had turned their backs on him. But Calvin handed Rubell a
blank check and told him to write in whatever figure he needed to
get started again. In the interim, New York businessman Mark
Fleischman had made a deal to purchase the defunct Studio 54
and reopen it under Steve and Ian's auspices. However, because
the partners were convicted tax evaders, the State Liquor Authority
(SLA) would not allow them to hold a liquor license, and a deal was
cut with the IRS and SLA that Rubell and Schrager would be paid
"consultants" to Mark Fleischman and almost all their earnings
would go to paying off their tax debt and penalties to the IRS.

Calvin offered to give a big party at his apartment for Rubell and
Schrager on the night of Studio 54's reopening, or as Rubell
grandly referred to it, the "relighting." New York by now was desperate for the return of glamour, and the party at Calvin's house
sparked the attendance of an array of stars, including Jack Nichol-
son and Boris Godunov. Andy Warhol gushed that "everybody was
either famous or beautiful—Brooke Shields and seventy-five other
models." After the party, all were off to Studio 54. The place was a
madhouse, with several thousand people mobbing both the front of
the club and the rear "celebrity entrance" on West Fifty-third
Street. Calvin alighted from a limousine with Brooke Shields on his
arm, dressed in a white shirt opened to his solar plexus to show off
his muscled torso. Intimidated by the size of the crowd, his eyes
narrowed in terror as the excitement of his and Brooke Shields's

presence caused the mob to close in on them. The photographers' strobe lights blinded them, and Shields, ever the trooper, punched Calvin in the ribs and said, "Come on . . . *smi-i-i-i-le.*

But Studio 54 would need more than Calvin and Brooke's attendance to regain its former appeal. Studio 54 was *déjà vu.* The door policy under the new reign was less discriminatory, the crowd less sparkling. When word spread that Rubell and Schrager were only consultants, the club's star appeal with fickle New York began to tarnish. The party was clearly over, and when Steve and Ian's "consultant" contracts with the new club expired around Halloween of 1981, they went off to stake out a new territory: hotels.

The two partners had considered going into many different businesses before they settled on the hotel industry. The hotel business in New York was not only thriving, but it was also "of the moment," as they explained. With backing from real estate investor Phil Pilevsky and National Westminster Bank, Schrager and Rubell bought a run-down Madison Avenue hotel called the Executive for just over $6 million. Like men possessed, the two worked 20 hour days at the hotel, learning the trade from an executive they had hired away from the Carlyle, networking with other employees in the hotel business, studying their new trade with fanatic devotion. Under Schrager's direction the Executive was stripped and cleaned and re-decorated from top floor to bottom by *moderne* French interior designer Andre Putnam. Renamed the Morgan, the renovated hotel opened on October 1, 1983, and from the start the old magic was back. The Morgan became the chicest, most desirable hotel in the city. Within two years it had a 96 percent occupancy rate, one of the highest in New York, and the property was valued at $14 million. Almost simultaneously, with the backing of former Madison Square Garden president Alan Cohen, Schrager and Rubell leased a fifty-seven-year-old, decrepit theater on East 14th Street called the Palladium, and with $10 million in capital turned it into a whimsical vision of the Japanese architect Arata Isozaki's computer-age disco.

But with Rubell's newfound success and notoriety, as well as the end of his probationary drug testing, he quickly regressed to his old ways of coke and Quaaludes, porno stars and hustlers. He also resumed his position as Calvin's primary carousing and drug partner. The pair spent endless nights on the prowl together, traipsing from party to restaurant to disco. Nothing seemed too wild for their tastes. One winter morning at 4:00 A.M. they were in the back of Calvin's chauffeured Mercedes when they spied a naked black man, wearing only his socks, standing on the corner in front of Radio City Music Hall trying to hail a cab. "Stop! Stop!" Rubell and Calvin yelled to the driver. "Stop and pick him up! That guy is really hung!" It took the unclouded mind of the driver to convince his passengers that it was not a good idea and that they should inform the police instead.

It was also at this time that Calvin became a regular customer of Jack Bianchi, one of New York's premier male madams. Bianchi was a short, muscular man with a lisp and an obvious blond wig that often sat askew on his head. He was for many years a delivery boy for Gristede's supermarket, until one of his customers, a rich old dowager who lived on Fifth Avenue, bequeathed him $50,000 in her will for his faithful grocery deliveries. Bianchi used the money to help set up his informal business of "giving people pleasure," as he put it. Over the course of several years, Calvin and his friends became some of Bianchi's best customers. "He was a darling," Bianchi remembered of Calvin, reporting that Calvin called him almost every week. "He really was the sweetest [customer] of them all. Calvin was so easy . . . He was very interchangeable. I'm not saying he went with short Puerto Rican dwarfs or anything. I remember once in the four years or so [he was a customer] he may have specified . . . something [specific], but [only] that one time out of fifty or sixty." The boys themselves agreed with Bianchi's assessment of Calvin as a complete gentleman. Universally, the call boys or porno stars who spent time with Calvin who were interviewed for this book draw the portrait of a shy, romantic man who needed great quantities of drugs and alcohol to initiate physical contact.

David Burns, a dark and handsome young call boy who spent one New Year's Eve for free with Calvin, believed that Calvin became dependent on the services of a madam because "he was afraid of failure, of public failure, of being made to look foolish. The idea that he might approach someone and be rejected was completely terrifying to him. That's why he used intermediaries like Jack Bianchi."

It was not unusual for Calvin to import fresh talent from out of

town. Sometimes Bianchi sent him eight-by-ten glossies of prospects, including one of a nude model hoisting himself out of a
swimming pool with a handwritten note across the bottom that
said, "I would love to model for you." Calvin would send his driver
out to Kennedy Airport to pick up the traveling "models." One of
them arrived wearing an army uniform and explained to the driver
that before he joined the service he had been a famous porn star.
"When I'm with Calvin," bragged the young recruit, "I get two
thousand dollars a night and all the coke I can get high with."

Calvin's driver dropped the soldier at Calvin's apartment and was
waiting downstairs when Steve Rubell arrived in his own chauffeur-driven Mercedes and went upstairs. The two drivers began to
gossip, and Rubell's chauffeur remarked, "Whoever this kid is,
Steve Rubell just dropped a dinner date with Bianca Jagger to rush
over here, so it must be somebody *hot*." The following night, Calvin's driver was surprised to see that his weekend date had not
changed into civilian clothes. "Calvin made the kid wear the army
uniform to Studio 54," said the driver, "to parade him around, to let
everybody know he had this guy just out of basic training."

Indeed, discretion had gone with the wind. Calvin was flaunting
his sexuality much more, particularly on Fire Island, where he had
a greater sense of security. Casual visitors to the community were
astonished to see him at Tea Dance surrounded by his favorite
models of the moment, and he even designed himself a flesh-col-
ored charmeuse swimsuit that turned translucent when it got wet.
In his *Diaries*, Andy Warhol describes finding Calvin's house with
"8,000 boys around it." His houseguests that weekend were David
Geffen, Steve Rubell, and Chester Weinberg. On Saturday night,
returning early from a party, Warhol wrote ". . . we walked in on
Calvin and Steve who were with those two porno stars Knoll and
Ford and so we were embarrassed and left and went back to the
party down the street. . . . Then we had barbecued steak and all the
talking was gay gay gay. If I'd had a tape recorder you wouldn't
believe it."

Warhol was so convinced that Calvin's decadent lifestyle had
given him AIDS that he was even afraid to be kissed by Calvin at a
party. "Calvin . . . kissed me so hard," wrote Warhol, "and his beard
was stubbly and I was so afraid that it was piercing into my pimple

and being like a needle and giving me AIDS. So if I'm gone in three years . . ."

3

Warhol wasn't the only one afraid of contact with Calvin. The AIDS rumor really hit home when one of his longtime friends in the press recoiled from touching him. "I just got the impact of the rumor," Calvin told Zack Carr. "I reached out to shake her hand or to kiss her and she backed off."

Remembered Zack Carr, "That's when I really knew that Calvin was in pain."

There was more pain to follow. Calvin's business had grown astronomically over the years, and it had taken a lot of borrowed money to do it. The company was heavily in debt to banks, in particular Manufacturers Hanover Trust, and the AIDS rumor had the same effect as taking a sledgehammer to his credit rating. Before long, every licensee, tradesman, and banker wanted to know "the truth" about Calvin. When stock in Puritan began to drop several points, allegedly because of the rumor, Barry's phone rang off the hook with calls from creditors and factors. Calvin was "fine," Barry would say, inviting the financiers "to come up and see for [themselves]." Zack Carr said, "Barry would bring down a lot of bank officials through the company. We were all introduced. They would come down periodically to see what was going on."

The first time that the issue was broached in print was by syndicated gossip columnist Liz Smith on March 25, 1983. She wrote that after two years of "people . . . calling, writing, tipping and telling me that Calvin is dying . . . two tipsters of usually high credibility told me in forty-eight hours that Calvin was in different hospitals at death's door. . . . The rumor bullies who've been kicking sand in Calvin Klein's handsome face for over a year reached their depth this week, to the point that Seventh Avenue's fashion king . . . has had it with stories he is ill, dying, 'with only three days to live,' 'down to forty pounds . . . ' " Smith went on to say, "Listen, I have just seen Calvin. He looks fabulous and healthy. . . . Whoever it is that wants him dead has caused a lot of concern and misery, but fortunately there's not a word of truth to it."

But Smith's denial did nothing to kill the rumors, and finally, at the end of May 1983, while Calvin was away on vacation with Chester Weinberg in Marrakech, Taroudant, Agadir, and Casablanca, a particularly virulent version of the story emerged; Calvin was *not* away on vacation; he had been spirited to a clinic in Sweden for emergency medical care. He could not be expected to return alive. This rumor burned up phone lines from coast to coast, until a week after Calvin had left for vacation it was announced on a West Coast radio station that America's great fashion designer, Calvin Klein, had died at age thirty-nine.

When word reached Flo and Leo Klein in their Riverdale apartment, they became hysterical. Flo called the office to discover that Calvin was in North Africa and not available personally to assure them he was all right. Flo would not rest until Barry called her and promised her that it was only a rumor and that Calvin was okay.

In Morocco, Calvin was furious and called columnist Liz Smith to again deny he was sick. On June 2, 1983, Smith wrote, "I have been receiving three and four calls a day advising that the designer is dying. . . . The person who calls is usually a responsible-sounding individual, invariably told the information by a 'reputable doctor.' " Smith wrote that she saw Calvin in the flesh shortly before he left on vacation at a dinner party given by Barbara Walters and that he insisted he was fine. "If Calvin was telling a white lie," wrote Smith, "he was the handsomest, sexiest, most successful looking person about to die that I'd ever seen." As for the stories that his trip to North Africa was a ruse, "If Calvin wasn't in Morocco," she wrote, "that was some heck of a performance and put-up job, making it sound as if camels were sitting on the telephone lines."

A few days later, the *New York Post*'s "Page Six" reported that since the moment Calvin was hospitalized with viral meningitis in 1981, "tipsters have been calling Page Six regularly . . . with variations of the story. Klein has been rumored to be undergoing treatment in a Swedish sanatorium, having blood transfusions in Switzerland, and bedridden in hospitals in New York, Boston and Minnesota." The gossip page added Calvin's denials, but it was like spitting in the wind.

Finally, in early June, after talking about it with Barry, Calvin decided to confront the issue head-on and gave what must be one of the most unusual interviews in the annals of American business to *Women's Wear Daily* and the *Washington Post*. "For a long time I wouldn't even discuss it," a "tanned and vibrant" Calvin told the *Women's Wear Daily* reporter on Wednesday, June 8. "People tend to believe that denials are a way of hiding the truth, but now it's gotten way out of proportion." Aside from a sprained ankle, Calvin contended, "I'm in great health. I don't even take vitamins." He went on to say that "I understand why I may be a target. I'm young, I'm successful, I'm not so bad looking and I enjoy living life in the fast lane. It's good gossip." Calvin also added that he did not intend to alter his lifestyle in any way as a result of the rumors. To make this denial even more unusual, Calvin had his personal physician, Dr. Kevin Cahill, deny the rumors as well. "Calvin Klein has been a patient of mine for years," the doctor said, "and there is no evidence that he is suffering from AIDS or any other serious disease. He's a healthy young man. . . . There is not a whit of evidence to support the rumors."

Not to put too fine a point on it, Calvin also asked his friend and fan, comedienne Joan Rivers, to allay the rumors on one of her guest stints, subbing for Johnny Carson, on the *Tonight Show*. Rivers took a moment to turn serious and tell a national TV audience that Calvin wanted everyone to know "he's not dead or dying. He's perfectly healthy."

Privately, although Calvin became resigned to the rumor, it continued to infuriate him. "The only way I can disprove this lie," he said, "is to go on living."

And live he did. If the rumors that Calvin had full-blown AIDS in 1981 or 1982 were true, that would make him one of the longest-living AIDS patients in the world and a medical anomaly. Or if the story were true that he had undergone a miracle cure or some type of blood-cleansing maintenance at a Swiss clinic, certainly Calvin would have shared this good fortune with his many friends who have wasted away amid terrible suffering from the disease. Yet no amount of logic or hard facts will stop the stories. The rumors about Calvin's HIV status persist to this day. "My real illness," Calvin said, "is that I always need a new challenge."

4

One Friday afternoon in the summer of 1982, en route from Manhattan to Fire Island, Calvin shared a public sea plane with other
passengers, and one young fellow on the flight was particularly star
struck at the sight of the world-famous designer. On his way to a
summer share, Calvin's fellow passenger stared at him the entire
twenty-five-minute ride to the Pines, taking in every detail to repeat
to his friends, but he was *really* blown away when at the end of the
flight Calvin bent over to wade out of the plane and his shirt rode
up to show his underwear band, which was imprinted with the
name "Calvin Klein" all around it. "This guy's so rich he even has
personalized underwear!" the young man told his friends.

The underwear Calvin was wearing that day was a sample, one of
a few dozen pieces Calvin had made up to wear himself so he could
check the fit and durability. Men's underwear was going to be Calvin's next excursion into the wonderland of designer clothing, and
in doing so, he would revolutionize American advertising.

For Calvin, underwear was pure sex. He even began collecting
articles of underwear, particularly T-shirts, preferably off the bodies of muscular young models. One athletically built male model
who visited Calvin's apartment remembered being more than
mildly surprised when Calvin admired his college T-shirt and asked
to trade for it. Calvin led the model to a large closet where very
carefully folded were dozens of worn T-shirts, shelved according to
style and color. The model chose one, pulled his own T-shirt over
his head, and gave it to Calvin, who folded it and put it in the
closet. A few days later, the same model was working on a Calvin
Klein men's clothing layout when Robert Ianucci, one of the stars
of Calvin's jeans campaign, showed up on the set and said, "Hey,
that's *my* T-shirt!" Ianucci said he recognized the shirt because of
the chlorine stains on the bottom and that he had given it to Calvin
Klein in a trade.

Calvin believed that most men were often much sexier with their
underwear on, and through the years he always thought it would be
fun to design them in a way that showed off the male physique to
its best advantage. But Calvin never went into business on an erotic
whim. The boy's and men's underwear market was a $900-million-

dollar frontier waiting to be claimed. Manufactured mostly by American firms, this previously mundane article of clothing was bought by wives and mothers on the basis of good fit and value and how many washings each pair could sustain. Up until now, only underwear made by European manufacturers had any sex appeal or daring.

Jockey International had begun to change all that in 1981 when they introduced an advertisement featuring thirty-seven-year-old Baltimore Oriole pitcher Jim Palmer wearing a form-fitting, albeit heavily airbrushed, pair of Jockey briefs. Palmer was a handsome man who appealed to woman, and by the end of a year Jockey International had sold $100 million worth of briefs, boxer shorts, and bikinis.

Calvin's brand of skivvies, a division of his Bidermann license, was to be produced by the same manufacturer as Jockey, and his underwear was basically of the same classic designs as Jockey's basic briefs and European bikini style, but maybe just a little snugger in the behind for that Calvin Klein touch. The most distinguishing feature about them was the name Calvin Klein encircling the waistband of the briefs. He also produced three kinds of undershirts: crew, tank, and V-neck, in either classic white or olive drab and grays, which gave the underwear an "enlisted man's" touch. The undergarments were considered outrageously expensive for the time; a bag of three Y-front jockey shorts or boxers was $14.50, and bikinis were $5.50 each.

Calvin intended to set himself apart not necessarily through innovation in garment style but with his hefty (for underwear) $500,-000 advertising campaign. There were many taboos in the specialty of underwear advertising, which was traditionally as antiseptic and as unerotic as possible. Even Jockey's Jim Palmer ads were couched in the pretense of showing the model getting dressed. But Calvin would have none of that. He intended to show underwear for what it really was: a turn-on.

Calvin's underwear venture marked the beginning of his collaboration with photographer Bruce Weber, who became wholly responsible for the striking eroticism of Calvin's print ads. Weber's photographs were a revelation to Calvin, so perfectly did they capture his vision. Not since Richard Avedon had a great talent tran-

scended advertising into pure art. Charging a day rate said to run
between $10,000 and $50,000, the thirty-seven-year-old photographer developed a "look" that became world famous. He combed
beaches and swimming pools and locker rooms for natural-looking
men and posed them in army barracks and public toilets. He shot
his models in natural light and sometimes ordered them to squint
into the sun so that they appeared to have been caught off guard by
his shutter. Although he photographed women as well, it was his
homoerotic studies of males that "made people wonder about their
own sexuality," said Weber. Indeed, one college student viewing
one of Weber's underwear print ads for the first time admitted to
his father that he found the photograph upsetting. "It makes a man
attracted to another man," he said.

Weber and Calvin tried to be good friends, but ultimately the
best that developed was an edgy working relationship. Although in
many ways the two were soul mates, they were very different personalities. Calvin was demanding and petulant to work with;
Weber was intensely private and protectively shy. Born in Greens-
burg, Pennsylvania, the charming and handsome photographer
had been a model himself after attending a prep school in Prince-
ton, New Jersey. But Weber did not like being the object of desire,
and comfortably metamorphosed from a stunning model into a
pudgy, middle-aged man with a trademark bandanna hiding his
balding pate. The molten center of his creativity was his gift of
being able to use his camera as an instrument of sexual desire.
Encouraged by photographers Diane Arbus and Lisette Model, his
pictures of men started to appear in art and fashion magazines in
the early seventies. He had, most of all, a keen eye for beauty and
discovered several of his models by prowling the swimming pools of
colleges and the shores of resort beaches.

Weber's "discovery" for Calvin's underwear campaign was the
lithely muscled, six-foot-three-inch tall, 185-pound Olympic pole
vaulter Tom Hintinaus. In September 1983, Weber's photograph
of Tom Hintinaus stood seven stories above the hurly-burly of
Times Square on a massive billboard previously used for one of
Calvin's jeans ads, forty by fifty feet high. Shedding any pretense
of photographing the model in a passing state of undress, Weber
shot the brawny athlete on a rooftop on the isle of Thera in the

Aegean. The pole vaulter was captured from below the apex of the bulging briefs, the corona of his penis clearly discernible through the soft cotton material. The crisp, clean white of the briefs, matching the pure white of the stucco behind him, stood out in brilliant relief against his tanned skin. The giant-sized, cotton-covered male member lording it over the crossroads of the world caused further public comment and outrage, setting off another wave of newspaper articles and TV reports decrying Calvin's shamelessness. "Can the name designer endow even the most prosaic product with the *ultimate* appeal?" *Advertising Age* asked. "This ad answers yes—especially when the model is so well-endowed."

Calvin blithely added to the controversy by renting twenty-five bus shelters throughout Manhattan to display the poster. In perhaps one of the most costly responses by the public to an advertising campaign, all twenty-five shelters had their glass shattered and the posters stolen overnight. It cost thousands of dollars to repair the glass and restock the poster on a continuous basis. Moreover, the Bruce Weber photograph of Hintinaus became one of the decade's favorite office-cubicle pinups for hundreds of thousands of secretaries across America, who bought their husbands and boyfriends undershorts by Calvin Klein.

Even before the posters went up, four hundred dozen pairs of shorts flew off the shelves at Bloomingdale's New York store, which was given an exclusive jump on the merchandise. Within two weeks the store's sales reached $65,000, and as the market spread to a hundred stores, twenty-thousand *dozen* pairs were sold the following month. Projected sales for the first year were $4 million, and although still only a small slice of the market, it was an impressive debut.

For Calvin watchers, his follow-up act wasn't hard to guess. One year after turning the men's underwear industry on its ear, he introduced a new line of underwear for women in what the fashion press called "the most talked about breakthrough in intimate apparel": *men's* underwear for women—that is, masculine boxer shorts or wide-waistband briefs that looked like jockstraps for girls. Priced well from six to twelve dollars, the line consisted of four tops and eight bottoms, all 100 percent cotton, in the usual white, pink, and baby-blue shades, as well as sweat grays and army khakis. "Calvin's New Gender Benders," *Time* magazine dubbed them. "And just a little strange, too." *Time* also pointed out that the women's boxer shorts curiously retained the fly front. When Calvin was asked why he retained an opening for an organ which women did not possess, he said in all earnest, "It's sexier with the fly. These things are seriously thought out."

The women's print ads, shot by Denis Piel, were only slightly less controversial than the men's, if only because the public had by now grown used to seeing women's bodies portrayed this way in the pages of *Playboy* or *Penthouse*. This ad series featured models with hard, athletic, but feminine bodies. In the most talked about photograph, the model is lying down with her pelvis arched skyward, wearing form-fitting Calvin Klein briefs and T-shirt hiked up to the bottom of her nipples. Another shot featured a silken-skinned young women with her back to the camera, in black briefs with a black undershirt pulled up above her head, exposing her breast as if for a mammography. "We shot black and white underwear," said Calvin, "but the night before the final shooting I had dinner with Diana Vreeland. She pointed at me with that finger—you know how she points—and said, 'My dear, think black. Its very sexy.' So we're only doing black for now."

Madison Avenue Freudians had a field day with Calvin's "locker-room" lingerie, and so did the customers.

"The consumer demand has hit a mania level," boasted Pam Gau, president of the line, to the press. Eighty thousand pairs of women's boxer shorts were sold retail in ninety days. One New York store sold $25,000 worth of undergarments in a month and another $150,000. Stores sold out by Christmas and were begging for shipments. Bloomingdale's and Saks reported that they sold twenty-thousand pairs at $7.50 each in the week before Christmas. Two hundred stores reordered their entire stock within three months.

Indeed, it got so big so fast, it quickly became impractical for Calvin and Barry to continue manufacturing operations themselves. In addition, their next logical expansion would be to move into hosiery and sleepwear, and it was decided that the whole line would be better off as a license. Therefore, in late August of 1984,

Calvin and Barry sold their women's underwear division to Kayser Roth, a cash-rich Gulf and Western company that was one of the largest manufacturers of women's underwear and hosiery in the world. Naturally, Calvin retained complete creative control of his product, especially the advertising, and in early 1985, he topped his earlier campaigns with a Weber shot that featured *two* men on a towel-covered mattress, with a naked woman lying between them. Each was dressed only in their tight scanty underwear, lying about exhausted and spent as if emerging from a torrid ménage à trois.

5

On August 8, 1983, fourteen months after learning he had cancer, Carl Rosen died. He left a total gross estate of $33,723,780. As much as it was expected, the news seemed to shock Calvin; all the money in the world couldn't buy an extra second on this earth.

It was the end of an era in the garment center. The death notices from friends and charitable organizations took up three columns in the *New York Times* obituaries. The funeral was held at Temple Emanu-El on Fifth Avenue and attended not only by hundreds of mourners who paid their respects but by both Rosen's mistress and wife as well as by the mayor of New York, Edward Koch, and New York governor Mario Cuomo.

The day after Carl Rosen was laid to rest, the control of Puritan Fashions Corp. was passed to twenty-seven-year-old Andrew, who now moved to the seat behind his father's big desk. "Obviously," said Andrew at the time, "I don't know everything." When Andrew was asked if he'd like it if Calvin took over the company and in the process made him a multimillionaire many times over, Andrew snapped, "No! I'm a young guy, I'm excited about the business. And we don't need it. . . . There's only one way I'm going to show anyone I'm competent. You get a report card every quarter. . . . If I do a good job—and that's the only thing I'm interested in—I'll be chief executive. That's what should happen. Or maybe it doesn't happen that way."

That second quarter the news was bad—although through no

fault of Andrew Rosen's. He hadn't been at the helm long enough to seriously affect the course of the company—not that he would have been able to do anything about the suddenly crumbling market for jeans. The designer blue jeans was a mother lode that had been quickly and thoroughly mined. Not only was the public losing interest, but Calvin's jeans were showing up in tawdry discount stores, cutting into his sales with prestigious retailers who carried the same jeans at twice the price. Calvin blamed Puritan executives for this "diversion" of his stock and was about to declare war on the company when fate intervened: On November 10, it was Andrew Rosen who was obligated to deliver Puritan's fourth-quarter earnings report, and the figures were even grimmer. Over the last three years the grosses for Calvin's jeans had been doubling, but this year there was no advance at all. Not only was the third quarter flat, but the fourth quarter looked worse, lower by a whopping 60 percent. Wall Streeters who were projecting $4.00 a share in dividends were now looking at a figure more like $2.65 a share. The day Andrew Rosen made the announcement, the stock dropped nearly 3 points to 13.

Calvin and Barry were outraged. "Andrew is a very nice young man," said Calvin, "but Puritan is a twenty-five-million-dollar company. . . . I have no personal animosity towards anyone in the Rosen family, but no twenty-seven-year-old has the experience to run a company that has a quarter of a billion dollars a year in sales."

On Monday, November 14, in what *Women's Wear Daily* called "a shrewd, opportunistic move," Calvin and Barry sent a carefully composed letter to the Puritan board, telling them of their dissatisfaction with Andrew Rosen's performance and lack of faith in him. They informed the board that they intended to buy Puritan Fashions Inc. and take it private. Their offer—take it or leave it—was a fair $16.50 a share, or nearly $60 million for the 3.5 million common shares. They wrote in a letter, "In deference to Carl and in fairness to Andrew, despite our misgivings, we did not seek to interfere with Puritan's affairs and Andrew's position as president. In the time that has passed, however, Puritan's actual and projected performance has declined sharply." If the Puritan board did not accept their $16.50 a share offer, the letter said, "we would have to review our alternatives for dealing with the concerns we've expressed. . . . We now realize that it is particularly unsatisfactory for sales of the major Calvin Klein product lines handled by Puritan to be under the control of others, and we do not feel that this should continue. As a result, we have concluded that it would be in everyone's mutual interest if we were to become more directly involved in Puritan's operations." They gave the Puritan board one week to accept their offer. If not, they stated, they would make a hostile bid for the company at a dollar less a share. Even with this threat, the offer drove the stock up nearly 4 points in a day to just over 16, before the hysteria faded and the stock settled to around 12, which meant that Calvin and Barry were offering shareholders a handsome 35 percent gain over market value.

Jeffrey Morris, research director for Evans & Co., said, "Who are Schwartz and Klein trying to kid that the third-quarter results were worse than they expected? The figures provided them with a perfect excuse for the takeover, and Andrew is being offered up as the sacrificial lamb."

The Puritan board of directors hired First Boston Corp., an independent investment bank, as well as the Park Avenue law firm of Kaye, Scholer, Fierman, Hays and Handler for legal advice. Calvin warned that his patience would be short, and on November 25, Barry let it be known that if the offer was refused, there would be a "full-blown war."

"You might say," said Jeffrey Morris, "the noose is around [Puritan's] neck and Calvin Klein is standing there ready to kick the box out from under them."

In the end, the final decision lay with the Rosen family. Andrew initially vowed to fight, but Carl's widow, Shirley, wanted to sell. The family would make as much as $6 million on the deal, and Andrew personally would be enriched by $1.5 million. To add to the pressure on the family, a shareholder, Harry Lewis, had brought suit against the company and its board, seeking to force the repayment of "unreasonable and unfair" payments that were made to Carl Rosen. The suit claimed that Rosen "created a board of directors who are subservient to his whims and wishes" and that the "excessive compensation . . . is a direct result of his domination. . . ." Finally, on a Sunday night, a despondent Andrew informed the board of his intentions to give in to the takeover offer and went off to Florida.

On Tuesday, November 29, the Puritan board unanimously accepted a $17.50-a-share bid, $1 more than was proposed originally, and the New York Stock Exchange announced it had suspended trading in Puritan Fashions. Calvin and Barry wound up owning 95 percent of the outstanding shares, with less than 600,000 shares remaining in public hands. In order to buy the stock, they borrowed a total of $105 million from Manufacturers Hanover Trust, using $75 million to purchase the company and pay off its long-term debt. The seven-year term of the loan carried a fee of up to 1 percent a year on the outstanding daily balance plus a $1 million origination fee. The interest was 1.04 percent above prime until the balance was paid down to $55 million, gradually reducing below that.

Andrew Rosen handled the situation with grace and aplomb, refusing to admit any animosity between him and Calvin. "There are a lot of things you can say about Calvin, but one thing is for sure," he said. "Calvin is an exciting guy, and he'll create an exciting company. Calvin is talented and creative, and he now has a $250 million company behind him. Combined, it [Calvin's company and Puritan] will be a powerful entity that could grow to $400 million overnight." He added, "The important thing is to look forward, not backward. I can't look backward."

Not many Puritan employees could look forward, either. First, Clavin buried the Puritan name, rechristening the company Calvin Klein Sport. Then he began a purge of almost all the Puritan executives, including, in particular, Andrew's sister, Lisa. In her position as head of marketing for jeans, Lisa adored Calvin in the beginning; her eyes would widen in star worship when she saw him. But Calvin barely noticed her—until she told a *New York Times* magazine reporter, doing a story on homosexual influences in the media, that "a gay element" attended Calvin's shows and was worth cultivating, adding, "I don't think it's politically smart for the company to be talking about this." Nor smart for Lisa; she was one of the first ones fired when Calvin took over.

Andrew Rosen himself was not fired. Initially demoted from president of the company to the mere head of one of the women's jeans-wear divisions, albeit well remunerated at over $500,000 a year, Andrew stuck it out, and in May 1987, Calvin restored him to the post of president. No question, reported *Women's Wear Daily*,

Andrew had grown to be worthy of the job, even if it was a job he seemed to be doing more out of respect for his late father than the innate enjoyment. "I can't say this was a life dream to run an apparel company," he told the industry daily somewhat wistfully.

6

By early 1983, Calvin had outgrown the Upper East Side and his ultramodern, low-ceilinged apartment at the Sovereign. The industrial-sleek style was dated, and so was the sensiblity of the glitzy building. Calvin was himself evolving into something less showy and newly arrived. He had a hankering for high ceilings and architectural drama, and that meant moving to the Upper *West* Side, the vogue address for nouvelle society.

Calvin's new duplex penthouse apartment at 55 Central Park West, which he bought from Broadway composer and lyricist Jerry Herman for $2.5 million, was a perfect reflection of the bachelor about town he had become. In this apartment there was no bedroom for his teenaged daughter, and if Marci wanted to sleep over, she would have to stay in the crowded gymnasium built just outside his bathroom. The top-floor bedroom was dominated by a huge fireplace, and just outside the double French doors was a garden in the sky twenty stories above Manhattan, complete with a real lawn, flower beds, and a small grove of willow trees. Off one wall of the bedroom was a greenhouse which contained not exotic blooms but a hot tub big enough for five people. The main floor contained a spacious living room with cathedral-like windows overlooking the park, a well-equipped kitchen with restaurant-quality appliances, and a laundry and utility space. One of the apartment's most striking features was a solid-pine staircase twenty feet long that led up to the bedroom. The staircase amazed most visitors not only because it was so steep; it was only thirty-three inches wide and had no sides or banister. A fall from the top could be fatal. Calvin already had it made wider—exactly one inch—not for safety's sake but because the minute difference in size pleased him aesthetically. "I said, this just has to be wider because I just know I'll never be able to live with it," Calvin recounted.

This apartment was decorated in the same minimalist mode as Calvin's last two residences, a style one visitor described as "militantly white," except for the beige industrial carpeting and sand-colored suede sofa draped with a red-and-indigo-streaked Indian blanket. "Even Max the cat," noted one visitor, "is charcoal colored." What also dominated this apartment was the presence of Georgia O'Keeffe. Calvin was having a love affair with the nonogenarian.

Over the last several years, O'Keeffe had become Calvin's greatest inspirational figure. The best-known woman artist of the century, at ninety-five, O'Keeffe proudly and magnificently flaunted convention. Everything about her was spectacular in his estimation, from the dignity of her lined face to the simplicity of the way she dressed in black-and-white pajama outfits. He loved the iconoclasm of her life, that she lived in the New Mexican desert in near isolation, that she had a companion younger by sixty years, the sculptor Juan Hamilton, and that she didn't care what society thought. Most of all, he loved her trademark bleached-animal-bone and flower paintings. The flower paintings in particular teased the public's eye, covertly erotic with their intertwined whorls. Calvin was so mad for the Santa Fe–based artist that he not only owned three of her canvases but kept several Stieglitz photographs of her in his bedroom. One massive O'Keeffe, of a bleached skull and brilliant white flowers, dominated one bedroom wall. "It's the last thing I see at night, the first thing I see when I wake up," he rhapsodized. "It's different in different lights. From the side you can see the brush strokes. There's a rhythm to them."

It was photographer Bruce Weber who introduced Calvin to O'-Keeffe's sexually enigmatic work when he persuaded the designer to accompany him to an exhibit of her work in a SoHo gallery. Calvin only dimly remembered that O'Keeffe had been married to one of his favorite photographers, Alfred Stieglitz, but was unfamiliar with her paintings. Calvin swooned when he saw his first O'-Keeffe 1930s abstract landscape, so simple and pale and luminescent. He felt an immediate creative and spiritual tie to the aging woman, and when he felt creatively impotent in the design room, he would browse through a book of O'Keeffe's paintings for inspiration. O'Keeffe's parched Southwest soon became one of

Calvin's favorite background locations for advertising shoots, and in the late seventies, he made a pilgrimage to the reclusive artist's beloved "Ghost Ranch." This was a sparsely decorated, strikingly simple, thick-walled white adobe hacienda near the tiny village of Abiquiu, New Mexico. Afraid to disturb her, Calvin left one of his sweaters as a gift on the front step but never rang the bell. A few years later, however, he owned several of her paintings and wanted more, and O'Keeffe's New York art dealer, Robert Miller, arranged for them to meet.

Calvin pulled an all-nighter the day before he met O'Keeffe, and he looked it. He was unshaven and disheveled the day he alighted from a private helicopter which landed outside of her small village. When he was ushered into her house, O'Keeffe, in failing health and memory, had no idea who Calvin was. Her awareness of fashion stopped with Elizabeth Arden. She did understand, however, that the effusive young man was a sincere and devoted fan of hers and that by the end of the day the "man in the print shirt" would pay her more than $1 million for some of her paintings, including *Summer Days,* in which a weather-beaten skull looms above the red earth. O'Keeffe warmed to Calvin even more when he told her that he once took a Matisse home from a gallery on loan and "after I lived with it for a few days, I realized it was just not me. I mean, while I think he was probably one of the greatest artists of our time, or any time, it was not something I wanted to live with."

O'Keeffe said, "My dear, I knew you had style."

The Ghost Ranch turned out to be an embodiment of Calvin's favorite colors and textures. Calvin loved every detail about the way O'Keeffe lived, the simple bed in her room, the wooden table around which she and her younger companion ate, the artistic way she folded her clothes. By the end of the day, after the anticipated $1 million changed hands for several of her paintings, Calvin begged the artist to allow him to use Ghost Ranch as the background for a photo shoot for his menswear line. The style and sensibility of the line, he said, had been inspired by O'Keeffe. The old woman was unhappy at the thought; she had never before opened her home to the press or public, but feeling beholden to the rich young man, she reluctantly agreed.

The shoot at Ghost Ranch (and at one other O'Keeffe home) had

an unusual model: Calvin Klein. It was decided that since O'-
Keeffe's home was practically a shrine in his eyes, he should be the
one photographed there by Bruce Weber. "I wanted to appear in
the ads myself," said Calvin. "It's the first time I've done that.
Bruce asked me where I would feel comfortable for him to take the
photographs [and] I said I'd love to go to Ghost Ranch. . . . I needed
just one ad for the menswear company. It was to be a picture of me
wearing a suit or sweater. . . ." A thousand shots and several days
later, Weber and Calvin had produced their most alluring and perhaps artistically enduring series of print ads. Calvin's contentment
and satisfaction in his surroundings comes through in each print.
He rarely looked more handsome than in these Weber photographs. The sepia-toned shots included one of Calvin reclining on
a bed, asleep or in reverie, his jacket carelessly thrown over his
torso. In another, Calvin lankily leaned against O'Keeffe's primitive
fireplace, his head back, eyes closed in a dreamlike trance, his long
arms and hands jammed in the pockets of a white linen double-
breasted suit. Several of the ads didn't show Calvin or even any
clothing, but only some architectural detail he had fallen in love
with, like a stucco archway. But perhaps the most fascinating shot
of all was Calvin stretched out on his side, resting on his arm in an
oversized sweater, one hand poised close to a square rattlesnake
hole. "I love it," Calvin said when questioned about playing with
danger. "I love having my hand in that spot. It is just very, very
beautiful."

CHAPTER FIFTEEN

Scandal sticks to rebuttal like tar.

—Mark Twain

B y the middle of 1983, Calvin found himself in the most turbulent of all his love affairs with men. Over the recent months, he had
become completely enamored of an ex–college athlete named Roland Hall* who worked for him as a menswear model. Hall was a
tall, chiseled young man in his early twenties with thick curly blond
hair and a long, aquiline nose. Ruggedly masculine and a straight-
arrow college graduate who eschewed drugs and alcohol, he had
been a star athlete at a prestigious university and was from a well-
off family. He had little interest in fashion and modeling but had
been lured into the field by the financial nest egg it promised when
a talent scout discovered him working out in his college gym. From
the first moment Calvin saw his photographs he was taken with
Hall; Calvin was used to making gods of men in his advertising, but
this guy already was a god. He was, at least in Calvin's eyes, perfect,
from the texture of his thick hair and the way it fell about his face
as he emerged wet from a swimming pool to the trace of high color
that developed along his cheekbones when he was angry or embarrassed. He moved like a big, loping gazelle, all long, sinewy arms
and size 11 feet, and when he pulled himself through the blue
water of a swimming pool doing his daily laps, the grace of his body
moving through the water was like that of a dancer. It was said that
the beauty of Hall in a swimming pool compelled Calvin to demol-
ish the house behind his in Fire Island and have built a black-lined

*A pseudonym.

307

lap pool in its place with a mirrored cabana at the far end. After
Calvin's years of searching, no other man quite stole his heart the
way Hall did.

There was only one problem: Hall was straight.

And not only was he straight, but other than his friendship with
Calvin, he barely tolerated "fags." Hall was a jock, the epitome of a
"real man." He liked swimming, rock and roll, and Italian food, in
that order. And to be adored. And that's what Calvin gave him.
Calvin plastered his face and body in magazines and newspapers
around the world, seeing to it that Hall was paid a small fortune in
the process.

The entire venture drove the people who loved Calvin crazy. Another *amour folle*. It was a re-creation of the relationship with Alphonso, played out nightly at Studio 54, chic restaurants around
town, and the Fire Island Pines. But at least Alphonso was have-
able. Hall was straight and clearly in great conflict over Calvin's
affection for him. He didn't want to reject the designer completely
for fear of repercussions, yet he could not bring himself to have a
physical relationship with Calvin, either—even if it meant damaging his lucrative modeling career. The net result was that while
Hall was frequently at Calvin's side, the young model was aloof and
mean to him. Calvin, in turn, acted like a "whipped puppy," according to a modeling agency executive who witnessed several of their
interchanges. There were frequent "spats" between the designer
and the model, and one Fire Island regular remembered Calvin and
Hall arguing publicly aboard the ferry coming back from the Pines.
As the months passed, Hall found himself in an untenable position,
and his relationship with Calvin turned explosive. By the end of the
summer of 1983, Hall had what has been described as a "nervous
breakdown." The model gave up his career and fled Calvin and
New York soon after, to begin a new life in the Midwest.

The end of his relationship with Hall left Calvin more depressed
than he had been in years, and his drug and alcohol use increased
accordingly. In the office, his unpredictability and sudden fits of
vitriol turned even blacker. "There were many missed meetings,"
Robert Taylor recalled. "You'd get a call from the secretary that he's
not feeling well, that he can't come in today, that he's got a bad
cold, or that he took off for the Bahamas and the meeting was going

to have to wait for two weeks. This shit went on constantly, constantly." Taylor never saw Calvin looking specifically drugged or stoned, but "he looked spent. He looked white. When you went into a meeting, you knew immediately whether he was going to be abusive or whether he was going to be passive." Employees began to notice that Calvin's moods were strikingly different after he returned from trips to his private bathroom. He also took infamous "walks to the freight elevator" or five-minute breaks in private in his office.

But it was only at night that Calvin really allowed himself to indulge in drugs to incapacitation. Chester Weinberg was so worried about him that he told one of Calvin's regular chauffeurs, "You have to keep an eye on Calvin. If you see him getting too high in one of the clubs, you have to snatch him out of there."

Yet frequently there was little anyone could do. One night, after attending a birthday party for the model Kim Alexis at an East Side restaurant, Calvin directed his driver to a brownstone building in the sixties and asked him to wait. This was the apartment of one of New York's premier drug dealers, now deceased, where it was possible to buy the finest-quality drugs available in the city, from cocaine to Quaaludes, as well as a wide variety of designer drugs and psychedelics. When Calvin emerged from the building an hour later, his hair was messed, his shirt was hanging out of his pants, and he was staggering. "He was really *stupefied* then," said the driver, who jumped from the car to help steady the designer and load him into the back seat. "Okay, I'm going home," Calvin managed to say, sprawled in the rear of his Mercedes.

When the car pulled up in front of Calvin's building, he asked if the driver would help him up to his apartment. "I need you to come upstairs with me and make sure that I get up the steps," Calvin said. "No one is home and I could fall and nobody would find me for a while."

For Calvin, gay life was turning out to be pretty empty. He lived under the Damocles sword of AIDS, he wasn't getting any younger, and every time he stepped into a nightclub, half the patrons looked young enough to be his children. One late night around that time, Calvin shared a joint with man-about-town-columnist R. Couri Hay at a trendy downtown nightclub. Calvin seemed unusually pensive and introspective that night. "He talked about how tired he was of going out in the night life," said Hay, "and the drugs and drinking and the scene and the sex."

Throughout most of 1983, hurt, confused, and embarrassed, he continued to brood. "I used to think it wasn't such a bad idea to live out your fantasies," he ruminated. "I'm not sure anymore. I think maybe a fantasy should remain a fantasy." Whatever it was he was looking for, whatever would make him happy, he hadn't found it.

And then, one day, he realized it was right under his nose.

2

Her name was Kelly Rector.

"There is someone in my life right now that I care a great deal about," Calvin joyously told the press in late 1983. "She's a lovely, wonderful girl, and I'm extremely happy. Although we've known each other for two and a half years, the relationship is a new one. Her name is Kelly Rector, and she works in my design studio. . . . I fell in love over a long period of time. . . . I didn't think another relationship was possible. Because of the health crisis . . . people are just so much more conscious of the fact that you can't go fooling around. You start . . . saying, 'I'm going to be more careful before I get involved.' Your values change! It didn't happen, bang!"

Kelly made her first appearance as Calvin's official girlfriend just after Labor Day, 1983, when syndicated columnist Liz Smith noted in her column, "Here's a hot new romance that should blow minds on Seventh and Madison Aves. as well as on Fire Island, where jealousy and envy are not exactly unknown. The handsome and super-successful king of clothes, Calvin Klein, has astonished intimates by turning to one of his most attractive employees, beauteous Kelly Rector, for companionship and much more. The twosome has been inseparable, and insiders report 'they can't keep their hands off one another.' Calvin is just full of surprises, as befits a well-rounded talent." *Women's Wear Daily* also noted in November 1983 that Calvin Klein and Kelly Rector were "arm and arm," and when he was asked about the relationship with Kelly, a reporter described him as "blissful."

Reactions varied among the "astonished intimates." Andy Warhol, for one, was outraged by the turn of events and labeled the whole thing with Kelly a "hot media affair." Giorgio Sant'Angelo moaned, "But Calvin likes *boys*," when he heard about Kelly. According to Giorgio's friend, Martin Price, Calvin made sure to introduce Kelly to Giorgio. "He wanted Giorgio's approval," said Price, but although Giorgio liked Kelly, he refused to pander to what he felt was a contrived situation and distanced himself. "Oh, it's just social climbing." David Geffen, Sandy Gallin, and Barry Diller were more sanguine about the new development. At one time or another they had all had heated love affairs with women. And although at first they thought Kelly was just a phase Calvin would pass through, they became more respectful of the situation as it became clear that Calvin was truly in love.

Kelly first walked into Calvin's life two years before as an applicant for a job as a design assistant in his studio. At first, he wanted to hire a recent graduate from the Fashion Institute of Technology, hoping to find the eighties version of himself, but according to one staff member, all the FIT students "had their hair dyed blue or cut in a Mohawk, and their clothes looked like they were from 1999." The search went on for several months until one night at a small dinner party, Helen Murray, a young woman who worked in Calvin's publicity offices, met Kelly, then a twenty-one-year-old design assistant at Ralph Lauren. Kelly seemed to have it all—style, class, and extraordinary natural beauty. Coquettish as a starlet, she could manipulate a man with her coy half smile, a seductive toss of her tawny brown hair cut in a swag to her shoulders, or a downcast look from her large ocean-blue eyes, banded with a ring of dark navy. There was an air of all-American fitness about her, and even her complexion radiated the outdoors and good health. When she spoke, it was in the soft, rounded tones of a Connecticut debutante. When Kelly mentioned over dinner to Helen Murray that she was thinking about leaving Ralph Lauren for greener pastures, Murray said there was an opening at Calvin Klein for which she would be perfect.

However, when Helen Murray recommended Kelly Rector to Zack Carr the next day, he shook his head and said, "Calvin will not hire anyone who's worked for Ralph Lauren, Halston, or Perry

Ellis." It was a rule, he said, "carved in stone." But as the search for
an assistant dragged on, Helen Murray begged Carr to ask Calvin
to meet this girl who seemed straight out of the pages of *Town and
County* magazine. Finally, Calvin relented and allowed Kelly Rector to come in for an interview.

No sparks flew. The half-hour meeting in Calvin's office was
businesslike and inauspicious. Sitting on the other side of a white
oval table from Kelly, Calvin was aloof but charming, his turtle-
green eyes alternately judgmental and cajoling. Kelly had a self-
contained protectiveness. Like so many women before her, she
melted in the presence of the handsome superstar. But she was
determined not to be wooed or cowed, and she told Calvin at some
length exactly what she thought about fashion, where it was going,
and what she could contribute to his staff. Unfortunately, she
didn't have a strong sketchbook of her own designs, which had always been a requisite to work in Calvin's design room, and Calvin
listened to her go on and on about herself with a bemused smile on
his face before thanking her and saying goodbye. A few minutes
after she left, Helen Murray popped into Calvin's office and asked,
"Well, what did you think of Kelly Rector?"

"The last thing I need," said Calvin dryly, "is another pretty face
around here with an opinion."

But the face and the opinions lingered in Calvin's mind, and two
weeks later, he surprised himself as well as Helen Murray by telling
her to call Kelly and say she was hired.

Kelly Rector was hardly just another ornamental fashion groupie
to be added to the pack of adoring female employees who worked
for Calvin. She had been bred since childhood for a fairy-tale future. Born in Detroit in 1957, she grew up in the Connecticut village of Westport, on the Saugatuck River where it flows into Long
Island Sound. Her mother, a former *Vogue* cover model in the fifties known as Gloria Kelly, got her dark good looks and prominent
cheekbones from her American-Indian heritage. Her father, Tully
F. Rector, was a handsome horseman from Texas who was one of
the highest-paid directors of TV commercials. They lived on a
quiet, tree-lined, twisty lane at 10 Charcoal Hill Road, in a house
built to resemble a small Normandy manor, with thick fieldstone
walls and French-style solid shutters. Kelly attended Coleytown El-

ementary school and then Coleytown Junior High, where her schoolmates were the children of other upper middle-class families with parents in the media or advertising. She was a popular and somewhat envied student, and all the kids at school knew she had an important father because one day a movie crew arrived in their neighborhood to shoot one of Tully's car commercials.

With an oval face, high cheekbones, and eager greenish-blue eyes, Kelly was a "sweet, lively, fun child," remembered a family intimate. Life seemed an endless round of pleasure to her. In 1960, when she was almost four, her mother and father built a large, rectangular aqua-blue swimming pool in the backyard, where she'd romp with her younger sister, Amy, who was born soon after they moved to this house. "My sister and I played for hours," Kelly said, "seeing how long we could hold our breath under water and swimming relay races to see who could swim the fastest. . . . When my friends came over, we would play Marco Polo, open our eyes under water, and scream and laugh until we were exhausted."

Aside from swimming, Kelly's other passions were Jessica, a basset hound that followed her everywhere, and horses. From the time she was old enough to sit up in a saddle, Kelly shared her father's love of thoroughbreds and jumpers, and she grew up able to handle the most skittish prize animals. The stable became her home away from home. "I always dressed in faded jeans and white shirts," she said, "and I always hung out with the guys. Horses took me away from my formal education because on weekends I was off to mop my horse stalls, clean my tack, and get ready for formal competitions on the eastern shore." Kelly's favorite steed was Fur Balloon, a championship jumper that her father bought for her in England when she was old enough to take care of a horse.

Then, in 1967, her world fell apart. Tully Rector had fallen in love with another woman, a model who shared his fondness for horses and Kelly's parents were getting a divorce. Kelly said, "At one point, when I was very young, my family had a lot of money. Then, I don't know, it just seemed to disappear." In the wake of the breakup of the marriage, Tully was forced to sell Fur Balloon. It nearly broke Kelly's heart to see him go. "It was a very sad point in my life," she said. "That's when I switched my interest over to fashion."

Indeed, Kelly buried herself in a fantasy world of fashion. After she grew out of her tomboy phase, she discovered that she had a talent for clothing, for putting outfits together and matching colors and styles. In her teen years she began to spend hours shopping for clothes in stores, and at home she carefully scrutinized every page of *Vogue* and *Harper's Bazaar*, daydreaming of the moment when her life would have a happy ending and she would live like the women in their pages. She stood in front of the mirror, fretting that she was too short, and always wore shoes with heels. "She was a clotheshorse," said a family member. "She was very aware of style and fashion. I just think she wanted to be a fairy princess."

In 1967, two years after divorcing Tully, Gloria remarried. Kelly's stepfather was a divorced New York psychologist, Dr. Murray List, who also lived in Westport. List had two girls of his own from his first marriage, and Kelly and Amy had a ready-made new family. Dr. List moved his newly combined tribe to a Manhattan town house at 116 East Eighty-second Street, where he also set up a practice. Kelly began to attend the expensively chic Dwight School, and although she still idolized Tully as well as his stylish new wife, she began to depend on Dr. List as a father. Although, said Murray List, Kelly was "totally self-absorbed" as a child, for a short time she felt the comfort and security of family life.

But three years later, when Kelly was fifteen years old, her mother's second marriage also came to an end, because, according to Murray List, Gloria "rejected my children." The divorce was unhappy, and Kelly's newfound security dissolved with it. Missing her stepsisters, she often wept. Her stepfather says he was denied any contact with her. Eventually, Gloria moved to California, and Kelly, not more than a young girl, set out on her own. "I think most children," said Murray List, "who go through two divorces decide that they're going to do what's in their best interests and take care of themselves first."

Having blossomed into a natural beauty, with glowing skin and a smile that boys compared to the Mona Lisa, from the age of sixteen to twenty-one Kelly dated Sam Edelman, the wealthy scion of a leather-goods and shoe manufacturing dynasty that licensed, among others, Ralph Lauren shoes. Kelly loved Edelman's warm Jewish family, and she frequently commuted between their big Ridgefield, Connecticut, house and FIT where she attended school. After she outgrew what was basically a schoolgirl relationship with Edelman, she shifted into higher gear. Her next affair was with Christopher Maytag, a tall, slender, fair-skinned boy of patrician stock whose great-grandfather founded the famous appliance manufacturing company. "They were desperately in love," said Maytag's mother, Mrs. Shirley King, "but Kelly broke off the relationship because Christopher was on drugs." Indeed, Maytag was in serious trouble, frequently drunk, shooting narcotics, and in and out of rehabilitation centers. While Kelly was no naif, drugs were not her thing. Maytag tried to placate her with beautiful presents like emerald bracelets, but after a year of broken promises, Kelly ended the affair. "I know that Christopher was devastated by it," his mother said, "but she warned him." Years later, when Maytag overdosed and was found dead in the hallway of an apartment building in lower Manhattan, Kelly attended the funeral at a Fifth Avenue church and sat in a back pew and wept.

Her next relationship was more upbeat and healthy, albeit brief, when she dated Yale graduate Cary Leeds, a ranked tennis player and the son of millionaire Manhattan Industries chief Laurance Leeds. But none of her boyfriends seemed to hold Kelly's attention more than her next flame, the flirtatious twenty-seven-year-old singer-songwriter John Leffler, who had written hit songs for Crystal Gayle and Joe Cocker. Leffler was slowly gaining a reputation as a noted advertising-jingle writer as well, yet he was perhaps equally known as an irresistible ladies' man. Kelly thought she was in love with the tall, good-looking fellow, and while she was dating him, she moved out of the West Side flat she shared with her sister and into her own small studio apartment in a doorman high-rise near Lincoln Center. Kelly decorated the apartment tastefully yet inexpensively in an easy southwestern style with folk baskets and Indian rugs that her mother had begun collecting. In 1979, after Kelly graduated from FIT, Sam Edelman helped her get a job as a receptionist at Ralph Lauren. But Kelly Rector was too talented, and too ambitious, to stay at the front desk for long, and she soon graduated to a position as assistant in Ralph Lauren's design room. When colleagues asked about her background at Ralph Lauren, she would say that Lauren had brought her in to be his "image creator."

By the time Kelly got her job at Calvin Klein Industries she was a seasoned pro. However, no amount of experience in the fashion business could have prepared her for a job with Calvin. He was like the "little girl with the curl" in the children's poem; when he was good he was very, very good—there was magic in the air around him—but when he was bad he was horrid. Kelly was determined to keep her distance from her alternately volatile and charming boss, yet with the passing of time, they both began to let down their guard around each other. The more Calvin watched her, the more he realized just how beautiful she was. Even better, he began to appreciate that she had the same indefinable talent that Eve Orton and Frances Stein had before her: infallible good taste. He came to depend on her as his editor, and she became something of a standard to him. "Kelly was Calvin's version of Ralph [Lauren's] homespun prairie girl," said one of Calvin's friends. "Kelly is Calvin's perfect shiksa." Even her complexion seemed so all-American to him—she hardly ever wore makeup, or needed to—that he would hold fabrics up to her face for contrast, and amused coworkers nicknamed her "the skin girl." Said one colleague, "All of a sudden she had influence."

The more Calvin and Kelly got to know each other, the more they liked it. However, the relationship remained strictly boss and employee, teacher and his favorite student. Indeed, it was in the absence of romantic or sexual pressures that the friendship was able to blossom naturally. That's not to say that Calvin wasn't flirtatious and provocative with her, but Kelly knew it was all a game, anyway. Sure, she thought he was dreamy, but dream was all she could do. It was no secret around the office that Roland Hall had broken his heart, and Kelly also knew that if Calvin was seriously interested in women, he had any number of high-powered beauties waiting in the wings. At public events, Calvin was often seen with one of his favorite female models, the classic, timeless beauty Lisa Taylor. They were together so frequently that *People* magazine even published the groundless rumor they would marry, to which one of Calvin's friends sniped, "They're both so beautiful, it would be like marrying themselves." Calvin also frequently squired the exotic Italian beauty Marina Schiano, now his in-house director of public relations, who for years had worked for Yves Saint Laurent, but no romance ever developed. According to Andy Warhol, Bianca Jagger had also recently fallen under Calvin's spell, after knowing him for many years. The artist wrote in his published diaries, "Bianca was trying so hard to marry Calvin because she doesn't have any money." Warhol went on to say, "[Bianca is] really after Calvin—I saw her just be so after him. But then, marrying Bianca wouldn't kill gay rumors."

Kelly knew she didn't have a snowball's chance in hell. "Of course, we thought Calvin was attractive," said one female staffer who worked with Kelly. "We thought he was *great,* and he was a lot of fun, but no one had any delusions . . . It was nothing sexual to it." But that didn't matter to Kelly. Calvin was turning into the best pal she ever had, and their relationship was so fulfilling—and so inno-cent—they even double-dated together, Kelly with her steady John Leffler and Calvin with Lisa Taylor.

In the spring of 1983, just as Calvin's friendship with Roland Hall was hurtling toward a cataclysmic end, Kelly unexpectedly broke up with John Leffler after six years together. A paparazzo shot of Leffler dancing with Cher was published in the *New York Post,* and Kelly told friends she felt humiliated. "[The photo] did wonders for my relationship," said Leffler sarcastically.

That summer, both Calvin and Kelly were wounded birds of sorts, nesting together, and their relationship subtly shifted into a more romantic mode, albeit not yet a sexual one. Tentatively, he invited Kelly out to his house in the Pines. He made sure the refrig-erator was stocked with champagne and told his houseboy, who was gay, to make himself scarce. Said one household intimate who was able to observe their romance bud that first idyllic summer, "Kelly came along at a time when he needed it badly. Kelly had proved to be there [for him], time after time, as a friend. . . . That simple, beautiful person that she is—he just felt really good with her. She took care of him, she made the weekends really special for him . . . out of genuine affection that they had for each other. Something was *so* special about it. . . . The way it grew was very special. . . . It was almost like two little kids falling in love with each other and not being really sure about how to make the next step. . . . You could tell that they both had [an attraction] for each other, but they didn't know where the boundaries were."

One day, while Kelly was assisting on a print-ad layout being shot in the Pines, another member of the crew remarked to Calvin, "Kelly's absolutely beautiful and such a good person to have on the team. I think I'm in *love* with her."

Calvin said, *"You* are? *I* am, too." There was a pause, and then Calvin added, "I'm in love with several people. Beautiful men, beautiful women. How can I choose? I just can't make any decisions."

Warren Beatty may have helped with that decision. At least it was Beatty whom Kelly credited as turning a platonic romance into an authentic love affair. It started in Los Angeles, where Calvin took Kelly on a business trip. While they were there, one of Calvin's Hollywood buddies invited them to an A-list, star-studded party whose guests included Warren Beatty. Calvin's attraction for Beatty had long been a joke among his close friends, and he was thrilled to meet the actor at the party, until, that is, Beatty began to flirt with Kelly. It burned Calvin royally—and surprised him with how much he really cared. But he said nothing, since he had no real claim on her. When Calvin returned to Manhattan the next day, Kelly told friends she stayed behind in Los Angeles at Beatty's behest.

When Kelly returned from the West Coast she had quite a tale to tell to her girlfriends in the office. The day after the party, she told others, Beatty called her at her hotel and invited her to his house, where they went to bed. After making love, she claimed to a girlfriend, Beatty confided in her that Diane Keaton—the only woman he really ever wanted—walked out on him.

Calvin was mightily chagrined to hear all the stories circulating around the office about Kelly's (or Beatty's) conquest. If she was good enough for Warren Beatty, she was good enough for Calvin. "It was as if," said an intimate of Calvin's, "by having Kelly, he'd have a piece of Warren." Kelly told friends that soon after the Warren Beatty incident, she and Calvin went out to dinner and then to her West Side high rise. But instead of dropping her off downstairs, this time he took her to her door and kissed her, his first sexual advance. One thing led to another, and the couple ended up in bed. Kelly said that at first Calvin was unable to perform, but later, when things were more relaxed, they made love for the first time. He was a wonderful lover—sensitive, caring, and adventurous.

Kelly said that later Calvin claimed she was the first woman he'd slept with "in God knows how long."

"But he's *gay,*" one girlfriend protested to Kelly.

"I know," Kelly said, "but . . . "

But . . . it felt very much like a real romance. While others could smirk, to Kelly and Calvin, it was one of the best times in their lives. It had been *decades* since Calvin felt that way, so happy and in love. That summer they took a romantic trip to England together to buy fabric, and one day Calvin promised to show Kelly the ancient university city of Cambridge. Bright and early on a sunny Sunday morning they set out from London in a chauffeur-driven Rolls-Royce. The countryside and meadows were the lushest green either of them had every seen, and on the way they stopped for lunch at a roadside pub. There was a mirror-topped lake nearby with two linen-white swans and boats for rent, and after lunch they wanted to go rowing. But while they were eating the heavens suddenly seemed to open, and it started to pour. Laughing like children, they decided to go to the lake, anyway; only the boats had been all covered and put away. That same trip, on another day, they wandered through the crowded, narrow streets of London holding hands, staring at houses and people, discovering out-of-the-way little shops. Without realizing it, the two got lost. "We found some odd street behind Kings Road," Calvin remembered of that day, "where every house is painted another color. . . . Kelly [was] all in white and looking incredibly beautiful and she's passing by each one of these little town houses, each one another pastel shade. I said, 'Look! . . . Here we are. Never heard of this street. And look at all of these colors! Do you realize if we just start chipping away what we have?' " What they "had" was the new colors for Calvin's spring and summer line. He and Kelly went up and down the block and, furtively keeping an eye out for the houses' owners, chipped away at the paint to bring home samples.

Although around the office the couple was determined to be discreet and treated each other with exaggerated politeness, they could not help ocassionally breaking into embarrassed smiles when they looked at each other. On the nights Kelly slept at Calvin's apartment, she would invariably show up at work the next day in the same outfit, which was like raising a signal flag to the fashion-conscious crew at the office. "Sometimes," a colleague recalled, "she'd look really tired in the morning and she'd say, 'I was out all night with Calvin.' They'd arrive together in the morning in his chauffeured Mercedes." Also, Kelly propped a silver-framed photo of Calvin against her office window. There were more subtle signs as well. When Kelly walked away from him, said the colleague, "Calvin would keep watching her." That first winter, he also gave her a floor-length fox coat from his collection, which she wore the entire season. Yet the couple was rarely physically affectionate in public. One night at dinner with the design staff, another employee said, "Kelly got up from the table to go to the bathroom, and she bent over to say something to Calvin and just put her arms around Calvin's shoulders. It was almost as if Calvin was startled, like Kelly forgot herself. You could tell she liked to be affectionate, she wanted to be, and yet he's not somebody who touches people."

Of all Calvin's friends, his new relationship had the most profound effect on Steve Rubell. When Kelly first kept appearing on Calvin's arm, Rubell expected she'd eventually go away, but now it had gotten *serious.* Rubell didn't like the situation at all. Kelly cramped his style. He liked her enough as a person—all of Calvin's friends liked Kelly—but having Kelly around all the time made Rubell self-conscious. "It made Steve look at himself," said one of Rubell's closest friends. "Whatever Calvin was going through made him look at himself in a certain way, and it made him feel uncomfortable with respect to his own life. I think that he would have loved to have had a companion. I think Steve was a very lonely person. And Calvin was a very lonely person, and suddenly Calvin wasn't lonely anymore. Calvin started living a fuller life."

Kelly, for her part, was distant and shy at first with Calvin's bachelor friends, although that did not mean she wasn't exposed to the gay side of Calvin's life. She became a frequent visitor to his house in the Fire Island Pines and seemed comfortable there. Two Studio 54 employees remember dropping in on Calvin's house to discover Calvin and Rubell stretched out on chaises longues poolside, inebriated and "mumbling," while Kelly swam bare-breasted in the pool. On another occasion, Calvin took Kelly to an all-boy party in the Pines, where they disappeared for what seemed like a long period of time. The host discovered them on a second-story deck, necking under a full moon, the beach and ocean behind them. The romantic interlude was broken, however, when Steve Rubell passed out on the floor, and Kelly watched disapprovingly as he had to be loaded into a red wagon and carted back to Calvin's house.

Eventually, Calvin began to see his chums less—in part because of Kelly's influence but mostly because she took up so much of his time. "By the point he was dating Kelly," said a close mutual friend of Calvin and Chester's, "he was starting to distance himself from gay friends. Chester said that Kelly disliked intensely the people associated with Calvin from those gay heydays."

The more their relationship as lovers solidified, the more Kelly's influence began to grow around the office, much to the chagrin of the rest of the staff. Kelly became the company booster, cheerleader, information gatherer, lobbyist, and gossip. After the news came out in the papers, "She wore Calvin on her arm like a medal," complained one veteran of the design staff. It seemed as if everybody who worked for Calvin Klein Industries had some Kelly and Calvin gossip to tell as her reign of influence began to extend throughout all the divisions. It seemed as if she had diplomatic immunity to come and go as she pleased. Kelly did "all kinds of very manipulative things," said one staffer. "She was famous for going through people's desks. She was known as the company spy."

Her most irksome prerogative, perhaps, was the new power she wielded over Calvin's taste in his collections. His clothing began to take on Kelly's stamp, and Calvin consulted her on the smallest decision, as if he couldn't make up his mind himself. One design executive from the Bidermann menswear license purchased fabric samples from the Orient and went to great trouble having several pairs of classic, double-pleated trousers made to be presented to Calvin. There was great enthusiasm at Bidermann that the trousers would become the leaders of the coming fall line. But when the designer arrived in Calvin's office for the presentation, his heart sank to discover that Kelly and another assistant were in on the meeting. Sure enough, the first pair of pants he showed them displeased Kelly. "I don't know, there's something about the pleats of the pants that are funny," Kelly said.

Calvin snapped, "Disapprove model 62431," and the pants were out of the line, all the planning and hard work for nothing.

"In my mind," said the designer, "I strangled Kelly. She turned blue."

But Kelly's emerging influence over Calvin didn't upset anyone more than Zack Carr. After nearly a decade working for Calvin, Carr had little to show for it. He was pushing forty and was still only a salaried worker paid $50,000 a year. For all those years the cherubic chief design assistant had been Calvin's right hand and confidant. He had watched in silence or clucked in dismay as Calvin went through his affairs and infatuations, always knowing that in the end, when the *garçon du jour* was gone, he and Calvin would still be together. And now, unexpectedly, there was a greater influence in Calvin's life, an influence with which he could not compete. Carr would make a suggestion about a garment or style, and Kelly would see it another way. Kelly's taste leaned to the countrified look of Ralph Lauren, whereas Zack was more influenced by the trendsetting European designers. As the clashes between them became more frequent, the resentment built, like a pressure cooker ready to explode. Calvin became the rivals' battleground as each vied for his attention and approval. He felt a real sense of loyalty to Zack Carr, but in the end he had no choice.

It all came to a head on Tuesday, May 1, 1984, during the hectic hours that led up to Calvin's important fall collection. The guest list for the collection was especially glittering that year—including pop superstar Michael Jackson, who would bring a hoard of paparazzi in his wake; Bianca Jagger; the society lioness Nan Kempner; Andy Warhol; writer Fran Lebowitz; society "walker" Jerry Zipkin— and the tension was running high. Calvin was in his usual paranoid, strung-out state, worried about the audience's reaction, frightened of taking a fall off the high wire in front of a sellout crowd. He had stayed up half the night before the show, taking Valium to calm down, as Zack and Kelly were at each other's throats. Carr disagreed strongly with Kelly about how the line should be presented, and Calvin was put in the middle. At one point Kelly had some harsh words for her boyfriend, and "whatever Kelly said to Calvin so devastated him that he could not deal with the show that day," Chester said later. Calvin stormed out of the building and disappeared. One executive remembered, "After the show there was cheering. It wasn't a great collection, but there was all this applause, and they wanted Calvin to come out and take a bow, and all the designers in the studio, Zack Carr, John Calgano, Kelly—and I don't remember who else—they all came down the runway. But Calvin never appeared. Calvin had walked out, and when everyone went back to congratulate him, he wasn't even there." Another employee claims that Calvin went "missing in action" for three days. "That's when Kelly realized what incredible control she had over this man," he said.

In its review of this show, *Women's Wear Daily* noted a peculiar new "horsey" sensibility to the clothes, a "brashly subtle, emphatically boyish collection . . . of understated style [which] gives free reign to his fantasies of thoroughbred gentility." It was almost a description of Kelly herself. The review went on to say that "the applause was loud and long at the end of the show but Calvin Clean wasn't there to acknowledge it. Calvin had left the building leaving only his assistants to take the bows and a bewildered audience without a cheek to kiss."

Ten days after the show, Zack Carr formally announced his resignation from Calvin Klein Industries. Carr's version of the parting was that "Calvin had asked me not to design anymore. He had asked me really to be a sort of 'head of studio' and just sort of organize . . . and I felt like . . . he was saying he didn't believe in anything that I have done in the past. I think this was out of the fear of not being American enough in designing, that he wanted to be much more American and he felt that I was too European . . . for him . . . which was probably true, actually. I felt that he wanted a new design team, and he asked me to put it together for him, and I think he wanted Kelly to be head of it and to be the inspiration for it."

Saying goodbye to Calvin was one of the most difficult experiences of Carr's life. "The last time I saw Calvin," said Carr, "the one thing that I told him was that 'I loved you.' That's all I could tell him. . . . " In retrospect Carr said, "I think that it's a very painful thing to come to [know] your own self. I think it's necessary in this life, that it's probably the only journey there is in life, actually. I couldn't help Calvin do that, and in some ways I think that's what Calvin was asking me to do."

Carr, however, was hardly bereft in terms of his career. The instant his resignation was made public he was besieged with offers from fast-talking promoters anxious to back him in a clothing line that would look just like Calvin's. After all, it was no secret in the industry that Zack Carr was the engine that drove the design room. "There is only one Calvin Klein," Carr snapped, "and I'm not him." Eventually, however, Carr did start his own concern, in the unlikely locale of Turin, Italy, in a joint venture with Gruppo GFT, the large Italian manufacturer, to design a signature collection of women's clothing. Although his star burned brightly at first, it burned quickly as well. The lines got rave reviews, but after three collections it was shut down. In December 1986 Carr requested that Gruppo GFT release him from his contractual obligations. By the summer of that year he was back in the United States, sitting in his West Eleventh Street apartment, thinking about Calvin Klein.

3

Of all Calvin's friends, nobody understood him like Chester.

Chester always said he knew Calvin better than his therapist. Kelly didn't mystify Chester at all. He knew exactly what Calvin was doing. Kelly was Calvin's future. A fork in the road had come in Calvin's life. While Chester had given himself over to the gay world and found his peace, Calvin had given himself over to the gay world and never really felt he belonged there. With men, there might be lust, but there was just not the same contentment Calvin found in a relationship with a woman. What's more, Calvin was keenly aware that changes were afoot in the world. A few years earlier it was considered chic to be bisexual; now AIDS was killing the chances of gay respectability. What was hip now were straight, aggressive, heterosexual businessmen with beautiful young second wives whom *Fortune* magazine dubbed "trophy wives." It was an ironic kind of respectability for Calvin, but that's what Chester thought Kelly held out to him. When he first met her, he thought, Oh, she looks exactly like a Ralph Lauren model. Nice, beautiful, but not talented.

Chester and Calvin's friendship had reached its ebb. Over the last few years Chester's role of mentor and confidant eroded, and

Steve Rubell and the Velvet Mafia had taken over the job. When Calvin had a problem to work out, he turned to David Geffen for advice. When he went out carousing at night, it was with Steve Rubell, and when he hopped on a jet plane at the drop of a hat, bound for exotic vacations, it was with David or Steve or Barry—not with Chester. Indeed, Chester was now a mere employee of Calvin Klein Industries. After Chester's latest venture, a sports-wear company, had failed, Calvin offered him a job designing for his casual-wear division. The job was a low point in Chester's career, "heartbreak," as his cousin Karen Mann called it. From designing for society belles under his own label to supervising the production of blue jeans for Calvin. He began to feel like Calvin's prisoner, totally indebted to him for his keep. Chester even had to borrow $115,000 from Calvin as a down payment on a co-op apartment that he wanted on West Twelfth Street in Greenwich Village, where he had recently moved with a handsome young lover, Patrick Lehman. At work, Calvin sometimes treated Chester cavalierly, once reducing him to tears by ripping apart a blouse he'd designed, scoffing that it would "look better torn." Soon after that incident, Chester bared his soul to a friend about Calvin. "I think he was madly in love with Calvin," said that friend. "He just *adored* Calvin. When I listened to the way he talked, I thought, Not only does he love him, but he is *in* love with him."

The same friend remembered a particular moment on Fire Island when Chester "violated a rule of behavior" in Calvin's eyes, deeply offending him. Just before Kelly appeared on the scene and the Fire Island house was still all stag, Chester brought a "trick," or virtual stranger, to Calvin's house as his weekend guest. Calvin was very warm and cordial to the young man, thinking it was a boy on whom Chester had a special crush. Sunday, after the boy was perfunctorily dismissed, Calvin was shocked to discover he was some anonymous pickup and became furious with Chester. "It could have been *anybody,*" Calvin complained later to a friend during Tea Dance at the Botel, "a murderer, a kidnapper—*anybody.*"

By the summer of 1984, having been expunged from Calvin's house, Chester took his own rental in the Pines. Calvin was too busy with Kelly and his new friends to notice that Chester seemed to sleep all summer. He slept late in the morning, took afternoon naps, and went to sleep early at night. Friends chalked it up to depression. But in October 1984, on a business trip to the Orient with other executives, it became apparent that Chester could barely keep his eyes open. He even brought a pillow with him on business appointments to catch quick naps in the backseats of taxis, and he once alarmed his traveling companions by falling asleep in the doorway of a Tokyo building. Back in New York, his weight began to ebb. The gym body vanished. He was always cold no matter how many clothes he wore, and suddenly he looked like a shrunken old man.

At New York University Hospital that fall, he was diagnosed with toxoplasmosis, a disease of the brain that is a primary symptom of full-blown AIDS. On November 8, Chester began intensive treatment with a combination of highly poisonous drugs. A month later, he returned gamely to the office, most of his hair gone, barely able to walk, "a whisper of himself," said one coworker.

Upstairs, behind the closed doors of Calvin's office, the anguish Calvin felt over Chester's illness could not have been greater than if he was his own flesh and blood. Chester having AIDS presented a nightmarish dilemma for Calvin. On the one hand, it crushed him that his stalwart friend and mentor was dying. It was bitterly ironic that after all the rumors that Calvin himself had AIDS, Chester was the one who got it.

On the other hand, it was lousy for business.

After all, half the jerks who didn't know any better thought *Chester was his lover.* Chester's dying was the last thing he needed right now; an employee highly associated with Calvin Klein in private and in the press *dying of AIDS.*

There was only one thing for Calvin to do: He fired him.

"He dismissed Chester as if he were the cleaning lady," said one former Calvin Klein executive. Chester was called into Calvin's office one morning, and when he tried to talk about the collection he was working on, Calvin cut him off. "Chester, look, we've got to talk about things," Calvin said. "This really just isn't working. For whatever reason, I just don't think you're performing the job that you need to. So I'm going to give you half your salary for six months, and you've really got to find something else."

Stunned, Chester stumbled back to his office, white as a ghost.

As it sank in, he began to cry uncontrollably. Only after the shock wore off was he able to compose himself. Before he left that day, he wrote a long letter to Calvin telling him how hurt and devastated he was, but Chester never mailed it.

Other voices have a different spin on this parting, even Chester's brother, Sydney Weinberg, who pointed out that Calvin sent a chauffeured car to take Chester to work after he got sick. "On some levels," said Weinberg, "Calvin tried to distance himself from Chester in terms of Chester's illness. I thought it was because Calvin couldn't deal with it, not because he was trying to shun Chester because he had AIDS. I think Calvin had a very hard time dealing with Chester's death. It's like any other member of your family that might die."

Whatever the motivation, Calvin was of little help. A few months later, after Chester had needle biopsies done on his brain to check the progress of the toxoplasmosis, he had a seizure at home, and Karen Mann rushed him to the hospital in a private ambulance. Unconscious and shuddering in petit mal fits, Chester lay on a gurney in the hallway of the emergency room for five hours waiting for a vacant room. In desperation, Karen Mann called Calvin's secretary at home and asked if she could use Calvin's name to help get Chester a room. Calvin wasn't in, but his secretary said, "Oh, just go ahead and do it."

Karen Mann went to the head of admitting and said, "Calvin Klein is Mr. Weinberg's good friend and employer, and I know he would appreciate it very much if you would take care of this." To her amazement, it worked. "They *did* it," she said. "They moved him up from eight on the list to first. I didn't think that would work in a hospital, I just didn't know what else to do." A few days later, when Chester was beginning to recover from this particular bout, Mann called Calvin from Chester's hospital room. When she told him that she used his name to get Chester a room, he said abruptly, "That's fine, if you have to do that, just feel free to do it."

Mann said, "I don't know that he liked it, but I didn't really care, either."

Calvin Klein didn't visit Chester in the hospital until the very end. It was a Sunday in April 1985, just around Easter, when Karen Mann got to the hospital and found him in the worst shape ever.

He was going blind, and it took him a long time to recognize her. In his lucid periods Chester repeatedly asked for Calvin, for news of him, when he would come. It was pitiful how desperate he was to know that Calvin cared. By the time Mann left the hospital, she was distraught. When she got home, she called Calvin at his apartment and was surprised when he picked up the phone.

"Chester doesn't know too many people anymore," Mann said, choking back tears. "I don't think he's going to know *me* much longer, so if you would like to see him and have him still know you, get yourself over there *right away*."

The following day, Chester's nurse told Karen Mann that Calvin Klein had showed up late the previous night to see his old pal. But when Mann asked her if Chester recognized Calvin, the nurse wasn't sure, and it bothered her that she would never know if Chester realized Calvin had come to visit.

Chester Weinberg died on Wednesday, April 24, 1985, at age fifty-four. The eve of his funeral, a few close friends were invited to attend a viewing at the Frank Campbell funeral parlor on Madison Avenue. It was late and crowded in the small parlor when Calvin showed up. "He was devastated," said Karen Mann, "and he was very tense."

Mann asked Calvin, "Do you want to go over and see Chester?"

Calvin nodded. The casket had been closed, but it was re-opened if friends wanted to say one last goodbye. When the lid was lifted by the attendant, the man in the box was virtually unrecognizable. Tears fell down Calvin's cheeks. "It's a good thing you called that night," he said. "I went to see Chester, and he knew me. We got the chance to say goodbye."

Chester's estate repaid Calvin the $115,000 he had loaned Chester to buy his apartment. Chester left no bequests to his brother or to his elderly mother and father, who contested the will. One of the many generous gifts Chester left behind, however, was a Rodin head he gave to Calvin. He had wisecracked when making up his will, "I'm going to leave Calvin the Rodin because he knows absolutely nothing about art."

Months later a memorial tribute was held for Chester at the Parsons School of Design, where he taught, and Calvin appeared to say some words about his late mentor. During his address, he delighted everyone by announcing that he was making a $100,000 endowment for a scholarship fund in Chester's name.

Chester had been dead a year when the fashion reporter for the *Washington Post*, discussing the way AIDS had decimated the fashion industry, asked Calvin, "How do you feel about the fact that people in your organization have died of it?"

"Nobody in my employ has died of it," Calvin said, and ended the interview.

4

It was not just Chester whom Calvin denied; it was the whole AIDS epidemic. It was an issue so thoroughly frightening to him that he could not confront it. For Calvin it was guilt by association. Denying AIDS was his strongest defense, and instead of fighting the disease, he became determined to distance himself from the death and dying. However, by the mid-eighties the gay community had risen like an assembled army in the face of an aggressor. Organizations like the Gay Men's Health Crisis (GMHC) in New York and God's Love We Deliver/Equity Cares were sprouting up all over America, one more desperate than the next for funding. But because AIDS at first seemed to affect only gays and minorities, the calls for help fell on many deaf ears.

So did the calls to Calvin.

To many close observers it didn't make sense. Friends of Calvin were dying right and left, including at least two of his houseboys, for whom GMHC provided care in their final months. Certainly, even if Calvin himself did not have AIDS, he had led a gay life, they reasoned. How could Calvin remain so aloof and removed in the face of this terrible crisis? Before long, gay activists like Larry Kramer, who helped found GMHC and later ACT UP, became outspokenly critical of Calvin. Said Rodger McFarlane, a founder of GMHC with Kramer, "Calvin was one of the first people we asked and asked most often for support. I was caring for many people around him, and he was bitterly ungenerous, vicious, and unresponsive."

In early 1986, a small group of concerned fashion leaders, including Donna Karan, decided to mount a huge fund-raiser for the American Foundation for AIDS Research (AmFAR), the groundbreaking research charity cofounded by Elizabeth Taylor, scientist-socialite Mathilde Krim, and businessman Jonathan Canno. Planned to take place at the mammoth Jacob Javits Convention Center on New York's West Side on April 29, 1986, "To Care Is to Cure," as they dubbed it, was touted to be one of the biggest fund-raisers ever held for AIDS. At the $150-a-person cocktail party the "World's Largest Photo Session" would be undertaken and include hundreds of fashion and movie stars photographed by Gordon Munro.

However, as the date of the event grew near, no fashion star stepped forward to participate, except for Donna Karan, who sent letters to all the big names in her field, including designers, photographers, and models—but few in the industry responded.

"What the event needed, quite clearly," said Sally Morrison, who was in charge of program development at AmFAR, "was Calvin Klein." The organizers felt that Calvin's endorsement of the event would ignite the dormant fuse. "But Calvin was resistant to our approaches for some time," said Morrison.

Two weeks before the event, hardly any tickets had been sold, and in desperation Mathilde Krim called David Geffen. Calvin's close friend had become an open and dedicated supporter of AIDS charities in Los Angeles and was proud of it. Krim explained the situation to Geffen and "asked him to intercede," she said. If Calvin would help, they had a surprise in store for him; he would personally escort Elizabeth Taylor to the event. Even an AIDS-phobic fashion designer couldn't resist *that* invitation. According to Krim, only an hour after asking for Geffen's help, Calvin Klein himself was on her phone asking, "What do you want me to do?"

Calvin not only agreed to cohost the evening with Elizabeth Taylor, but he underwrote the entire cost of the event so that all the money from the ticket sales would go directly to the foundation. The announcement of Calvin's sponsorship and generosity stunned the fashion community, which scrambled to fall in behind him. Among those who became sponsors included Bloomingdale's Marvin Traub, Peter Allen, Jeffrey Banks, Claudette Colbert, Brooke Shields, Gloria Steinem, Albert Nipon, Fabrice, and Mary

McFadden. By the day of the fund-raiser it had become one of the hottest charity tickets in the industry and because tickets were also being sold at the door of the Javits Center, several thousand supporters unexpectedly showed up at the last moment. Two hours after the event had begun, Elizabeth Taylor and Calvin Klein walked into the vast convention center, arm in arm. The sight of the two stars together caused such a commotion that the crowd and press began to stampede them, nearly knocking Elizabeth Taylor off her feet. As the mob grew in ferocity, a human circle of security police had to be formed around the frightened couple to prevent them from being trampled.

"To Care Is to Cure" grossed $300,000 for AmFAR, but for years to come it was one of the few times that Calvin lent his name and clout to the war against AIDS. From the way he continued to behave, AIDS had nothing to do with him.

CHAPTER SIXTEEN

It's much easier to get to the top than it is to stay there.

—Calvin Klein

O n a rainy Friday morning, September 26, 1986, a radiantly happy Kelly Rector, twenty-nine, married Calvin Klein, forty-three, in a quiet civil ceremony in the mayor's office of the historic Campidaglia City Hall in the Eternal City of Rome. After producing documents from the American embassy and paying a marriage fee of 40,000 lire, the couple were led into a spectacular marble chamber, designed in the mid-sixteenth century by Michelangelo. A luminous gray light penetrated the dusty beauty of the ancient room through its huge windows, and the lush poetry of the Italian ceremony gave the wedding a dreamlike effect. When the bride and groom turned to each other to say, "I do," there were tears in their eyes. "It was so-o-o romantic," Kelly said.

It was also very spur-of-the-moment, although the decision to get married had been talked about and analyzed at length. Conversations about marriage began the previous summer, but neither of them took it up as a cause. Ultimatums, even cajoling, would have wrecked their relationship. However, as time went by, Calvin became more convinced that he was truly bewitched by Kelly. He felt wonderful when they were together. And he believed she truly loved him, for himself. She had tremendous patience with him. She had seen him at his worst—drugged and stoned or a simpering nervous wreck before a show—and still she loved him and came back for more. She put up with the AIDS rumors and with the stories of his checkered sexual history and never complained. No, it wasn't a conventional arrangement, but in many ways they made an even deeper commitment to each other to make so delicate a situation work. Calvin later explained, "Our relationship is obviously not going to be about who does the dishes. It's far deeper than what most couples would experience. I believe in marriage and family, about the kind of love that makes you care more about someone else than yourself."

And she did love him selflessly. Of course, she was thrilled with his fame and fortune, but that's not why she loved him. She knew he needed her. She knew he could choose the pick of the litter, men and women, and he wanted her. In return, she understood that she must let Calvin be himself. However, she wasn't going to hang around forever. She was a determined spirit who longed to have a family and a home. She was giving her life up to him, and she wanted his ultimate commitment. The marriage conversation went on for over a year, into the summer of 1986, when Calvin and Kelly were overheard talking about a prenuptial agreement at Melon's, a Bridgehampton hamburger restaurant. Calvin had gently warned Kelly, "I have a lawyer; you should get one, too."

Then, in late September, they were both going to Italy on business together, and the idea came to them that they should elope. Explained Calvin, "We thought the best thing, since we had to be in Europe to work on fabrics, anyway, was to sneak off," pointing out that the decision to marry was so spontaneous that he didn't even think about buying wedding rings until he was on his way to the airport. "I ran into Tiffany's," Calvin recounted, "and I said, 'I've got to be out of here in five minutes.' I was trying to keep it quiet, you know, so [a Tiffany executive] took me upstairs, and in the elevator was [model] Cheryl Tiegs. 'Hi, Calvin,' she said. 'What are you doing here?'" Calvin thought, Oh, God! There goes the secret.

The secret held a little longer, at least until the Italian embassy, which had helped arrange the wedding, leaked the news to the local press shortly before the late-morning event. The scene outside the ancient stone building was a madhouse. Rows of carabinieri kept a hive of press and photographers at bay in a drizzling rain as they waited impatiently for the couple to emerge from the ceremony. When Kelly appeared on the marble steps leading out onto the large square, she was radiant, her cheeks flushed, a smile on her face. She wore an ivory double-breasted suit and bone-colored lace and silk top. Two strands of pearls circled her neck, and she clutched a pair of white kid gloves as she tripped through the rain next to her husband. Calvin wore a dark suit and striped tie, a gardenia in his lapel. Unfortunately, the groom was not having a good day, and he appeared bloated and lined from his alcohol consumption. They were accompanied by Kelly's co–design director, Melissa Huffin, and her Venetian boyfriend, Count Nuno Brandolini, who witnessed the marriage. As they all descended the steps of city hall, reporters shouted up to Kelly, "Who designed your outfit?"

She flashed a bright smile and said proudly and bell-clear, "Calvin Klein, of course!"

After a light wedding lunch at one of Rome's best restaurants, the newlyweds went on a sightseeing spree, holding hands in the backseat of a limousine. "We went to the Vatican and St. Peter's, and we saw every museum in three hours," Kelly said. The U.S. ambassador, who helped arrange the wedding, offered them the VIP suite at his palatial residence to spend their honeymoon night, and Kelly was thrilled. The next day as well was spent shopping and sightseeing in Rome, and on Sunday afternoon the couple rendezvoused in Como with members of Calvin's staff who were already ensconsed in the Villa d'Este, a luxurious hotel in a Renaissance villa at the edge of Lake Como. That night, Calvin's other staffers were invited to join the newlyweds in a celebratory dinner. There was much toasting and drinking and bonhomie that night. One dinner guest recalled, however, that no one quite knew how to behave around the couple, who tried to remain studiously casual about their formalized relationship.

When word flashed back to New York about the nuptials, W magazine dispatched a team of hairdressers, makeup artists, and stylists to the Villa d'Este, where Calvin, beaming, agreed to an interview and two-page photo layout. The handsome couple posed on a veranda, with haze-draped Lake Como behind them. All through the photo shoot and interview the couple were obviously longing for each other, restrained only by the reporters and cameras. "Kelly Klein," Calvin said, rolling the name over his tongue as if it were the most wonderful thing he ever heard. "Mrs. Calvin Klein." Kelly sat at her husband's side, said *W*, "searching his face for cues. He frets over her shyness. She quietly coaches him on where he has absently left papers and datebooks. . . . He touches the cashmere shawl thrown over her shoulder. 'It matches her eyes,' he says with pleasure. Unable to stop himself, he softly then touches her shoulder. 'Should I touch her?' he appeals to his guests decorously, wanting to."

"This relationship has totally changed my life," said Calvin. "I can't remember when I felt like this. I certainly am in love."

Kelly added, "I'm very happy. Calvin is a regular man, fun to be with. There is never a dull moment with him."

The story of Calvin's marriage hit the headlines of New York newspapers while the newlyweds were still in Europe. Flo Klein was stunned. "Flo hated it," said a family member. "She was hysterically angry. She liked Jayne." As far as Flo was concerned, he should live with the shiksa, but why marry her? Though Calvin's daughter, Marci, was also kept in the dark by her father about his forthcoming nuptials, she was philosophical about his decision, said a friend. "She wanted her father to be happy." Kelly's parents were equally as sanguine. "Kelly has always wanted a family," her father, Tully Rector, said. "She's that kind of girl." When someone who knew Calvin during his wild disco days asked Kelly's sister Amy, "What about Calvin's gay life?" Amy responded coolly, "There was no gay life."

After Kelly Rector became Mrs. Calvin Klein, there was a dramatic change in the office. Already a catty and gossipy place, the office now turned into a den of vengeful harpies. Many of her colleagues were resentful of her new authority, and it rang like a shot through the office when Kelly called from the airport the moment they returned from the wedding to tell an assistant she wanted her name changed on her stationery to "Kelly Klein." Since she was now a pipeline straight to Calvin, all the employees watched their every word around her, increasing the already unpleasant tension. Despite her low, politely hesitant voice, "when Kelly became Mrs. Klein she became your worst nightmare," said an executive, "this monster . . . this . . . demanding princess, very aggressive . . . and rude to people. It was very difficult, and nobody wanted to work." She developed a kind of proprietary sassiness around the office. One of Calvin's chauffeurs claims she once playfully pinched him in the behind as she walked by him in a narrow hallway in the office.

Being Calvin's wife gave Kelly immunity from all but Calvin himself. Calvin had a sharp word for almost everybody in the office, including Kelly. "For the most part she would say nothing, but sometimes you could see that she'd almost want to cry," remembered a coworker.

"Well, what do *you* know about this?" Calvin goaded Kelly in front of a roomful of people when he disagreed with her opinion at a design meeting. Kelly looked as if she wanted the floor to open up and swallow her. On another occasion, when Kelly mentioned to Calvin in front of a group of staff members that she wanted to buy a certain coat she had admired in a store window, he snapped, "God forbid if I didn't have the money!" and Kelly visibly recoiled. One time, Kelly bit her lip and held back tears when a business associate mentioned to Calvin how beautiful he thought Kelly was, and Calvin responded offhandedly, "Well, she's beautiful, but she does have wide hips."

As the weeks went by, it became clear that it would be best for all concerned if Kelly wasn't around Calvin day and night, and the decision was made to keep her as a wife but let her go as a design director. In November 1986, two months after their marriage, Kelly left the company. She was hardly relegated to the position of hausfrau, however. She was quickly snatched up by *House & Garden* magazine as an editor. Some wags found it amusing that her first assignment for the magazine was to do an article about closets.

Kelly's immediate replacement at Calvin's was the talented fashion director of British *Vogue*, Grace Coddington, who assumed the title "director of design." Coddington brought in three primary assistants, each brilliant in his own right: Stephen Slowik, Edward Wilkerson, and a gifted upstart with big ideas named Isaac Mizrahi. However, Calvin was rude and unreceptive to Coddington's young design team, and although Coddington was a genius at magazines, she was a novice in the garment center. It was next to impossible to please Calvin, whose moods seemed to swing as frequently as he changed his mind. Her brief reign at Calvin's company was unremarkable and lackluster, and one collection featured many taffeta floral prints, which staffers called the "Shower Curtain Collection" behind Calvin's back.

Calvin longed for the days of Zack Carr, and now, with Kelly out of the way at the office, maybe it was possible. Coincidentally, Carr was feeling the same way about Calvin. After his venture in Italy had folded, he remained unemployed, and he wasn't surprised—or disappointed—when the phone rang one day and it was Calvin offering him his job back. Zack Carr has happily worked for Calvin ever since, remaining the master's primary surrogate in the design room.

2

While Kelly's presence might have been expunged from the design room, her influence in Calvin's personal life could not be denied. A new Calvin began to emerge, his final metamorphosis into married landed gentry. Gone almost overnight was the collegiate look of Top-Siders and T-shirts and jeans, replaced with a more elegant British style of bespoke Savile Row shirts and suits and suspenders to hold up his pants. It also became clear that it was uncomfortable and inappropriate for Kelly to spend time in the Fire Island Pines, surrounded by the memories of her husband's old flames. Thus, the "gay houses" in the Pines and Key West were sold, and Calvin and Kelly began to rent houses in various hamlets in the monied, manicured, old-guard summer enclave of East Hampton. While Calvin got close to $1 million for his house in the Pines from an American Express executive, he was so anxious to unload his Key West hideaway that he took a huge loss. He had paid $975,000 for the house but put it on the market for $750,000 and finally unloaded it for $400,000. (Years later, David Geffen had such longing for *le temps passe* that in 1991 he bought Calvin's former Fire Island house from its new owner.)

The *New York Post* noted coyly that "it was a four-legged creature that led Calvin to sell his houses on Fire Island and Key West . . . the horse his wife, Kelly Rector, keeps in the Hamptons." Calvin explained the shift in location of his vacation home by saying, "Kelly rides all the time. She rode in the Southampton Classic last summer. . . . We had been spending the summers in the Hamptons for a few years, and we never used the other houses, so . . ."

The Hamptons are a series of pristine beach communties a hundred miles from Manhattan along the south fork of Long Island. Gatsbyesque in its grandness and splendor, for years only artists, poets, and the Waspy patrician names of great wealth like the Astors and Vanderbilts and Morgans summered there in "beach cottages"—rambling thirty-room mansions set on the dunes behind a mile of dark green lawns. Bordered by ponds and bays on one side and endless stretches of beaches and the Atlantic Ocean on the other, the legendary quality of light bouncing off the water brought some of the century's great artists to work there, including William Merritt Chase, Willem de Kooning, and Jackson Pollack. But in the seventies and eighties came an influx of New York's wealthy yuppies, stockbrokers and lawyers, fashion moguls, and Hollywood directors and stars. The seven primary hamlets had become a seasonal beehive of social activity, the newest stage on which nouvelle society would parade itself. Calvin had wanted to buy a home in the Hamptons, but he wanted a showplace, no easy task in a sea of mansions and beach houses. Each year they rented a different gorgeous home; once, a sprawling, gray-shingled New England house on a duck pond in Wainscott and in another year a five-bedroom cottage in the estate area of Georgica, tucked away from sight down a quarter-mile drive of privet. There was one summer season when the man who owned the house, hearing Calvin Klein wanted to rent it, upped his price from $75,000 to over six figures. Calvin didn't even flinch, because Kelly liked the house so much. In summers and autumn, the couple made East Hampton their second home, and he loved it so much that instead of going back into Manhattan, he commuted to the office in his new toy, the company's $5 million Gulfstream jet, outfitted in English walnut and roomy beige leather armchairs and with its own private stewardess, or a seaplane that would deposit him near Georgica Pond, not far from home. Kelly stabled two horses in the Hamptons at the world-famous Topping Riding Club, where she rode almost daily in a corral overlooking the fields and ocean, and Calvin began to try to share his wife's interests by taking riding lessons. They were seen in restaurants with other upstanding couples, like James and Linda Robinson, the CEO of American Express and his wife, or billionaire Revlon owner Ronald Perelman and his wife, gossip queen Claudia Cohen.

The honeymoon lasted longer than most. Calvin loved being married, loved having that other person to shower with attention, and he couldn't stop himself from lavishing on Kelly a series of romantically beautiful gifts. He secretly located her aging horse, Fur Balloon, the one she had been forced to sell as a child, and surprised her with him one day at a stable. They boarded him to live out his life contentedly at the farm north of New York that Barry had acquired for his thoroughbreds. At Christmas, Calvin gave Kelly a full-length fur coat. He refurbished her antique Volkswagen Beatle as a surprise and bought her a Nikon camera so she could study photography. Perhaps the most unusual present was Calvin's thirtieth birthday gift to her of model Christie Brinkley's former million-dollar Central Park West apartment, just a few blocks north of his own. Albeit a generous gift, people smirked that the couple still lived separately, reinforcing the perception their marriage was an arrangement, an *amour blanc*. Calvin added fuel to the speculation when he confided to a reporter, "It's not a good time to talk about the way I live, because we're living in limbo. . . . I mean, Kelly has an apartment. I have an apartment."

Calvin's present apartment was in actuality an elaborate one-bedroom, not big enough for the two of them. Kelly's apartment was only a trifle larger. Calvin wanted to buy one of the most fantastic and unique apartments in New York city, the triplex in the south tower of the fortresslike San Remo building farther north on Central Park West, with its commanding 360-degree view of the city. Calvin had offered music business impresario Robert Stigwood $6.5 million for the co-op, in a building whose other tenants included Dustin Hoffman, Diane Keaton, and Bruce Willis. But the San Remo co-op board didn't want Calvin and Kelly and turned them down. Too much publicity, it was said. "They were afraid of wild parties," claimed one resident. Calvin and Kelly had the distinction of being the first couple the board turned down since Madonna and Sean Penn.

And so they lived apart, their chauffeured limousine each night depositing Kelly Klein on her doorstep and then delivering Calvin Klein to his, where he could be left to his own devices.

3

By 1986, Calvin Klein was at war with Maurice Bidermann and the menswear division. The discord was ironic, however, because the menswear line had turned into a certified hit, one with which most designers would be deliriously happy. Grosses topped out at around $100 million a year wholesale, paying a very handsome royalty to Calvin.

But Bidermann did something for which Calvin would never forgive him: He signed a contract with Ralph Lauren to manufacture a line of women's sportswear—in direct competition with Calvin's bread-and-butter line. And Bidermann didn't even have the courtesy to tell him about it. The evening before the Lauren deal was announced, Calvin and Barry had drinks with Zelnick. The new business venture was never mentioned, although it would be all over the next morning's trade papers. As far as Calvin was concerned, he had been deliberately double-crossed. "Calvin sure didn't like it," Michel Zelnick said. "He got very pissed." Calvin was so angry with Zelnick that he returned the Frenchman's Christmas gift, an antique Japanese book, with the wrapping paper intact.

Calvin's cooperation in the menswear line seemed to wane as his anger with Bidermann increased. "He became much more of a pain in the neck," said Zelnick. "In the beginning Calvin was probably more involved [in the design] than not," said Zelnick. "Then he became less involved, and then he became totally negative. . . . We couldn't get approvals. We couldn't get him to sign off on anything. Suddenly, whatever we were proposing to him was wrong. . . . It became very, very complicated."

There was something else wrong, the executives at Bidermann believed. "All one would know," said one executive, "is that Calvin's moods would go up and down, and he could go from being incredibly pleasant to being an absolute monster." One Bidermann executive, who pointed out that there was a strictly enforced antidrug policy at their company, remembered, "His mood would swing. He wouldn't arrive for meetings, or he would be late. He'd cancel. This happened again and again."

In fact, Calvin's menswear line changed its point of view dramatically over the years, moving from its original Americanized European style in 1984 to a silhouette that looked so much like Giorgio Armani that when the Italian designer saw Calvin's suits in the window of Saks Fifth Avenue, he remarked, "I didn't know I had windows at Saks." Lately, the look had swung to Calvin's new fashion image, that of a very proper British gentleman—peaked lapels and intricately textured Donegal tweed suits with natural shoulders. The *New York Times* reported, "One gets the feeling Mr. Klein spent hours studying those 1930's Cecil Beaton photographs of Gary Cooper." More probably the influence was Kelly's, who encouraged Calvin's three-hour shopping trips to London on the Concorde to have his clothes made at Anderson and Sheppard. Bidermann executives worried that Calvin's fleeting infatuations with different influences would hurt revenues.

What was hurting revenues, Calvin contended, was that Bidermann was making and selling his suits far too cheaply, for around $400, while an Armani suit was priced at almost double that. But Bidermann didn't want to raise the price or make better-quality suits; his money was made on volume. Bidermann didn't care to spend the money to deliver the impeccable quality Calvin wanted, and just as Calvin anticipated, myriad manufacturing problems developed. The sportswear, for instance, which Calvin expected would be manufactured in Hong Kong, was instead manufactured in Singapore, where there was a much lower quality of workmanship. The suit-and-pants line was made in a Bidermann-owned factory in the south of France, and according to Bidermann menswear designer Don Robbie, "Everything was glue, not stitches, everything was fused. It just had a cheap, dumpy, clunky look to it." On one occasion, Stanley Kohlenberg bent over at a public relations meeting and split his Bidermann-manufactured pants up the back. "Barry nearly had a hemorrhage," said Kohlenberg. "I had to take my clothes off and have the seams closed. It was the worst manufactured stuff in the world."

Calvin also claimed that he would approve one fabric and then

the garment would be manufactured in a cheaper fabric. Allen
Tucker, who was president of the men's sportswear division, remembered, "I would show Calvin a suit, and he would like it, and I
would take it back to Bidermann, and they would say, 'Buy something cheaper and don't tell Calvin about it.' Calvin would see the
suit Bidermann produced and go crazy. He knew he hadn't approved that quality."

Zelnick disputes this practice. "As a rule, no," said Zelnick,
"what we showed him was what we made."

The retail sales figures seemed to reflect the growing problems.
Gross wholesale sales bottomed out at $60 million, and Calvin's
menswear boutique at Bloomingdale's was made smaller and
moved near the elevators "because the clothes weren't selling," reported the *New York Times*. Soon, according to Calvin and others,
Bidermann was shipping the goods to unapproved accounts to keep
up grosses. "He was dumping the Calvin Klein label inventory in
some not-so-desirable locations [like the discount store SYMS],"
said one menswear executive, "which in itself could break the license. . . . It was Bidermann law [to unload returns on discoun-
ters]. You had X amount of inventory at the end of the season—you
better get rid of it."

"Towards the end," said Zelnick, "Calvin would say he didn't
have the time to see our designers. But everything was presented to
one of his assistants for approval." By 1985 and 1986 the tension
was so great that Bidermann hired a liaison, a young designer
named Harold Streitman, who, while his title was design director
of Calvin Klein menswear, spent much of his time trying to recon-
cile the sparring camps. Streitman was walking on eggs. Calvin
would say, "I want you to make all these sweaters in Italy. They
should be fine needle, they should be beautiful, and I want you to
use this twill." Streitman would know that the twill Calvin wanted
was four times more expensive than the yarn Bidermann was prepared to use, and when the sweaters were made and sent back to
Calvin, he would hit the roof. "I *hate* this," he'd shriek. "Why are
they doing it this way? It's *cheap!* I disapproved this last year. Why
are they doing this?"

It got to a point where "Calvin had a legal secretary in his office,"
claimed Streitman. "If I was showing him this stripe [for a polo

shirt], I had a form that was dated, that said what the stripe was, my comments, his comments, and 'approved' or 'not approved.' See, I could show . . . this stripe for the quality, [or] . . . for the color, [or] . . . I could just show it for the setting and stripe. Calvin would say, 'Well, Harold, I like the navy, [but] I think the stripes are a little too narrow, and I don't like the quality at all.' " Then Streitman would go back to Bidermann and report what Calvin had said. "Bidermann would say, 'Tough shit, because we just bought six zillion yards of this shit, and that's what we're making the polo shirt out of. . . . " Streitman would return to Calvin and plead that there were production commitments already in place for the fabric, and Calvin would say, "Fuck the production commitments."

At an impasse, an inevitable lawsuit ensued. In the spring of 1986, Calvin hired renowned litigation attorney Arthur Liman to bring the issue to arbitration. Bidermann countersued, claiming that Calvin was depriving him of his services and interfering with his business. "But it wasn't a question of the lawsuit," contended Zelnick. "It was a question of Calvin wanting to get his license back. Just like with Puritan. He saw that when he was making a buck a pair on the jeans, Puritan was making two bucks. He said, 'Why should they make two bucks? It's my name.' "

In April 1987, the pending arbitration was settled by terminating the licensing agreement with Bidermann and purchasing the existing inventory and related businesses for an aggregate $13.6 million. Barry and Calvin immediately forked out $11.4 million in cash, and additional payments totaling $2.2 million were made the first of each month from June 1987 to April of 1988. In the spring of 1987, Calvin unveiled plans to begin manufacturing his own line of menswear, in-house, and began to hire a design staff to work on it. But there was little time and even less money to implement the plan, and by the middle of June, Calvin announced that he was abandoning the idea of reopening his menswear line and fired his newly hired staff. Even as the stunned employees were clearing out their desks, Calvin was telling *Women's Wear Daily*, "There is no men's company. One day we will be in the mens' business. When I intend on going into the business, I'll make an announcement."

4

At the same time the Bidermann lawsuit was raging, the arbitration between Calvin and Barry and Minnetonka's Robert Taylor dragged on for two years. "Do you think Barry and Calvin liked us?" Taylor asked, "They *hated* us. I knew that if I sued my licenser, life was not going to be a bed of roses. But it wasn't a bed of roses, anyway." Nevertheless, throughout the arbitration, Taylor was determined to stick to the terms of the deal, which allowed him to create a new Calvin Klein fragrance. Taylor believed unequivocally that the right fragrance would pump more cash than a field of oil wells. He hired as consultants two industry veterans, Alice McKnight and Jean Kirksey, who were running a small, mostly mail order company called Cosmetique from offices at 9 West Fifty-seventh Street, which Taylor took over. His first order of business was to try to close the cosmetics line, which never really took off, and revive the original scent by giving some of Calvin's famous pizzazz to the advertising. Second, he would introduce a new men's fragrance, simply called "calvin," with a small "c," in late 1980.

A grueling nightmare ensued. It was beginning to dawn on Taylor at this point that it was really Calvin who ran the show. "Barry is completely a tool of Calvin," Taylor claimed. Calvin makes *every single decision and uses Barry like a whipping boy.* . . . This partnership bullshit is not, in fact, true. Calvin ran the show lock, stock, and barrel. . . . We would sit with him like little children and be whipped and just be humiliated, like he was so good at doing. . . ." On one occasion, Taylor presented Calvin with an idea for the advertising campaign for the new men's cologne, an illustration of a woman in a wheelbarrow which was pushed by a muscular man in overalls with "a bit of a gay look to him," said Taylor. The woman was ecstatically pouring a huge, unmistakably seminal drop of perfume onto herself. When Taylor first unveiled the illustration at a meeting, everyone stared at it for a second and then turned to look at Calvin for his reaction. "I could just see the blood come up," said Taylor.

Calvin roared, "Never. Never would I do that." He told Taylor that the chairman of a company should have better things to do with his time then meddle with advertising.

Of course, the advertising campaign that Calvin chose was far more provocative than any woman in a wheelbarrow. Calvin promised to "shock the world" with the campaign, and he pretty much succeeded. Even *Advertising Age* said, "The designer's latest fragrance ads may go too far." The ad in question was a gauzy photograph featuring a tautly muscled man wearing only white jockey shorts. He is lying on his right side in bed, his face hidden in a swirl of sheets, with his right leg bent forward so that his buttocks stick into the air. A woman with a masculine haircut is pressed across him, the nipples of her bare, round breasts hidden in the nape of his back. There was no copy, no hard sell, just Calvin's name, with the product line in subdued type underneath. But sex alone could not sell. The old scent was a loser, and the women's and men's fragrances limped along, grossing $7 million a year and losing $2 million in the bargain.

On October 27, 1983, the arbitration board handed down a decision in favor of Taylor and Minnetonka. According to the decision, not only didn't he owe Barry and Calvin a red cent; they owed *him* $668,352. The two of them were fit to be tied, but they had no choice but to hand over the money. The day the arbitration decision was handed down, Taylor went to see Barry in person to "bury the hatchet." He told him, "We're your fragrance licenser and we're trying to build the business. I need you as a partner if we're going to make it a success. Let's shake and be friends." Barry shook hands with Taylor that day, but he warned that Calvin would not be so forgiving, and just as he predicted, Calvin said he would personally have nothing further to do with anyone who had sued him.

With maddening impertubability, Calvin maintained that if Taylor wanted to build the business, it was his legal right and contractually Calvin would not stand in the way. In order to help things move forward, Taylor would simply have to find a new president for Calvin Klein Cosmetics who could be a liaison between them.

Alice McKnight and Jean Kirksey resigned their posts at Calvin Klein Cosmetics even as Taylor ran through a list of likely candidates who might find favor with Calvin. One night, having a drink at the Plaza Hotel, a long shot came to him. There was a fast-rising executive named Robin Burns who was the cosmetics division merchandise manager for all Bloomingdale's stores. She was involved

in the launch of Calvin's men's fragrance, and Taylor remembered
one meeting in particular at which Burns "made people want to do
things rather than force them," said Taylor. Burns was also an attractive young woman with a good figure and great sense of personal style—just the kind of handsome young career woman Calvin
liked to surround himself with. She was born in the old gold-min-
ing town of Cripple Creek, Colorado, and she worked her way
through Syracuse University on partial scholarship, shored up by a
job as a waitress. She joined Bloomingdale's in 1974 and quickly
worked her way from a fabric buyer to her current title. She was
such a tiger, said one colleague, that "I think her fingernails grew
an inch an hour."

When Taylor suggested to Burns that she become president of
Calvin Klein Cosmetics, her eyes widened, and she said, "You must
be kidding me." It took Taylor three months to convince her. "I
thought he was out of his mind," said Burns. "I was just thirty. I
kept saying to myself, 'What's the worst that could happen? I could
go back to retailing.' I believed the company couldn't get any worse
but also that the Calvin Klein name was magic."

When Calvin discovered that Taylor had hired a thirty-year-old
department-store executive as president of his cosmetics company
without consulting him, he swore he wouldn't even consider meeting with Burns. The young woman doggedly called his office for an
appointment for two and a half months without a return call. She
even asked Marvin Traub, president of Bloomingdale's, to intervene and implore Calvin to meet with her. But Calvin would not
hear of it. "It's not that easy with me," he said haughtily. "Even
Marvin [Traub] said it was hard to believe that Robin would have
gone to the company without meeting me first."

Running out of avenues to pursue, Burns had a brainstorm. She
called the office and invited Kelly Rector, then still Calvin's assistant, out to lunch with her to explain her dilemma. Calvin wasn't
fond of this idea, but Kelly wanted to meet with Burns, and Calvin
began to grudgingly respect the young executive's determination.
Over lunch, Burns outlined a marketing plan for Kelly. She wanted
Calvin to develop a new, sexy, in-your-face perfume, something
very strong and distinct, hate it or leave it. And she wanted him to
devise an overtly sexual but tasteful advertising campaign to go

with it. Burns had already talked Taylor into putting up major dollars for the campaign. By the end of lunch, Kelly was impressed enough to endorse a meeting with Calvin, who reluctantly agreed to give her an audience in his office.

As much as Calvin was ready to hate Robin Burns, from the moment she opened her mouth, he decided she had an almost telepathic understanding of him and his market. "I would say something, and she'd get it," Calvin enthused to the amazement of executives who hadn't heard such compliments pass his lips in years. "She's very bright, and suddenly I realized I was working with someone who was on the same wavelength as me. We got past the hard stuff right away. Everything is so intelligent and well thought out. . . . She always says the right thing to everybody. She's really an extraordinary woman."

With Calvin's blessings, Robin Burns's first task was to develop the sexy new scent she had envisioned. Set for a March 1985 launch, this time Calvin didn't meddle in the choice of the scent. Instead, Burns hired *parfumier* consultant Ann Gottlieb, one of the best-known "noses" in the business, to help concoct the odor. Gottlieb asked three different fragrance companies to submit samples, but only one of the scents, a burst of exotic flowers made by the firm of Rourge-Bertram Du Pont, was immediately right. In the jargon of *Women's Wear Daily*'s fragrance expert, the long-lingering scent's "top notes blend mandarin, bergamot and a subtle green note with jasmine, rose and orange blossoms. The mid notes are a blend of spices of coriander, taget, and armoise, and the base is a warm amber mingled with oakmoss."

The bottle was designed by the noted French packaging designer Pierre Dinand, who was invited to Calvin's apartment to gain inspiration from Calvin's personal collection of oval *objets*. Calvin wanted a design with no hard edges and a "good feel." The final product was a stubby, clear crystal bottle with a thick, amber-colored stopper. Because the perfume itself was a dark amber color, the shapely bottles showed the fragrance like liquid gold. It cost almost as much as gold too. Packaged in an ivory box with indigo type, it would sell for $170 an ounce—and $30 for an ounce of cologne. The men's scent, which would follow later, had a pricey tag of $35 for its top-of-the-line cologne.

One of the most crucial elements, as always, was choosing the perfect name for the new perfume to convey its sexual essence. Robin Burns was away on vacation, fishing in the Rocky Mountains, when she called Taylor to say, "I've got it! I know what the name is. Climax!" But Calvin hated that name and the images it conjured. Then Taylor's wife, Mary Kay, made up a list of her own favorite names, and at the top of the list was "Obsession." Calvin resisted this name at first, but after talking about it with his staff, he tentatively agreed. It was only a slight hitch that the name had already been copyrighted by a fragrance company called Nestlé LeMur and wasn't available to use. Taylor bought the name from Nestlé LeMur for only $10,000, telling them that he wanted to use it for a bubble bath for Minnetonka.

While Robin Burns remembered that the gestation of the perfume was "like having a baby," Taylor felt as if he were getting an ulcer. Calvin chose Bruce Weber to shoot the Obsession print ad in Alcapulco, for which Taylor had to cough up $50,000 for one print. It was an extraordinary print, however. Tastefully erotic, the blue sepia-toned photograph showed several naked bodies confusingly swirled together in a hot tub. The viewer had to pause and study the picture to discern that the occupants were two men entwined around a single female, the finger of the woman poised at the lips of one man about to nibble on it. "It's a passionate and sensuous photograph which says if a woman wears Obsession, men will be totally obsessed," explained Calvin. A later ad featured a naked couple in the middle of a deep forest, standing up on a swing facing each other, their groins pressed together. The sepia-toned ads for the men's fragrance, also shot by Bruce Weber, featured three naked women, limbs entangled, the print distressed by scratches. "The scratch marks," explained Calvin, "could imply that a man has torn this out of a magazine and hidden it in his coat." For the Obsession body-lotion ads, Weber captured a chiseled male model kissing the bare midriff of a naked woman, her breast pressed into the side of his face. When 24,000 consumers were asked what the most memorable advertisements of the year were, Calvin Klein's Obsession ads ranked number one, and he would stay number one for four years in a row.

Calvin went back to the team that had created his jeans commercials—director Richard Avedon and writer Doon Arbus—to come up with the concept for his TV campaign. It fell to Robert Taylor to negotiate the price. Avedon told Taylor that he had a great idea for the TV spots but that it would cost Taylor $100,000 just for Avedon to tell him what it was. "One hundred thousand dollars for me just to *hear* the idea?" Taylor humphed. "I'm a country boy from Minneapolis, and I don't quite understand that. How much is it going to cost me to *own* it?" Avedon said it would cost another $100,000 to own it, plus probably $1 million to film the idea, which Nestor Alemendros, the famous cinematographer of such feature films as *Days of Heaven* and *Kramer vs. Kramer* would shoot for them. Moreover, Avedon wanted to fly in Shakespearean actors from Great Britain. At first, Taylor was aghast at the cost and refused. But Calvin insisted that Avedon and Arbus were crucial to the campaign, and with the encouragement of Robin Burns he took a deep breath and okayed the budget.

Four different TV commercials were made featuring the exotic South African model José Borain, whom Calvin signed to an exclusive contract. The series of surreal vignettes drew the viewer into a diffuse white limbo, with recurring Daliesque motifs and sparse set pieces reminiscent of the villa of some rich, decadent clan. José Borain dances and swirls through the commercials, the object of impassioned, obsessive love by four other characters: a young beautiful boy, a young man who cries, a troubled older man, and an older woman. In each of the spots she implores, "Save me!" to these people, who respond with heated phrases: "She was a fever from which I'll never recover." . . . "Love is child's play once you've known obsession." . . . "Once she had devoured my very soul, she abandoned me." . . . "Between Love and madness lies Obsession." At the end of each spot, an anguished voice cries, "Oh, the smell of it!" The campaign had a haunting ambiguity, with its implications that a prepubescent boy or an older woman each would be obsessed with the same beautiful young woman. The commercial Avedon made the following year for the men's version of Obsession was no less intriguing. In the single black-and-white commercial, a neurasthenic actor from Iceland stands trial in disjointed limbo backgrounds before a variety of judges, including José Borain. In his final defense, he says, "I rest my case . . . If living with Obsession is a sin, let me be guilty."

Calvin kept the women's commercials under wraps, even from

Robin Burns and Robert Taylor, who were both sent copies to view on the same day. When Taylor played his copy on his office VCR, he screamed aloud, "Ahhhhh! These are the best fucking commercials I've ever seen! I absolutely love it! I don't understand it, but I love it."

As the momentum grew, Taylor gave the fragrance one of the most spectacular launches in the annals of the perfume business. Over $17 million was poured into the advertising and marketing budget in the first ten months alone, with the TV ads in saturation schedules in twenty-seven markets across America. The print ad caused a sensation when it appeared in fashion magazines, and when Obsession for Men was released, another $6 million was poured into the budget, which included thirty million scented magazine strips. The woman's launch was accompanied by an unprecedented series of in-store, personal promotions by Calvin himself, something he had balked at doing for other licensees. But this time he had Robin Burns to go on the road with him. "I reluctantly [agreed] to make appearances," Calvin said. "I'm always frightened no one will come to see me. But Robin has a wonderful way with people, and she calmed me down."

The fragrance burst into the field as one of the biggest sellers on the market. "Obsession's sales run wild," burbled *Women's Wear Daily*'s page 1 headline. "Calvin Klein's newest . . . fragrance shows signs of becoming a national Obsession. Clearly the launch of the year." The first day, it sold $7,000 worth at Bloomingdale's, and after one week, the store reordered $90,000, then the next week placed a second reorder, "substantially larger than the first," said Onute Miller, the fine-fragrance buyer.

By the end of its first year on sale, Obsession's *wholesale* income would top $30 million, outselling popular standards like Joy three times over. Robin Burns was rewarded with a dramatic salary increase into the mid-six figures, and her office was moved out of the cramped Fifty-seventh Street space and into spacious quarters in the Fifth Avenue splendor of Trump Tower. It was also Robin Burns who Calvin insisted accept the award when the Fragrance Foundation honored Obsession as the "best women's prestige fragrance introduction of the year." The impact of Obsession on Bob Taylor's Minnetonka company was just as uplifting. "Instead of breaking even," said Taylor, "we made three million dollars." Analysts expected the value of the company to grow over 200 percent every year for the *next five years*, and signs were that they wouldn't be disappointed.

By 1986, along with Obsession for Men and a line of body products, sales soared to $74 million and by 1987 broke $100 million, making Obsession the second-bestselling fragrance in the world, right behind Giorgio.

5

"We were never late with our royalty check," said Robert Taylor. "We were paying him seven million dollars in royalties, straight, no expenses."

However, the income from the fragrance was hardly enough to cover the debt of Calvin Klein Industries. Calvin and Barry had encumbered themselves with mind-numbing obligations to swallow up Puritan Fashions, and slowly but surely the market for its one big asset—blue jeans—practically evaporated. The public had already tired of high-ticket designer blue jeans and was returning to the standard brands of Levi's and Lees. "After Calvin and Barry bought Puritan," said a banker they consulted in the period, "the whole denim market went to hell. They bought the company during an era when ladies were wearing their mink coats and their blue jeans walking up and down Park Avenue, almost going to lunch at Le Cirque in them, and suddenly the world changed, and people stopped wearing their blue jeans." In 1984, for the first time, Calvin Klein Industries, pulled down by losses in the Puritan/Sport division, suffered a pretax loss of over $11 million, even though Calvin and Barry were still pulling down $12 million a year in salaries. But they were dancing in the eye of the hurricane. Over at Manufacturer Hanover's headquarters, an alarm signal went up that the Puritan/Sport division was in financial trouble, and according to sources at Manufacturers Hanover, the bank sold "a piece" of the loan to Chemical Bank. "Chemical put it in the 'workout' group," said the source, "which means it may require restructuring or foreclosure." One day, out of the blue, "Calvin and Barry got a call from a guy at Chemical saying, 'I'm your new account officer,' and that was the first they knew [the loan] had been sold." Reportedly, the new loan officer was "panicky" about the loan.

Barry and Calvin needed money—a lot of it, and fast. They considered, for a moment, taking the company public, only to recoil when their advisers quoted a total price far less than they expected. One night, over dinner, Calvin poured his heart out to his friend Barry Diller. Then still chairman of Paramount Pictures, Diller's tight-fisted financial acumen was becoming legendary in the film industry, and his financial influence had begun to reach far beyond Hollywood. Diller had previous business connections to Drexel Burnham Lambert, the Wall Street company making a name for itself in the flotation of "junk bonds," and within days Calvin was meeting with the new grand sorcerer of corporate America, Drexel's junk-bond guru Michael Milken.

Driven by a monkish fanaticism, the Queens-born, thirty-eight-year-old financial wizard put in twenty-hour days arranging private placements of "high yield" bonds for companies. Naturally, investors who bought these bonds, so risky they were dubbed "junk," would demand a sizable reward, in the form of interest rates typically 4 percent above those on bank loans or bonds that had the blessing of Wall Street's fusty credit-rating agencies. With junk bonds, principal repayments could be postponed for several years, supposedly freeing up the company's cash flow to take care of the staggering interest.

In March 1985, under Mike Milken's auspices, Calvin and Barry attended the first of three Drexel High Yield Bond Conferences, or the "Predators' Balls," as these conventions jocularly came to be known, at the Beverly Hilton Hotel. This annual financial jamboree mingled two groups of Milken clients: those issuing junk bonds and potential investors or "predators"—financiers and bankers from all over the world looking to make a killing in companies desperate for cash. "It was an opportunity for Calvin to meet with a lot of people who would be selling his bonds," said a Drexel executive, "and it was an opportunity for him to meet with some of the prospective buyers over lunch or dinner." The first morning of the conference, opening ceremonies were held in the ballroom of the Beverly Hilton Hotel, emceed by Mike Milken before an audience of fifteen hundred financiers, bankers, their wives, girlfriends, and assorted hookers. Milken announced that the combined buying power of his audience equaled 3 *trillion dollars*. On the black-tie-only closing night of the festivities, the same audience was treated to a private performance by Diana Ross, who, for the finale, perched on the lap of one of Calvin's potential investors, insurance magnate Carl Lindner, and sang to him.

Both at the Predators' Ball and after it was over, Barry and Calvin appeared at a series of Drexel-arranged presentations, or "road shows," at which the partners proved themselves master salesmen. "He knows his business," a Drexel official said admiringly of Calvin after hearing Calvin sell his company's potential. But even better than being impressed by his knowledge, being sold junk bonds by Calvin was like being wooed by a movie star. "The first time I met Calvin," recalled a CenTrust executive, "I spent two hours in his office talking with him, and he was charming. The next time I was there, I met Calvin and Barry, who were going to do a presentation to potential bondholders, and Calvin came over to me and said, 'Are you married? Does your wife wear Calvin Klein?' I said, 'No, my wife is only five feet,' and he said, 'The next time you come to New York, have your wife come to my showroom and we'll give you the best price.' "

Robert Taylor also saw Barry and Calvin in action at the Predators' Ball three years in a row. "One of Mike Milken's provisions," said Taylor, "was that [Barry and Calvin] had to stand up in one of the conference rooms and give a presentation on how they got the money from Mike and how good [Drexel] was to them and what they did with the money and how successful they were. . . . But in the meantime they weren't doing well. The business was headed south. They were losing money, and they were scrambling to cover their asses."

Participants remember that it was Calvin, not Barry, who haggled in the fall of 1985 over the final interest rates that the bonds would pay. "He started at the "very, very skinny end of what was possible," recalled the Drexel executive accompanying Calvin on the road, who came away thinking, This is a very, very, very bright businessman. Eventually, Drexel issued a prospectus for $80 million in high-interest bonds. There were two issues of notes, one series priced at $45 million, with eight-year terms and a 13⅞ percent interest rate, the other at $25 million in ten-year notes at 14⅝ percent. David Paul's Floridian savings and loan bank, CenTrust, bought the lion's share, investing $20 million. Other investors included Dort Cameron's Bass Investment Limited Partnership for $15 million, Carl Lindner and the Great American Insurance Company for $5 million, and Guy Dove III's Atlantic Capital Corporation for $4 million. Mike Milken himself walked away with $3.3 million for his efforts, and Calvin and Barry were so grateful to Barry Diller for making the initial introductions that Barry Schwartz named a prize colt after him, "Killer Diller," who won $461,000 in purses.

Calvin and Barry gleefully repaid the banks. Instead of having to make stiff principal payments to Manufacturers Hanover Trust, their new bonds required interest payments only for the first five years. "This is a chance for us to breathe," Barry said.

Not for long, however. Over the next few years, Barry and Calvin would go back to the well of junk bonds, adding considerable additional debt to an already faltering company.

6

Market research in the fragrance industry held that while oriental fragrances, like Obsession, made up a majority of the market, many women still would not wear a scent unless it was flowery, and by having only one kind of perfume, Calvin was missing out on a huge slice of his potential market. Thus, after the success of Obsession, a second, floral scent went into production, planned for release in the spring of 1988. This particular floral, however, would not be for old ladies. It would also be "distinctive and modern," promised Robin Burns. The same team that developed Obsession was assembled, including top "nose" Ann Gottlieb to help choose the scent, Pierre Dinand to design the hand-polished, rectangular crystal bottle, Bruce Weber to photograph the print ad, and Richard Avedon to produce the TV commercials. Developed by International Flavors and Fragrances (IF&F), the perfume was a blend of all white flowers—freesia, white lily, and muguet, underlined by bottom notes of narcissus and sandalwood—and would retail at $175 an ounce.

This time around, however, not only would the perfume be distinctively different from Obsession, but so would the message. "Spirituality . . . love . . . marriage . . . commitment," said Calvin. "I think that is a feeling that is happening all across the country."

He explained, "I'm thinking about love, and I'm thinking about . . . what Obsession represents . . . [and] that kind of advertising is the exact opposite of what I want to do now. I want something completely different, something softer, something much more romantic, much subtler. . . . I'm projecting where America will be, what people will be thinking in the next five years. So I tried to think, What's happened after the sexual revolution? After all, with AIDS, with people now being afraid of having sex with a lot of people, [people are] thinking about romance and thinking about commitment."

The idea solidified when Calvin bought Kelly perhaps his most lavish and romantic of all gifts, $1.4 million worth of jewels from the estate of the duchess of Windsor, including a $1.25 million pear-shaped necklace and a set of pearl earrings the size of marbles, one white, one black. "The duchess was the first one to [deliberately] wear mismatched earrings," said Calvin. But most poignant of all was a gold-and-diamond friendship ring that King Edward VIII of England gave Wallis Simpson when he decided to abdicate his throne for the woman he loved. Calvin said the ring epitomized the strength of his devotion to Kelly. She wore the ring on her pinkie, because the duchess had such narrow fingers. Up until now, Kelly and Calvin had sported only the temporary gold wedding bands which Calvin had bought at Tiffany on his way to Italy.

"Everybody talked about the fact that I bought her the pearls and that I bought her the earrings," said Calvin, "and I loved the way Kelly looked in these things, but as I was going through this catalog, I saw this ring. I thought it was an absolutely beautiful ring. It was an eternity ring. Well, in England an eternity ring is before the engagement ring, and it means 'forever.' I thought, My God, I've got the next name. I've got the whole idea for the next perfume. It all makes so much sense." Robin Burns, however, claimed that it was Barry who came up with the name "Eternity" after bidding on the ring for Calvin at the Sotheby auction in Geneva, Switzerland. Whoever thought of the name first, "We all went crazy," said Burns. "Eternity takes us into the late eighties and is very consistent with what's going on in Calvin's life."

Again, it turned out that another company had already trademarked the name Eternity, this time the cosmetics giant Coty. Robert Taylor paid them $25,000 for the rights, which was only a nibble at the $18 million launch budget. Calvin himself chose blond supermodel Christy Turlington as his Eternity girl. "I love you so much, I would marry you," he told Turlington, "but I already got married. So I want you to be the girl for my new fragrance. Just do me a favor. Don't break me." Turlington squeezed a $3 million contract out of Calvin for eighty days' work a year. She would become the exclusive face of Eternity.

In June the first advertising was scheduled to break with a four-panel magazine insert of a product shot taken by Irving Penn, printed on paper that mimicked Eternity's own pale white packaging. In June and August there would also be 14 million scented strips inserted, along with an order form. The Bruce Weber print ads, which were scheduled to begin appearing in magazines in September, featured a diffusely lighted couple, this time fully clothed, sometimes pictured with their children, often hugging or reclining in romantic rather than erotic poses. Complete photographic portfolios of the Weber series running as long as ten pages were scheduled for prestige magazines, and ten different thirty-second TV spots were filmed, again under the helm of Richard Avedon. The TV commercials, set to break the second week of September, also featured a young couple, Christy Turlington and actor Lambert Wilson, whom Kelly chose for the spots, explaining, "He's got a great nose." The series of ads "tell a story about love," said Robin Burns. Equally as fascinating to watch as Calvin's previous commercials, if less compelling, these take the viewer through the trials and tribulations of romance—fighting, reconciling, parenthood—each commercial color-tinted according to its mood; cool blue, warm red, steely white. In each, love triumphs eternal. The only slightly controversial hieroglyphic in the series comes when Lambert Wilson asks a supine Christy Turlington, "Would you still love me if I were a woman?" and Turlington responds languidly, "Forever, if I could always be your man."

Robin Burns had developed a unique marketing strategy for the launch, officially set for April 6, when Calvin Klein would make a personal appearance at Saks Fifth Avenue's flagship store. After that, Burns had decided, the perfume would only be sold at Saks Fifth Avenue stores in Manhattan and Southampton, presumably driving the rest of the country wild until, in September, it would be released nationally in seven hundred stores. It was an encouraging sign that when the fragrance was first set out and displayed at Saks counters in Manhattan two weeks prior to the launch date, eighteen hundred bottles were sold without any publicity.

As the release date drew near, an accompanying media campaign was also mounted. This vast undertaking was to include a series of important one-on-one interviews with the press by Calvin himself, including rare television appearances.

The pressure mounted as the launch date grew near, when—suddenly—all of Calvin's interviews with the press were called off. Business appointments as well were canceled or put on hold.

Calvin "wasn't available," his office responded to hundreds of calls. Calvin couldn't see anyone. Calvin was away on vacation, said the publicity department.

Everyone kept wondering, Why would he go away on vacation a month before the launch? Why had Calvin disappeared?

In the blink of an eye, the huge rumor machine was cranked up to full gear, and the gossip was all over Seventh Avenue and the media. Only this time it was no rumor, they said. His time had finally come. Calvin Klein, they said, was dying of AIDS.

CHAPTER SEVENTEEN

I'm in the first year of my second life. I feel reborn.
—Calvin Klein

Calvin wasn't dying. He had gone to save his own life.

On April 27, 1988, feeling more miserable than he could ever remember, the forty-six-year-old designer flew to Minneapolis–St. Paul International Airport, where he was told to wait by luggage carousel 14 for a representative of the Hanley Hazelden Center at St. Mary's for Alcohol and Drug Rehabilitation to come meet him. He was then driven by station wagon forty-five minutes to Center City, Minnesota, and onto the six hundred-acre "campus" of Hazelden, which looked for all the world like a small college nestled by the serene Center Lake, often referred to by patients as "Lake Librium." For the next thirty-one days, it was as if Calvin had disappeared from the face of the earth.

Psychiatrists say that societal drug use of mood-altering substances is cyclical and that in the early phases of the decline period of the cycle, when the use of recreational drugs first begins to be considered outré, it is always the people with the most to lose who give up drugs first. And Calvin had a lot to lose. For over three or four years his cocaine use was wildly out of control, often turning into binges of days in length, the ragged coke high mollified by vodka and Valium. He was so dependent on cocaine that on a trip to England to inaugurate his first British Calvin Klein boutique on fashionable South Moulton Street, the first chore he assigned one of the staff was to find him a gram of cocaine so that he could bear to attend the opening. On his way out to the Hamptons, he was sometimes so strung out that he had to stop at a friend's house on the way for a reviving toot.

While most of Calvin's inebriated periods were confined to private moments, his overindulgence began to cause him public embarrassment. On September 16, 1986, at a charity event in behalf of the restoration of the Pulitzer Fountain in Manhattan's Grand Army Plaza, Calvin drank an entire bottle of Stolichnaya vodka, and everybody at his table noticed. And that same year, on a business trip to Paris with Kelly and several of his staff members, he got flamboyantly drunk in front of the whole party. "In Paris he drank straight vodkas before we went out," said a participant, "and he got mean if we didn't join him. He drank his dinner that night while Kelly picked food off his plate as well as her own. She loved to eat, and he loved to drink." After dinner, he insisted on going dancing. Tactfully, Kelly made her apologies and went back to the hotel. Calvin and the rest of the group went off to a chic Parisian night spot, Les Bains Douches. At first, the doorman didn't recognize Calvin and wouldn't let him and his party inside. Calvin turned loudly indignant, insisting, "I'm *Calvin Klein!*," until the manager recognized him. Once inside the club, Calvin stumbled among the tables, staring at people. After he grew bored with this, he gathered his group to move on to the next hot spot. "He just kept wanting to go out to clubs," said a staffer, "and we were exhausted, and he was high as a kite, so he was having a good time."

Sometimes there was a stiff price to pay for being drunk. At a Washington, D.C., benefit held by the Washington Fashion Group, Calvin joined dignitaries from the business and political establishment for a black-tie dinner followed by an auction. "Calvin got quite blotto," said one participant from the Washington Fashion Group. "It was most unpleasant." He got so drunk he didn't seem to realize when he bid $50,000 on a Hermès horse saddle for Kelly and later denied it. "Calvin *did* bid fifty thousand on the saddle," said one man who was there, "and then there was a scuffle afterwards because he claimed he had bid *fifteen* thousand." Eventually, however, Calvin coughed up the dough. "He was sort of shamed into paying the fifty," the man said.

Perhaps the most chilling story of his abuse comes from a close associate of Donald Trump's. In the winter of 1987, Calvin and

Kelly rented Lilly Pulitzer Rousseau's Palm Beach house for three months—just a few blocks away from Donald Trump's spacious compound, Mar-a-Largo. Calvin wasn't fond of the formal and rigid town of Palm Beach, but Kelly liked to ride at the Palm Beach Polo Club. One freezing cold winter night in New York, Donald Trump was awakened by a call on his private line from Calvin Klein, says Trump's close associate, "screaming and ranting and raving like a lunatic." Calvin was saying, "I don't know what's happening, but people are coming at me from all directions and they have guns and submachine guns, and it's really a very serious situation. Could you help me?"

According to the associate of Trump's, the developer assumed Calvin was "pretty fucked up at the time with drugs." Trump persuaded Calvin to give him the address where he was staying and then called trusted aides at his own estate. "[Donald's people] went over and found Calvin, who was totally drugged out and fucked up," said the intimate of Trump's, "and they took very good care of him." The Trump aides avoided taking him to the hospital, fearing reporters would get wind of the episode. Instead, they stayed with him until the morning, and he calmed down.

People were afraid to confront Calvin about his drug use. "In a lot of ways," said Zack Carr, "I thought that Calvin was indestructible. It was difficult for me to see Calvin in any kind of pain, so that I was really always trying to comfort him. Sometimes the comfort really should have had . . . more discipline . . . someone to say, 'No, I don't think you should do this anymore. Let's stop this, it's not good for your health, it's just not good.' " But, explained Carr, "we were in a time where nobody was saying no to anything. To say yes to everything is what was supposed to be done. It was [considered] damn wrong to say no. Well, it was stupid. There were [people] that did think they were indestructible. They could stay up all day, all night, they could have sex in every way imaginable, and they could still work and produce and do everything."

Kelly Klein's beautiful life was turning into a hell. She was a prisoner of Calvin's illness. It was like Christopher Maytag all over again, but this time with much higher stakes; Kelly was in love with Calvin. She understood the self-recrimination, the impossible, tortured quest for perfection that made him turn to drugs and alcohol in the first place. Only now enough was enough. He was turning into a tyrant, and she found herself half frantic not to do anything that might offend him, literally trembling in the face of his anger. Her father, Tully Rector, said, "Kelly told me she wanted to see him 'nip it in the bud.' He had a lot to lose. He didn't want to lose control of his business—and my daughter."

Kelly didn't exactly lay down the law to him, but in his sober moments she made it clear that his drinking and drugging had become the biggest problem of his life. He was hardly in denial about his disease by now, and he balefully agreed that the time had come to stop. Believing all it took was willpower, Calvin quit all his indulgences at once and went on the proverbial wagon. But without support, even the iron will of a superman was powerless over addiction to drugs and alcohol.

In the end, it was Barry Schwartz, not Kelly, who forced a showdown. One day in April 1988, Barry and Calvin had a long talk about his problems, and carefully stopping short of an outright ultimatum, Barry pointed out that Calvin's substance abuse was hurting not only his mind and body but threatened the welfare of the company. Calvin agreed to find help.

The hardest moment was when Calvin decided he had to tell Flo and Leo that he was seeking treatment, fearing that otherwise they would read about it first in the newspapers. He drove to his parents' Riverdale apartment to see them. "He was high" when he got there, an intimate recalled. "Coke, a little alcohol, and I don't know what else. You know, coke was his choice of drug. This was just before he went to Hazelden. And he was desperate, the poor kid was . . . he *knew* he was going downhill, he *knew* he was in big, big, trouble. . . ." Calvin told his mother he needed to lie down, and she brought him a blanket and covered him on the living-room sofa.

"Mom, I feel *so* sick," he told her. Said the intimate, "He didn't confide in her that it was drugs until . . . I think it was the next morning."

In late April of 1988, with the encouragement of Hazelden graduate Liza Minnelli, Calvin made arrangements to enter the midwestern clinic, the granddaddy of all rehabs and the model upon which the Betty Ford Center in Rancho Mirage, California, was based. Hazelden's thirty-day program cost about $5,500 at that time, and it was racking up a list of celebrated alumni, including reportedly Kitty Dukakis, the wife of Democratic presidential candidate Michael Dukakis; William Hurt; Sharon Gless; and various sports stars, airline pilots, physicians, plumbers, and priests. The program was totally anonymous, and many of the patients at Hazelden were so famous that they used fictitious names or went by their initials.

Calvin was immediately admitted into Ignatia Hall, the detox building where all patients stay for initial assessment and observation. A few days later, he was transferred to one of the four men's units, where he would live and bond with twenty-two "peers." This was no easy feat for Calvin, who had to shed his mantle of superstar and admit he was in the same fix as everyone else on his unit in order to begin the recovery process. He was also assigned a case manager–counselor to see him through his introspective odyssey. In this rigorous, disciplined program, the patients attended lectures on drug and alcoholism in the three-hundred-seat Bigelow auditorium three times a day. The program also stressed medical, psychological, and spiritual development and promoted meditation as a stress-reducing technique. There were also individual and group therapy sessions with psychologists as well as motivation therapy. Although Calvin completed only a monthlong program, frequently a stay at the main facility is followed by a period of several months in a halfway house. Some patients are also treated for a common coaddiction to drugs and alcohol: sex addiction.

Meanwhile, back in Manhattan, Calvin Klein was missing in action, and the AIDS rumors were reaching pandemic proportions again. Calvin's publicity department's insistence that "he's away on vacation" was like waving a red flag. It didn't make sense. Why would he suddenly cancel all his important Eternity interviews to go on vacation? Eventually, Steve Rubell began to blab to friends that Calvin was in rehab and, before long, news leaked to the press. Notified at the center that his office could no longer contain the news, Calvin decided it was best to get it out in the open in a press release. One company executive said, "It was the stylish thing to do."

It was also the bravest. It was terrifying and embarrassing for someone with Calvin's pride and ego to announce publicly that he was an addict and an alcoholic. Although he probably didn't realize it at the time, his admission was inspiring to others. His public statement read in part, "A little less than two weeks ago, I checked into the Hazelden Foundation in Center City, Minnesota, for treatment of alcohol and prescribed drug abuse. I imagine that for almost anyone going through something like this, it would be a private matter. In my situation, I feel compelled to make this public statement because of the many friends and colleagues who've supported my work over the years. Finally, I wish to say that I have never felt better, and I look forward to the completion of the program at the end of May."

"Nothing Came Between Drink, Drugs and Calvin Klein—Until His Wife Rode to the Rescue," screamed the tabloid *Star* in a full-page headline. The *New York Post* offered "Calvin Klein's Obsession—Pills and Booze: Fashion kingpin cleaning up act in rehab center." But perhaps the most provocative reporting came from William Norwich, the *New York Daily News* society columnist. "Calvin Klein Has Designs on Sobriety" read the headline. The columnist went on to say that the "forty-six-year-old billionaire" had checked himself into a rehabilitation center. "But news of his stay at Hazelden also has stirred a gossip mill that has always turned heavily on the subject of the celebrated designer," wrote Norwich. "This includes the open nature of his marriage. . . . According to friends, Calvin and Kelly have never completely nested in the same abode, ostensibly because they've never been able to find the right spot. Kelly still maintains a residence in an apartment on the upper West Side that had belonged to Christie Brinkley before she married Billy Joel. Klein lives in a West Side triplex."

This public evaluation of their separate living quarters greatly upset Kelly Klein, and two days later, syndicated *Daily News* columnist Liz Smith, the grande dame of columnists and a respected voice of reason, took her colleague Norwich to the woodshed. In a column headlined "Gossip Standards Are on the De-Klein," Smith chided a "cheeky" Norwich for his "gratuitous speculation" in questioning the open nature of the marriage. "What is served by putting such in print?" Smith demanded. "As soon as Calvin and Kelly had a problem [his addiction] and openly announced it, they got this other load of stuff thrown on them. . . . It appears Mrs. Grundy still thrives, and she is racist, sexist, homophobic, mean-spirited, hypocritical and petty. Of course, I admit I haven't seen the Kleins in flagrante delicto (nor do I want to). It is enough for me to know how upset and disturbed Kelly is by these stories. . . . Let's just say I know Calvin and Kelly a lot better than Mr. Billy does, and I think they're one of the most loving, caring and devoted of twosomes. They honestly seem to be proud of and concerned for each other. They are real friends. . . ."

Without further bother from the press, Calvin completed his stay at Hazelden on Friday, May 27, 1988, and left with a thirty-day "clean and sober" medallion in his pocket and hope in his heart for the first time in a long while. The medallion was with him that weekend as he sat in the audience at Brown University on May 30, and proudly watched his daughter, Marci, graduate from the Ivy League school—proud for Marci and proud for himself. Calvin, who continues to follow a twelve-step program, has remained clean and sober ever since, one day at a time.

2

There was a sad footnote to that Memorial Day weekend when Calvin left Hazelden.

His old friend and supporter, Eve Orton, died by her own hand. Calvin and Eve had drifted apart fifteen years before. She always believed that when Calvin "turned gay," as she put it, he was embarrassed by it and shied away from seeing her. "He almost turned his back completely on her, and it hurt her very much," said one of Eve's dearest friends. In truth, he let his friendship with Eve lapse not only because he had moved beyond needing her help in the fashion world but because of her constant kvetching, which had earned her the nickname of "Contessa de la Complaint."

For a time, Eve had become the *directrice* of the Valentino boutique in Manhattan, but over the years her health began to decline, and when Calvin bumped into her at a fashion-industry gathering, she looked old and frail. "Soon after that," said Eve's friend, "clothing and a watch arrived at the apartment as gifts from Calvin, and he called her up to edit the next collection before he showed it." But Eve was unsure of herself and gently turned him down.

As time passed, she had run out of money and worried constantly about her bills. In December 1986, for the first time, Eve Orton was not deemed important enough to be invited to Diana Vreeland's annual costume show at the Metropolitan Museum of Art, and that night she tried to kill herself with an overdose of sleeping pills. When word raced around the museum's Temple of Dendur, where the gala dinner was being held, a covey of Eve's old friends jumped into their limousines and sped the few blocks over to Lenox Hill Hospital, where Giorgio Sant'Angelo, June Weir, Nancy White, and Sally Kirkland sat vigil by her all night. When she came to eight days later, her left leg was permanantly paralyzed. Calvin sent flowers but never came to see her again.

In 1988, the day after Calvin was released from Hazelden, Eve Orton was found dead in her apartment from a second overdose of sleeping pills, alone and forgotten.

3

Robin Burns had a joke about Calvin's rehabilitation at Hazelden: "I hope that it does for Eternity," she said, "what Elizabeth Taylor in the Betty Ford Clinic did for Passion."

For Calvin, it wasn't so funny. On June 6, just a scant week after his release from Hazelden, he was scheduled for his first public appearance at Saks Fifth Avenue to help promote the launch of Eternity. Amid suspense and almost presidential security precautions, Calvin descended on an escalator onto the crowded main floor of Saks wearing a khaki poplin suit, red tie, and penny loafers, looking apprehensive but tanned and healthy. He was surrounded by security men, guns bulging under their navy blazers, while dozens of his own employees milled through the throng of over four hundred people waiting to see him, including fourteen reporters from publications all over the world. The mob seemed to just gape at him as he stepped onto a gray-marble platform and made a short speech. "I hope I get a chance to meet you all," he mumbled shyly, and then quickly sat down behind a table to sign autographs for customers. The press, meanwhile, was forbidden questions and was kept at bay from the designer behind velvet ropes. When a few of the fourth estate had the audacity to shout questions to him about his stay in Hazelden, Calvin pretended he had an ear problem and couldn't hear. Finally, a persistent United Press International reporter waited in line with the customers. When she got up close to Calvin, one of his public relations men stood in her way. "What about the new morality?" she yelled. Calvin said awkwardly, "I'd need a press conference to do that one." Calvin finished his autographing and was whisked away.

At least Robin Burns was right. The publicity attending Calvin's rehabilitation focused international attention on his new perfume. It was as if his fragrances had begun to symbolize the chapters in his unfolding life story, and the public was captivated. Eternity had the largest initial sales of any fragrance in the history of Saks Fifth Avenue, including any of Calvin's other scents, and by the end of its first year, it grossed $35 million—and was growing.

Back in the office, when Calvin first got out of Hazelden, "He was a very different person," said one staff member. "It didn't last very long, but it was very impressive. He spoke to people for the first time. I thought this man had miraculously turned around his personality. He was lovely. He actually thanked Zack and I swear Zack almost dropped over."

There were also other, more portentous changes evident. Now that he didn't need a drug den in which to get high, Calvin and Kelly were going to live together full-time. Calvin sold his Central Park West bachelor apartment to his friend David Geffen and bought the former "Gucci mansion" on East Seventy-sixth Street for $7 million. This handsome limestone town house, which the Gucci leathergoods family had bought in 1979 for $750,000, was a deep, five-story building with its own elevator. Since the front door faced the street, the couple felt insecure enough in their new abode to hire round-the-clock shifts of armed security guards for protection. The house was classic and formal in design, with a grand staircase lined with a Persian runner, rising from an entrance hallway that was dominated by a black granite sculpture of a hard, lean male torso. There was a spacious wood-paneled library, and the third-floor master bedroom had a wood-burning fireplace. In the living room, which overlooked Seventy-sixth Street, two brown leather sofas faced each other across an antique coffee table which was neatly stacked with oversized photography books by Bruce Weber and Georgia O'Keeffe. Calvin's favorite artist was also represented in the living room by a beautiful Stieglitz photograph of her as a young woman, which leaned against a standing easel. The furnishings were a mixture of contemporary and antique, and in keeping with Calvin's taste, hardly anything had any rough texture or sharp color. The house was kept so clean, it was almost antiseptic. There was a butler, two housekeepers, alternating cooks, and a full-time laundress who washed and ironed Calvin's shirts by hand (never starched, steam-ironed only). Even Calvin's closet had a fanatical orderliness to it, with the shirts and pants, grouped by color, spaced exactly one inch apart on hangers. Across from Calvin and Kelly's bedroom, there was a large room, originally meant to be a second bedroom or nursery. But it was completely empty except for a large, blown-up photograph of Calvin leaning up against the wall, looking handsome and suntanned, wearing jeans and white socks, and sitting on his bed in Fire Island.

Although rumors continued to persist that Kelly kept a secret, separate apartment, the couple actually lived together in the East Seventy-Sixth Street town house. However, it was too big for them, and a few years later, when Calvin's cash flow tightened dramatically, the Gucci mansion was put on the market and sold. Calvin and Kelly moved instead into the $1 million Central Park West apartment Calvin had given Kelly as a gift. This stylish, prewar, two-bedroom duplex overlooked the Tavern on the Green restaurant, where the tree limbs are gaily wrapped with thousands of feet of sparkling white lights, like a faerie garden. On the first floor of the apartment there is a living room and dining room as well as a substantial kitchen. On the second floor there are two bedrooms, but one was so small that it was converted into a massive closet to house the couple's extensive wardrobes. And so, with great compromise, Calvin and Kelly were finally sharing their lives together completely.

4

Not all of Calvin's relationships improved with his newfound sobriety. It is a staple of recovery that the alcoholic and addict must avoid "people, places, and things" associated with drugs and alcohol, and Steve Rubell signified all three to Calvin Klein. Rubell was Calvin's chief enabler and mischief maker. Calvin's entire relationship with Rubell was about the pursuit of sex or drugs. Yet Calvin could not bring himself to cut Rubell off altogether. He had watched in sincere admiration as Rubell resurrected himself from the ashes of a tax-cheating jailbird to one of the foremost hoteliers in the world, with a personal worth of more than $200 million. His nightclub, the Palladium, was raking in $10 million a year alone. He and Ian Schrager had recently bought the huge, run-down Barbizon Hotel on Lexington Avenue for $50 million as well as a condominium apartment building on Central Park West for $90 million, with intentions to renovate both into luxury buildings. At the same time, they were already busy redoing the old Paramount Hotel on West Forty-seventh Street at a cost of $30 million. With bankers competing to lend them money, the partners had bought themselves a $2 million summer house in Southampton. Although Rubell was a frequent visitor to Calvin's East Hampton home, the closeness never resumed. Rubell blamed the distance on Kelly. "Gay—it's an empty life," he said. "Everybody gay is getting married."

But it wasn't Kelly who kept Rubell away; it was the drugs. An intimate of Steve Rubell's explained, "Steve had a big problem he didn't want to deal with, and people were dealing with their problems and facing up to things. I don't know if Steve could really cope with that. And I don't think he could cope with his huge drug problem. And it's difficult when you look around and you see your friends dealing with it."

The long-term effects of Rubell's abuse of his body were obvious just to look at him. While preparing for the opening of Morgan's Hotel and the Palladium, he suddenly lost all of his hair, and there was a sallow tinge to his skin. Most people assumed that he either had AIDS or some form of cancer and that he was undergoing radiation therapy, but over the years Rubell maintained that it was just

a nervous condition. His friends smiled and nodded sympatheti-
cally and went away believing what they wanted. The truth was that
not only did he really have a nervous disorder; he was also suffering
from chronic hepatitis, and by the summer of 1989 he was a very
sick man. He was battered by a bad case of bronchitis, and nau-
seous all the time, he even eschewed his usual diet of colas and
junk food. In early July, diagnosed with a recurrence of hepatitis,
he went out to his Southampton house to rest. But he never
seemed to get any better, and on Saturday, July 22, he went back to
Manhattan to consult with the doctor again. This time he was diagnosed with a severe peptic ulcer, and that day, practically coerced
by his brother and Ian Schrager, Rubell checked into Beth Israel
Hospital. By that evening, his kidneys began to fail, and septic
shock set in as he drifted into a coma. On Tuesday, Schrager said,
"everything that could go wrong went wrong. It was irreversible."
He died Tuesday night, July 25, 1989, of hepatitis and septic shock
without ever regaining consciousness.

Still, many people continued to speculate that those causes were
only the side effects of HIV infection. Perhaps the greatest irony in
Steve Rubell's sad story is that, according to insiders and intimates,
it was *not* AIDS that lead to his death but the years of drug abuse
that sucked his body dry. "He just couldn't stop," said a friend, "he
was *so* lonely."

On a hot July morning police barricades were set up outside the
Riverside Memorial Chapel on Amsterdam Avenue in Manhattan,
with a red velvet rope to hold back uninvited mourners. A loud-
speaker system had been erected in the street so that the expected
overflow crowd could hear the service. But people didn't turn out
for a funeral as they did for a discotheque, and a surprisingly mod-
erate number filled the pews, Calvin and Kelly prominent among
them, as well as Donald Trump, Bianca Jagger, and author Carl
Bernstein. Calvin sat stone-faced in the audience as Steve Rubell's
brother, Don, told the mourners, "Steve always said he could talk
to a lamppost. What he didn't know was that afterwards it would
feel better than any lamppost on the block."

When the services were over, Calvin walked outside with Kelly.
He stopped for a moment on the sidewalk under the marquee of
the funeral parlor and, unable to contain himself, broke down and

sobbed in front of photographers. His picture appeared in the next day's papers, holding his head in his hand as he wept.

That was not the end of Calvin's grief that summer. The following month, Giorgio Sant'Angelo died.

Calvin and Giorgio had not been close for many years. Giorgio had a temper as fiery as his creativity, and eventually Calvin's boorishness provoked his anger. The breach began years before over Calvin's behavior at a Lena Horne concert. Horne had long been Giorgio's biggest and most important private customer. When things were tough financially for Giorgio, the singing star would sometimes order dozens of garments in different colors just to help him out. Giorgio was also frequently backstage at her New York performances, helping the diva into the stage outfits he designed for her. It was to one of those appearances, at the Westbury Music Fair in Long Island, that Giorgio invited Calvin and their mutual friend Marina Schiano. According to Giorgio, Calvin spent the entire performance criticizing and ridiculing Horne. Giorgio was so infuriated by Calvin's mockery that at the end of the show he rushed outside and jumped into his limousine, stranding Calvin in Westbury, thirty miles from New York, without a way home. "I'm finally finished with Calvin," Giorgio announced.

"I don't think he talked to Calvin for a very long time after that," said Martin Price, Giorgio's friend. Then, in 1987, Giorgio suffered an aneurysm of the heart, which doctors attributed to his smoking of unfiltered cigarettes since he was eleven years old. Later that year, it was discovered that he had lung cancer as well. According to some intimates, doctors believed that the poisonous spray called paraquat, which the U.S. government sprays on marijuana crops as a deterrent to growers and smokers, caused the cancer in Giorgio's lungs. Several long hospitalizations followed his diagnosis, during which Giorgio needed constant care and round-the-clock nurses, depleting his cash reserves. When Calvin heard how sick Giorgio was, he offered his old friend the use of his Key West beach house in which to recuperate, but Giorgio demurred. What he needed was an infusion of money to help him stay alive. Giorgio was at first too proud to ask his millionaire friend for it, but he was convinced by mutual acquaintances that Calvin would help him. It was a painful moment when, in June 1989, Giorgio asked Calvin to come

to his Park Avenue apartment. Calvin arrived in his English bespoke suit, now the picture of landed gentry. Calvin and Giorgio sat
at opposite ends of the sofa while Giorgio swallowed his pride and
explained that he was badly in need of $25,000 to keep his head
above water.

Martin Price, who was sitting on a chaise longue across the
room, remembered the tense silence that followed. "Calvin never
said the word 'no,' " said Price.

Instead, he suggested, "Don't you think that you can ask all of
your clients for an advance on your collections?"

Giorgio had a blank expression as he said, "That has already been
looked into, and it was not possible."

Calvin changed the topic of conversation before he excused himself and left. Giorgio got up from the sofa, walked into the bathroom, and began to comb his hair. Martin Price followed him and
stood in the doorway in silence for a time before asking, "How
about *that?*"

"Disappointing," Giorgio said in his clipped accent, "very disappointing."

Giorgio never spoke Calvin Klein's name again. He was not,
however, without the aid and comfort of his friends. According to
Martin Price, heiress Doris Duke and jewelry designer Elsa Peretti
saw to it that Giorgio wanted for nothing in his final months and
that he felt comfortable and secure. "They were brilliant, brilliant,
brilliant," said Price.

Giorgio died on Tuesday, August 29, 1989, at St. Luke's–Roosevelt hospital, three months after asking Calvin for money. Calvin
phoned once, "at the very, very, *very* end," said Price, but by then
Giorgio was too sick to take the call. "It was too late." At Giorgio's
funeral, Calvin made a point of giving Price his condolences.
"Giorgio really loved you," Price said.

And Calvin answered, "I loved him as well."

The old guard was all dead—Eve Orton, the baron, Chester
Weinberg, Giorgio, and Steve Rubell—but a new life awaited
Calvin.

5

Over the years, as the sales of their perfumes drove up the value of Minnetonka stock, Calvin and Barry cannily began to buy up shares themselves, both privately and through their Puritan/Calvin Klein Sport division, until by 1989, they owned $59 million worth, nearly *double* Robert Taylor's stake of 7 percent. When the quantity of Barry and Calvin's combined stock rose beyond 5 percent of Minnetonka's total, they were obligated to file disclosure statements with the Security and Exchange Commission, a practice the partners found abhorrent, since it let everybody in on the details of their finances. Indeed, nestled within these disclosures was a paragraph that stated Calvin Klein Industries might seek control of Minnetonka Inc., although Barry scoffed at the idea, characterizing it as "standard boilerplate to keep his options open."

"Fat chance!" Taylor cried at the thought of Barry and Calvin taking over his company. "Give me a break. What are they going to buy it with?" Taylor contended that Calvin and Barry were already leveraged to the teeth by their Drexel bond deal and could never muster the cash for a takeover. Nevertheless, the financial press made much of this option, speculating that Calvin and Barry would try to wrest control of Minnetonka from Taylor, just as they had claimed Puritan from the Rosens. The rumors persisted until April 1989, when Barry and Calvin announced they were transferring their personal holdings in Minnetonka to the Calvin Klein Sport division, signaling the beginning of a chess play.

Taylor promptly shocked Calvin and Barry to the core by announcing that Minnetonka was up for sale to the highest bidder. This would foil their takeover bid, he figured, if only because of their greed; if Taylor sold Minnetonka, Barry and Calvin would make a small fortune on the stock they owned. Equally to the point, it would put an end to their association. Taylor had had enough of Calvin and Barry, and he wanted to start over fresh at a brand new company. "One hundred percent owned by me . . . and that I can make as big as I want or as small as I want," he said. He was also influenced to sell the company just then, he said tactfully, by a buoyant financial climate, in which the prices "that were being paid for cosmetics companies were so excessive."

Taylor's announcement that Minnetonka was for sale immediately sent the stock blasting up 8 points in one day to over twenty-one dollars a share, creating a paper profit of $18.2 million for Calvin and Barry. However, the partners were still appalled by this turn of events. Not only could they not afford to mount a takeover of Minnetonka against one of the giant conglomerates that would be bidding for it, but chances were that a perfect stranger was going to take over their most precious license. Yet Barry and Calvin also had a very powerful weapon left. If Minnetonka was transferring the fragrance license, the partners had the right to approve the new owner or break the agreement, and since Calvin Klein Cosmetics was the gem of Minnetonka's crown, Taylor wasn't selling it to anybody without them on board.

"Suitors Line Up in Lively Chase For Minnetonka" was the *Women's Wear Daily* headline only a week after Taylor made his announcement. A satisfied Taylor reported that "many handfuls" of companies had contacted him, including "a very nice mix of European, Far East, and domestic companies." Among the callers were financier Meshulam Riklis, the husband of pop star Pia Zadora, and the Elizabeth Arden company. There were some suitors, however, who arrived on Taylor's doorstep convinced they could buy the company at bargain-basement prices because its namesake would soon be dead of AIDS. Once Calvin died, one of the interested parties reasoned to Taylor, the company wouldn't be worth very much.

"No, *no*," Taylor said. "He hasn't got AIDS. He's cleaned up his life, and he's got Kelly."

But the buyer didn't believe it and dropped out of the bidding.

Of all the buyers interested in Minnetonka, the most feasible in terms of money, professionalism, and staying power was the Unilever Company NV. This $50 billion Dutch-based company sold soap and detergent products worldwide. In America, it owned Chesebrough-Pond's, which manufactured, among other cosmetics products, Elizabeth Taylor's fragrance White Diamonds. Barry and Calvin got along well enough with the president, Robert Phillips, and on July 1, 1989, Minnetonka was sold off in two pieces with Barry and Calvin's blessings. Its Vitabath, Claire Burke, and La Costa Spa lines were sold to Japan's Tsumura & Co. for $70 million, and the other part, consisting of Calvin Klein Cosmetics

Corp., was sold to Unilever's Chesebrough-Pond's subsidiary for $376.2 million, or $22.86 per share, realizing for Calvin and Barry an instant cash bonus of $21 million.

Robert Taylor never saw Barry Schwartz or Calvin Klein again. He now runs Tsumura's highly successful La Costa Spa division and divides his time between estates in Minneapolis, San Diego, and Palm Beach. Robin Burns resigned as president of Calvin Klein Cosmetics soon after it was sold to Chesebrough-Pond's, and is now president of Estee Lauder.

Unilever left Calvin alone, and in September 1991, with the enormous international clout of the conglomerate behind him, his company released yet another fragrance, this one called Escape. Although Escape was based on a theme of vacation and "getting away from it all," it also represented Calvin's new outlook on life. Escape was the final evolution. For Calvin, the word conjured relief, away from the office and its pressures and from being Calvin Klein all the time. It was about the beach and East Hampton, about letting down his guard and not having much left to prove to the world.

It was also unusual to be introducing a third fragrance on the market, since conventional wisdom held that designers could only sustain two "master brands." But Calvin contended that modern women wore "a wardrobe of fragrances" and would buy a third one of his. This $115-an-ounce "fruity, floral" scent was developed by the fragrance firm of Mane, and in line with Calvin's romantic new mode, Pierre Dinand modeled the bottle after an antique cream jar owned by Kelly. The bottle's hinged top and unfussy lines fit the travel motif. "After work, you get away," Calvin explained of the concept. "You escape, and you do it with style." Calvin also said that the scent is "an extension of Eternity, which was about family, commitment, children, and romance. . . . Escape goes beyond that." Although it was said that Calvin intended to spend 30 percent more on advertising than he did for Eternity, industry estimates were that Unilever would pour $40 million into Escape advertising its first year, and then the six-hundred store launch would be supported by another set of TV commercials, print media layouts, and scented strips in 40 million copies of fashion magazines. Despite Calvin's earlier disavowal of high-voltage sexual sells, the print campaign was much more carnal than the one for Eternity, with a signature photograph of a couple in skimpy white bathing suits, lying in embrace, the woman on top, on a rocky shore. The series of black-and-white TV commercials, however, featured fully dressed couples, often hoisting children joyously up in the air in slow motion. With the addition of Escape to his fragrance repertoire, the combined wholesale volume of Calvin's fragrances climbed to $300 million and would creep even higher as they entered more foreign markets.

6

Still, they could not stanch the hole from which their money bled.

Looming ahead of Calvin and Barry on the financial horizon was a staggering amount of junk-bond debt, payable in whopping chunks of $10 and $15 million a piece in each of the coming years. One way for them to satisfy the debt that would have been previously abhorrent to them was to sell Calvin Klein Industries outright to a large conglomerate, just as Taylor had done with Minnetonka. The company might easily fetch $400 million, which would pay off the debt in total and leave them each as much as $100 million profit. Undoubtedly, any new owner would allow them to retain a chunk of stock and control over their own division. However, they would be contracted employees, not owners. Still, they needed the bucks, and although Barry insisted "that the company isn't for sale," he entered negotiations with Triangle Industries, the largest can-manufacturing and vending-machine conglomerate in the world. If the deal went through, Barry and Calvin would walk away with "something in the $400 million range," said a Triangle representative. Wall Streeters scoffed that there was "little synergism" between a can manufacturer and Calvin's chic operation. However, one common bond was that Triangle's Nelson Peltz and Calvin shared Mike Milken as an adviser. "It was an interesting opportunity," Barry commented. "We explored it." Calvin even began looking forward to the idea. He and Barry were in the midst of hammering out a deal in the fall of 1987 when, on October 19, the stock market plunged to the depths in its greatest one-day decline since 1914. The Dow Jones Average slumped 508.32 points as Triangle's stock price was nearly halved. Peltz and his company's president, Peter W. May, took the opportunity to buy up their own company's shares, but once Triangle got through with its own restructuring plan, it would no longer have the money to buy Calvin Klein Industries. Calvin was distraught. He told another businessman, "Losing this deal was the worst thing that ever happened to me." He was "terribly depressed" as the pressure began to bear down on him.

The nineties did not greet Calvin and Barry with much better news, although there were a few bright spots on the business picture. The men's underwear line, which Calvin got back when he bought out Bidermann, was still a winner, with $50 million in wholesale sales. The fragrance division also was thriving under Kim Delsing's leadership at Unilever, but the royalty payments of all the licensees together reportedly only came to $21 million. Calvin's flagship "Collection" line, grossing $37 million, accounted for only 11 percent of the company's income, nowhere near large enough to put the company into the black. In 1990, the entire company was only reporting annual sales of $200 million, losing $4.3 million in the bargain. In the coming year sales were expected to fall another 7 percent.

At the heart of the problem was Calvin and Barry's management style, attested to by the high turnover of executives at the company. They had brought in Bob Suslow, the former chairman of the Batus chain, which included Saks Fifth Avenue and Marshall Field, as president of Calvin Klein Industries at a $200,000 a year salary and even made him an equity partner. But while they were perfectly able to get along with him when he was their most important customer, as a coworker they squabbled repeatedly, and after two years Suslow abruptly resigned and sold his shares back to Calvin and Barry. The partners even asked Robin Burns to analyze what was wrong with their business, but she allegedly demurred because she knew they didn't want to hear what she would have to tell them. It wasn't only the unhappy atmosphere at headquarters, but over the years the tough return policy had taken its toll, and instead of being friends with many of the retailers, they were in a cold war. The difficulty in keeping executives damaged continuity and respect in the trade. They could not put together creative teams to implement business ideas without meddling. "They didn't have what Ralph Lauren had," said Robert Taylor, "which was a strategic plan. And not only that, I'm not so sure that they wanted one, because the bigger the company got, the less control they had. Barry Schwartz liked running that business like a corner grocery store."

Another reason for the money hemorrhage was the Puritan/Calvin Klein Sport division, which lost $14.2 million in 1990. By this time the Sport division covered casual clothes as well as jeans, yet Calvin seemed to have lost his uncanny touch with the customer. Many younger women who could not afford his Collection line were not buying his clothes at all, and newcomers like Donna Karan were seizing the spotlight. "Calvin Klein is not offering anything new," insisted one buyer from the Dayton Hudson store chain, saying that the prices were consistently high and the styling too minimal for the consumer. Blouses similar to eighty dollar items in the Sport line were only forty-two dollars at the Gap, a chain that was crucifying Calvin's casual wear and jeans business.

In October 1991, Calvin tried to revive the dying jeans business with what the *Wall Street Journal* called "shock therapy": a whopping 116-page advertising supplement, wrapped in plastic, in the October issue of *Vanity Fair* magazine. Called a "polybagged outsert" in the trade—because it was meant to be removed from the magazine and saved—this lavishly produced booklet of black-and-white Bruce Weber photographs cost more than $1 million to produce and place, making it the single most costly ad supplement in consumer history. Photographed mainly at the old Warfield Theater in San Francisco, the lengthy photo essay told the story of a "day in the life of a rock band," mostly offstage and mostly undressed.

Indeed, in what seemed like desperate pandering, Calvin's jeans appeared tertiary to the erotic and provocative photographs themselves. "Calvin Klein Shocks Even Madison Ave" was the *New York Times* reaction. In another searing critique, *Time* magazine called it "a jumbled pastiche of naked bodies, black leather jackets, Harleys and tattoos, with cameo roles by a crying baby and a urinal. Biker chicks straddle their 'hogs' and rough up their men. Rippling hunks wield electric guitars like chain saws, grab one another, sometimes themselves. Oh yes, there are even a few incidental photographs of jeans, most of which are being wrestled off taut bodies or used as wet loincloths." Indeed, Calvin seemed to have gone full circle, from Brooke Shields to Eternity and now this. The most controversial photographs in the collection included two male members of the band in what seemed like the beginning of a passionate kiss; a band member urinating and smiling over his shoulder; and a blatantly erotic photograph of a muscular band member under the shower, holding a wet pair of Calvin Klein jeans strategically over his genitals. The *New York Times* even tallied the nudity for its readers: "nude male posteriors, 2; nude female posteriors, 4; barechested men, 27; topless women, 2."

But as widely discussed as the outsert became, it didn't work with the consumer. The *Wall Street Journal* reported, "Klein Jeans Sexy Insert Didn't Spur Sales." The photo supplement, said the *Journal,* "didn't have any noticeable impact in sales." Roger Farah, chairman of merchandising services at Federated Department Stores, told the paper, "Denim is a hot commodity right now, but Calvin jeans-wear isn't doing so well." The majority verdict was that even as Calvin rhapsodized about his own newly old-fashioned personal life, he was still selling the public sex. Calvin, finally, was out of touch with the retreat from sex in the nineties. "It projected the mid-1980's 'everyone-is-flush' sensibility. Now . . . the country is going back to basic values." Ron Frasch, senior vice president at Neiman-Marcus, predicted: "The ads are likely to change in the future."

With the expensive advertising having no effect on sales, the figures for 1991 were even grimmer, and because of the necessity of Security and Exchange Commissions filings, they were no secret. "Debt Burdened Calvin Klein Is Faltering," said the headline in Crain's *New York Business.* The filings disclosed that in the first nine months of 1991 the company earned only $2,655,000 on sales of $138,774,000. Long-term debt stood at $54,649,000, and from 1990 to 1991 cash reserves dwindled from $27.9 million to $9.2 million, most of the difference going to repay the junk-bond principal. In September 1992, Barry and Calvin owed another $15.3 million repayment on the bonds plus another $7 million in interest. The following September they would owe yet another $15 million, followed by repayments of $12.5 million due in 1994 and again in 1995. Post haste, Calvin and Barry dropped their salary to a little over $2 million each—still too generous, jeered Wall Streeters, who prophesied inevitable bankruptcy.

Adding to the partners' headache was that the junk-bond market, riddled with illegal activities and insider crimes, had all but crashed by 1990, and their Drexel Burnham Lambert prophet, Mike Milken, was at the center of a federal government investigation. In March 1989, U.S. prosecutors unveiled a ninety-eight-count indictment against Milken, and a year later, he pleaded guilty to six felonies involving securities law violations. He agreed to pay $600 million in fines and was sentenced to ten years in prison, of which he ultimately served a mere twenty-two months. But Milken's real victims were entrepreneurs like Calvin and Barry, who had succumbed to his easy-money siren song. In the next few years, their bonds were bought and sold like penny candy, and they had no control over who their debtors were.

Worse, the bonds had drawn Barry Schwartz into an ugly scandal. In April 1988 he had accepted an invitation from David Paul to become a member of his CenTrust Savings and Loan board for a token $18,500 fee. This was an innocent courtesy to Paul, whose bank had invested $20 million in Calvin Klein junk bonds and who sat on the board of Calvin Klein Industries. The forty-eight-year-old Paul was a smooth-talking former real estate developer from Connecticut. In just five years he had taken an ailing Florida bank called Dade Savings and Loan and turned it into the glamorous $9-billion-dollar CenTrust, the largest—and least conventional—thrift institution in the southeastern United States. Paul ruled his flashy financial empire with a meaty fist from behind bullet-proof walls in his $90 million CenTrust Tower in downtown Miami, which boasted twenty-four-karat gold-leaf ceilings, gold toilet fixtures, and a $1 million spiral staircase. Although his impressive résumé included two degrees—a "Harvard Ph.D. in city planning" and an "M.B.A." from Columbia University—his deportment was more appropriate to a fishmonger than an alumnus of an Ivy League business school. However, Miami's social set, Washington politicians, and banking regulators flocked to Paul's estate on the exclusive LaGorce Island in Miami, where they dined on Cajun cuisine prepared by guest chef Paul Bocuse as the music of twenty-foot waterfalls cascaded into a lagoon-style swimming pool. Moored at the house's teak deck was Paul's $7 million yacht, *Le Grand Cru*.

At the time Barry served on the board, from April 1988 to August 1989, Paul was embarking on an art-buying spree, letting it be known "that virtually no piece was too costly to be considered by CenTrust," reported the *Wall Street Journal*. In December 1988, Barry journeyed to Miami for a board meeting where, according to the directors' minutes, "the board expressed satisfaction" at the purchases to date—an art trove that included a $1.4 million Willem-Claez Heda still life, a $1.89 million pair of François Boucher dovecotes, a $2.2 million painting of a table setting by Jan Jansz. den Uyl, and most stunning of all, the $13.2 million *Portrait of a Man as the God Mars* by Sir Peter Paul Rubens—which was hung not in the CenTrust Tower but in Paul's own home.

Even as Paul proudly displayed his new collection to guests, a rash of scandals at other savings and loan institutions began breaking around the country. As one bank after another went down, David Paul's CenTrust came under close scrutiny, and in the winter of 1989, provoked by reports of Paul's spending, the Florida state comptroller's office began to take an interest in the treasures being acquired by a federally controlled bank. That March the comptroller's office gave Paul thirty days to sell the Rubens. Barry resigned from CenTrust's board in August 1989—too late not to be smeared. As the thrift's operating losses spiraled upward to $119 million—and Paul continued to collect nearly $5 million a year in compensation—dozens of federal banking examiners descended on the CenTrust Tower armed with warrants. After an examination of CenTrust's records, it was determined that the thrift had a negative worth in the *billions*. Among other disclosures made, it turned out that David Paul's Harvard Ph.D. and Columbia M.B.A. were fake and that even after being ordered to sell the $13.2 million Rubens painting, he defiantly bought a $315,000 sailboat called the *Bodacious*. The Resolution Trust Corporation, the government agency overseeing the cleanup of the savings and loan industry, blamed CenTrust's financial state on such "excessive and inappropriate expenses and investments" as its junk-bond portfolio and art collection. Paul was slapped with two massive criminal indictments accusing him of raiding CenTrust as well as civil charges filed by the Resolution Trust Corporation seeking more than $250 million in damages from Paul and fifteen of his former officers and directors—including Barry Schwartz. The complaint accused Barry and other ex–board members of "gross negligence and/or conscious disregard" of their duties in permitting "enormous expenditures that were totally inappropriate for a federally insured savings and loan." The suit also claimed that Barry, "who owned a substantial interest in Minnetonka . . . benefited when CenTrust purchased 200,000 shares of Minnetonka stock for nearly $3 million in January 1989." This transaction, maintained the *Wall Street Journal,* boosted the stock price. Barry Schwartz has repeatedly denied any wrongdoing, but the case brought horrible publicity. The mere mention of CenTrust during an interview, wrote one reporter, was "enough to cause Mr. Schwartz to bolt from his chair and nervously pace the room" before pouring a glass of water from a silver-plated carafe.

Sometime before it went under, CenTrust divested itself of its holdings of Calvin's junk bonds, which were sold among various speculators in the field. Because these kinds of bonds do not have to be registered—or officially valued—the records of the transfers of bonds are not public. Suffice it to say that by 1991, when over $50 million worth of Calvin Klein junk bonds wound up in the hands of an insolvent company called Executive Life Insurance Co. of California, it was possible that the bonds had passed through a half-dozen hands, a dizzying and scary scenario, as Barry and Calvin watched helplessly. In 1991 most of Executive Life's $6.9 billion junk-bond portfolio was seized by the insurance commissioner of the state of California and publicly auctioned by the insurance commissioner to the highest bidder. In 1992 Calvin's debt surfaced in the hands of a familiar face, Leon Black, an investment banker and former head of mergers and acquisitions for Drexel Burnham Lambert, who had once described his relationship with Mike Milken as "hero worship." However, just because Black was familiar didn't mean he was friendly. Payments were due on the bonds, and he wanted them.

Calvin and Barry's latest unfortunate financial circumstances became public knowledge on November 22, 1991—three days after Calvin's forty-ninth birthday—heralded by a front-page *Wall Street Journal* article headlined "Calvin Klein Is Facing a Bind as Magic Touch Appears to Be Slipping." The story explained in gruesome detail his many debts and failures. "Mr. Klein appears to have lost his Midas Touch with young consumers," the article said, pointing out that "marketing missteps reflect turmoil within the house of Klein." The article also discussed the many firings, resignations, and defections in the company over the last ten years, quoting one former employee saying, "You live with paranoia."

How would Calvin find the cash, asked the *Journal,* to continue to retire tens of millions in junk-bond debt as his business declined? The debt hung over the faltering company like a death sentence. Up and down Seventh Avenue, the vultures alighted on the building tops.

7

A friend in need is a friend indeed.

There was only one person Calvin knew who was so rich that he could afford to help him out to the tune of $50 million and not even feel it: David Geffen.

Since Steve Rubell's death, David and Calvin had drawn closer. They were an odd couple to be seen together, tiny David with his big head and long, tall Calvin, huddling down to hear what David was saying to him. Although there was a competitive edge that never subsided with time, Calvin trusted David more than anyone in his life except for Barry. David might have been insufferably confident in his many opinions, but there were few people more insightful to talk over problems with, no one more dedicated and loving to Calvin as a friend. Although over the years Calvin remained close with Barry Diller and Sandy Gallin, only David had power over him.

Through the years Geffen had emerged as one of the most talented and powerful men in the entertainment industry, and certainly one of the richest. His business endeavors encompassed not only his ultrasuccessful, eponymously named record company but scores of hit movies, including *Risky Business, Little Shop of Hor-*

rors, and Broadway musicals like *Cats* and *Miss Saigon.* He was also beginning to amass one of the world's great private collections of abstract expressionism, and he counted among his friends publisher S. I. Newhouse, art dealer Leo Castelli, and one of the most respected financiers in America, Felix Rohatyn. Geffen became a power broker in the Hollywood community, and his Beverly Hills house became a staging area for Democratic candidates on the hustings in Los Angeles, including Bill Clinton before his 1992 election to the White House.

Truly, Geffen was a genius in many arenas, except at understanding human nature. Although he had come out of the closet by officially announcing he was "gay" rather than "bisexual," as he had claimed to be for years, he could not form a personal relationship. "It's difficult to be in a relationship with someone as well known and wealthy as I am," Geffen explained. Some in the gay community suspected he had decided to publicly discuss his sexuality to defuse repeated—and potentially embarassing—attempts to "out" him by journalists. But Geffen asserted that his candor was designed to liberate himself personally and to encourage other gay men. "He just seems so relieved," Calvin said. "He felt he could be a role model. Gay men are not necessarily thought of as the shrewdest businessmen in the world. He felt he should do this publicly as well as for himself, and he's really much happier."

In mid-March of 1990, David Geffen sold his record company to the Music Company of America (MCA), the entertainment conglomerate that also owned Universal Pictures and G. P. Putnam's Sons publishers, for $550 million worth of stock. Yet only seven months later, in January 1991, the Japanese electronics giant Matsushita swallowed up MCA, instantly transmuting Geffen's already formidable holdings into $670 million worth of cold cash. By now his total net worth was over $1 billion, making him the first billionaire in show business. One of the first things he did was drop $47.5 million on Jack Warner's former Beverly Hills estate, and he didn't even know the money was gone: Geffen was so rich that the monthly interest on his holdings alone is estimated to total $10 million.

And what good was all that money if it couldn't be used to help take a monkey off a friend's back?

On May 6, 1992, in a stunning gesture of friendship, David

Geffen acquired approximately $62 million dollars' worth—in face value—of Calvin Klein Industries junk bonds—not just the bonds that were due but all the outstanding debt securities of Calvin Klein—for an amount believed to equal between $41.3 million and over $50 million. However, the price he paid was at such great discount that when the bonds were redeemed, Geffen would allegedly make a $20 million profit. But the likelihood of Geffen's ever calling in the bonds was remote. Geffen would not even admit that future payments on the bonds were due: "When it's comfortable for Calvin and Barry to pay" is all he would say. "It's of no concern to me. . . . I believe Calvin is one of the smartest people I know and is a guy whose talent I not only believe in but admire and respect. . . . There is no downside for me. . . . I don't think they can blow it. Calvin is a total winner."

"David is an incredible person," said Calvin. "To have him buy our bonds is the greatest thing to ever happen."

David was modest about it. "I made an extraordinarily good investment while being able to help out one of my closest friends," Geffen said. "It's a win-win situation for both of us." Shortly after bailing Calvin out, Geffen told a reporter, "Look, honey, it doesn't represent five percent of my net worth."

Geffen's pledge was that he would have nothing to do with the day-to-day running of the company. The money was a hands-off investment for him. He didn't know anything about fashion. But he did know about marketing and image and positioning, and before long he couldn't help putting in his two bits. As brilliant a predictor of trends as Calvin was, some of Geffen's suggestions were home runs. It was Geffen's idea that Calvin hire Marky Mark, the muscle-boy rap star, as his next underwear model. The beefy nineteen-year-old rapper from the streets of Boston was already giving Calvin a free ride by wearing his jeans so low on his hips that the waistband of his Calvin Klein underwear showed. Mark was causing a sensation at his personal appearances by dropping his jeans to his ankles to reveal just how well he filled out his shorts. Geffen helped Calvin make a deal with Mark over chops at the Old Stove Pub in Bridgehampton. A $100,000 contract was negotiated with Mark to become Calvin's official poster boy. The ads of Marky Mark were certainly eye-popping, making Calvin's original Tom Hintinaus underwear poster seem demure in comparison. Mark almost burst out of his sixteen-dollar button-fly shorts, twenty-one-dollar cycling shorts, and old-fashioned Y-fronts. In one, he stretches his already tight underpants across his crotch so snugly that the shot had to be airbrushed before it began appearing in magazines and bus shelters in October 1992. Calvin also rushed into production two 30-second TV spots that featured the butch bodybuilder alternately grabbing his crotch or pressing a bare-breasted, teenaged model named Kate Moss into his chest. Mark hit a live nerve with the public, and in just three months, sales shot up 34 percent over the previous year. Within twelve months the men's underwear division was grossing a remarkable $85 million per annum. "Marky Mark," said Kal Ruttenstein, vice president of Bloomingdale's, "is the male equivalent of Brooke Shields." Unfortunately, Mark didn't like his newfound pinup boy status overshadowing his recording career, and he liked gay men ogling him even less. After several widely reported gay slurs, his contract with Calvin Klein wasn't renewed. Nevertheless, sales continued to soar, and in January of 1994, Calvin sold his men's and women's underwear business to the Warnaco Group for $64 million. The New York–based group already manufactured some of the top names in the business, including Fruit of the Loom, Chaps by Ralph Lauren, and Christian Dior, and, as always, no matter who was making the goods, Calvin retained ultimate control.

Because of his investment in the company's outcome, Geffen became a self-styled adviser and image manager to Calvin. As the man who had successfully constructed and repaired the careers of stars like Joni Mitchell, the Eagles, and Cher, he thought he understood exactly what Calvin should be doing for his public image. One thing was that it was time for Calvin to stop being afraid of associating himself with AIDS charities and gay causes. It was Geffen, along with Barry Diller and Sandy Gallin, who convinced Calvin to allow himself to be honored by AIDs Project Los Angeles (APLA), an AIDS service group, at a fund-raiser to be held at the Hollywood Bowl on June 3, 1993. Up until this point, except for his appearance with Elizabeth Taylor at the Jacob Javits Center, the most public instance of Calvin's philanthropy to AIDS causes was a five-figure donation for tickets the previous year when APLA's

Commitment to Life Awards honored David Geffen, and then it was mumbled by gay activists that Geffen himself paid for Calvin's tickets. When AIDS activists heard that Calvin was to be honored by APLA, the reactions were unequivocal. "It makes my skin crawl," said Rodger McFarlane, executive director of Broadway Cares/Equity Fights AIDs. "I will not give absolution to people who colluded in genocide." Added AIDS activist and author Larry Kramer, "It's beyond gross. . . . Here we have a man who's done so little to fight AIDS but is being given a major award, solely—I would imagine—because he is David Geffen's close friend. It's like the Jews honoring David Duke."

The event became one of the most successful fund-raisers APLA ever held, bringing in $1 million, double the previous year's receipts. But when the final figures were totaled, it turned out that the event had been so expensive to stage that only forty cents of each dollar was left after accounting for costs. The spectacle included cocktails, dinner, a Calvin Klein fashion show with three hundred models, mostly bare-chested, and an appearance by Tina Turner. Calvin himself appeared onstage at the end of the event and made a rambling, lackluster speech in which he thanked a long list of people. It was noted that he only said the word AIDS twice and never mentioned gays or lesbians. Nevertheless, Kelly and his daughter, Marci, both in the audience, wept while Calvin spoke, unleashing a new wave of speculation about whether or not Calvin himself was HIV positive.

Only three days after the Hollywood Bowl event, David Geffen pressured Calvin to open his East Hampton home for another fund-raiser, this time in support of allowing gays in the military. It was a shock to those who knew Calvin abhorred the loss of privacy in holding such an event in his own home. The $500-minimum-per-person ticket proved too high even for the monied gays of the Hamptons, and only sixty people turned out to stand in a drafty and wet striped tent on Calvin's lawn. Calvin himself stayed indoors for most of the fund-raiser, only to make a brief speech in which he announced, "David Geffen talked me into this."

Indeed, Calvin had had enough of Geffen's influence in his life and became determined to get out from under his thumb. In mid-June of 1993, Calvin and Barry announced to the press that they had borrowed $58 million from Citibank to buy back their bonds from David Geffen. Taking advantage of low interest rates, their loan from Citibank carried only 6 percent interest, saving the company $4.7 million in payments each year—and getting them away from Geffen. "I bought the bonds at a discount," said Geffen, "I sold them at a discount, and I made a profit. . . . I'm delighted that he was able to buy them back so quickly." Wall Street insiders noticed that the assets of a trust were guaranteeing the loan. They assumed the assets were put up by Geffen, since Calvin wasn't known to have anything like $58 million to stake as security. "All they have done is rearrange the deck chairs," said one financial commentator. But they were rearranged in a way that ensured that Geffen no longer could meddle in Calvin's daily affairs. With Calvin's tenuous self-respect restored, the bond repayment only strengthened the friendship between the mogul and the superstar designer.

CHAPTER EIGHTEEN

Only a weak mind seeks ultimate answers.
                                    —Agnes Thorton

T he only sound at Calvin and Kelly's beachfront East Hampton
home is the distant percussion of the ocean rolling to the shore.
Occasionally, there is the sound of a small private plane landing or
taking off at the town's tiny airport, but mostly there is just silence
and sea grass and piping plovers nesting beyond the dunes.

Escape.

Their house is the last on a street that is unusual not only because it is a dead end but because it funnels into a narrow promon-
tory, affording the house a sweeping view of the Atlantic Ocean as
well as the shimmering, halcyon Georgica Pond across the road
from it, the far shore dotted with sprawling mansions and timbered
boat houses. This road is perhaps the most private and exclusive
slip of property in all the Hamptons, and their immediate neighbors include Revlon heiress Lynn Revson, Cox Communications
heiress Katherine Johnson Rayner, director Steven Spielberg,
screenwriter and director Nora Ephron, and former *Washington
Post* editor Ben Bradlee.

The huge 1891 gray-shingled Klein residence was once owned
by Juan Trippe, the founder of Pan American Airlines, and Calvin
bought the eight-parcel piece of property from his heirs. When he
and Kelly first laid eyes on the mansion, it was "just a big old
wreck," she said. But Calvin thought the faded old house was "kind
of sweet" even if it was "falling apart." They set about refurbishing
it in a makeover that would top $10 million. "We wanted to keep it

as much as possible like 1891," said Kelly, "in that old, rambling East Hampton shingle style." But the shingles were about all that was kept the same. The entire house was lifted off its wooden pilings, and a new foundation was poured and built underneath it. Calvin hired internationally renowned French architect and designer Thierry Despont to redesign the existing cluster of small rooms into an airy, open environment, with lots of paned windows to let in the light. Naturally, there were battle royals between Calvin and Kelly and Thierry Despont. *W* magazine reported that "towards the end, the couple and their very grand French designer-architect were ready to strangle each other."

Despont agreed. "Working with them was like playing tennis with a great partner. They push you, and you push them." To allow the couple careful control over what Despont was doing, the design for the house was not only rendered in architectural blueprints, but a scale model was also created by Despont's office so Calvin and Kelly could get a visual sense of the proportions. As soon as Kelly laid eyes on the model, she thought the giant-sized living room looked too big in relationship to the rest of the house. She repeatedly told Calvin and Despont that they were making a mistake. "But *nooooo*," Kelly said, "Thierry and Calvin had their very grand days." While the house was being built, the couple would pay weekly visits, and Kelly kept up her lament about the size of the living room. Rumors ricocheted around the sedate beach community that Calvin intended to use the room as a discotheque. Then one day while Kelly was taking a stroll along the beach, a stranger recognized her from her photographs and asked her exactly what it was that Calvin and she were building: an indoor tennis court or a swimming pool? That was all Kelly had to hear. She had a firm talk with Calvin and "finally we decided the living room had to come down," she said. The structure itself was already in place and shingled, with a work crew banging away on the roof, when Calvin took the contractor aside and said, "We have to make a change here." The builder was shocked; they had been building the room for a year, but Calvin had it ripped down the next day.

Yet no one aspect of the house was given as much attention as the floors. "Floors make a house look old and lived in," said Calvin. "We always knew we wanted dark, old, wide planks." Unfortunately, no planks readily available could pass Calvin's muster, and Despont commissioned a search for three hundred-year-old aged wood. Teams of carpenters were dispatched to scour the Northeast, and eventually an old Vermont farmhouse with just the right wood was located, purchased, and carefully pulled apart. The wood was then sent to a warehouse, where each plank was individually numbered and photographed. Then the photos were sent to Calvin so he could approve each plank. When enough planks were chosen, a master drawing was made indicating exactly where each individual plank would be laid for Calvin's assessment. Finally, the floor was laid. Next came the staining. It turned out that because of the different density of each plank, it would be necessary to hand-stain each piece individually so they would all have the same deep, even eggplant color Calvin wanted. This exercise had to be repeated many times on each plank until every last one of them was perfect. Finally, the wooden toilet seats in the bathrooms were dyed to match the floors.

Other than the dark floors, there is no color scheme to the house except for white. Almost everything except the antique wood furniture or occasional tea table is white, beckoning the diffuse beach light. Even the servants are requested to dress in white. In the living room, the overstuffed club chairs, purchased in Paris, as well as the plump sofa, are draped in fitted white slipcovers with tailored skirts, and so are the high-backed chairs around the oval mahogany dining-room table. Throughout the house all the windows are framed in sheer white curtains that billow like spinnakers in the gentle ocean breeze. The mixture of Calvin's love of Santa Fe and Kelly's Mexican and Anglo-Indian religious artifacts is evident from all the wooden pieces scattered on tabletops. "I keep putting things away," Calvin said, sighing, "and Kelly keeps bringing them out." Kelly's favorite tabletop objects are crucifixes, and there are many different shapes and sizes about. Very little art hangs on the walls; most of it—priceless photographs—are leaned on shelves, including original prints by Alfred Stieglitz, Robert Mapplethorpe, and Bruce Weber.

For the master bedroom, Despont converted seven smaller rooms into one graciously sized suite, outfitted with his-and-her dressing areas. This room got Calvin's special attention. He had the moldings and doorknobs and nail heads changed and removed numerous times, until it nearly drove the workmen crazy. When Calvin told one frustrated contractor that an artist friend of his suggested that the bricks around the fireplace be changed yet again—this time because the texture was too rough—the contractor exclaimed, "You and your cocksucking friends!" Calvin looked not too pleased but let it slide by.

The finished bedroom is almost elegiac in its beauty. It is dominated by a stately four-poster, canopied queen-sized bed that Calvin bought from the estate of Andy Warhol. The bed is draped in a gauzy white crown of mosquito netting, and Calvin sleeps on the left, the same side as his father slept on, nearer to the large windows and French doors overlooking the Atlantic horizon. The southern exposure brings the morning sun streaming through these windows, enveloping the bed in warm yellow light. A lush duvet covers the puffy down mattress, and the laced-trimmed Pratesi linens are changed each day by the maid. There is very little on the walls except for small mirrors over the Flemish dressers, and opposite the bed, leaning on the fireplace mantel, are two black-and-white photographs along with one of Kelly's primitive Mexican crucifixes. The his-and-her wainscoted bathrooms are almost as roomy as the bedroom itself. Both have long dressing mirrors and abundant shelving for toiletries. The shelves, however, have precious little on them save for Calvin's perfume that Kelly displays. In Calvin's bathroom, a deep, old-fashioned, claw-footed tub stands next to a square, white-paned window. Taking his morning bath, Calvin can choose between a view of the ocean or a David Hockney drawing hanging over the towel rack.

The guest bedrooms, each outfitted with a double bed, are in a separate building, attached to the main house by a portico and deck. There are three bedrooms for guests to choose from, with a common sitting area in which is found the only TV in the house. Not only is there a dearth of television, there is also no swimming pool. At the start, they intended to redo the house's existing pool. Built in the early 1950s, the pool "was situated between the house and a dune that sloped down towards the ocean," said Kelly, "and disrupted the beautiful ocean view we had from the house." So before they finished restoring the house, the existing pool was filled with soil and sodded over with grass. "Our friends thought this was a strange thing to have done," Kelly conceded. Kelly decided to research pools before they designed a replacement, but when she tried to find a book about swimming pools "that might inspire me and help me to decide what kind of pool to build [in its place], I realized there weren't any." So Kelly decided to put together a retrospective book about pools herself. In the fall of 1992, the publisher Alfred Knopf released her handsomely designed $100 coffee-table book. Called, simply, *Pools,* the volume had a brief text by Kelly herself as well as 187 photographs of pools, from Coney Island to Hadrian's Villa. The extravagant book was only a modest success, but it was the first time that Kelly endeavored beyond Calvin's sphere of influence and marked a small personal triumph. In the end, they never did build another pool in East Hampton. "With the ocean and the pond," Calvin said, "it didn't seem right to look at something artificial."

The house was inaugurated on its hundredth anniversary with a late-summer party whose guests included Diana Ross, Barry Diller, Hampton residents Christie Brinkley and Billy Joel, *Rolling Stone* publisher Jann Wenner and his wife, Jane, and Sandy Gallin, among others. The food was served buffet style around the big dining-room table, simple country fare like barbecued chicken, ribs, roasted new potatoes in rosemary and olive oil, and Caesar salad. It was cool that night by the beach, and the house was lit by long white taper candles that flickered in the breeze. They played soft rock and roll over the stereo system, and when it got late and the crowd had thinned down to just a dozen friends, Billy Joel took his place at the black grand piano in the living room and gave an impromptu performance. For the finale, he was joined by Diana Ross. Calvin was "enthralled," said one participant, "just enthralled."

Daily life at the beautiful house is precisely prescribed by habit and taste. Kelly is usually up before Calvin, around 6:00 A.M. most mornings, with her husband rising about an hour later. Neither is ever seen in a robe by the servants, and they both get fully dressed before they go downstairs for breakfast. If they eat together, they sometimes sit at a round antique wood table in the country kitchen or, weather permitting, out on a bleached-wood terrace at a wooden table with an Italian market umbrella, set with straw mats and heavy green drinking glasses. Calvin drinks only bottled water or cranberry juice. They eat in silence most of the time, staring at the view of birds fishing in Georgica Pond or the rolling surf. No butter or eggs are served. Four or five boxes of cold cereals are laid out on the kitchen table for Calvin to choose from. Raisin Bran is his favorite, but sometimes he has crunchy granola or Nutrigrain. Coffee and 1 percent fat milk are offered in thick white pottery from Portugal.

Dinners are usually grilled, mostly chicken and fish, with fresh vegetables. Calvin prefers that fish be served whole, not fileted, with the head intact, and that only Northern Italian preparations be used. Three different types of bread are served with the evening meal, set out in an antique wooden bowl. Berries are the only snack that Calvin approves of between meals, and the kitchen staff buys several pints and examines each small berry to find only the most perfect to serve to him. Although he insists that the professional, steel-faced refrigerator in the kitchen is stocked at all times with lobster and chicken salad (made daily from free-range chickens raised at a local chicken farm and slaughtered fresh for Calvin), neither he nor Kelly eats much. Kelly in particular is afraid of gaining weight, and Calvin monitors her like a hawk. "You're getting fat now," he has been overheard goading her.

Each guest bedroom is outfitted daily with a bowl of fruit and a pitcher of ice water. Every bathroom throughout the house has a completely stocked medicine cabinet as well as a vase of cut flowers. Kelly does the flowers herself, following Calvin's preferences. Flowers of several types are never mixed, and they can be only one color, white, with the exception of a small bouquet of pink tea roses that Kelly places on her side of the bed. She grows most of the flowers herself in the cutting gardens on the southeast side of the house, but she buys the more exotic blooms at a Hampton's florist.

The couple own two trendily pretty Tibetan terriers and in a dubious gesture of honor named them after Calvin's folks, Flo and Leo. The dogs' namesakes themselves are seldom invited out to see the place, for it is Calvin and Kelly's retreat, and there are no visitors from outside their inner circle. Calvin keeps his distance from his mother, who still has the capacity to "push his buttons," as a friend says. Still, Flo is on call when Calvin feels ill, because there is something about the consistency of her matzo balls and her chicken soup that his many cooks cannot duplicate. He once sent a limousine to Flo's apartment in Riverdale to pick up a Tupperware bowl of soup and *alkes,* which nestled by itself in the backseat of the car as it was driven out to East Hampton.

The handsome couple are one of the darlings of nouvelle society, so called because, like Calvin's, most of its fortunes are only one generation old. Yet try as he might, Calvin has never quite fit into the role of East End gentility. He doesn't play tennis, and he is less than adept at most sports. Once when he was doing sit-ups, he gave himself a hernia that needed surgery. When he went skiing in Italy with Kelly, he broke his leg and had to wear a cast. While learning how to sail, he sprained a ligament in his left wrist and was in a brace. While taking horseback-riding lessons at the Topping Riding Club in Bridgehampton, he fell off the horse, hit a post, split open his head, and tore a hole in his esophagus. Sometime after the accident, he had surgery to repair his throat at New York's Lenox Hill Hospital in February 1991. Again, the AIDS rumors spread, in particular a well-circulated story that the hospital had marked all his blood and tissue samples "Infectious." Calvin's public relations department tried to soothe fears about the designer's health by announcing that the designer was "peppy and talkative" and planned to be back at work by the end of the week. Therefore, the most athletic Calvin gets these days is to take a gym class with fitness trainer Radu or to paddle one of his canoes out on Georgica Pond and daydream. At night, he and Kelly sometimes go the movie theater in town or play a word game, "Topics," in which they challenge each other to guess a subject drawn from a hat. "I never had the patience before to sit still for very long," Calvin says. He is still at his most relaxed and ebullient when he is among his old friends— David Geffen, Sandy Gallin, and Barry Diller. Author Fran Lebowitz, upon whose searing wit Calvin dotes, has also become a close friend, and Kelly is grateful for the companionship of another woman in Calvin's all-male inner circle. The group tries to be kind to Kelly, and Sandy Gallin is so fond of her he even keeps a picture of her on a table in his living room. But in Kelly's presence they often appear to be "walking on eggshells," said one observer, afraid of offending her with their frank conversation.

Soon after they were married, there was some talk of children. "This is a big house," Calvin said, "and I would like to have more of a family." Said Kelly, "I want a little boy and a little girl." But that idea now seems remote. "I don't wake up thinking about [children]," said Kelly. "I like my job, riding, and traveling with Calvin. I don't want to give that up. I'll be thirty-six soon, so I'll have to take my chances. There's nothing wrong with adopting." When Calvin was asked about the possibility of having children, he blushed and said, "We're not there yet. But when we are, there will probably be a perfume called Baby."

Kelly's friends and family say she got what she wanted, "to be a fairy princess," as her stepfather Dr. Murray List, put it. But Kelly herself does not seem so sure of that. Sometimes she will proudly declare, "I am Calvin's muse. . . . I love him. I love everything he does." Yet when she heard about the breakup of Princess Diana and Prince Charles, she sighed, "So nothing's sacred, I guess. I'm losing all my fairy tales." Then she added wistfully, "Life isn't fairy tales at all. It's not for anyone. Everyone is the same. Everybody's got the same problems no matter what you have."

Some intimates see the marriage as a happy compromise, others, an uneasy truce. Almost all agree the couple truly love each other, if for reasons so different that life cannot be easy for either of them. She remains in his shadow and much of the time appears terrified of making a mistake or sounding stupid. Yet Calvin seems aware of the price she is paying, and there are hugs and kisses of encouragement. "To have someone who loves you and cares about you truly is what life is all about," Calvin maintains.

Said one intimate, "He probably feels a little guilty, and I think he tries to make her as happy as possible." Sometimes, however, Kelly finds herself dwelling on his past. One thing that provokes her is the occasional call that comes from a young man who claims to know Calvin. If a man calls one of the five private numbers at the beach house, Kelly snaps to the servants, "Hang up!" One friend who had dinner with the couple at the Sappore di Mare retaurant in the Hamptons hamlet of Wainscott remembered that "we were having this perfectly civilized dinner conversation, and . . . Kelly transformed into a real bitch. . . . She was horrible to Calvin, and she kept interjecting remarks about boys . . . real nasty and kind of cutting reminders about men . . . insinuating, basically, that he'd been sleeping around with men."

Most of the time, however, Kelly swallows her feelings, as she did one recent Thanksgiving. Autumn is Kelly's favorite time of the year in East Hampton. The house is perhaps more beautiful in the fall than in any other season. The light is more melancholy, but the ocean is at its warmest, the beaches are empty, and the sky is filled with migrating wild ducks. As the foliage turns to brown and gold, the orange sunsets over the pond seem to be filled with a poignant sense of waning. This Thanksgiving Day Kelly cooked dinner, telling the cook and the Portuguese housekeeping couple that she was going to do everything herself except serve it. She spent two days in the kitchen, making her own stuffing and yam purée, basting the turkey to a golden brown, and baking a pumpkin pie for desert.

The dinner guests that Thanksgiving were all "rich, obnoxious Jewish gay guys," said one of the guests. "At least he could have invited one other woman, like a girlfriend of hers. . . . It was an awkward situation, all gay men and Kelly, making this fabulous meal for us." David Geffen was among their number that day, and much of the conversation centered around his recently acquired status of billionaire. Kelly said nothing as she listened to the conversation going on around her as if she weren't there—competition about business deals or boys, chatter that the guest described as "one ego flaring after the next." He remembered that watching Kelly and Calvin interact during dinner was like trying to solve a conundrum. "They really *do* love each other, but basically he's *gay*. I think he would love to be one hundred percent [hers], but he can't because . . . he's bisexual, but he's mostly gay."

Kelly continued to play with her food in silence for several minutes and then excused herself from the table and disappeared into the kitchen. Few people in the dining room seemed to notice she was gone. In the pantry, ignoring the staff, she fussed over some platters for want of something to keep busy. But her hands were shaking, and her eyes welled with tears, and for a moment, it looked as if she would cry.

Instead, Kelly turned and looked out at the ocean, and the distance in her eyes made the expanse of the Atlantic seem small.

BIBLIOGRAPHY

Among the thousands of source materials referenced for this book are Federal Bureau of Investigation files; federal Organized Crime Task Force documents; House Banking Committee documents; internal CenTrust Bank documents; the office of Thrift Supervision/Resolution Trust Corp. documents; New York City Police Department files; New York State Supreme Court records; the Bronx Historical Society archives; the *New York Post* and *New York Daily News* libraries and morgues; the New York Public Library; the *Miami Herald* library; the New York City Health Department; the Massachusetts Secretary of State's office, Boston; the New York City Board of Education; Dunn & Bradstreet; *Women's Wear Daily* library; the Fashion Institute of Technology library; State Liquor Authority Records; P.S. 80; the High School of Art and Design library.

The chapter on the Marci Klein kidnapping was constructed from interviews, the complete FBI files, New York Police Department files, transcripts of FBI tape recordings, transcripts of the trial, as well as confessions and statements. Every quoted word is verbatim.

Periodicals and newspapers:

Ad Age
The Advocate
Adweek
Allure
The American Lawyer
Business Week
The Chicago Daily News

397

The Chicago Sun Times
The Chicago Tribune
Crain's New York Business
Current Biography
Daily News Record
Entertainment Weekly
Fame
Forbes Magazine
Fortune
GQ
Interview
Los Angeles Magazine
The Los Angeles Times
Miami Herald
Miami Review
New York Daily News
The New Yorker
New York Magazine
New York Post
The New York Times
Newsday
Newsweek Magazine
Outweek
Parade
Playboy
The San Francisco Chronicle
Time Magazine
Tobe Report
W
The Wall Street Journal
Washington Post
Women's Journal U.K.
Women's Wear Daily

Books:

The Andy Warhol Diaries, edited by Pat Hackett (Warner Books, 1989)
The Beautiful People, Marylin Bender (Coward-McCann, 1967)
Chic Savages, John Fairchild (Simon and Schuster, 1989)
The Designing Life, W staff (Potter, 1987)
DV, Diana Vreeland (Knopf, 1984)

The Encyclopaedia of Fashion, Georgina O'Hara, (Abrams, 1986)

The Fashion Conspiracy, Nicholas Coleridge (Harper & Row, 1988)

Fashion: The Inside Story, Barbaralee Diamondstein (Rizzoli, 1984)

History of 20th Century Fashion, Elizabeth Ewing (Barnes and Noble, 1986)

Inside the Fashion Business, Jarnow, Judelle, Guerreiro (Macmillan, 1986)

The Man Who Was Vogue, Caroline Seebohm (Viking, 1982)

O'Keeffe: The Life of an American Legend, Jeffrey Hogrefe (Bantam Books, 1992)

Perry Ellis, Jonathan Moor (St. Martin's, 1988)

Pools, Kelly Klein (Knopf, 1992)

The Predators' Ball, Connie Bruck (Simon and Schuster, 1988)

Ralph Lauren: the Man Behind the Mystique, Jeffrey Trachtenberg (Little Brown, 1988)

Simply Halston, Steven Gaines (Putnam's, 1991)

Tarnished Crown: The Quest for a Racetrack Champion, Carol Flake (Doubleday & Company, Inc., 1987)

INDEX